THE ESSENTIAL HOLMES

THE ESSENTIAL
HOLMES · *Selections from the Letters,*
Speeches, Judicial Opinions, and Other Writings of
OLIVER WENDELL HOLMES, JR.

Edited and with an Introduction by
RICHARD A. POSNER

THE UNIVERSITY OF CHICAGO PRESS
Chicago and London

Richard A. Posner is a judge on the U.S. Court of Appeals for the Seventh Circuit. He has taught at Stanford University Law School and the University of Chicago Law School. The most recent of his numerous books is *Cardozo: A Study in Reputation* (University of Chicago Press, 1990).

Frontispiece: Oliver Wendell Holmes, Jr., circa 1920. Harvard Art Collection.

The University of Chicago Press, Chicago 60637
The University of Chicago Press, Ltd., London
© 1992 by The University of Chicago
All rights reserved. Published 1992
Printed in the United States of America
01 00 99 98 97 96 95 94 93 92   5 4 3 2 1

ISBN (cloth): 0-226-67552-1

Library of Congress Cataloging-in-Publication Data

Holmes, Oliver Wendell, 1841–1935.
  [Selections. 1992]
  The essential Holmes : selections from the letters, speeches,
judicial opinions, and other writings of Oliver Wendell Holmes, Jr.
/ edited and with an introduction by Richard A. Posner.
      p.   cm.
  Includes bibliographical references and index.
  1. Holmes, Oliver Wendell, 1841–1935. 2. Judicial opinions
—United States. I. Posner, Richard A. II. Title.
KF8745.H6A4 1992
347.73'2634—dc20
[347.3073534]   91-23035
                                                 CIP

⊗The paper used in this publication meets the minimum requirements of the American National Standard for Information Sciences—Permanence of Paper for Printed Library Materials, ANSI Z39.48-1984.

CONTENTS

INTRODUCTION

Oliver Wendell Holmes[1] is the most illustrious figure in the history of American law. He is also, to an extent no longer fully appreciated, a major figure in American intellectual and cultural history generally.[2] It is high time that his essential writings (both judicial and nonjudicial, including epistolary and bellelettristic), which are widely scattered, were brought together in a single volume.[3] My goal in this Introduction is to introduce the reader to Holmes and to explain the principles of selection and arrangement that inform this anthology.

Born in 1841, Holmes was the eldest son of Dr. Oliver Wendell Holmes, the famous physician, poet, and man of letters—author of *The Autocrat of the Breakfast-Table*, "Old Ironsides," "The Deacon's Master-piece" and other works. On his mother's side, the future Supreme Court justice came from families (the Wendells and the Jacksons) that had played a distinguished role in the history, including legal history, of Massachusetts. Raised in Boston, a childhood friend of William and Henry James and Henry Adams and (through his father) acquainted with Emerson, Holmes first displayed literary gifts as a student at Harvard College, becoming class poet. The Civil War erupted in his senior year. A fervent abolitionist, Holmes sought and obtained a commission in the Twentieth Massachusetts Volunteers, a regiment that was to distinguish itself in the war, suffering enormous casualties in the process. Holmes served with courage, rising to the temporary rank of lieutenant-colonel, but he did not reenlist when his three years were up. He had been seriously wounded three times; the first two wounds—

---

1. He was born "Oliver Wendell Holmes, Jr.," but, as was customary in those days, dropped the "junior" when his father died in 1894. I include "Jr." in the subtitle of this book, not because the selections are confined to things he wrote before his father's death (they are not), but to distinguish him from his father.

2. See, for example, Edmund Wilson, *Patriotic Gore: Studies in the Literature of the American Civil War*, ch. 16 (1962).

3. The only previous anthology of judicial and nonjudicial writings by Holmes is *The Mind and Faith of Justice Holmes: His Speeches, Essays, Letters and Judicial Opinions* (Max Lerner ed. 1943). Compiled in the first decade after Holmes's death, it presents the materials from an outdated point of view and contains too few selections to convey a rounded picture of Holmes's thought. *Justice Holmes ex Cathedra* (Edward J. Bander ed. 1966) is an amusing collection of snippets from Holmes's opinions and of anecdotes by and about Holmes.

shots through the chest and the neck, received at Ball's Bluff and Antietam, respectively—missed killing him by fractions of an inch. He had had his fill of war.

Returning to Cambridge, Holmes entered Harvard Law School and received his LL.B. in 1866. For the next fifteen years he combined the practice of law in Boston with legal scholarship, though only at the very end of this period did he have a full-time academic appointment. He was an active participant in the broader intellectual life of Boston and Cambridge (and England, which he visited frequently until his last visit in 1913), as part of a circle that included Charles Sanders Peirce, William James, and other founders of philosophical pragmatism. Although Holmes was a competent and respected legal practitioner, his bent was academic. Considering that most of his working time was devoted to practice, his scholarly output during this period was prodigious: a distinguished edition of Kent's *Commentaries,* the leading legal treatise in America; many articles, brief notes, and book reviews; and finally *The Common Law* (1881)—widely considered the best book on law ever written by an American.

A brief stint as a professor at the Harvard Law School ended, shortly after *The Common Law* was published, with Holmes's appointment to the Supreme Judicial Court of Massachusetts in 1883. He served for twenty years on that court, the last three as chief justice. From this period come several speeches that figure largely in this volume (not all of them on legal subjects), and among them—to complement his achievement in *The Common Law*—what may be the best article-length work on law ever written, "The Path of the Law," published in the *Harvard Law Review* in 1897.

Holmes wrote many fine opinions as a state court judge, some of which foreshadow the themes of his Supreme Court years. Yet he did not, during those many years on the Massachusetts court, make anything like the impression on the law that Chief Justice Lemuel Shaw of his court had made before him or that Judge (later Chief Judge) Benjamin Cardozo of the New York Court of Appeals was to make after him. It was only with his appointment by President Theodore Roosevelt to the United States Supreme Court at an age when most men would have been preparing for retirement—he was about to turn sixty-two when he took his seat on the Court in 1903—that Holmes fully found himself as a judge. He served almost thirty years on the Court, and while most of the opinions that he wrote either have been overtaken by events or engage the interest only of legal specialists, a number of them made a durable contribution at a more general level.

Holmes continued to do some occasional writing during his years on

aged: 62 - a 1= on U.S. Supreme Court

the Supreme Court. He retired in 1932 (with a nudge from his colleagues—for although his mind remained sharp, he could no longer handle his share of the Court's workload and, God be praised, the modern practice of having law clerks ghostwrite opinions had not yet caught on). He died three years later, days before his ninety-fourth birthday.

It is conventional to divide Holmes's career into three phases. The first, or scholarly, phase (for no one has been much interested in Holmes the practicing lawyer) dominated until his appointment to the Massachusetts court in 1883, but did not end then; the high points are *The Common Law* and "The Path of the Law," the latter written many years after he became a judge. Book and article are similar in theme as well as in distinction. Together they supplied the leading ideas for the legal-realist movement (more accurately, the legal-pragmatist movement)—the most influential school of twentieth-century American legal thought and practice—although backslidings to formalism are evident in a number of Holmes's judicial opinions and other writings.[4]

The pragmatist method is well illustrated by Holmes's treatment of contractual obligation. There is, he suggests, no duty to perform a contract, as such. Since the usual remedy for breach of contract is simply an order to pay the promisee his damages, the promisor's practical legal obligation is to perform *or* pay damages, and the promisee's practical entitlement is to performance or damages, at the promisor's option. Thus Holmes, consistent with the pragmatist program, tried to shift the focus of inquiry from the duty to keep one's promises to the consequences of breaking them. Holmes's famous prediction theory of law (law is merely a prediction of what judges will do with a given case), announced in "The Path of the Law," is a fruit of his pragmatic preference for analyzing law in terms of consequences rather than of morally charged abstractions such as "right" and "duty." Likewise his contention that law concerns itself only with behavior rather than with inner states and his attempt to trace the origins of law to revenge—both prominent themes of *The Common Law*. Finally, in Holmes's denial of a legal duty to perform promises as such, we see the severance of law from morals—the "bad man" theory of law (law viewed from the standpoint of persons who care nothing for moral duty) that is a basic element of Holmes's jurisprudence. The bad man is interested only in the consequences of violating the law; it is from his standpoint that the obli-

---

4. See my discussion of Holmes's jurisprudence in *The Problems of Jurisprudence* (1990), esp. Introduction and ch. 7. "Formalism" refers to the style of legal argumentation that purports to derive conclusions by logical or quasi-logical processes and thus to minimize politics and personality in judicial decision-making. For present purposes it may be considered the opposite of pragmatism or realism.

gation of a contract is merely to perform or pay damages for nonperformance, rather than to perform, period.

The third phase of Holmes's career, in the usual view, is his service on the U.S. Supreme Court—his service on the Massachusetts court (the second phase) being viewed as interlude and preparation, a lull having no great interest in itself. His major contributions as a Supreme Court justice were in four areas.

1. In the *Lochner*[5] dissent and other famous opinions opposing the use of the due process clause of the Fourteenth Amendment to prevent social and economic experimentation by the states, Holmes created the modern theory of federalism, the theory of judicial self-restraint (though here he was borrowing heavily from James Bradley Thayer), and the idea of the "living Constitution"—the idea that the Constitution should be construed flexibly, liberally, rather than strictly, narrowly. A better metaphor for Holmes's own view of the Constitution, however, is not that it is alive, but that it should not be allowed to kill the living polity in obeisance to the dead hand of the past. Since interpretation is a two-edged sword—a license for judicial intervention as much as for judicial forbearance—there is a latent tension between Holmes's emphasis on judicial restraint and his emphasis on flexible interpretation. And although he wrote pathbreaking opinions in defense of flexible interpretation (see chapter 9), he also wrote a well-known essay on interpretation, reprinted in that chapter, that has provided ammunition to the advocates of strict interpretation. The sheer bulk of Holmes's oeuvre evidently precludes complete consistency, which may make the skeptical reader wonder whether there is, as my title posits, an "essential" Holmes.

2. In his opinions in *Schenck, Abrams,* and *Gitlow,* which launched the "clear and present danger" test and the "marketplace of ideas" conception of free speech,[6] Holmes laid the foundations not only for the expansive modern American view of free speech but also for the double standard in constitutional adjudication that is so conspicuous a feature of modern constitutional law: laws restricting economic freedom are scrutinized much less stringently than those restricting speech and other noneconomic freedoms. Here, as in the case of interpretation, we again find Holmes seeming to work both sides of the street—rejecting the protection of economic freedom in *Lochner,* insisting upon the protection of freedom of expression in *Abrams* and *Gitlow.* If it is a crooked

5. Lochner v. New York, 198 U.S. 45 (1905).
6. Schenck v. United States, 249 U.S. 47 (1919); Abrams v. United States, 250 U.S. 616 (1919); Gitlow v. New York, 268 U.S. 652 (1925). In both *Abrams* and *Gitlow,* Holmes's opinion was a dissent.

path, still it is one that most judges and mainstream legal scholars have been content to walk with him. He could have argued that freedom of speech had a solider textual grounding in the Constitution than freedom of contract; but, consistent with his general although not uniform preference for flexible interpretation, he did not so argue.

3. Holmes mounted an influential challenge to the idea that federal courts in diversity of citizenship cases (cases that are in federal court because the parties are citizens of different states, rather than because the case arises under federal law) should be free to disregard the common law decisions of state courts and make up their own common law principles to decide the case. The challenge succeeded, shortly after Holmes's death, in the *Erie* decision, which ended "general" federal common law.[7]

4. And finally, in his dissent in *Frank v. Mangum*[8] and his majority opinion in *Moore v. Dempsey,*[9] Holmes established the principle that state prisoners convicted in violation of the Constitution could obtain a remedy by way of federal habeas corpus. Although Holmes's conception of the scope of habeas corpus for state prisoners was far more circumscribed than the modern view,[10] it was an expansive interpretation of the Habeas Corpus Act of 1867, under which these state prisoner cases were (and are) brought.

In all four categories, the primary vehicles of Holmes's innovations were dissenting opinions that, often after his death, became and have remained the majority position. Holmes's success in dissent made the dissenting opinion a popular and prestigious form of judicial expression. His majority and dissenting opinions alike are remarkable not only for the poet's gift of metaphor that is their principal stylistic distinction, but also for their brevity, freshness, and freedom from legal jargon; a directness bordering on the colloquial; a lightness of touch foreign to the legal temperament; and an insistence on being concrete rather than legalistic—on identifying values and policies rather than intoning formulas. The content is sometimes formalistic, the form invariably realistic, practical. Unfortunately, Holmes's principal legacy as a writer of judicial opinions was not to make well-written opinions

7. Erie R.R. v. Tompkins, 304 U.S. 64 (1938). The precursors are Holmes's dissents in Kuhn v. Fairmont Coal Co., 215 U.S. 349 (1910), and (especially) Black & White Taxi Co. v. Brown & Yellow Taxi Co., 276 U.S. 518 (1928).

8. 237 U.S. 309 (1915).

9. 261 U.S. 86 (1923). All of the opinions by Holmes that I have cited, except *Kuhn*, are reprinted in this volume.

10. Holmes to Harold J. Laski, Aug. 18, 1927, in *Holmes-Laski Letters: The Correspondence of Mr. Justice Holmes and Harold J. Laski 1916–1935*, vol. 2, at 971 (Mark DeWolfe Howe ed. 1953).

fashionable—a change that would require a revolution in the legal and
political culture of the United States, which disdains good writing and
even articulateness—but to make dissent fashionable. Modern judges
are quick to dissent in the hope of being anointed Holmes's heir, but
they lack Holmes's eloquence and civility. Most of them do not realize
that the power of Holmes's dissents is a function in part of their infre-
quency; he was careful not to become a broken record.

If all Holmes had been was an influential legal scholar and, later in
his life, an eloquent and (in the fullness of time) highly influential
Supreme Court justice, that would be plenty; but there is much more.
Only after Holmes's death did it become widely known that he had
conducted for upwards of half a century a voluminous, erudite, witty,
zestful, and elegant correspondence with a diverse cast of pen pals.
Several volumes of this correspondence have been published; the
vast bulk, however—amounting I am told to more than ten thousand letters—remains unpublished. The published letters reveal that
Holmes was a voracious, indeed obsessive, reader, of extraordinarily
eclectic tastes, in five languages;[11] a loving collector of prints; an astute
student of human nature—in short a versatile, cultivated intellectual.
Only recently has a set of love letters seen the light of day, addressed to
one of Holmes's English friends, Lady Castletown.[12] Holmes may have
been America's premier letter writer.[13]

A tall, commanding figure, his looks flawed only (and slightly) by his
too-long neck (for which his father liked—nastily—to tease him),
Holmes had the unusual good fortune to grow more handsome with
age, becoming a magnificent octagenerian. He was also a considerable
wit, like his father, and although he had no Boswell to memorialize his
table talk, a number of his best sallies appear to have been repeated in
the letters; others are in the Bander volume (note 1). One of the most
famous is apocryphal. Holmes did *not* say of Franklin Delano Roosevelt, "A second-class mind, but a first-class temperament." As many let-

11. English, French, German, Latin, (ancient) Greek. But, by his own admission,
Holmes was no linguist. He read works in foreign languages laboriously, with frequent
resort to ponies.

12. Excerpts have appeared in Sheldon M. Novick's fine biography of Holmes
(*Honorable Justice: The Life of Oliver Wendell Holmes* [1989]), and more will appear in G.
Edward White's forthcoming biography of Holmes.

13. All the letters reprinted in this volume have been published previously, with
the exception of the letters to Alice Stopford Green, which were transcribed by
Mark DeWolfe Howe. Apart from the Green letters, kindly drawn to my attention by
Philip Kurland, I have not attempted to explore Holmes's voluminous unpublished
correspondence—most of which remains, untranscribed, in Holmes's virtually inde-
cipherable handwriting.

ters make clear, this was Holmes's opinion of Theodore Roosevelt, though it is not clear that he ever stated it so pithily.

Holmes lived to a great age with remarkably little decline in intellectual zest and power, and faced the indignities and deprivations of old age—"wreck of body, / Slow decay of blood, / Testy delirium / Or dull decrepitude, / Or what worse evil come— / The death of friends, or death / Of every brilliant eye / That made a catch in the breath"[14]— with great courage and gallantry, so that his last years completed a circle with the military heroism of his youth and earned Frankfurter's description of Holmes's great natural gifts as having been "accentuated by his long, dashing career which enveloped him as though in a romantic aura."[15] Holmes was childless, so left no proofs of the regression phenomenon; and notwithstanding his (apparently harmless, i.e., noncoital) flirtations, his marriage of sixty years to Fanny Dixwell remains a monument to the institution of companionate marriage. Not only was Holmes a great jurist, a great prosodist, a great intellectual; he was a great *persona,* a great American, a great life.

Legal scholarship being inveterately and indeed obsessively political (and that regardless of the point on the political compass from which it comes), Holmes's reputation has fluctuated with political fashion, though never enough to dim his renown. Although many of his opinions took the liberal side of issues, the publication of his correspondence revealed—what should have been but was not apparent from his judicial opinions and his occasional pieces—that, so far as his personal views were concerned, he was a liberal only in the nineteenth-century libertarian sense, the sense of John Stuart Mill and, even more, because more laissez-faire, of Herbert Spencer. He was not a New Deal welfare state liberal, and thought the social experiments that he conceived it to be his judicial duty to uphold were manifestations of envy and ignorance and were doomed to fail. He had, moreover, a hard, even brutal, side, conventionally ascribed to his Civil War experience, that is found in few of the English libertarians (none of them soldiers). It is the side shown by his friend James Fitzjames Stephen (of which more shortly), a critic of Mill. Hostile to antitrust policy, skeptical about unions, admiring of big businessmen, Holmes was a lifelong rock-ribbed Republican who did not balk even at Warren Harding. His "objectively" liberal efforts as a Supreme Court justice to loosen the federal judicial hold over state legislation, and his advocacy of judicial self-restraint generally, have less appeal to liberals of all stripes today, to whom many con-

14. W. B. Yeats, "The Tower," pt. 3 (1927).

15. Felix Frankfurter, "Foreword," in *Holmes-Laski Letters,* note 10 above, vol. 1, at xiv.

temporary state legislative innovations seem retrogressive—and repressive—as in the occasional attempts to restore the sexual morality of the nineteenth century by banning pornography and abortions. Holmes's advocacy of free speech has set him on a collision course with the efforts of today's feminists and spokesmen for minority groups to repress sexist and racist expression. And habeas corpus and *Erie* are old hat, and Holmes's role in them largely forgotten.

Nor has Holmes a secure following among conservatives, although they are happy enough to quote those snippets of his prose which support their agenda—the snippets endorsing judicial restraint and strict construction. Atheist, Darwinian, eugenicist, moral relativist, aesthete, and man of the world, Holmes is not a figure with whom modern social conservatives, whether of the Moral Majority or of the *Commentary* variety, can feel entirely comfortable; and those who like his libertarian economic views are prone to dislike the decisions in which he dissented from the judicial imposition of those views on the states. Legal realism and pragmatism are alive and well but most of their practitioners are modern liberals, who are not comfortable with Holmes's views of social policy. (Most conservatives, having forgotten that Sidney Hook was a socialist, consider pragmatism a socialist creed.) Although still a deeply respected and even venerated figure, Holmes today lacks a natural constituency among lawyers and others interested in legal and public policy, while to the broader public he is only a name.

It is natural to suppose that Holmes's place in history depends on the magnitude, soundness, and durability of his contributions to law and to thinking about law. Perhaps it does, but this volume has been constructed on a different premise, or rather premises: that Holmes's true greatness is not as a lawyer, judge, or legal theorist in a narrowly professional sense of these words, but as a writer and, in a loose sense that I shall try to make clear, as a philosopher—in fact as a "writer-philosopher"; and that his distinction as a lawyer, judge, and legal theorist lies precisely in the infusion of literary skill and philosophical insight into his legal work.

I anticipate two objections. The first is to an aesthetic perspective on law, a perspective implicit in assigning a big role in the evaluation of a judge or legal thinker to his skill at writing. I imply by "aesthetic" a suspension of ethical or political judgment. A review by Peter Teachout of a previous book of mine[16] takes me to task for praising the rhetoric of Holmes's much criticized opinion in *Buck v. Bell*[17] ("Three generations

---

16. Peter Read Teachout, "Lapse of Judgment" (Review of *Law and Literature: A Misunderstood Relation*), 77 *California Law Review* 1259, 1293–1295 (1989).

17. 274 U.S. 200 (1927).

of imbeciles are enough") while criticizing the reasoning and result. To Teachout, rhetoric is intrinsically moral, making it a contradiction in terms to call an opinion good (i.e., beautiful) rhetoric but bad law or morals.[18] This is semantic quibbling. There is no reason the word "rhetoric" cannot be attached to writing or speech viewed, evaluated, as an instrument to a given end—the persuasion, edification, mystification, entertainment, or whatnot, of its audience. The quality of "rhetoric," so defined, has nothing to do with the merits of the rhetorician's end. And that is the offense: to those whose bent is strongly ethical—a common American tendency, puritanism and philistinism being salient features of our culture—the aesthetic conception of rhetoric is not only unworthy but insidious, a seductive art at the disposal equally of good and evil. These solemn moralizers will never appreciate Holmes, or credit such distinction as they are willing to grant him to his writing skill. I in contrast have no compunctions about separating the moral and aesthetic dimensions of expression and seeing in Holmes one of our greatest writers, however much one may disagree with the content of some of his finest prose.

I go further. I claim that some of Holmes's best opinions, notably the *Lochner* dissent, possibly the most famous and influential of all his opinions, owe their distinction to their rhetorical skill rather than to the qualities of their reasoning; often they are not well reasoned at all.[19] In part at least, Holmes was a great judge *because* he was a great literary artist. And in part because he was a philosopher—a suggestion that invites a second objection to my argument that Holmes's distinction as a jurist derives mainly from his being a writer-philosopher. This objection is that law, surely, is an autonomous discipline, practical in character, and not a parasite on other disciplines, especially one as nebulous as philosophy. Many lawyers, at least, will think it denigrates Holmes to associate him with so dubious an academic activity, surely little better than navel-gazing, as philosophizing.

I shall try to indicate what I think Holmes's work in law owed to his being a philosopher, but I must first explain what I mean by calling him that, what his philosophy was, and, indeed, what philosophy is. "Philosophy" is a collection of problems and suggested (but often, as it now appears, deeply inadequate) solutions found in a body of texts that

18. "To say that a 'poorly reasoned' and 'vicious' opinion also represents 'a first-class piece of rhetoric' impoverishes immeasurably our sense of what is meant by rhetoric and by excellence in rhetoric." Teachout, note 16 above, at 1294. The interior quotations are from my book *Law and Literature: A Misunderstood Relation* 289 (1988).

19. *Law and Literature: A Misunderstood Relation*, note 18 above, at 281–288, discussing *Lochner;* cf. Richard A. Posner, *Cardozo: A Study in Reputation*, ch. 7 (1990).

(setting aside the important but fragmentary contributions of Heraclitus and other pre-Socratic philosophers) begins with the works of Plato and the nonscientific works of Aristotle and culminates, or perhaps peters out, in the specialized and often hideously technical and obscure writings of present-day professors of philosophy. The problems that define works as philosophical tend to be of a general and fundamental character, not amenable to systematic empirical investigation; and the suggested solutions tend, therefore, to be quasi-theological, aspiring to final and comprehensive, but empirically untestable, understanding. The ambitions of the philosophical system-builders regularly provoke a skeptical backlash, so that the history of philosophy is the history both of the philosophical problem-solvers and of the antiphilosophers nipping at their heels. We have philosophers and antiphilosophers, and together they make up philosophy.

Among the fundamental questions that philosophy worries are questions about the meaning and purpose of human life, including the meaning and purpose of human life in a cosmos from which God has departed. Nietzsche, a contemporary of Holmes, said that God is dead. (Dead *for us*: Nietzsche was making a sociological rather than a metaphysical observation.) God had been killed among the thinking class by physics, geology, the "higher criticism" of the Bible, and the theory of evolution—systems of thought that had undermined Christianity's appeal to the rational intellect—and had been badly wounded among the common people by the growth of security and prosperity, which had shifted people's attention from the next world to this one. Christianity had been the foundation of Western civilization. Its disappearance as a living source of metaphysical certitude and ethical foundations was the crisis of modernity. Holmes agreed; and by the depth and eloquence of his belief he became part of a diverse cast of moderns that includes (in addition to Nietzsche and Holmes) Heidegger, Kafka, Gide, Camus, Sartre, Wittgenstein (in his later work), and, among our own contemporaries, Richard Rorty. All these thinkers have been concerned with the personal and social implications of taking seriously the definite possibility that man is the puny product of an unplanned series of natural shocks having no tincture of the divine, and they have been suspicious of efforts to smuggle in God by the back door (perhaps by renaming him Progress, or Science, or Technology, or History, or the Class Struggle) in order to recreate the certitude and the sense of direction that Christianity had provided. Pragmatism and existentialism are characteristic, and related, manifestations of this influential current in modern thought, the first typically American, the second typically European.

It is no accident that a majority of the persons in my list were not professors of philosophy and that all, even those who were not literary artists, had literary or artistic interests and, with the possible exception of Heidegger, wrote with great distinction (present tense, of course, in the case of Rorty). For when we speak of "the meaning of life" we speak of a topic about which literary artists seem to have more to say than philosophers. When modern secular intellectuals seek consolation for a loss, for aging, .for the indifference, immensity, and caprice of the universe, or for the cruelty of man, it is to literature rather than to philosophy that they turn. It should come as no surprise that the most penetrating insights into the philosophical topic that I am calling "the meaning of life" come from individuals who fuse philosophical and literary attributes, writing in a form equally remote from academic philosophizing and imaginative literature: notably Nietzsche and Wittgenstein, but also, though in a minor key, Holmes. It is a matter not of sheathing philosophical analysis in graceful language but of aesthetizing philosophy—of seeing in it the materials for conceiving of a life on the model of a work of art.[20] Holmes, most like Nietzsche in this regard, was, then, a "writer-philosopher."

There are affinities in content as well as in form between these great contemporaries. I shall not explore those here.[21] I have tried to explain how I think Holmes ought to be approached, and the arrangement of materials in this volume is intended to assist the reader in taking that approach. I leave it to the reader to discover what is to be found at the end of the journey.[22] The filaments of his thought are astonishing in their variety (I have touched on a few already). One can find pragmatism, atheism, (nineteenth-century) liberalism, materialism, aestheticism, utilitarianism, militarism, biological, social, and historical Darwinism, skepticism, nihilism, Nietzschean vitalism and "will to

20. Cf. Alexander Nehamas, *Nietzsche: Life as Literature* (1985).

21. I discuss them in *The Problems of Jurisprudence*, note 4 above, at 239–241.

22. The scholarly literature on Holmes is impressive in sophistication as well as bulk. Places to begin include the two volumes of Mark DeWolfe Howe's uncompleted biography: *Justice Oliver Wendell Holmes: The Shaping Years 1841–1870* (1957), and *Justice Oliver Wendell Holmes: The Proving Years 1870–1882* (1963); the endnotes in the Novick biography, note 12 above; and several recent essays: Patrick J. Kelley, "Was Holmes a Pragmatist? Reflections on a New Twist to an Old Argument," 14 *Southern Illinois University Law Journal* 427 (1990); Thomas C. Grey, "Holmes and Legal Pragmatism," 41 *Stanford Law Review* 787 (1989); G. Edward White, "The Integrity of Holmes' Jurisprudence," 10 *Hofstra Law Review* 633 (1982); White, "Holmes's 'Life Plan': Confronting Ambition, Passion, and Powerlessness," 65 *New York University Law Review* 1409 (1990); Robert W. Gordon, "Holmes' Common Law as Legal and Social Science," 10 *Hofstra Law Review* 719 (1982); and Mark Tushnet, "The Logic of Experience: Oliver Wendell Holmes on the Supreme Judicial Court," 63 *Virginia Law Review* 975 (1977). For my own, distinctly more favorable view of Holmes, see index references to Holmes in *The Problems of Jurisprudence*, note 4 above, and *Law and Literature: A Misunderstood Relation*, note 18 above; also the scattered discussions of Holmes in *Cardozo: A Study of Reputation* (1990), esp. pp. 138–140.

power," Calvinism, logical positivism, stoicism, behaviorism, and existentialism, together with the explicit rejection of most of these "isms" and a sheer zest for living that may be the central plank in the Holmesian platform. Whether the elements of his thought coalesce to form a coherent philosophy of life I doubt—because I range Holmes in the ranks of the antiphilosophers—but leave to the reader to decide. What I do not doubt is that the variety of intellectual influences that played upon Holmes's subtle and receptive intellect, together with his power of articulation and the daring with which he brought his intellectual storehouse and rhetorical imagination to bear on his professional tasks, makes Holmes a central figure in the intellectual history of this nation, and one who deserves to be more widely and appreciatively read than he is.

I said "intellectual history *of this nation*"—not of the world, and I want now to explain this qualification. Holmes's thought, and the fundamentals of his literary style, were pretty much fixed by the time *The Common Law* appeared. Indeed, the most famous sentence he ever wrote—"The life of the law has not been logic: it has been experience"—graces the opening paragraph of that book. And in Holmes's formative years America was, intellectually, a province of England. How likely is it, then, that Holmes was an *original* thinker and writer? I think his was a syncretic rather than a profoundly original mind, and that is why I used the word "minor" when comparing him to Nietzsche and Wittgenstein. I suspect that he borrowed greatly and to great advantage from the people he met in England as a young man, notably John Stuart Mill and James Fitzjames Stephen, and that by doing so he helped to make American thought cosmopolitan and (paradoxically) to liberate American jurisprudential thought from slavish adherence to English models. He did more than translate English into American. He enriched where he borrowed; his creative imitation was a species of greatness, like that of Shakespeare though on a much smaller scale.

Mark DeWolfe Howe, in his uncompleted biography of Holmes, discussed Holmes's intellectual debts in great detail. But so deferential was Howe toward his subject that he downplayed Holmes's indebtedness to predecessors lest he be thought to be accusing him of lack of generosity toward them—but that *was* one of Holmes's sins, although a venial one. Among Holmes's creditors was, as I have said, James Fitzjames Stephen,[23] a prolific English jurist of the generation before Holmes,

23. Howe, *Justice Oliver Wendell Holmes: The Shaping Years*, note 22 above, at 213, 227, 267–268. For illustrative works by Stephen—who incidentally was the (elder) brother of Leslie Stephen, and thus Virginia Woolf's uncle—see *Liberty, Equality, Fraternity* (R. J.

whom Holmes met shortly after beginning his own legal career. To the extent that Stephen is remembered today it is for his book *Liberty, Equality, Fraternity*, first published in 1873, an attack on James Stuart Mill notable for its advocacy of using law to shape morals. This might seem to place Stephen at the antipodes from Holmes. Not so. Stephen was a Benthamite, a skeptic, a tough-minded, no-nonsense antisentimentalist, and a master of plain, forceful prose enlivened with apt metaphor. I imagine that Holmes learned much from Stephen—especially how to write English English, which is to say good English, rather than American English, which in Holmes's formative years and indeed long after was, with a few notable exceptions such as that of Lincoln (but was not Lincoln's English the English of the King James Bible?), bad English. Stephen advocated the use of law to back up the moral teachings of Christianity because he thought supernatural sanctions alone were not enough to coerce good behavior. His ground, then, was utilitarian, and his whole approach to law was practical, instrumental. The germ of Holmes's "bad man" theory is in Stephen, who disparaged Mill for the hints of egalitarianism, and for what Stephen considered the overvaluation of liberty, in Mill's later writings. Also like Holmes, Stephen emphasized the importance of revenge in shaping the criminal law. Stephen was unwilling to abandon *all* belief in the Judeo-Christian God, however, and in this he differed from Holmes. A related difference is that Stephen was untouched by Darwin. Holmes was the more thoroughgoing skeptic, was far more influenced by science and, in a word, far more modern. Yet if the philosophy of life of Holmes and of Stephen had each to be summarized in three words, it would be the same three words: Calvinism without God. "Nirvana," Stephen wrote "always appeared to me to be at bottom a cowardly ideal. For my part I like far better the Carlyle or Calvinist notion of the world as a mysterious hall of doom, in which one must do one's fated part to the uttermost, acting and hoping for the best and trusting" that somehow or other our admiration of the "noblest human qualities" will be justified.[24]

How well this sums up Holmes's view of life I hope this volume will make clear. I do not suppose he took it from Stephen or any other one person. It must have welled up from the depths of his being; it was the interaction of his temperament with his social and intellectual environment. He did borrow ideas, metaphors, even perhaps poses from

---

White ed. 1967), and *Essays by a Barrister* (1862), especially the essay "Doing Good," in id. at 78.

24. From a letter quoted in Leslie Stephen, *The Life of Sir James Fitzjames Stephen* 458–459 (1895).

Stephen as from others, but he formed them into a personal philosophy and system of jurisprudence unmistakably his own, and by doing so he made, incidentally, a far greater impact on the law than Stephen had done through his voluminous writings and his judicial opinions (Stephen was a judge of the English High Court for twelve years). As one acquaints oneself with Holmes's predecessors, surprise at finding many of Holmes's insights and even expressions anticipated gives way to awe at the power and ingenuity with which Holmes synthesized, reformulated, and extended the ideas and expression of those who had gone before him.

I have been emphasizing literary flair and philosophical insight. But there is more to Holmes's achievement than this. The functional, evolutionary, policy-saturated perspective of *The Common Law* was a considerable innovation in legal scholarship. Nor should we neglect his proficiency as a working judge. He was a deep student of the common law and a skillful legal analyst, and—much like Learned Hand, the greatest lower-court judge in the history of the federal judiciary—he had a considerable intuitive feel for the economic and other policy implications of legal doctrine. His sterling judicial character—serenely and steadfastly detached from the parochial values of his class and the political fashions and pressures of the time—is an underemphasized dimension of his distinction. His detachment has often been confused with coldness. There were indeed times when he seemed to look at his fellow man through the wrong end of the telescope. In a letter quoted at greater length below, he wrote, "My bet is that we have not the kind of cosmic importance that the parsons and philosophers teach. I doubt if a shudder would go through the spheres if the whole ant heap were kerosened." But in his judicial opinions as in his letters, warmth, charm, even sweetness are conspicuous.

Holmes's judicial performance exhibits great variance, owing in part to the impatience with which he attacked judicial assignments; and recent legal scholarship, having cast off the exaggerated, almost hagiographic, deference of Howe's generation, focuses on the vulnerable aspects. Then too, much of any judge's work, even that of a justice of the Supreme Court, is ephemeral—indeed, when viewed from the distance of a half century or a century, a bore. Yet I think a careful and (if such a thing is possible) disinterested study of Holmes's opinions would produce a sharp upward revaluation of his judicial performance. This is not the place to attempt such a study, but I have included in this volume a few of Holmes's less famous opinions to indicate the scope and vitality of his judicial oeuvre.

But it is not for his gifts of legal reasoning (narrowly understood) or judicial temper that he is, or should be, chiefly renowned as a judge, let alone as a scholar. It is for the general principles, such as legal positivism and judicial self-restraint and freedom of speech, that his opinions and his pre-judicial and extrajudicial writings helped to shape, and for the unequaled literary power in which he articulated and applied those principles. And—to return at last to my suggestion concerning the springs of his greatness—he owed those principles not to legal texts or other traditional sources of law but to the possession of a philosophical mind that saw the Darwinian struggle, for example, instantiated in the labor movement, the social-welfare movement, and even communist agitation; that insisted on subjecting legal doctrine to the pragmatic test of meaning; that built judicial restraint and freedom of speech on the surprisingly robust foundations of skepticism, relativism, and pragmatism; that distinguished with unprecedented clarity between legal positivism and natural law.

Nor should Holmes's literary skill be thought merely a bright coat of verbal paint on a philosophical chassis that does all the real work in enduing his judicial opinions with depth and resonance. Remember that I called him a writer-philosopher. Language is the gate of perception, and its masters therefore see farther than the rest of us. The insight that invests Holmes's judicial work with depth and resonance is literary as well as philosophical, the writer-philosopher being at work in his opinions as well as in his extrajudicial writings. To the literary side of Holmes we owe the poetic concreteness, the metaphoric vividness, of his opinions; to his philosophical side, the sense of the general in the particular—the sense that Holmes "had one foot on the finite and the other on the infinite" (unpublished letter to Alice Stopford Green, June 18, 1911).

Given my aims, the reader will not be surprised to discover that the selections are not grouped by genre (letters, occasional writings, judicial opinions, etc.); do not attempt a representative sampling of Holmes's writings (for example, I have included almost nothing that Holmes wrote before *The Common Law*); are not in chronological sequence; and are minimally annotated. The groupings are broadly thematic, and the general movement of the volume is from general to specific, so that the selections dealing with the life struggle and other metaphysical topics precede those dealing with the social struggle, politics, and personalities, with law bringing up the end. But as I have not wanted to split up individual works, placing a fragment in one part of the book and another fragment elsewhere, there are many departures from the sequence just outlined. To avoid solemnizing the man, I have included some selections for their charm and zip rather than for their depth and have rather loaded them toward the front of the volume, under such headings as "Joie de Vivre" and "Aging and Death" (an exhilarating bunch of letters—don't be put off by my chapter title!). To enhance readability, I have indicated ellipses only when something of substance (as distinct from a citation, cross-reference, bibliographical footnote, "yours truly," or other triviality) has been omitted, and I have also surreptitiously, though very slightly, modernized Holmes's punctuation and corrected an occasional misspelling or typographical error.[25]

The impossibility of arranging Holmes's writings in watertight subject-matter compartments without damaging their flavor by breaking them into fragments stems from the kaleidoscopic variety and succession of subjects in a single document. The tendency is especially pronounced in the letters, as two examples (not printed elsewhere in this volume) will illustrate:[26]

Beverly Farms, September 15, 1916

My dear Laski,

. . . I should drop pragmatic and pluralistic. Perhaps I am the more ready to say so because after honest attention I don't think there is much in either of those parts of W. James's philosophy. But in any event, though Pound also talks of pragmatism, the judging of law by its effects and results did not have to wait for W.J. or Pound for its existence, and to my mind it rather diminishes the effect, or checks the assent you seek from a reader, if you unnecessarily put a fighting tag on your thought. So as to the other word. As to the thing last involved I don't know that I could do more than repeat what I have said or im-

25. Primarily in papers and opinions that he wrote before the 1890s, there are commas in odd places (such as before the direct objects of verbs and before dashes), which I have deleted. The letters contain an eccentric number of dashes, which I have pruned slightly, following Howe's lead. Apart from these changes and those noted in the text above, the letters appear exactly as in the published volumes from which I have taken them; I do not vouch for the accuracy of the editors' transcriptions of Holmes's scrawl. This is not a critical edition of Holmes's works, in which the editor tries to establish an authoritative text. In this regard I should note that there are numerous although mostly minor discrepancies between opinions by Holmes published in the official reports of the Massachusetts Supreme Judicial Court or the United States Supreme Court and the same opinions as published in unofficial, but normally highly reliable reports, such as the *Northeastern Reporter* or the *Lawyers' Edition* of U.S. Supreme Court decisions. I have used the official reports except where the version in the unofficial report appeared to be more accurate. I have also, as with the other materials reprinted in this volume, taken some liberties with capitalization, punctuation, and spelling, in order to eliminate archaisms.

26. The first letter is to Harold Laski and is reprinted from the Holmes-Laski correspondence, note 10 above, vol. 1, at 20; the second is to Lewis Einstein and is reprinted from *The Holmes-Einstein Letters: Correspondence of Mr. Justice Holmes and Lewis Einstein 1903–1935* 49 (James Bishop Peabody ed. 1964).

plied before. The scope of state sovereignty is a question of fact. It asserts itself as omnipotent in the sense that it asserts that what it sees fit to order it will make you obey. You may very well argue that it ought not to order certain things, and I agree. But if the government of England or any other first class European power, or, under a changed Constitution, the Congress of the U.S., does see fit to order them, I conceive that order is as much law as any other—not merely from the point of view of the Court, which of course will obey it—but from any other rational point of view—if as would be the case, the government had the physical power to enforce its command. Law also as well as sovereignty is a fact. If in fact Catholics or atheists are proscribed and the screws put on, it seems to me idle to say that it is not law because by a theory that you and I happen to hold (though I think it very disputable) it ought not to be . . . All my life I have sneered at the natural rights of man—and at times I have thought that the bills of rights in Constitutions were overworked—but these chaps remind me if I needed it, and I am not sure that Croly doesn't, that they embody principles that men have died for, and that it is well not to forget in our haste to secure our notion of general welfare . . .

Turning to your letter, I hadn't been aware of a difference between us concerning H. Spencer but if I should take you literally should feel quite sure that you didn't do him true justice. I think myself that he was something of an originator, but at all events his great influence as a *vulgarisateur* may not be realized by you, coming after the accomplishment of the results. A great many things that he said were very far from commonplace when he said them, although I have no doubt they would seem pretty thin now. When I remarked that concerning *The Scarlet Letter* to W. James he replied, of course it does—it was an original book . . .

Beverly Farms, August 19, 1909

My dear Einstein,

. . . Before he came I also had read Henry James's *The Ambassadors*. All the characters as usual talk H. James, so that I regard it rather as a prolonged analysis and description than as a drama. It brought up Paris to me; but more especially, by a kind of antagonism that it provoked, made me reflect, contrary to Münsterberg's book (*The Eternal Values*), how personal are our judgments of worth. If a man debates for half an hour whether to put his right or left foot forward while he stands in a puddle, he will think me stupid when I prefer to brusquer the decision. For all I know the fate of the cosmos may hang on it, but I think him stupid as to the growth of ideas, or the law, or whatever my hobby may be. I was struck as usual by the exclusiveness of his criteria and interests. He lives in what seems to me rather a narrow world of taste and refined moral vacillations; but in them he is a master. I can't help preferring him in description and criticism, but he has a circle that thinks him great as a novelist. My general attitude is relatively coarse: let the man take the girl or leave her. I don't care a damn which. Really, I suppose, he, like his brother and the parsons, attaches a kind of transcendental value to personality; whereas my bet is that we have not the kind of cosmic importance that the parsons and philosophers teach. I doubt if a shudder would go through the spheres if the whole ant heap were kerosened. Of course, for man, man is the most important theme; but it makes a difference whether one thinks one is a relation or not with the absolute. As I probably have written before I define truth as the system of my limitations, and don't talk about the absolute except as a humorous bettabilitarian (one who treats the Universe simply as bettable). Man of course has the significance of fact; that is he is a part of the incomprehensible, but so has a grain of sand. I think the attitude of being a little god, even if the great one has vanished, is the sin against the Holy Ghost. Like other grounds of salvation this one is intellectual not moral. Man is damned, and I should like to see him executed for being inadequate . . .

The letters hop around in the liveliest possible fashion from topic to topic (the two letters just quoted—and not in their entirety, either— touch on character, personalities, philosophy, religion, law, literature, and the nature of originality), depending on what is on Holmes's mind at the moment or on the topics mentioned in the letter to which he is responding, or both. It is impossible to assign such letters to one department of Holmes's thought.

I do not share all of Holmes's beliefs, philosophical and otherwise, and I do not think that the most important thing about a judicial opinion is that it be well written. But I would not have undertaken this volume if I did not think that there was much of permanent value in what I am calling Holmes's philosophy of life. The rise of the ghostwritten judicial opinion and the ghostwritten judicial speech or article marks a sad declension in the quality as well as the eloquence of American law, just as ghostwriting and television have combined to debase political rhetoric generally. All educated Americans, and especially American lawyers in all branches of this alarmingly powerful profession, have much to learn from Holmes, and my overriding aim in this volume has been to make the learning easier.

The selections represent only a small sample of a corpus that includes more than two thousand judicial opinions as well as thousands of letters and about a hundred articles, speeches, and notes; only *The Common Law* and the occasional speeches are generously sampled. But because Holmes repeated himself a lot, because many of the early articles are in effect reworked in *The Common Law*, and because many of the letters and opinions deal with ephemera, the title I have chosen for this anthology can be defended. I hope, though, that the reader will be stimulated to search out the other riches in Holmes's writings, especially the letters, of which my sample is particularly meager.[27] Perhaps this

27. The best of the letters, in my opinion, are in the Holmes-Laski correspondence. The other collections of published letters from which I have borrowed are *Holmes-Pollock*

volume will even encourage progress toward an edition of the *complete* works of Holmes, encompassing all the opinions and all the letters, including the unpublished ones. Meanwhile, the vastness of the corpus makes a book like this essential (so my title has a double meaning) for bringing Holmes before that larger public, within as well as outside the legal profession, that has not taken much interest in him.

At a minimum, these selections should persuade the unprejudiced reader not to dismiss Holmes as a man not of our time. The impulse to do so is evident in a stream of belittling, at times hysterical, criticisms of the man and his ideas that has flowed steadily since the publication in 1945 of "Hobbes, Holmes and Hitler."[28] Much of the early criticism was by Catholic jurisprudents writing in the natural law tradition[29] and is readily explained by their instinctive antipathy to Holmes's legal positivism. Holmes's enthusiasm for eugenics, evident in *Buck v. Bell* and in his correspondence, is offensive not only to Catholics (who to

---

Letters: The Correspondence of Mr. Justice Holmes and Sir Frederick Pollock 1874–1932 (Mark DeWolfe Howe ed. 1941) (also two volumes); *The Holmes-Einstein Letters*, note 26 above; "The Holmes-Cohen Correspondence," 9 *Journal of the History of Ideas* 3 (Felix S. Cohen ed. 1948); *Progressive Masks: Letters of Oliver Wendell Holmes, Jr., and Franklin Ford* (David H. Burton ed. 1982); *Holmes-Sheehan Correspondence: The Letters of Justice Oliver Wendell Holmes and Canon Patrick Augustine Sheehan* (David H. Burton ed. 1976). The principal articles are in Oliver Wendell Holmes, *Collected Legal Papers* (1920), and the principal speeches in Oliver Wendell Holmes, *Speeches* (1913). Those speeches and more appear in *The Occasional Speeches of Justice Oliver Wendell Holmes* (Mark DeWolfe Howe ed. 1962), while a number of the very early articles, which do not appear in *Collected Legal Papers*, are reprinted in *The Formative Essays of Justice Holmes: The Making of an American Legal Philosophy* (Frederic Rogers Kellogg ed. 1984). The University of Chicago Press is soon to publish a four-volume collection, edited by Sheldon Novick, of all of Holmes's articles and speeches plus *The Common Law*. A number of Holmes's opinions for the Massachusetts Supreme Judicial Court are reprinted (and others excerpted) in *The Judicial Opinions of Oliver Wendell Holmes: Constitutional Opinions, Selected Excerpts and Epigrams as Given in the Supreme Judicial Court of Massachusetts (1883–1902)* (Harry C. Shriver ed. 1940). And a number of Holmes's opinions for the U.S. Supreme Court appear in *The Dissenting Opinions of Mr. Justice Holmes* (Alfred Lief ed. 1929), and *Representative Opinions of Mr. Justice Holmes* (Alfred Lief ed. 1931). Novick's biography of Holmes, note 12 above, at 400–407, contains a complete bibliography of Holmes's published writings.

28. Ben W. Palmer, "Hobbes, Holmes and Hitler," 31 *American Bar Association Journal* 569 (1945). "If totalitarianism comes to America . . . it will come through dominance in the judiciary of men who have accepted a philosophy of law that has its roots in Hobbes and its fruition in implications from the philosophy of Holmes." Id. at 573.

29. A good example is Harold R. McKinnon, "The Secret of Mr. Justice Holmes: An Analysis," 36 *American Bar Association Journal* 261 (1950). McKinnon takes Holmes to task for failing to recognize that "the foundation of our law" is "the recognition that it *is* a father-controlled world in the sense that infinitely above the strivings of men is the Providence of God." Id. at 346 (italics in original). Holmes would have been nauseated by this passage.

their great credit opposed the movement for sterilizing the unfit that gave rise to the statute upheld in *Buck*) but also to those who remember eugenic sterilization as one of the policies of Hitler's Germany.[30] Holmes's military experience supplied metaphors for his writing that grate on the sensibilities of the modern intellectual, as do his "my country right or wrong" patriotism, his Social Darwinism, and his hostility to most social reform outside of the field of eugenics. Holmes's most recent biographer has found it necessary to apologize to his reader for Holmes's sexism, racism, and other affronts to contemporary sensibilities.[31] I daresay my suggestion, even duly qualified, that Holmes is the American Nietzsche[32] will not endear him to those for whom Nietzsche is the philosopher of Nazism—nor even to those for whom Nietzsche is the philosopher of postmodernism.

The picture of Holmes as a reactionary monster is an enormous distortion. It is true that he held basically conventional views—today regarded by some as vicious—of women, and in particular that he sometimes belittled their intellectual capacities; yet he also valued their conversation to a degree unusual in his day. Nor can it all have been flirtation or small talk because a number of his letters to women have the same intellectual content as his letters to men, as the letters to Alice Stopford Green that I reprint in this volume show. It is true that after his youthful abolitionist phase he displayed no marked sympathy for black people; but he was remarkably unprejudiced for his time. He had none of the snobbism, the anti-Semitism, and the contempt for American culture and institutions held by his childhood friends Henry James and Henry Adams; it is impossible to imagine him an expatriate. Steadfast in his belief in capitalism (a belief that is seeming rather prescient at the moment), he nevertheless was utterly willing to allow socialist experimentation, abhorred "red scares," had a soft spot for unions, and cultivated the friendship of Jewish radicals (as they appeared to proper

30. Forcefully denounced (don't be put off by the bland title) in "Sterilization Law in Germany: Statistical Survey concerning Obligatory Sterilization in Germany," 95 *Ecclesiastical Review* 50 (1936). See also Ingo Müller, *Hitler's Justice: The Courts of the Third Reich*, ch. 13 (1991).

31. "Justice Holmes proved to be a shadowed figure, marked by the bigotry and sexism of his age, who in personal letters seemed to espouse a kind of fascist ideology. He was a violent, combative, womanizing aristocrat." Novick, note 12 above, at xvii. Novick has gone overboard. Every substantive term in his list—"bigotry," "sexism," "fascist," "ideology," "violent," "combative," "womanizing," and "aristocrat"—is imprecise and misleading as applied to Holmes; and it is apparent from the title of Novick's book and much else besides that Novick's own view of Holmes is altogether more favorable than the use of these terms implies.

32. *The Problems of Jurisprudence*, note 4 above, at 239–242.

Bostonians) such as Brandeis, Frankfurter, and Laski. Tolerance, largeness of spirit, scientific curiosity, and liberalism in its most cosmopolitan form: these are the abiding characteristics of Holmes's thought, along with that fundamental and, I think, deeply creative and energizing sense of existential commitment that he shared with James Fitzjames Stephen. Holmes was no pacifist or one-worlder—quite the contrary—but I cannot recall anywhere in his writings an expression of enthusiasm for American imperialism, gunboat diplomacy, or "the white man's burden." His devotion to civilization, democracy, free speech, and the rule of law gives the lie to attempts to find affinities between his thought and the ideology of totalitarian or authoritarian thinkers—which is not to deny that at a sufficient level of generality such affinities exist. (Define "fascist" broadly enough, and we are all fascists.) We may find Holmes's eugenic enthusiasms shocking, although with the renewed interest (stimulated by modern medicine's ability to keep people alive in a vegetative state) in euthanasia, and with the rise of genetic engineering, we may yet find those enthusiasms prescient rather than depraved. We should remember that belief in human eugenics was a staple of progressive thought in Holmes's lifetime;[33] for example, it was one of the motivations behind the Planned Parenthood movement.[34] The fact that Holmes thought war necessary will not endear him to the modern intellectual, but we must remember that the particular war he thought necessary was our Civil War, that there is at least one more necessary war in our recent past, World War II, and that at this writing we have just finished another war that most people in this country think just. Holmes believed in blind commitment, and in this we can see folly if we like, or an echo of Kierkegaard and an anticipation of Sartre and Camus, or merely an admission of human fallibility: all our commitments must be blind because we are blind.

For those whose only heroes and heroines are men and women who think just like themselves, who refuse to make allowances even for *autres temps autres moeurs,* nothing I have said will mitigate the charges against Holmes. For those of less confined and parochial tastes, Holmes should satisfy Hamlet's description of his father: "He was a man, take him for all in all,/ I shall not look upon his like again." We are more skeptical than the Elizabethans, and to our ear it sounds as if "take him for all in all" is an acknowledgment of human frailties rather than the simple superlative that Shakespeare apparently intended ("the [best] man of all"). Holmes was human, and had frailties, though not those

33. See, for example, Bertrand Russell, *Marriage and Morals,* ch. 18 (1929).
34. Linda Gordon, *Woman's Body, Woman's Right: A Social History of Birth Control in America* 274–290 (1976).

conventionally or anachronistically ascribed to him. He was catty about prominent contemporaries of his, notably the James brothers (who reciprocated) and Charles Sanders Peirce; he exaggerated the originality of his ideas; in this and other ways he was rather unscrupulously ambitious in his youth; he was susceptible to flattery; he wrote judicial opinions too quickly, and with insufficient research; in his later years especially, he leaned too heavily on Brandeis for guidance in technical cases; a related point is that he overstayed his welcome on the Supreme Court by at least three years—although he wrote some splendid opinions in that period, as you will see. So, he wasn't perfect; he was only great. His massive distinction has not been dented by his many detractors.

A word, now, on how to read this book. The selections from *The Common Law* and from Holmes's articles, speeches, and judicial opinions should be self-explanatory, and it has but rarely been necessary to drop a footnote to explain a reference for readers unschooled in law or in the particulars of Holmes's thought. To minimize clutter, I have indicated the source of those articles and speeches first published in Holmes's *Collected Legal Papers* (1920), or in his *Speeches* (1913), or in Professor Howe's expanded edition of the speeches (see note 27 above), as *CLP, S,* and *OS,* respectively, together with the page number. Where the article or speech had been published previously, normally in a law review, I have used the first-published text.

The letters that I have reprinted were written to Frederick Pollock (or his wife), Harold Laski, Lewis Einstein (or his daughter), Morris Cohen, Patrick Sheehan, Franklin Ford, or Alice Stopford Green. Pollock was an approximate contemporary of Holmes and a distinguished English legal scholar. Laski, a much younger man, was an English socialist who had some legal training (at the Harvard Law School), wrote on legal as well as social and economic matters, taught for many years at the London School of Economics, and eventually became a leading member of the British Labour Party. Einstein was an American diplomat. Cohen taught philosophy at City College in New York. Sheehan was an Irish priest whom Holmes met on one of his British jaunts, and who died in 1913. Ford was a journalist-savant-crank interested in social credit and news gathering. Green was an English historian and the wife of another English historian. Holmes visited the Greens in England, and they visited the Holmeses at Beverly Farms, Massachusetts (north of Boston), the Holmeses' summer residence.

Equipped with the addresses and date of each letter, the reader can easily find the full text in the appropriate volume in Holmes's correspondence cited in note 27, except the letters to Mrs. Green (see note 13). After moving to Washington to serve on the Supreme Court, Holmes summered in Beverly Farms and I have retained his address when he was writing from there because the change of locale is a frequent topic in the letters. The reader should also know that Holmes had a protracted hospital stay in the summer of 1922 (for a prostate operation), to which several of the letters allude.

In reading the selections, do not forget the advanced age at which Holmes wrote so many of them. He turned seventy in 1911, eighty in 1921, ninety in 1931. The quality of some of the work he turned out in his eighties and even nineties is remarkable.

I want in closing to thank Lawrence Lessig, Cass Sunstein, G. Edward White, and two anonymous readers for the University of Chicago Press for their helpful comments; Paul Freund, Philip Kurland, and Stephen Holmes for advice and encouragement; and my wife, Charlene, for editorial assistance. I acknowledge permission generously granted to reprint writings of Holmes in which copyright still subsists: Selections from *The Occasional Speeches of Justice Oliver Wendell Holmes,* edited by Mark DeWolfe Howe, are reprinted by permission of the publisher, Harvard University Press, © 1962 by the President and Fellows of Harvard College. Selections from *Holmes-Laski Letters: The Correspondence of Mr. Justice Holmes and Harold J. Laski 1916–1935,* edited by Mark DeWolfe Howe, are reprinted by permission of the publisher, Harvard University Press, © 1953 by the President and Fellows of Harvard College. Selections from *Holmes-Pollock Letters: The Correspondence of Mr. Justice Holmes and Sir Frederick Pollock 1874–1932,* edited by Mark DeWolfe Howe, are reprinted with the permission of the publisher, The Belknap Press of Harvard University Press, © 1941, 1961 by the President and Fellows of Harvard College. Selections from *Progressive Masks: Letters of Oliver Wendell Holmes, Jr. and Franklin Ford,* edited by David H. Burton, are reprinted by permission of Associated University Presses. Selections from "The Holmes-Cohen Correspondence," 9 *Journal of the History of Ideas* 3 (1948), edited by Felix S. Cohen, are reprinted with the permission of the *Journal.* Selections from *The Holmes-Einstein Letters: Correspondence of Mr. Justice Holmes and Lewis Einstein 1903–1935* (1964), edited by James Bishop Peabody, are reprinted with the permission of Macmillan (London) and St. Martin's Press (New York), © 1964 by James Bishop Peabody. Holmes's unpublished letters to Alice Stopford Green, transcribed by Mark DeWolfe Howe, are reprinted from the Oliver Wendell Holmes, Jr., Papers in Harvard Law School Library, with the permission of the librarian.

THE ESSENTIAL HOLMES

1 • AGING AND DEATH

To Alice Stopford Green

October 14, 1911

My dear friend,

Your letter was forwarded to me here and has warmed my heart. Bless your flattering Irish tongue! No matter, I always believe you mean the dear things you say, and gain confidence from them. You have done me no little good in that as well as other ways—for the American public does not waste much time in praising judges, though I have no right to complain. I had expected to end a fatiguing week by a laborious conference of the judges this p.m. but this morning Harlan the Senior Justice died and everything is put off. The old boy had outlived his usefulness—but he was a figure the like of which I shall not see again. He had some of the faults of the savage, but he was a personality, and in his own home and sometimes out of it was charming. On my 70th birthday who but he bethought himself to put a little bunch of violets on my desk in Court? He dissented alone in the Standard Oil and Tobacco cases and showed most improper violence towards his brethren, but I regarded it as partly senile. Peace to his ashes. This is a year of anniversaries—Saturday the 21st, about the time that you will receive this, will be 50 years from my first battle and wound—Ball's Bluff. I have just been looking up a letter from old Francis Lieber dated June 16, 1872, in which he says "57 years ago our company came out of the battle (of Ligny) with but 18 men whole and hale." So that the two of us cover nearly a century. Yet when I am talking with my secretary (as usual a lad fresh from the Harv. Law School) I don't feel much older than he. Well—Sunday p.m. I was interrupted yesterday afternoon— and then came the news of the death of my dear though rarely seen friend Owen Wister (grandson of Fanny Kemble) and this morning has begun with letters to his widow and Mrs. Harlan—not a cheerful start. However as one grows older one gets like the eels accustomed to being skinned. Indeed the war accustomed me to it when I was young, and it makes one feel that perhaps it is time to take the lesson home—but I hardly believe it. I dare say that the best way is not to bother about death until it comes, but just crack ahead. I often say that to live sublimely the line of one's life must end outside the frame like a Japanese drawing. I remember getting the same impression as a little boy before Japanese drawings were heard of from the cover of my copy of Jack and the beanstalk; the beanstalk was cut off by the top of the cover and Jack was climbing—to one could not see what mysterious end. The picture has stuck by me through life. Everything seems an illusion relatively to something else—as green relatively to vibrations—until on further thought one sees that the whole great illusion is all of a piece and that the root and perhaps the flower of [——] are not for us . . . What of it? The cell has its life as well as the larger organism in whose unity it is a part—and our subrealities are no doubt in some sense part of all the reality there is. I am told that the Papuans delight in cat's cradle—and if they have become uneasy from your looking too hard at a human head or a stick you restore good humour by producing a string. Philosophic race! Perchance when the cosmic pull is given to all the knot of personalities and worlds they will all disappear and comfortable nothing will reign supreme—though Bergson says there ain't no such thing as nothing and that it's a bogus conception. "To what a depth my spirit is descending." While the illusion lasts I send you my love and gratitude. Let us hang on while we can.

Reflections on the Past and Future

Remarks at a Dinner of the Alpha Delta Phi Club,
Cambridge, September 27, 1912

OS 163

When I was a small boy and was allowed to see the celebrations of the day—it may have been on the introduction of the Cochituate water into Boston, or the funeral of John Quincy Adams, or I know not what—I was most impressed by the part played by a carload of veterans. I got the notion, which has persisted, that the glory of life was to be carried in a civic procession, in a barge, as a survivor—I did not inquire too curiously of what. Now I am beginning to realize that somber joy, and to feel something like the old gentleman of whom I overheard Judge Hoar tell, who remembered George Washington before dinner—and after dinner remembered Christopher Columbus. Take this Club. In my day, after having been saved from extinction by two members of the Class of 1860, it used to meet, I think rather oftener than elsewhere in my room, at Danforth's in Linden Street, which had the advantage of being outside the College Yard. If I am not mistaken, the last meeting that I attended before this was there in 1860 or 1861. In those days the Club used to listen to essays by its members before the business of the bottle began. Without yet going back to Columbus it may connect you with the past if I mention that at that time my grandmother was alive and that she remembered moving out of Boston when the British troops came in, before the Revolution. I spoke of the introduction of Cochituate water. When I was a boy there were pumps in the back yards. The closets that depend upon the pipes were not—we had no such luxuries even at Danforth's—and the illustrious Gayetey and his compeers had not yet replaced the newspaper with their tissues. The light was from candles and whale oil lamps that it always was a bore to get started. The water of the Back Bay came up to Arlington Street and the Public Garden was a dreary waste. You got from Cambridge by omnibus—and might return part way by rail from the Fitchburg station and then by horse car (not street car) to the neighborhood of the Law School Building. This was all before the war, when I was a boy. Some things that happened after it would seem rather ancient history to most of you. It would seem remote to the lawyers when I say that I have sat on the Bench with Lord Chancellor Cranworth and have dined with Baron Parke. It will have a meaning to everyone when I say that I have talked with a schoolmate of Byron's and a friend of Charles Lamb's—Barry Cornwall. The war itself, though it started the changes that almost have made a new art of warfare—such as the field telegraph, breech loaders, and ironclads—sounds nowadays pretty remote in its methods. We fought in two close ranks, the rear rank firing over the shoulders of the front. A regiment would be wiped out if it tried it now. Yet I remember seeing what I suppose was the germ of that which made it impossible, in the shape of a little go-cart with a gunbarrel on top that it was said would grind out a stream of bullets like a hose, on the Peninsula, at Malvern Hill. I never heard that it succeeded and at the time I supposed that it stood on the plane of Christian Commission Crackers that I also saw, with Come to Jesus printed on their side.

But after all our interests are in the present and the future—not in the past. They are our real topics and for any man who is not superannuated the question is what he has to say about them. I have learned to distrust the melodramatic completeness of simple formulas and do not put much faith in prophecy. Twenty years ago I was much stirred by Pearson's prediction that by mere spread of population in the torrid and middle zone the yellow race would come out ahead of us in the long run and that we should be put on the defensive. And to this day I am by that of James J. Hill as to the exhaustion of our resources. But Pearson's denouement is too far ahead and I console myself even when I think of Mr. Hill's. If he is right we shall support a smaller population than otherwise and there may be less scope for abilities like his which seem to me one of the greatest types of human power. But little peoples and small populations have done things in their day and may again. Athens could not have kept New York going for ten days, I suppose, but it counts for more than the United States. Perhaps in the future we shall care less for quantity and more for quality and try to breed a race. There would be compensations even if we had to drop from James Hill to Aeschylus and Aristotle. Perhaps by the self-defeat of nature to which Hegel called attention civilization will cut its own throat, or as Flinders Petrie thinks there may [be] discoverable cycles of its rise, decline, and fall. But even then we hope that some survivors will pass on the torch as the two men of '60 passed on the vital current of this Club. Whatever else we learn from nature we learn from it a mystic faith.

I have been reading lately a golden book, or rather books, for there are ten volumes of it: Fabre's *Souvenirs Entomologiques*. It is a seed book. There I am very sure is the source of that echo from behind phenomena that for a moment we think we hear in Maeterlinck's *Bees*. I think it must have inspired one of the most noticeable traits in Bergson's philosophy. It is simply the exquisitely told tale of a life-long watch of beetles and wasps, but from it we learn the faith I spoke of if we had it not before. I heard the doctrine years ago from Dr. Bartol. He spoke of the hen hatching her eggs in obedience to a destiny she did not understand. Fabre tells us of grubs born and having passed their whole lives in the heart of an oak that when, after three years, the time for metamorphosis comes, build a chamber that as grubs they do not need with a broad passage for the beetle that is to be. They obey their destiny without any sight of the promised land. The law of the grub and the hen is the law also for man. We all have cosmic destinies of which we cannot divine the end, if the unknown has ends. Our business is to commit ourselves to life, to accept at once our functions and our ignorance and to offer our heart to fate. When one is drawing near the end it is a great happiness to be assured for a moment by friends such as I see around me that one has borne one's part and has not failed in the faith.

To Lewis Einstein

Beverly Farms, August 30, 1908

My dear Einstein,

. . . Life seems very short to the old, the past part of it, but the length of the future (*ici bas*) after all is but an induction; perhaps our case will be the exception. Newman I believe was less sure of the sunrise than of his faith. One may be wrong even in thinking one is a poor creature.

To Patrick Sheehan

Beverly Farms, September 3, 1910

Dear Canon,

. . . Sadness comes with age—or ought to, I suppose. I sometimes try to force myself to feel worse than I do remembering that my next birthday will make me 70. When you speak of infirmities and my friends here die, I really do feel gloomy, but my interest in life is still so keen, I still want to do so much more work, that in the main I feel pretty cheerful. Especially candor compels me to admit when I am led to think that my work is valued as I should like it to be—and here you will discern the [vanity] I am afraid—but as I believe I said I meet him [death] with a grin and cut under him by recognizing that vanity is only a way to get any work out of me, and that my only significance is that which I have in common with the rest of things, that of being part of it.

October 18, 1912

My dear friend,

Your letter gives me the heart ache. I have been thinking so much about you and hoping so much for good news. I wrote from Beverly Farms to you a letter that you seem not to have received, directed to Doneraile. Of course I agree with your dislike of money as an ideal, a domination for which I fear the upper strata of the world are more responsible for than the lower—but unlike you I should not express my dislike in terms of morality. It seems to me that a general fact rather is to be regarded like a physical phenomenon—accepted like any other phenomenon so far as it exists—to be combated or got around so far as may be, if one does not like it, as soon as fully possible. I always say yes—whatever is, is right—but not necessarily will be for thirty seconds longer. I don't know whether I ever mentioned my impressions from rereading Plato—that it was the first articulate assertion of the superiority of the internal life. This summer I was interested to see this point of view more fully developed and no less keenly felt by Epictetus. And if you find yourself able to read books, I got the greatest pleasure from Zimmern's *Greek Commonwealth* which contrasts strikingly our modern ideal of comfort with that of the Greeks who knew little of it but built the Parthenon and did all the other wonderful things. I feel like repeating to you Hamlet's "Absent thee from felicity a while"—you give such comfort and joy to one at least who loves you. I am old though I can't realize it, and I hope you will stick it out as long as I do, to help in maintaining the high hearted feeling about this life. I tend towards gloomy views from time to time, but set it down partly to age—and partly content myself by reflecting that I am not running the universe—and am not called on to lie awake with cosmic worries . . .

To Lewis Einstein

April 17, 1914

Dear Einstein,

. . . I dined last night with Charles Adams. We mentioned that Howells, he and I were the three or three of the four oldest men now living of the Saturday Club in Boston. We are so near the edge of the void that we can spit into it. But though I say so I don't feel or realize it except by the dropping of leaves from the tree between us and the sky . . .

To Harold Laski

March 31, 1920

My dear Laski,

Your decision sounds right to me. Of course I cannot judge with knowledge of all the elements—but it seems plain that you will be in a better *milieu* for your work and that is the first thing to consider so far as you are concerned. I gather that your wife will like the change, or at least does not object to it, and that being so, I should think the case was pretty clear. But oh, my dear lad, I shall miss you sadly. There is no other man I should miss so much. Your intellectual companionship, your suggestiveness, your encouragement and affection have enriched life to me very greatly and it will be hard not to look forward to seeing you in bodily presence. However, I shall get your letters and that will be much. I shall do my best to hold up my end of the stick, though while the work is on here, as you know, it sometimes is hard to find time or to get free from the cramp to the law—I should say, of the law, in the sense that one's mind after intense preoccupation only slowly recovers its freedom—as the eye only gradually readjusts itself to a new focus— especially with the old. I feel as if I were good for some time yet, but I used to think that the mainspring was broken at 80 and in any event as that hour approaches one is bound to recognize uncertainties even if one does not realize them—as I don't. If we should not meet again you will know that you have added much to the happiness of one fellow- being.

To Frederick Pollock

November 19, 1922

Dear Pollock,

. . . A while ago I wrote as if writing were impossible; it was the discouragement of having to live in a hotel and lose much time in the adjustment between two places, coupled with the pressure of beginning work. Now I am back in my house and although at this moment I have two decisions to write I am much more serene. I still am rather weak in the joints and perhaps am more tired than I used to be when I come from Court. I drive each way and walk but little. But everything seems to be going as well as possible. I simply avoid all extra fatigue or tasks. Putting in an elevator to save going up the steep front stairs to library and bedroom displaced some of my folios and left less room for them, but I have sent off the 9th English edition of the *Encyclopaedia Britannica* and Rees's *Cyclopaedia* dear to my boyhood and got more room. The title *Low Countries, Engravers of the* was my delight in my teens, and I can recite the abbreviations on the back from *Dec–Deg* to *Yam–Zol*. For some reason the first few volumes didn't fix themselves in my memory. I kept them from filial piety, but now have sent them to the Pittsfield Library to which long ago I sent a lot of my father's books. Last year I sent his MSS and autographs etc. to the Congressional Library and in this way gradually am cutting down, and giving permanent place to things of interest. I am not contemplating death and still aim some years ahead, but I had to contemplate it last summer. It isn't the same thing to an old man that is it to a young one—he has had his whack and can't complain. Metchnikof's suggestion of a parallel between the destiny and desires of living creatures illustrated by the *éphémères*—which I saw once at Niagara Falls—seems to hold good, but living is very pleasant and I mean to do as much of it as I can. What a divine gift is fire. In the clearing up that I have nearly finished I have cut short a thousand hesitations and shut out many fool vistas of possible interest by burning odds and ends. Civilization is the process of reducing the infinite to the finite. I could dilate, but refrain. I have enhanced the circulation in the extremities as one does by cutting one's nails. But I must stop and go to work. This is merely a wiggle of your friend to show that he is still alive.

December 31, 1922

Dear Pollock,

A happy New Year to you and yours. It promises to begin happily at this end. I have just finished reading your *Essays in the Law*—or rather rereading, for the most part, and have done it with admiration of the learning mastered and vitalized and the happy and luminous exposition. I tell you what: for a young fellow you are doing well. My reading was delayed by my work, but I have had time not only to read that but to do a bigger chore (do you have the word?), in the form of Frazer's *Golden Bough* in the one volume edition, pitilessly compact print, ideas that had become familiar to me, Salomon Reinach *et al.*, and the immense mass of facts that mostly vanish from my mind—but a book to be read for the Day of Judgment. I should suspect that his latent motive was to show that all the great doctrines of Christianity were survivals or transfigurations of universal superstitions of the most primitive times. Perhaps I should put it stronger than suspect . . . I forget whether I have told you that the 8th and 15th respectively were the 20th anniversary of my taking my seat here and the 40th of my going upon the Massachusetts bench, and that I was surprised to receive a number of letters—increased by a puff in the *New Republic*, that made me repeat that when you get to the top of a hill there is nothing left but to come down . . .

Beverly Farms, August 2, 1923

Dear F.P.,

It is a great satisfaction to get a letter from you feeling reestablished except as to legs. I am with you on that. I don't work mine very much. A mile is the maximum. I don't know whether it is heart or what (the doctor in Washington said I had a good pump) but I don't find it wise to press exercise as much as I should like. Even a short walk takes time however, and what with that and drives about (there are wondrous sights on this cape) and solitaire and snoozes I don't have such a lot of time for reading. I haven't quite finished the 7th Vol. of Sainte-Beuve even now. If I didn't avoid mental improvement this summer I might have taken his *Port-Royal* instead. But he is just what I want; you finish a subject by the time you have had enough of it; most of those he talks about I want to know better than I do, and it is an added pleasure when you don't admire excessively the man you read. I have told you I think of a young Chinaman who writes to me from Berlin. His professor Stammler is deeply occupied with the forms of thought—like a true German. I wrote the other day, though not to Mr. Wu, that infinite meditation upon a pint pot wouldn't give one a gill of beer, and that I was more concerned with the contents than the forms. I think you will agree. The other day Laski wrote glorifying your saint Miss Austin [*sic*], I must get *Pride and Prejudice:* but have I dared confess to you that the last time I tackled her I found her—let me whisper it very softly—a bore?

I envy you your environment and possible, I suppose before this actual, journey to France. The old world is the place for those who are more interested in the works of man than in those of God, but I am very happy here, and as even the old is relative I can get the mystery of the past if I go to Boston and look at the steps that lead from Bosworth Street—formerly Montgomery Place—to Province Street. By there I was born and they have not changed, and with memory they call up a Boston of two centuries ago. Two centuries are not as good as two millenniums—but beyond an early point a man can't count the difference. They say that crows can't count above three. A billion and a million miles or dollars are much the same for ordinary thought—and so of years.

December 1, 1925

My dear Pollock,

Welcome to old age—which begins at 80. So you are a child again in a new zone. I wish I were to be or to have been at your birthday party. If you had given the date I should have cabled unless the time has gone by. No doubt those present appreciated the story of your fruitful and gallant life. I hope we may keep on together for a good time yet. If I pass the line of 85 in March I shall set 90 as a goal. When I turned 80 my wife sprang a dinner party with nearly all my old secretaries on me. I didn't know anything about it until I entered the dining room.

Your tail piece bothered me for a moment—as to "H.M." I said to myself I didn't know that Her Majesty wrote books, unless he means Queen Victoria and I didn't think he would write about her quite in that tone. At last the glimmering light came to me from the context and I remembered that I had written of Harriet Martineau.

The book I mentioned is:

Michael-Neo Palaeologos
His Grammar
By his father Stephen N.
Palaeologos.
London and Toronto—J. M. Dent & Sons Ltd.

I couldn't be sure whether you would be tickled by the whimsicalities and funny illustrations (I don't mean the pictures) as I was, or whether you would be repelled by the humorously intended but rather overworked fantastic terminology. I think on the whole that the book is quite amusing and acute. In its criticisms of other writing I think it loses sight of its own insistence that everything depends on the context and finds obscurity when from that point of view there is none. Also you may think that he says things that are old to philosophers. But I recur to the opinion that I haven't had such a peck of oats for some time.

I am very hard at work again as we are sitting, but in good shape and enjoying it, preparing small diamonds for people of limited intellectual means.

To Frederick and Lady Pollock

May 24, 1929

True thanks dear friends for your kind and affectionate words. Of course I knew I could rely upon your sympathy. I am reconciled by the certainty that a continuance of life would have meant only a continuance of pain and suffering of which my wife had had too much before the final accident. (She fell and broke her hip bone.) We have had our share. For sixty years she made life poetry for me and at 88 one must be ready for the end. I shall keep at work and interested while it lasts—though not caring very much for how long.

To Harold Laski

May 30, 1929

My dear Laski,

A dear letter from you has just come—you will have heard from me before this, but I reiterate: please keep on writing and I shall do the best I can. I don't lose my interest in my friends or affairs of the mind or in my job—although it may be, as I wrote to someone yesterday, like a man's beard growing after he is dead. My wife's death seems like the beginning of my own—but I am confused and hardly know what I think about anything. It hasn't prevented my writing. Frankfurter wrote to me highly praising something that I wrote in the midst of anxieties—and I have just turned off a dissent about the refusal to admit a pacifist to citizenship that Brandeis liked and joined in. There seems to be a distinct compartment in one's mind that works away no matter what is going on with the rest of the machinery. I have been delayed in reading W. Lippmann's book but have it at my elbow, probably to be finished between here and Beverly—to which I go via the Touraine on the night of June 5—arriving Boston 6:50 AM and I hope Beverly Farms by Saturday. The women behaved like bricks and gave up their usual holiday at this time—go with me and straight on to B.F. where things will have been prepared for them and they will put on the finishing touches, and notify me. I have been reading a curious book called *The Confusion of Tongues* by Charles W. Ferguson—an account of the best known come-out sects, Spiritualism, Theosophy, New Thought, Christian Science, Ku Klux, Mormonism, Mennonites—and other less known by name to me but he says maintaining great establishments—ending with the Atheists (not the quiet scientific un-believers but people on fire with the same enthusiasm as the others only with inverted values—or colors) . . .

To Lewis Einstein

Beverly Farms, June ?, 1929

My dear Einstein,

My affectionate thanks for your kind and feeling letter. It was better that my wife should die than live in suffering and pain which I am sure was the alternative. I think too that it was better that she should die be-fore I do; she was of the same age as I, and I think would have been more at a loss than I am if left alone. I like solitude with intermissions, but she was almost a recluse. I have my work and a fair number of peo-ple whom I like to see. She shocked Gifford Pinchot once by saying, "I have no friends"; and it was true that there was no one except me with whom she was very intimate. Things hurt her that I didn't mind. We have a lovely spot at Arlington where she lies.

I may last even a year or two; but my work is done, though merely as a *jeu d'esprit* I shouldn't mind writing decisions in my ninetieth year and still better at ninety. I have had my reward, especially in these last years in the form of letters and articles. I wrote to a man yesterday, who had said supersuperlative things, that if the devil came round the corner and said: You and I know that that isn't true, I should believe him. Still so long as he didn't appear in person, such letters kept alive my hope that I had lived my dream . . .

June 5, 1928

My dear Einstein,

I am too old to start into any new field. I still want to keep on a little longer in the law. Perhaps one always wants a little more, but my grounds are somewhat more specific. I am so nearly old (ninety is old) that people are kind to me. I think I have told you how impressed I was as a boy to see carried in civic procession a barge full of survivors, I don't know exactly from what, the revolutionary men were almost all dead. I seem to see a role for myself in that way. The boys will come and poke up the old man and I will growl a little, mention some remote fact, and send them off with something to tell.

To Harold Laski

Beverly Farms, June 15, 1929

My dear Laski,

Here I am—settled quietly—it is now a week since I arrived. Everything is pleasant and I drive, see my friends, and read a little and sleep in the process. Frankfurter and his wife made a very satisfying call. He relieved my mind by telling me that there was no danger of his leaving the Law School for Chicago—which I had heard rumored. I have a faithful follower, James Doherty, who thinks it his special duty to look after me. Some of my wife's relatives thought it well that he should come on to the funeral and he somehow established himself in charge of a good deal and managed things admirably. He drove down here with me last Saturday and didn't leave till Monday, after he had taken me to walk and satisfied himself that I was safe—solemnly exhorting me not to come to Boston without notifying him. He seems to think that I oughtn't to be trusted in the streets alone. I must tell you too that the moment he heard of my wife's death the Chief Justice at once communicated with Arlington and made sure that everything was ready. How can one help loving a man with such a kind heart? I have a lovely spot in Arlington toward the bottom of the hill where the house is, with pine trees, oak, and tulip all about, and where one looks to see a deer trot out (although of course there are no deer). I have ordered a stone of the form conventional for officers which will bear my name, Bvt. Col. and Capt. 20th Mass. Vol. Inf. Civil War—Justice Supreme Court, U.S.—March, 1841—His wife Fanny B. Holmes and the dates. It seemed queer to putting up my own tombstone—but these things are under military direction and I suppose it was necessary to show a soldier's name to account for my wife . . .

Beverly Farms, September 29, 1929

My dear Laski,

You miscalculated a little, for your letter that expected to meet me in Washington was forwarded to me here and reached me yesterday. But tomorrow morning I do leave for Boston—and hope to be in Washington Thursday morning. I believe that I have told you that my expected last two weeks of idleness have been cut up by standing for a full length portrait by Hopkinson for the Harvard Law School. Hopkinson has a gift for catching a likeness and for vividness I think—and I am quite proud of his results. As to Buckle—it must be over 60 years ago that I read him—and I only have referred to him once, when writing about Montesquieu, to make sure of his having dwelt on climate. My general impression is like yours. I think on reopening him I found him abler than I had anticipated but I hardly had regarded him as a pathfinder although he more or less indicated the direction of future paths. Your musical dame and sexual reformers give me great pleasure—why am I denied these glimpses of a higher aether? To have a woman asking about your *medias res* is more amusing than ten *certioraris*.* Your German historian Burckhardt I know not—ought I to before I die? As a result of the portrait I have read nothing since rereading *Anna Karenina* except part of Swift's *Diary to Stella*—not so good reading as Pepys and even perhaps a trifle squalid, but still interesting. I shall take it with me. Books like that and Pepys and Walpole's letters fill a niche in life very pleasantly.

I think that my wife's death, although I cannot regret it, because life would have meant suffering and pain, keeps the thought of my own before me, so that I want to add; if I am alive, when I say that I go to Washington Wednesday night. It makes me think of the time when all life shall have perished from the earth, and tests the strength of the only comfort I know—the belief that the I know not what, if it swamps all our human ultimates, does so because it is in some unimaginable way greater than they, which are only a part of it. But I also think that our demands for satisfaction are intensified by exaggeration of the belief in the unity of ourselves and a failure to see how they change in content and contour—as is natural if consciousness is only an electric illumination of cosmic currents when they make white light. Lord, Lord, I have said all this so many times before that I ought to be ashamed. But the thought must needs repeat itself daily and so the expression may be pardoned if not more than once a month. Also every litany has its repetitions.

I envy you your acquaintance with Birrell. I was just referring to a page in *Obiter Dicta* and found it hard to lay the enchanting volume down. Happy the man who can take books leisurely, like a soaking rain, and not inquire too curiously for the amount of fertilizer they contain. It takes robust and staying power to get adequate pleasure out of even the greatness of the past. It takes other and richer gifts to find all the good there is in the second rate. But I fear that I drool—farewell.

To Frederick Pollock

May 20, 1930

My dear Pollock,

You fire me by your bet on the judgment of posterity as to [Robert Bridges'] *The Testament of Beauty.* I read it very inadequately, with all

---

*A petition for certiorari is a request to the Supreme Court to accept a case for review.—Ed.

manner of interruptions and distractions but even so I bet that posterity will let it calmly die. It seemed to me the Cosmos arranged to suit polite English taste. I would not deny passages of some beauty but I did not see the great lines in it (I mean the lines of greatness). You almost compel me to read it or in it again but I don't much want to. What do you think of other candidates for immortality like Browning's *The Ring and the Book?* I find it hard to believe that the world will take the trouble it demands. Other things that received superlatives when we were younger seem to me to have sagged a little like *In Memoriam,* and Ruskin and Carlyle. The only firebrand of my youth that burns to me as brightly as ever is Emerson, and I am bound to admit that for many years I have read but two or three pieces of his, coupled with *The Heart of Emerson's Journals* (I am not sure of the title) which impressed me a few years ago. Well, here is a battleground if we jaw together this Autumn. I speak cautiously of that because I don't venture to look far ahead although I now am rather hoping to reach my 90th birthday. It makes a difference as one gets near to that time. People are very kind to so old a man and make much of him. I suppose it makes their own horizon seem wider . . .

Beverly Farms, June 9, 1930

My dear Pollock,

Here I am once more and was welcomed by your letter. You discourse with a learning that I do not attempt to emulate as to Montesquieu and the balance of political powers. The little I ever knew is, I am afraid, pretty well forgotten. So I accept your remarks in respectful silence. I read Kinglake's *Crimean War* when I was in the army, but that is some time ago. I met Kinglake, who said he had a question to ask—I knew what it would be. Did our men fight in line? I grinned and said I remembered his speaking of that as an Anglo-Saxon prerogative, and asked if he really believed it, to which he—yes, he certainly did. I said of course our men fought in line, and that I believed you could make baboons do it if you had the right sort of officers. That is my chief association with the author and the book nowadays. As to India also I am blank. You keep up with public affairs; I now avail myself of old age to excuse what in fact has been the neglect of a life-time. My adieu to the last Term was a dissent on the requirement in the 14th Amendment of due process of law from the States. Of course it is too late to prevent the extension of the phrase to an artificial meaning but the Court has gone farther than I can possibly believe to be warranted on the question of the right of the States to tax, and in opinions by McReynolds has overruled decisions written by me and others, when I thought authority, logic and settled practice authorized the tax. I am on most friendly terms with all the judges, but I suspect that if I should be gathered to Abraham's bosom some of them would think it an advantage to the law, even if they missed a friend . . .

To Lewis Einstein

My dear Einstein,

It must be over a month since I have written. Lumbago, colds, and work are my excuses. I won't dilate upon it beyond saying that little burdens weigh heavier as one nears ninety. That is just four weeks off now. A fortnight ago when I had a cold I told the Doctor that I wanted to take every precaution to live until I rounded the cape. Not that it matters in any way except that one makes goals for oneself to reach and then wants to reach them. Solitaire seems always an epitome of life. One says to oneself why do I care whether I win the game or not, and then one answers, why do you care to live, or like beer (not that I ever drink it), or why do you work? I know no answer except that that's the way I'm made. As Frenchwomen in novels frequently justify their foibles by generalizing them, *Je suis comme ça.* One can take oneself solemnly or lightly. One has to be serious when at work. When at leisure one surmises that it will not matter much to the Cosmos whether one turns to the right or to the left, but one doesn't know. It may be that one's act is a cosmic necessity and has the whole weight of the universe behind it. It may be that there is no necessity, but that one's unimaginable spontaneity takes now this turn now that. We may be important. It may be that the universe would be in ruins were not this paper on the table now in front of me a nodus that has the illusion of personality and in its freaky moments fancies itself distinguishable from the before and after of the stream of energies that for the moment is able to say: "I." I recur to my old formula. Having made up your mind that you are not God don't lie awake nights with cosmic worries. Here endeth the First Lesson.

Of events not much to tell since you left. The usual routine, made less comfortable by the above mentioned lumbago and colds and alleviated by my secretary reading to me when I was too tired to work. *Inter alia* he read *The Newcomes* to me, which I have been wanting to reread for ten years. At intervals I read *Medieval Latin Lyrics* by Helen Waddell whose *Wandering Scholars* I read with much pleasure last summer. She writes with feminine enthusiasm but is a scholar and translates loosely but well into pretty verse. Also two amusing books that I can recommend: Hoffenstein's (I think) *Poems in praise of practically nothing,* some of them very good indeed, and D. B. Wyndham Lewis and Charles Lee *The Stuffed Owl,* an anthology of good, bad verse, showing the bathos, platitudes etc., of which our most highly gifted men have been capable with a few samples of the less highly gifted like the Sweet Singer of Michigan. Also a volume of essays from the *Spectator* by Addison & Steele showing where Thackeray got some of his pleasantness, although the hidden music of his style is his own, and counts for much. Style, I think, is sound, a matter of ear. I liked Siegfried Sassoon's book. No special comment to make.

My love to the two charming ladies.

May 29, 1931

My dear Einstein,

In your letter of May 17 you say, perhaps prophetically, that you are glad to think of me back on the North Shore. But not yet. We adjourn on Monday next, June 1, and June 3 I have taken tickets for the North. Meantime there has been pretty constant work. Last night a lot of stuff coming in for a wind up on which we had to be ready to recite at our conference today. However it is over now.

I shall go out to Arlington tomorrow, Memorial Day, and visit the gravestone with my name and my wife's on it, and be stirred by the military music, and, instead of bothering about the Unknown Soldier shall go to another stone that tells that beneath it are the bones of, I don't remember the number but, two or three thousand and odd, once soldiers gathered from the Virginia fields after the Civil War. I heard a woman say there once, "They gave their all. They gave their very names." Later perhaps some people will come in to say goodbye.

It is beginning to be very hot and if it goes further will take the life out of one. It is very different from the North. It is easier to live there in the summer. I like to live, but feel that it does not matter much.

My secretary has been very good in reading to me out of working hours, more serious matters finished. We began yesterday Wodehouse, *Very Good, Jeeves* which makes me roar. That chap is master of a light rather original slang that makes life joyous when all the carbonic acid gas seems to have fizzled out of it. Few benefactors can be compared with him.

Turning to what you say I respect laziness and probably have said to you more than once that those who make the most of themselves don't make much. I regret my limited capacity for it. A sinister sign, but not, I hope, conclusive. You speak of the Americans in England at and after the Revolution, and among them Gilbert Stuart. I thought he was an Englishman. As to the spark of art, poetry, and philosophy being passed on and kept alive, I bet it will be, though when I wanted to be disagreeable to White and McKenna (Catholics) I used to suggest that perhaps in two hundred years Mongolian ideals would be in the ascendant.

Well, I am a rag now, but hope to be different in a fortnight. My love to the ladies. I hope the ball you speak of will be or has been a success.

To Frederick Pollock

Beverly Farms, August 16, 1931

My dear Pollock,

Will this letter hit you as you sink to shore from the billows of the Baltic, or how otherwise? I know not. It is hard to deal with such sports as you two. But I owe a line to both of you. I have read nothing of Dickens except *Our Mutual Friend* for many years. I have given *Vanity Fair* my first adequate reading. It seems to me to be a great novel—very great. The greatest drawback to me in this and *The Newcomes* is that mundane motives and interests seem to be Thackeray's own ultimates, *non obstant* pious ejaculations when he talks of Amelia. Of course I am not talking religion but of the scale of intellectual preoccupations. I admit that the bias is more natural in London than elsewhere. The prizes are greater—and there was splendor in Thackeray's time—and even in mine.

I don't think Plato's *Laws* is dull, except as all antiquity is, and I don't see why it should be thought to have been a compromise. Perhaps what seems queerest to us in his infinitesimal state is that the citizens never have to think about making a living. That is left to the slaves and foreigners. I think one likes the old fellow as he drools on (I speak as a modern). I await your address about the Inns of Court with interest. The last few days my secretary has been away and I have taken the opportunity to read some detective stories for which I have an ignoble liking. I have read four running. My wife used to remark that many could begin a novel well but few could end one well. That struck me with all these—the conclusion generally impotent and one that one didn't like.

I also have read Strachey, *Portraits in Miniature.* For the most part (one or two exceptions) they did not seem to me up to his earlier work. Also I didn't care much for his *Elizabeth & Essex.* The only moment that I remember when Essex interested me was when he spoke ill of the figure of his Mistress. A minor work by Willa Cather (American). She seemed to me really great in *My Antonia.* Except for the interjection of slumber I really should have had some of those longed for hours when I wondered what to do, but such hours are very rare. Apart from all else more people come than I want, though each individual is welcome. Perhaps I make a mistake in not trying to walk but it is an effort and I doubt if it is wise to try even an eighth of a mile. Time is slowly taking down the house. I suppose next month the American Bar Association intends to give me a medal and I am expected to say a few words by radio—details not yet settled—at any rate, not a very exciting occasion.

In view of uncertainties I will write no more. My love to my dear Lady Pollock . . .

Yours ever,
O. W. H.

I have been accompanying Rémy de Gourmont in some of his *Promenades philosophiques*. He is so clever that he ought to have been a little bigger.

To the Federal Bar Association

February 29, 1932

Gentlemen of the Federal Bar Association:

Your kind invitation for March 8 has been answered, I believe, in due form. But I cannot say Farewell to life and you in formal words. Life seems to me like a Japanese picture which our imagination does not allow to end with the margin. We aim at the infinite and when our arrow falls to earth it is in flames.

At times the ambitious ends of life have made it seem to me lonely, but it has not been. You have given me the companionship of dear friends who have helped to keep alive the fire in my heart. If I could think that I had sent a spark to those who come after I should be ready to say Goodbye.

Radio Address (1931)*

In this symposium my part is only to sit in silence. To express one's feelings as the end draws near is too intimate a task.

But I may mention one thought that comes to me as a listener-in. The riders in a race do not stop short when they reach the goal. There is a little finishing canter before coming to a standstill. There is time to hear the kind voice of friends and to say to one's self: "The work is done."

*On the occasion of a national celebration of Holmes's ninetieth birthday.—Ed.

But just as one says that, the answer comes: "The race is over, but the work never is done while the power to work remains."

The canter that brings you to a standstill need not be only coming to rest. It cannot be while you still live. For to live is to function. That is all there is in living.

And so I end with a line from a Latin poet who uttered the message more than fifteen hundred years ago:

"Death plucks my ears and says, Live—I am coming."

To Frederick Pollock

April 21, 1932

My dear Pollock,

Probably you will have returned from your I hope successful trip to and on the Mediterranean. I envy you, but I am being happily idle and persuading myself that 91 has outlived duty. I can imagine a book on the law, getting rid of all talk of duties and rights—beginning with the definition of law in the lawyer's sense as a statement of the circumstances in which the public force will be brought to bear upon a man through the Courts, and expounding rights as the hypostasis of a prophecy—in short, systematizing some of my old chestnuts. But I don't mean to do it or to bother about anything. We are reading Spengler, *The Decline of the West,* a learned, original book, written with incredible German arrogance, and not in all believed by me, but wonderfully suggestive—an odious animal who must be read. A lot of other stuff is being waded through and I am lightly skipping through the little book on Marcel Proust. The cherry trees around the Potomac basin have been as beautiful as ever but probably are near their end. My love to Lady Pollock.

2 • JOIE DE VIVRE

To Alice Stopford Green

November 9, 1913

My dear fighting friend,

Your letter has waited a day or two for Sunday morning, my only breathing time, and now my answer will be interrupted by having my hair cut as I overslept myself. Your militant animosities strike me as a little wholesale—you include peers and preachers. The latter I grant you—the dimple chinned parson is my type of fatty degeneration— but I should make reserves as to peers. Naturally I don't believe in the institution but individually a good many of them seem to me not bad specimens. Nature is an aristocrat or at least makes aristocrats, e.g. the cat—and one recognizes certain bloods that generation after generation turn out superior men with here and there a genius. But this is a platitude that I ought to apologize for uttering to you. I don't know enough about the [Irish] home rule business to be entitled to an opinion. I should think that the Carson manifestations were ill judged, but I suspect that if I were an Englishman I should be against home rule. You have taught me something of the wrongs that have been done, but I have not quite as much respect for abstract human rights as you have, and I think the welfare of the Empire would outweigh all other considerations. I believe in the iniquitous doctrine of my country right or wrong. Don't throw me over for my speculative wickedness. I assume that you won't, and turn to other themes. I thought I had written to you since getting home but as I'm not sure I will mention that I had an upset for a week and then a happy three weeks before coming on here. Here again I have had a fall down that hasn't prevented my sitting in Court, but that made me unable to get up from my chair after I had sat there two hours—without help. Lumbago however is the least demoralizing of pains and now that it has nearly disappeared I rather smile at it. It has not prevented, either, my writing two decisions last week and two the week before in addition to my other work—I send you the two that have been delivered. You wouldn't think that those few pages are our answer to printed arguments that made two considerable 8vo volumes, not to speak of oral discourse of an hour and a half to a side. If you look at them I think it will strike you how on the hair trigger they live in New York. At 1 o'clock worth half a million dollars, at 12 a million to the bad.

Also how all the complex life is built on trust. No doubt a cautious and scrutinizing trust but still trust. Of course the banks know the circumstances of those they lend to—and how they must watch the ticker that tells of the ups and downs of the stock in which their borrowers have invested. My last cases concern, one, the hours of labour law (whether there is a separate offence for each man kept overtime when all the cases are due to the same delay), and the other the liability of a judge in the Philippines to an action for some of his judicial doings. So you see that I have variety. Fanny read to me the other evening extracts from the correspondence of Charles Eliot Norton—friend of Ruskin and all the illustrious in letters. I used to know him. I must say the letters present an amiable side—and he preserved what seems to me a Boston tradition when he made a speech and did it like a gentleman, and he belonged with the refined of the world. Why then does one hate a precieux? Why does any circle of culture almost inevitably make one want to stay outside? Culture of course often means having more wood in your woodpile than you have in your furnace, and of a size that won't go in. I suppose the want of actuality that one detects in details—the recognition of shibboleths to which is given an artificial value—are part. Perhaps there is some natural cussedness in oneself to account for part—I dunno—but so it is. I always thought better of my father that he never belonged to a set. In fact I think he used to remark how even a small one worked as a buffer between you and the shocks of life and made you feel like a king because a little crowd pronounced you a boss (I put it in my own way). Washington is a good abridgement of life—the way that mighty men appear here, have their day and are forgotten, is really striking. Each cabinet thinks itself a halo and in a puff the sunlight vanishes and they are but obscure moths. The whole world except a very few outside of politics has changed since I have been here. Even of the Justices only two are left who were here when I came. And no one cares—and to tell the truth I don't see why any one should very much. To jump to a more general aspect—when you realize my great formula no doubt often repeated to you that friendship, property, and truth have a common root in *time*—when you hear a great scientific man say apropos of science and Calvinism—oh yes I know all about that, but I *believe* this—presumably simply because he was shaped to his theology before he ever heard it questioned—how can you take man seriously on the speculative side—as the friend God needed in order to find out that he exists? Seriously for practical purposes, yes—but when one looks at him with the devitalized thought of contemplation may one not smile, if one includes oneself and also recognizes that the smile postulates a fulcrum outside that does not exist and therefore should include not only the smiler but the smile itself? If I fail to carry scepticism far enough, correct me! But this is only Sunday amusement when one plays with God out in the back lot of the void. When one is at work one is keen enough—and you who have the soul of a martyr and so much more human sympathy than I, I am afraid will think it unprofitable—but simplicissimus has its place.

Well, I have allowed myself a letter flogging the spirit in your company, my well beloved friend, and now will go to work. Did you know or know about Canon Sheehan, my friend at Donerail, who died the other day? a beautiful spirit—I am afraid I should not have talked quite so freely to him!

To Harold Laski

December 15, 1923

Dear Laski,

This will come late to wish you a Merry Christmas but I am wishing it. A bully long one from you December 1. You speak of Curzon. I saw him once or twice with the Souls when they were in full blast. I mainly remember thinking that Little Peddlington was everywhere, from the interest taken in some verses of his in which he chaffed some of them—or somebodies' else. His "Simple Man" remark is A-1, if perhaps obvious. Hardy is a deity whom I have not worshipped. I have not read his later books, and the earlier ones read long, long ago with pleasure but without so far as I remember adoration. Croce I think a pretty big chap—at least I read his *Aesthetics* (tr. Ainslie) with that impression—before I knew you. I glanced at his *Goethe* in the Boston Athenaeum with impressions similar to yours so far as they went. I have just finished volume 1 of Ferrero, *Greatness etc. of Rome* of which I think I spoke heretofore. I read (present tense) no more of that—though it gave me some pleasure and suggestion. Also *Ariel ou la vie de Shelley*—lightly touched—just—but giving that impression of squalor in Shelley's points of contact with the world that is disagreeable. I always have believed that he could not have made his adorable excursions into the fourth dimension if he hadn't been something of a damned fool. I am on the point of having a little time for reading and wish you were here to give me a tip—for I can't remember those that you have given me in the past. I envy you your Augustine *De Civitate Dei*. W. Lippmann dined here a couple of nights back—and was most agreeable. He told me of a man speaking to another on the train—"Did I meet you in Albany?" "No, I never was there"—"Neither was I—it must have been two other men." My work is done—substantially. My cases were disposed of on

Monday—I was given but one new one which was written and has been approved by the brethren. The dentist and a morning of business are my only preoccupation for the next two weeks, except my expected young Chinaman and an afternoon to hear Mme. Duze in *Ghosts*. But it is astonishing how many fool letters one has to answer and fool books to acknowledge. Yesterday *inter alia* it was a young woman who wanted to paint my portrait—later in the morning another who found me in the street said I had better wait till she could paint me, then at luncheon a chap, from whom I once bought an etching that I never have known what to do with, had me from the luncheon table to the telephone to know if he could do an etching of me—to which I, "No!" "Oh, but I want to do it for myself" (hum-hum). "I am afraid that I am too busy." As I write there comes a copy of my opinion on an alleged conspiracy, anti-trust, which I enclose. Not that it is anything remarkable but the Solicitor-General (Beck) fulminated on the wickedness of the combination, misquoted Shakespeare, unless I greatly err, and I regretfully fear was disappointed.

I think I must have written since Learned Hand dined here—also very pleasant. Pursuant to my plan of not going out I stayed away from the reception at the White House, the other evening. I am in good shape except coughing especially at night—an ancient trouble—but which makes my eyelids now droop—so I will leave your most agreeable society for a half hour slumber. Homage to your missus.

To Lady Pollock

January 10, 1904

Beloved Lady,

As usual I have about a minute and a half before doing something else. But it is ever thus. I love seeing your dear handwriting again—and, of course, I am always your dear Judge. In formal converse we are always Justice but I should hate to have you change . . .

I still read nothing, and at times like other people I feel discouraged. My mode of thinking and doing things sometimes seems to me academic to the point of unreality, but after all it is not my own shortcomings alone of which I am conscious. I find people pleasant—I will change the order and say I find pleasant people here as elsewhere, and am amused with the dining out which now is pretty constant. I don't twang the tremolo very much—hardly at all—but there is a good deal of a kind of pleasantness which one can appreciate before the final collapse. When people wish to be polite they express the hope that I still have 10 or more years of activity ahead, which is accurate but sounds short. We always exempt ourselves from the common laws. When I was a boy and the dentist pulled out a second tooth I thought to myself that I would grow a third if I needed it. Experience discouraged this prophecy. Good-night my dear friend. I hope you have recovered from the fatigues of the voyage etc., and should like to be sure of it. My love to Fred.

Always affectionately yours,
O. W. Holmes

It seems to me that we did nothing for you when you were here and yet we wanted to do so much. You must take affection for deeds and have faith.

To Lewis Einstein

January 6, 1908

My dear Einstein,

I have been hoping to hear from you, to learn where you were, and to thank you for your last book, the *Erasmus against War,* as well as again for the Leonardo, which I read the other day with equal admiration at three or four wonderful prognostics and pungent sayings and surprise at the drool that makes up the body of the book and which he seemed to take pleasure in repeating.

At the risk of being too personal I must felicitate you on the growth of your power of expression. Perhaps you have been helped by the critical taste of your wife, but certainly your writing is a different thing from what it was when I first knew you. You have grown to your own style, and I only hope I may have many like the last. Forgive my freedom and set it down to the real interest I feel in all that concerns you.

I have not read any of the books you mention, but under your leadership I have recurred to Anatole France and the works you recommended, with the result that I have got more pleasure from him than ever before. He has some of the wisdom of scepticism although he, like other Frenchmen (as we agreed in our talk), is a dogmatist at bottom. The Mussoos never seem to realize that cosmic criticism changes the critic's relation to the object fired at only by the kick of the gun. When one damns the weather he only signifies that he is ill adjusted to his environment, not that the environment is bad. And when A. F. makes his M. Coignard talk on the baseness of mankind, one says to oneself pray do you regard yourself as a little God outside of the Show? Where do you get your που στῶ, your criterion to condemn the whole?

Since I wrote the last word I have had my day in Court, fired off my decisions, and been bored with listening to those of others. We waste two thirds of the day in solemnly spouting our views and our differences, when it all goes into print and the real audience is the "videence" that reads. But it is usage and not without a touch of pompous impressiveness. The custom was established before the days of intellectual breechloaders and magazine guns. And once in a while it rather tickles one to have something imperturbable and slow. The Chief* twigs things as well as another, but you don't get him to change what has been, one jot. The man who puts my robe on to my shoulders did it for Taney thirty years ago. In the same way when I went on the bench in Massachusetts twenty-five years ago and said I wanted a quill pen, the old messenger (who had been on Lafayette's guard of honor when he returned to the U.S.) took a bunch from a drawer and said, "If you don't mind cutting them here are some that Chief Justice Shaw left." C. J. Shaw had been dead for a quarter of a century.

But I must dress and go out to dine. A happy New Year to you and yours.

To Patrick Sheehan

November 23, 1912

My dear friend,

Your new story came a few days ago. I have begun it and am impatient to read more as soon as the stress of work permits. There is a slight anxiety in writing you for fear that you don't receive my letters. If you could get some one to send a line just saying that the two I have sent as I shall send this to the South Infirmary are received, I should feel freer in snatching a moment when I can send you my love. I have just made up my mind that I can not go to Richmond and Petersburg tomorrow for the funeral of the wife of a friend of mine, an old Confederate officer, and it has reminded me that I am of the age when one must be prepared for one's self and one's dearest—yet I can't feel so. Life still seems vigorous both in my wife and me. I only hope to meet the inevitable like a philosopher when it comes.

Let me turn to more cheerful themes, though I must add that at those moments when one fleetingly feels as if one has done one's work nobly and adequately, death doesn't seem so hard. But whenever for a minute and a half I feel cocky and as if I had done the trick, I at once

*Chief Justice Edward Douglas White.—Ed.

begin to anticipate the revenge of fate and expect to get jolly well taken down within twenty-four hours. It must be so as long as one is taking part in the fight. I was sorry for Taft in the recent election, and I apprehend trouble from what the Democrats may do with the tariff. I think that probably Taft was the best man, but he made every political mistake—from the beginning when he put Democrats and doubtful Republicans in his cabinet. I said of the Roosevelt movement that it seemed characterized by a strenuous vagueness that made an atmospheric disturbance but transmitted no message. To prick the sensitive points of the social consciousness when one ought to know that the suggestion of cures is humbug, I think wicked.

I have been writing away at decisions. One of the queer aspects of duty is when one is called on to sustain or enforce laws that one believes to be economically wrong and do more harm than good—but as I think we know very little as to what the laws pronounced good; as there is no even inarticulate agreement as to the ideal to be striven for, and no adequate scientific evidence that this rather than that will tend to bring it about if we did agree as to what we want, I settle down on simple tests. I look at it like going to the theatre—if you can pay for your ticket and are sure you want to go, I have nothing to say. But I think the crowd would not want what they now do, if they saw further into the facts.

Dear friend, I talk at random, and I fear this ill suits the atmosphere of a sick room, but as I can't see and don't know exactly how or where you are, I fire away, and simply follow my pen, hoping that it may give you a moment's distraction. Whatever I write about it is merely a roundabout way of saying I am thinking of and with you and of sending you my love.

December 15, 1912

Dear Canon,

It is a joy to see your handwriting as firm as ever and to see the heading, Doneraile. As to your "not forgotten" I don't believe you doubt that you never are very long out of my mind. I must tell you before I forget to mention it that two ladies whom I frequent (at the rare odd moments when I have a chance to call) are great admirers of *Under the Cedars and the Stars,* and always inquire about you. I have been so very hard at work that I read nothing and so haven't finished M. Lucas. This last week, for instance, besides sitting in Court 4 hours each day, except Saturday which is Conference and more fatiguing, I have written 2 decisions to be delivered tomorrow, had to be ready at yesterday's Conference to vote on about 50 cases, including those argued, and dined out nearly every night. I like to work at high pressure, but it leaves time for nothing else, as I neither work nor read after dinner. I do so like to think of the band and illuminations for your return. I don't wonder they all love you—one doesn't have to be of your parish for that.

Again to interrupt, lest I forget, don't bother about writing except to let me know once in a while that my letters are received, unless you feel like it. I will try to slip in a letter to you between cases from time to time, irrespective of answers.

Last Sunday, Dec. 8, my ten years since I took my seat were up, and I am now free to retire when I like. But (apropos of some suggestions of yours) while only the philosophical side of things interests me I don't care to write except on subjects which I think I know to the bottom, and therefore I think it wise, while my powers seem unabated, to try to put a touch of the infinite into the law, rather than turn to other fields. That sounds rather swaggery, but if I have succeeded at all, what I have aimed at throughout has been to exhibit the particular in the light of the universal, so far as may be . . . Here I was interrupted for luncheon and after it I find the usual little slip from the Chief Justice allotting decisions to be written. I have two and shall have to bestir myself. You say you wish the President would make me Ambassador. English friends sometimes used to suggest that years ago, but even when I was a judge in Massachusetts I wouldn't have taken it—very much less would I take it now. That is not a career; my work is—to give it up in order to be an ornamental umbrella handle! No thank you. But people differ so. Last night at dinner at Justice Hughes's, McKenna (of our bench and a Catholic) evidently thought, indeed, I believe, said, that four years of the Presidency was worth a life on the bench. To which I replied that to my mind, 4 years on the Bench was worth a lifetime in the Presidency. I then said to Senator Root (who you may remember has been Secy of State, etc., etc.) that I never had regarded any office as an object and he said neither had he. I think he meant it and I know that I did. I have told you of our Regimental Surgeon's distinction of external and internal men. I don't see how any internal man can regard an office as anything but an incidental advantage (when it is one). The thing I have wanted to do and want to do is to put as many new ideas into the law as I can, to show how particular solutions involve general theory, and to do it with style. I should like to be admitted to be the greatest jurist in the world, but I wouldn't do much more than walk across the street to be called Chief Justice instead of Justice—though I think the difference has affected the present incumbent. I no longer hear him wishing that he could retire! You see, I talk ahead just as usual, hoping that you will prefer that to conversation on the invalid footing—but I am thinking of you always with constant affection.

To Harold Laski

December 31, 1916

Dear Laski,

You are a dear and your letters give me great pleasure—but even an acknowledgment has to be written at a gallop as there always is some demand upon my time hopping in—just now it was 17 pages of opinion that I don't agree to. I grin with raging envy when you speak of a week's reading. Apropos of the books you mention, the life of Marshall is easy and interesting. H. Taylor I think of as you do, the interest such as it is is in Cicero, of whom I know less than I should. It did those chaps a lot of good to live expecting some day to die by the sword. Who is Judge Bruce? I never heard of him—I should expect a book of that title to be platitudes. But indeed I never have heard of most of the people you mention, e.g. Ker's *Dark Ages*—(mem. for future inquiry). I have a secretary who has socialistic velleities, though with a very rational nature, and I see in him the tendency common to the time to believe in regulating everything—against which I am as prejudiced as you are—not *a priori* but because I don't have sufficient respect for the ability and honesty of my neighbors to desire to be regulated by them, and because, though I don't believe in H. Spencer, I do believe in *The Fable of the Bees*. I must go out to luncheon, and send you my love. I wish I could write peaceably and at length. I told my sec'y that there was no injustice in death or in being born a toad rather than an eagle. I added that I desired to stand as the upholder of the respectable and commonplace.

There is no short cut to fame or comfort and all there is is to bore into it as hard as you can. But many of our friends seem to believe that they can legislate bliss. I have been so busy that I haven't opened even last week's *New Republic*.

November 30, 1917

Dear Laski,

You are a splendid young enthusiast and make me feel more alive. Your letter finds me in a happy humor to receive it for my work is done, for the moment. I have sent round an opinion in which I take three pages to say what should be said in a sentence, but which Brendeis thought ought to be put in solemn form because of its importance. It is hard to dilate upon the obvious even when one is in a bare majority and may by one's efforts turn it into a minority. Also I have finished Marsilio and in a few minutes expect to return it to the Library (I hate to have other people's books) whither I am going, to compare the etching over which I am hesitating—Van Dyck—3d state—with the first state or reproduction of the same. I expect to find that it has lost nothing by the additions and that the work is as fresh as when it was born—I can't believe that it could be more vivid. That done, I recur to the *Harvard Law Review* and your article in the Fall *Literary Review* of the *N.R.* [*New Republic*] on The Literature of Politics. I sympathize with the young as you know, but I have the foibles of the old. It riles me to note the air of having it all for the first time that is so common in the contributors to that noble sheet.

Later: It is done—the book returned—the etching compared—your article and some others in the *N.R.* read. Yours to my mind the only good one of the first four . . . You I think are open to a slight criticism for airy references to things that you know damned well your readers don't know about. Do you know anything about Prof. Goodnow's "Splendid book on Social Reform & the Constitution" (Beard p. 4)? It sounds as if I ought to read it. I hoped to dilate more at length but I must go back to my printseller—with my etchings under my arm and buy (one or both?) and otherwise bustle, but I would give one dollar and twenty-five cents for a comfortable jaw with you about nothing in particular this afternoon. You delight me by your reference to Hobbes in your letter. I think you seem to overrate Figgis—who seemed to me a useful worm rather than a flyer.

A bientôt.

December 22, 1922

My dear Laski,

No news since my last recently sent—so my answer to yours of the 5th received yesterday p.m. will be short. I found that Douglas and Orage *Credit, Power and Democracy* was short and I am through it without waiting for you. I didn't follow its reasoning clearly, but felt that I could see the outside limits of its use to me and so put it in the shelves. To free me from scruples, the same or the next evening your Mr. Martin (clever chap) turned up and gave me an account of an evening with the authors at the Webbs with Bertrand Russell *et al.*—and brought peace to my spirit. The next evening he dined with us and I enjoyed talking with him very much, though I am far from sharing all his views. All manner of details present themselves as soon as one has a little leisure down to the clearing out of corners and making more room in one's bookshelves. My! I feel so clean—the result is that the days go by with little reading done. I have just passed the middle of the one volume *Golden Bough,* the pages pitilessly snug with compact print, the ideas—I dare say to a considerable extent originating with Frazer—but familiar, the illustrations for the practice of the Bugaboos, the Wee Wees, the Beshitkas and manifold other savages making—as my father used to quote the Scotsman for saying about the calf's (sheep's) head—fine confused eating, the whole rather a reinforcement than an illumination, and heartbreaking to one who wanted to get through it—even though content to read. I can't bring my conscience to skimming—I have to read every word, though probably with no better result than if I just took the tips of the asparagus. So I shall be lucky if I have finished the damn thing by the time we go back to Court. You meantime will have eviscerated 100 pamphlets, and skun six folios, and eaten X octavos, all *en route* for a *magnum opus.* Fired by that thought I resume Frazer. My love and Christmas wishes to you both . . .

To Frederick Pollock

May 21, 1922

Dear Pollock,

. . . In the summer I always expect to improve my mind, but a reference of Saintsbury's led me to take down a cheap edition of Pepys's *Diary* and I think that as a preface to more serious employment I must get from the Athenaeum or buy the later unexpurgated edition and read it through. When you open Pepys you get one leg on the fly paper at once and it is hard to get away. A while ago I read George Willis, *The Philosophy of Speech,* with pleasure. I should suppose that he was very bold in linguistic hypotheses. He tumbles all the languages round in his lap like puppies but you don't have to believe a man implicitly to be stimulated. Quiller-Couch on *The Art of Writing,* which I read just before, barely repaid the reading—not much more. But a book that I read earlier and think that I have not mentioned heretofore, W. Lippmann on *Public Opinion,* seems to me really extraordinary. Perhaps he doesn't get anywhere in particular but there are few living I think who so discern and articulate the nuances of the human mind. There are some other things in this year's list worth mentioning but I won't write a catalogue. I must say a word for Radcliffe *Fishing from the Earliest Times* which filled a day when I was shut up by the doctor, with joy. Did you ever read anything by Francis Hackett who lately has left the *New Republic?* I think that in literary matters he has more power to utter the unutterable than anyone I can think of, but the gift hardly if at all appears in his *Story of the Irish Nation,* which seems to be written with enforced simplicity. One discounts somewhat any partisan account, but he tells a moving story well. One who is interested in the writer can say that, without accepting his point of view.

. . . We are very happy with the present Chief,* as I may have told

*Chief Justice William Howard Taft.—Ed.

you. He is good humored, laughs readily, not quite rapid enough, but keeping things moving pleasantly. His writing varies; he has done some things that I don't care for but others that I think touch a pretty high level. A slight difference at times is good, and I thought the other day that he expressed the movement of interstate commerce in a large and rather masterly way. Well, *sat prata biberunt* as the Latin Grammar says. Goodbye for the moment. My love to your wife.

November 5, 1923

Dear Pollock,

Your letter has just arrived and allows me to infer that you are as well as ever and feel no traces of your accident. I hope this is true? How I envy your being able to go to a thousand interesting places that echo of the past. I love the old. I like to have books in my library that were on shelves before America was discovered. I prefer prints that go back two or three hundred years and show one the same human feeling that we have today. Apart from "the grand old masters" I have hanging here a little Ostade that brought tears to my eyes until I became accustomed to it. A little peasant family sitting around a table with a bowl of porridge over which the father is saying grace—the little boy standing with the same reverential shoulders that one sees in Millet's *Angelus,* with no self-consciousness or melodrama . . . Last spring I got a rather below par impression of Rembrandt's portrait of himself in a felt hat—after he got religion—that I long had wanted and that I think very fine. My colleague Butler always reminds me of it in the modeling of his face . . .

Do you ever see my young(ish) friend Laski? He is a *heluo librorum,* reads a paragraph at a time and remembers it. I read much more slowly and forget. One does not forget the limits—one remembers that Hegel or Marx could not affect this mind beyond such and such points—but the articulation of their arguments or systems disappears.

I have interrupted myself at this point to consider a case in which Brandeis wants me to be ready with a dissent, because it weighs on my mind, and so I am no longer the careless and happy boy that began this. Please give my love to Lady Pollock. I drop with a shriek of adieu into the gulf . . .

To Morris Cohen

January 30, 1921

My dear Cohen,

Your generous notice of my book [*Collected Legal Papers*] touches and moves me deeply. There is no one whom I was more anxious about— for there are very few for whose judgment I care so much. But I wanted

you to feel free to "pass with your best violence" and so did not want you
to show me what you wrote before it appeared. I will not expatiate on
the happiness it gives me to read what you say. It makes life easier. An
odd phrase for a man who will be 80 in March. It seems as if at that date
one might tie up the past into a neat package, insure it with Cohen as
valuable, and take an irresponsible rest. But as soon as a corner is
turned the road stretches away again and ambition to go farther returns . . . With regard to your criticisms I may not have expressed in
writing the reserve that I often have expressed in talk—that I was
speaking only of the economic aspects of the regime of private property. I always have recognized that there might be an emotional issue
and that people might say I don't like it and I want a change even if it
costs me more—what I think a mistake is the giving of an emotional
attitude the aspect of an economic one. That I believe to be a humbug
and while I fully agree that it involves an issue of fact I have not failed to
talk with some economists who could give me light and for thirty years
have expressed to more than one of them the wish that we might be
furnished diagrams—expressed in money, labor hours or by whatever
unit was best of the different consumptions

R R Travel	Meat
Cereals	Luxuries of the few as I believe
	it would turn out, &c. &c.

As to the purposes of the cosmos—on the last page but one (bottom)
I leave open whether there is a plan of campaign. But as I don't believe
that I am a little god, I do in a sense worship the inevitable—although
in an unpublished speech at the Tavern Club (for Paul Bourget) I spoke
of "man's most peculiar power—the power to deny the actual and to
perish."

Of course you are right in taking me up on everything being connected with everything else—I know that you have your reserves on
that and are far more competent to speak than I am—I know that the
hypothesis is not proved. But it seems to me that it is almost the postulate in thinking about the universe and that the great advances in
thought have come from betting that there is more connection than has
been established up to that moment.

But I bow to you on that. Also I think it likely that early associations
affect my emotional attitude toward the mystery of the world. Well, I
expect a fall soon, for I begin today proud. I hope to avert the irony of
fate by recognizing that self feelings are a bait by which nature gets our
work out of us, but still I am very proud of such words from a philosopher whom I so deeply respect.

To Harold Laski

January 12, 1921

Dear Laski,

An even more than usually delightful letter from you came yesterday—(date 28th December). It told of a luncheon with Bryce and a dinner with Haldane—which I mention on the principle of a bit of cross-examination that Devens used to recite: "Merely to fix a date, your Honor—was this before or after you were burnt in effigy by your neighbors?" But having mentioned it I will add that your estimate of one of them seems to me correct, if you add, most loveable and having a to me—probably not to you—appalling omniscience. Industry is a dangerous virtue. I hardly need add how tickled I was by your account of the dinner. If you hadn't said between ourselves I should have read it to my wife and my secretary. I think you know the latter—Day Kimball—the politest and most agreeable of companions. I think having a certain hardness of intelligence that makes him less sensitive to atmospheric elements than to logic but doing his work as well as his play with me in first-rate style. By repercussion that makes me think of Landau a former one whom you knew . . . He had few goods in his shop window but gave one a good deal of spiritual companionship—and that makes me think of Disraeli and the affection that he inspired, and that makes me ask whether loveableness is a characteristic of the better class of Jews. When I think how many of the younger men that have warmed my heart have been Jews I cannot but suspect it, and put the question to you. Brandeis, whom many dislike, seems to me to have this quality and always gives me a glow, even though I am not sure that he wouldn't burn me at a slow fire if it were in the interest of some very possibly disinterested aim. I don't for a moment doubt that for daily purposes he feels to me as a friend—as certainly I do to him and without the above reserve. This, of course, *strictissime* between ourselves. I pause to remark that I have a scarf pin that gives me immense pleasure—it looks so like a cockroach hiding in a corner with a gleam of light upon his back. While interrogating you let me ask also whether you think as it sometimes is said that the Jews always have No. 1 at the bottom more than the rest of the world. I put these things to you as one capable of detached opinions. I find it hard to imagine of Cohen, for instance, who seems to me, whatever his foibles, to have a kind of holiness about him. We are listening to arguments on all sorts of cases rather more important than the average. The C. J. has been down with a cold for a few days which makes it inconvenient in a number of ways. I think he will be up in a day or two now.

Must be off for Court in a moment now. At odd minutes I am reading the *Confessions* of St. Augustine with much gusto. But I ought to be spending the time I have taken to write this upon some of the cases that have been argued: It is "consumed in the neglect of my duties." I send you a thousand longing thoughts.

March 15, 1917

Beloved lad,

The book arrived yesterday and your letter this morning. I read the first chapter last night with very great pleasure and of course with substantial agreement. Possibly there is an implication of a slightly different emphasis from my own. I am reminded of what I said at Langdell's dinner—that continuity with the past is not a duty, it is only a necessity. It seems to me rather a necessity than a duty for sovereignty to recognize its limits—its own limits. It very well may recognize the limits of another sovereignty. I forget whether I ever called your attention to *Cariño v. Insular Govt.* 212 U.S. 449, 458. Probably I did. I hardly need to tell you how pleased and flattered I feel at your preface and quotation. I suppose that I see from what I have read and the titles of the other chapters the scope of your understanding and I have no doubt that the book deserves and will bring you great credit.

The birthday was a great surprise and a great pleasure to me—but I would not have had you come on for a thousand dollars (payable to me). I couldn't have put you up and I should have been most anxious . . . I should like to follow your steps in Virgil (I stick to the old-fashioned spelling), but there is not much chance. If there are any crevices your book will fill them for the present. I am not a slow reader but I can't read a page or even a paragraph at a glance like you, and moreover although I take a few spoonsful of the classics now and then I never can get rid of a feeling that I am wasting time when there is much new to be read—witness the dazzling stream of names that you fire off at me, perhaps to keep me in my place as a worm. To be sure such reading as I have done—e.g. the *Banquet* of Plato a few years ago, or the *Oedipus* last summer, or a little Homer—has given me interesting reflections, but the interest is apt to be more in the reflections than the thing. I am somewhat subdued to what I work in, I want to read what bears in a general way on my path and I feel the want of a certain tension. I don't read as many novels as I used to and I care less for them I think. Now I am sketching possible dissents in various directions—sometimes with, sometimes against my brother B[randeis]. It is a fine sport as one is freer and more personal than when one is speaking for others as well as for oneself. To them I return. My love to you and homage to your wife.

March 29 [23?], 1917

Dear Laski,

A moment snatched for a word or two of answer. *Imprimis*—Joy to be ahead of you on any book. Unless the *Orpheus* is a recension I had it years ago, recommended it to others, and I doubt not have it on my shelves. 2. I send the Adamson opinions by this mail. They are all together. I thought Day's dissent wrong but the most rational. My own opinion goes the whole hog with none of the C.J.'s squeams—but I don't care to say more than is necessary. As I put it after the argument, I think if Congress can weave the cloth it can spin the thread. 3. Why did you call Ross a bad writer (in *Social Control*)? I thought it had considerable literary power. 4. I was delighted at your compliment to Peter Plymley. There is a cheap ed. of this at Beverly Farms and I remember being much impressed by their power and their style. 5. Why use the word pragmatist unless you adhere to W.J.'s philosophy on that matter. I never could make anything out of his or his friends' advocacy of his nostrum except either that in motives depending upon human conduct effort affects the result—which we have heard—or that by yearning we can modify the multiplication table, which I doubt. His whole attitude on the will to believe &c presupposes something that we can't change as the basis for recommending the will. Otherwise he has no answer if I say, "I don't want to." But I think as little of his philosophy as I do much of his psychology. He seems to me typically Irish in his strength and his weakness. 6. Which lastly reminds me of what you say of Francis Hackett. Of course I should be proud to have him really want a photograph of me (Oh Laski dear you said "autographed photograph" a vile phrase) but I never supposed he would care a damn for me, my ways, works, or machinery. So I am open to command but need a little reassuring. His and Wells's remarks led me to get Joyce, *Portrait of the Artist as a Young Man*, of which I have read a part. Certainly a singular picture—on the whole not carrying me away—but worth reading. Many pages are impressionist blots—you have to stand two rooms off to see the solid intended. Homage to madam and love to you.

February 19, 1920

Dear Laski,

Your article on Keynes I had read, with the usual and expected pleasure, before your letter came. I am waiting for the book. W. Lippmann asked me not to get it as he proposed to send it to me. If you look into George Ade read some of the *Fables in Slang*. I don't exactly understand who Beveridge's John Lowell was. I understood him not to be the judge. If I was wrong, I remember my father telling me that my grandmother said that the old Judge had brains enough to furnish three generations. You make me sick with your odious way of nabbing the books that *nous autres* would like to have got—if we had the eyes to see them. It is like my wife who will find a flower or something that is beautiful in a vase where the rest of us see only a dirty tangle. However, you are young and I am old and being old am less keen than I should have been when younger to possess books and engravings that reason tells me will soon be in the hands of my executor. If I understand Cardozo's remark it indicates what I may say without personal application that many American judges cannot get very near to their insight in words. I always say in conference that no case can be settled by general propositions, that I will admit any general proposition you like and decide the case either way.

My *New Republic* for the 18th hasn't come yet. Yesterday p.m. my business affairs having been attended to and the books of improvement on hand having been read I sought a moment of literary irresponsibility and took up at random a little volume of Hugo's *Choses vues*—happening on a visit to the *Conciergerie* and a mention of Louvel. So I went to Larousse for Louvel and to Paris guide books for the *Conciergerie* and had a delightful hour in gossiping about places and people in Paris. I suppose it is the *tourelles* of the *Conciergerie* that I see through the bridge in my Méryon etching. I think one could spend months delightfully in reviving literary and local gossip of this sort with regard to Paris—and local with regard to London. I remember hearing of an M.P. whom I knew slightly but whose name I have forgotten saying that after the adjournment he meant to devote two weeks to London with a Baedeker. If it were not a principle that the joy of life consists in the neglect of opportunities I could grieve that I didn't make a point of seeing this and that in England. But after all, as with the other parts of the globe, one has seen specimens enough, and I do not share Bryce's desire to engollobate the whole show. I must repeat another chestnut of mine that he who makes the most of himself doesn't make much. Well—I leave you for Victor Hugo once more.

February 25, 1921

Dear Laski,

A letter from you this morning brings the usual joy. (February 11). You tell of the Asquiths *et al.* As you know I retain an affectionate recollection of Mrs. Asquith and an abiding respect for her, *non obstant* her lamentable want of reserve to the public. I hadn't read her book, but have seen extracts and/or subsequent communications to the papers.

Wells's book (*Outline of History*) I have not quite finished—interruptions have been constant—but nearly, and with profit in spite of his asm for isms. He has the artist's gift. We don't go to artists for the discovery of truths but that they should make us feel and realize. That I think Wells does. He makes us feel, as I may have written, the continuity of history with pre-history, and feel the world as one. As I draw near the end I find more dominant the tendency to expound and illustrate his opinions which I don't care much for. I am indifferent to his philosophy of life. Cohen, who was here the other day and delightful, was disgusted with his lack of appreciation for the Greeks—and of Alexander the Great (Wells seems *ex industria* to belittle all the most famous—Alexander, Caesar, Charlemagne, Napoleon). Cohen discoursed most interestingly about what Greece taught the orient and the Jews. Now the recess draws to an end—with as usual less leisure than I hoped, but at least with the dentist done with for the present and also with some pleasant moments, though I haven't had a chance for a jaw with Rice, the head of the print department in the Congressional Library. The few days when it was possible my throat has been in such condition that to talk meant to cough at night. The Doctor came in yesterday (summoned by my wife to look at me) and gave me a sucker for my throat that really seems to do good. I had the best night for a fortnight last night. Incidentally he inspected me as I have puffed and panted more than I used to and said I was all right in heart and lungs. These physical details are unpardonable. Do you regard abbreviations in a letter as equally so? I don't. *The Nation* had a very flattering review of our book—by a lawyer, Professor Thomas Reed Powell of Columbia—and altogether I am on the look-out for something that will take me down badly—for P.L. also put in a little puff in the N.R. (I have mentioned Cohen's notice.) This egotistical excursus must be forgiven—if one can't think about oneself a little as he reaches 80 when can he? It makes me tired to read of the mellifluous days when it is to be all SERVICE—and love of our neighbor and I know not what. There shall be one Philistine, egotist, unaltruistical desirer to do his damnedest, and believer that self, not brother, was the primary care entrusted to him, while this old soldier lives. If A lives for B and B for C and so on there must be an end somewhere. Let's be Ends—you as well as I. I am proud of you.

Aff'ly yours,
O. W. Holmes

N.B. I always have insisted that the above vaunted egotism makes us martyrs and altruists before we suspect it.

To Frederick Pollock

April 6, 1924

Dear Pollock,

A good letter from you came yesterday to cheer me on my return from conference preliminary to sitting again on Monday. Apropos of "journalese jargon" of which you speak I remember once saying: profanity is vitriol, slang is vinegar, but reporters' English is rancid butter. I don't know that you have the thing to which I refer in England—an intrusion into the language of sentiment, as when they call a house a home. It abounds here. No, I never saw *Faust* (i.e. Goethe's) on the stage. I agree that B. Taylor's translation is much the best, but he does take the edge off and the poetry out of many passages. As to part 2, I wait for better days—though I have read it.

I have taken a very little turn at the classics while I had some leisure. I found that I had Seneca and turned over his pages for a few hours, got some really good things and said goodbye—too much crumbs. Then a little Plutarch in translation and then the *Menaechmi* of Plautus, as I didn't remember ever having read one of his plays—the Latin easy to my surprise—the fun rudimentary, not to my ditto. Then I took up Tacitus (for [?] the Day of Judgment), as I never had read anything but his short pieces. I read two books of the *History,* all I had time for, with great delight. The intense compactness of his writing is a lesson. I must add him to Rousseau's *Confessions* as one that is as good as ever was. I think I have not written all this to you before, but my memory wobbles. Have I uttered the fundamental blasphemy, that once said, set the spirit free? The Literature of the past is a bore—when one has said that frankly to oneself then one can proceed to qualify and make exceptions. Now I have opened Santayana *Scepticism and Animal Faith.* He is not a bore, but I think he improvises and obscures the foundations of his thought with too many tickling words. *Au fond,* unless I mistake, he takes much the same view that I have taken *en passant* in one or two of my things. His philosophy is much nearer to my way of thinking than James's or Royce's. But my moments of reading will be cut off for a month now.

I was amused by a question of taste yesterday. In one of my opinions I give a short account of a statute and say that there are amplifications "to stop rat holes" that need not be stated as the plaintiffs admit that they are within the Statute. The C. J. criticised. I said our reports were dull because we had the notion that judicial dignity required solemn fluffy speech, as, when I grew up, everybody wore black frock coats and black cravats (I didn't say that to them). I didn't care for the phrase but do for the principle. . . .

To Harold Laski

February 20, 1925

Dear Laski,

. . . In these last moments of unexpired leisure, in which there still are daily jobs, I have been reading Hind's *Short History of Engraving and Etching*—and renewing my youth when I pored over a dictionary of engravers by one Shearjashut Spooner—"Phoebus, what a name"—until I could recognise prints by their remembered description. It is a very pleasant pursuit of useless knowledge—most of which I shall forget forthwith. Now I miss Rice (of whose death I wrote to you lately). I put the magnifying glass on to my Dürers and Mantegnas—(school of—if the elephants and two others were by his hand according to current judgment they would have cost many more hundreds than they did tens). But I don't try to follow in detail the minute distinctions of method that these conoshures take.

Adieu pour le momong.

Affectionately yours,
O.W.H.

No, I must add a word or two. How characteristic of the Virginian (generally provincial) to think more of Jefferson than of Washington. Washington had the nation in his belly. It is many years since I read Bossuet but my recollection is of really moving eloquence. You don't expect to be moved by the thought of anyone of that time. If I remember rightly, Jhering at the beginning of his *Geist d. R. R.* has remarks on the dangers of specialists, but I always have thought it best to get at the universe through some definite door. I am surprised at what you say of those who have joined the monarchical Catholics. Unless this is merely a political move I should think it threw a very discrediting light on the faculties of the youth in question.

To Frederick Pollock

June 10, 1923

Dear Pollock,

It is a joy to see your noble fist again and to know that no permanent harm was done. It is hard for old sportsmen to avoid the perils of the highway. I have come devilish near to running into an automobile. Keep the aquiline orb peeled. However, you are not old yet. Age begins with 80. Tomorrow morning we come in for our last opinions and adjourn for the summer . . . I shall have a dissent in two suits by *Pennsylvania and Ohio vs. West Virginia* to prevent the enforcement of a W.V.

statute intended to give a preference to the inhabitants of W.V. in the use of the natural gas produced in the State. As the case has not yet been decided I say no more. Otherwise I have nothing. My cases all have been written and delivered. I am pleased to think that I have done my full share of work—the doctor thinks it remarkable that I was able to—but as I don't know how narrow the margin may be I have not volunteered as I generally do to take some extra cases and relieve those who are hard pressed, and generally I have avoided all additional taxes. As a result I feel in good case, though none of us knows how tired he may be. I told you I believe that late in life I have discovered Montaigne and have read him with enormous delight. The beast knows a lot of things that I had fondly hoped had been reserved for me . . . I got a letter this morning from a girl asking what were the requirements for a stenographer. I told her that I never employed one. If it weren't for my wife I doubt if I should have any modern improvements. She put in electricity, the telephone, and now the elevator—and the queer thing is that she never will go to the telephone or use the lift. Our women go north this evening and leave us as usual with a female caretaker who will get our breakfasts, and two colored men. I rather like the change for a few days.

Don't overtax yourself while you are getting thoroughly well and give my love to your wife who I dare say has felt the burden of your accident quite as much as you . . .

April 2, 1926

My dear Pollock,

. . . I was overwhelmed with letters, telegrams, and papers on and after my birthday, and they with my work drove me to the limit of my powers. I was surprised and no little pleased at some of the articles. But that is over now and for the rest of this and next week I am as near the feeling of leisure as I am likely to get. I need it and mean to be as idle as I can. The only book I read, at odd minutes, is Horace Walpole's Correspondence—just the thing for such moments. He once in a while is surprisingly ahead of his beef-eating contemporaries, and his style is so pleasant that one can read on indefinitely without fatigue. For all round, I think you might put him at the head of English letter writers, of course Charles Lamb is more pungent and has more genius, and very possibly Byron whom I don't remember so well, but take the world he tells you about and the way he tells it, I think one could read him longer with undiminished pleasure. But, oh, my dear Pollock, I began talking about leisure and since I began this letter three opinions have come in that I must read carefully, and a man has called to jaw with me about writing something to be engrossed on parchment and put under a corner stone! (a decent chap though) and one of my brethren is coming later, and I have a polite letter from Belgium with a signature that I can't read but concerning which I must consult the Belgian Embassy. I may say with Betsy Prig—leisure, I don't believe there's no sich a person. Even when I am ready to be idle I say to myself what duty am I neglecting? I turn to your last letter. I think I met your brother in former days but I knew only his name. You speak for the need of a certain modicum of intelligence for justice. It seems to me that the whole scheme of salvation depends on having a required modicum of intelligence. People are born fools and damned for not being wiser. I often say over to myself the verse "O God, be merciful to me a fool," the fallacy of which to my mind (you won't agree with me) is in the "me," that it looks on man as a little God over against the universe, instead of as a cosmic ganglion, a momentary intersection of what humanly speaking we call streams of energy, such as gives white light at one point and the power of making syllogisms at another, but always an inseverable part of the unimaginable, in which we live and move and have our being, no more needing its mercy than my little toe needs mine. It would be well if the intelligent classes could forget the word sin and think less of being good. We learn how to behave as lawyers, soldiers, merchants, or what not by being them. Life, not the parson, teaches conduct. But I seem to be drooling moralities and will shut up and go up to the Belgian Embassy as I said. My love to Lady Pollock.

To Harold Laski

Beverly Farms, July 1, 1927

My dear Laski,

This morning there comes a delightful and desired letter from you busy about many things to me as near idle as I can be. I have read little—the most serious book: Morley's on *Diderot*. Morley seems to me a razor not a sting—and the finest edge of his thought a little blunted by respectability. I did Haskins, *The Renaissance in the Twelfth Century*—a great wrong by the first impression that I told you of. I found him very interesting and instructive—although already it seems years since I finished the volume. Yet I believe my last letter, answering your last, was written as I was beginning it. It seems as if I had mentioned *The Road to Xanadu*—I can't have. I didn't read the whole of it but the best 100 pages, a search into the materials for "Kubla Khan" in what Coleridge had been reading is an admirable bit of work. Not a name, not a thought, hardly an adjective that is not traced, so that all that was needed was a dream, opinion and genius—and the writer fully appreciates the genius needed to produce the poem. Then a French tale—*La nuit kurde,* by Bloch—of which I do not see much use, depicting the melodramatic doings of a young warrior, of which it is enough to mention his emulating a spider by screwing a woman while he killed her by biting and, put in as an extra, chewing her throat. Then a few pages in a long book about a woman who writes would-be poetry and tales by the ouija board. Pretty much drool to my mind—but exciting the admiration of the commentator. It is a comment on man. When he absorbs himself in a system or an atmosphere—Catholicism, Hegel, Spiritualism, it doesn't matter what—he soon loses all relation to outside standards, and becomes a satellite of the sun around which the system turns. I don't see how we can help smiling at ourselves—so arbitrary, irrational and despotically given are our ultimates. I feel as if I were wasting my patrimony when I am not producing articulate words and merely receiving impressions that lose their form when I turn my back. An artist would feel just the opposite—each yielding to a compulsion of nature as he yields to the outside world, and having no better justification than that he desires to live. Why? Why do I desire to win my game of solitaire? A foolish question, to which the only answer is that you are up against it. Accept the inevitable and do your damnedest. Meantime I do receive impressions in my daily drives that are full of charm and that at least enrich life if they don't enrich me. I can't get it quite straight in my memory whether Redlich came to us last winter—but I agree to all that you say about him. Frankfurter and Mrs. called the other day and gave me much pleasure. His *Progress Report of Harvard Survey of Crime and Law in Boston* impresses me greatly and makes me believe when heretofore I have been a sceptic. I should rejoice if he produced what promises (at least to my ignorance) to be a great and noble work. I had only a glimpse of Gooch and wished that I had seen more—but I suppose he was busy and so my talk ends in the doubtful hope that this will catch tomorrow's boat.

January 23, 1928

My dear Laski,
   This begins a letter that I don't know when I can finish seeing that I have a five to four case just assigned to me in which I am the doubting fifth. But I must say that you stir depths when you speak of showing me your Paris and your Antwerp. Also I am charmed by your old Belgian Jesuit and delighted at your experience with Shaw and Chesterton. I have told you often that I didn't care what Shaw thought about anything—that I regard him as he once described himself as a mountebank—good to make you laugh but not to be taken too seriously. When Chesterton tackles fundamentals he seems to me incom-

petent. When he utters paradoxical epigrams he amuses me—but as to him also I don't care what he thinks.

'Tis done—my opinion has gone to the printer and I hope even that it may convince Brandeis who took the opposite view. Two generations ahead of me there was a well known lawyer in Boston, Charles G. Loring, whom my mother-in-law pronounced a really good man because he never took a case that he didn't believe in—perhaps a more sardonic way of putting it would be that he believed in every case that he took. My senior partner was a student in his office and one day Loring working on a brief said "I pursue this investigation with increasing confidence"—a good touch of human nature which I now illustrate, having convinced myself quite comfortably. Dear me—how can man take himself so seriously—in view not only of the foregoing, but of the fact that a change in the wind or the electrical condition will change his whole attitude toward life. Of course he can't help being serious in living and functioning, but I mean in attributing cosmic importance to his thought and believing that he is in on the ground floor with God. This interjection comes up to me so often that I can't help repeating it often as I probably have uttered it before.

I was amused last night by a number of the *Mercure de France* sent to me by Gerrit Miller with an article intended to show the Casanova when he wrote his memoirs in his old life was an omnivorous reader, and as the reporters say in their rancid language—abreast of the times—that therefore various coincidences with a work by Diderot then attributed to the Chevalier de la Morlière, with Faublas and with Restif de la Bretonne, indicate that he had read the works referred to and heightened his memoirs with high lights from those sources. If you are a Casanovan this may interest you. C's book did me good at a critical moment—just when I had got out my *Common Law* and had some symptoms that for the moment I mistook for a funeral knell. It is an amazing work as no doubt you know . . .

February 18, 1928

My dear Laski,

Two A-1 letters from you—one closely following the other and ending with the admirable tale of Matthew—I suppose it was his father that took me to Court one day to witness a trial before Sir A. Cockburn—in which M. was counsel on one side. Cockburn seemed to be busy correcting proof—it was supposed of his charge, in the *Tichborne* case, while the trial went on. I was much struck by the way it was conducted. One side stated the facts—the counsel on the other side at a certain point: "I shall have to trouble you to put on evidence upon that." If he did it didn't take long and Cockburn said he would direct a verdict. Thereupon one side said that he should like to be allowed to address the jury—which he did in a short argument—and then Cockburn charged strongly on the side for which he had been inclined to direct the verdict and the jury found accordingly without leaving their seats. Then one juryman stood up and said, "I understand"—(a certain fact, I forget what) to be so and so." "No, no, no" said the others—but he had put his finger on what seemed to me the point in the case—which I thought the judge and lawyer had overlooked. The jury put their heads together—discussed a little among themselves, and then brought in their verdict the other way—I thought rightly—with little help from Judge or lawyers. My memory may have distorted things, but that is the way I have remembered it for many years. I don't believe that I need to explain why it seemed to me to illustrate what Judge John Lowell said to me when I was a young lawyer: "They do everything on honor in England." Well, this p.m., our last conference before going in again on Monday for 4 weeks of argument. I had but one case to deliver—a majority opinion of no great interest—Brandeis dissenting—but at the last minute McReynolds said that he wanted to write something (against the op.) and so it went over. It is rather aggravating to have things hang up in that way because the Judge doesn't take the trouble to be ready. He has three weeks of vacation for it. I tried to put a shovel full of coals on his head by handing him my prospective dissent where we stand 5 to 4 unless he changes his mind, and where he has the majority opinion to write—which he has not started on yet. I despise the notion that I think some of the last generation had that it was like opposing counsel in Court and that it would be fine to spring something unforeseen on the other side. I read them my views in another case in which the following vote showed that I was in the minority but on which I will have my whack if I live, if it is my last word.

Brandeis and I are so apt to agree that I was glad to have dissent in my case, as it shows that there is no preestablished harmony. I have had almost no time to read—having had two hours of driving on pleasant days. I have finished Greville's *Diary* and that is about all. I think I mentioned Demogue, *Notions fondamentales du droit privé*—which I was compelled to get hold of by the remarks of Morris Cohen in an essay. Demogue is a good man evidently—but for 100 pages he has told me nothing that I didn't know—substantially, has illustrated to me that some problems are not dug down to the foundations as well as with us—and yet I haven't the moral courage to stop, but feel obliged to toil on through 559 more pages in a print that tires my eyes for fear of missing something—or because I don't like to back out. Your last letter but one was the first news I had had of the death of Felix [Frankfurter]'s mother. I referred obliquely to it in writing to him—but could not do more.

I vehemently disagree with the "contempt for the jingles of Kipling." I agree that Kipling's attitude toward life seems to me wanting in complexity and not interesting—but it will take more than Sassoon to convince me that Kipling ought not to stir the fundamental human emotions. I think he does—and that simple thinkers often do. A student of mine long dead spoke with contempt of the fighting lines in *Henry V.* His widow was a mainstay of the sympathizers with Sacco and Vanzetti. I was not with him.

3 • CULTURE AND PERSONALITIES

Dr. S. Weir Mitchell

Remarks at a Tavern Club Dinner,
March 4, 1900

OS 119

. . . I shall venture for a moment away from the field of personal reflections. It seems to me that in one sense the sphere of literature is narrowing. Art and religion, in spite of their kinship, long have lived under separate roofs. Law left the hands of the priests even further back. Today the whole domain of truth concerning the visible world belongs to science. One half resents sporadic *aperçus* about the universe because he discerns that they are fragments of an actual or possible science. It no longer would be possible for any but superficial persons to repeat Mrs. Browning's attitudinizing exclamation concerning the poets: "I speak of the only truth-tellers now left to God." We know that God is not so hard up as she professed to think. We yield but scant sympathy to Tennyson's posing

> Vex not thou the poet's mind
> With thy shallow wit

We know that the epoch-making ideas have come not from the poets but from the philosophers, the jurists, the mathematicians, the physicists, the doctors—from the men who explain, not from the men who feel. We realize that explanation and feeling are at the opposite poles of intellectual life, and require and come from opposite interests and opposite gifts. We no longer ask of *belles lettres* that they should be a "criticism of life," in Matthew Arnold's phrase, or that they should help us to fix our attitude toward the world. We do not read novels for improvement or instruction. We do not want "medicated fiction"—to quote what once was said to my father—we want only to be amused, to be moved, to be uplifted, and to be charmed.

To my mind the great realistic movement is perfectly consistent with what I have said. The end of art is to pull the trigger of an emotion. But what will pull the trigger depends upon the audience. If they know too much to believe a ghost story even for half an hour, there is no use in telling them ghost stories. If the instantaneous photograph has made them notice more exactly how animals move, the old pictures of races, in which the horses' legs stuck out straight fore and aft, no longer give them this feeling of speed, and the pictures miss their end. Realism seeks more truth, not because truth is the end of art, but because at the present day more truth is the condition of our feeling what the artist wants to make us feel.

So I say that there has been a further differentiation of callings; that art no longer is a handyman about the house, with a general business of imparting useful information, but that it more and more definitely is and will be confined to the function of making us feel what it is for others to prove and in the main to discover. For the most part thinkers belong in the opposite camp. Few indeed are the men who unite in any degree the power to disclose truth and the power to make it live in our hearts. Few are they who at once can reveal and charm.

I have made these general reflections, partly because they naturally came into my mind when I think of literature, and because, while no general proposition is worth a straw, the chief end of man is to frame them, but mainly in honor of our guest, who presents so very unusual an example of success at both the poles. A man must indeed command large forces who can turn both flanks of the enemy and not himself be cut in two.

To Harold Laski

March 26, 1925

Dear Laski,

. . . As to poor Norton it is hard to be exactly just. He had a fine side to him. He was cultivated and gave of his cultivation to those who needed it. When I was in college I got him made an honorary member of the Hasty Pudding unless my memory deceives me, but he was only a parasite of literature. Bill James once said that in another century they would think Norton the great dark sun around whom the eminent of his time revolved, as he published the letters to him and had the intelligence not to print his replies. On the other hand Woodberry, a somewhat more than local poet, told in teaching verse how Norton opened to him a world of beauty and cultivation that otherwise would have been closed. Let us be just to him while not expecting him to say anything to us. It is said that he began a lecture once—"probably none of you ever has seen a gentleman." He had a good Boston tradition as a speaker, and in his later years certainly spoke like a gentleman, with a certain personal distinction. In middle life I found it hard to be just to him, but age has mellowed my revolt just as it has brought back kindly feelings to Charles Eliot of whom at one time I might have complained—we are good friends now. I wrote to him on his 90th birthday and got back a regular schoolmaster's letter in which he considered and summed up his former pupil. What you say about H. James in connection with the others perhaps has in view the same thing that I had when I used to say that I thought it underbred to discourse on and make literary capital out of the social position of the important American in Europe. That is a matter solved by the individual and best not made a matter of consciousness. A man of intellect ought to take society *de haut en bas,* i.e., recognizing its value and charm, and at the same time its unimportance as compared with his superlatives . . .

To Alice Stopford Green

June 7, 1914

My dear friend,

. . . I see little of the Chief [Chief Justice White] in these days. Like most of the Southerners I have known you have to take him on his own terms. You can't expect as one does with men of the great world a reciprocity of interest. The things and points of view that most occupy me he cares little for—so that I listen to him a good deal more than he does to me—and his view of life and of the law naturally does not hit me. How that sentence illustrates the passing of metaphor into abstraction from which all sense of the original figure has vanished. To talk of a view hitting one is almost as bad as speaking of the *confluence* of the English *school* with the *first fruits* of German historical knowledge—as I once did in my hot youth. You see the same thing in design. What once was a human face or a bird's head degenerates as portraiture but grows as ornament until it becomes an arabesque in which the original motif can be detected only by history. Such things interest me. I have been amused at an illustration of the theory of conventional manners in a squirrel. He drops his nut through the bars of the floor of his cage— and then gives the regulation scratches and pats, as if it were earth. So man takes off his hat . . .

To Frederick Pollock

October 13, 1921

Dear Pollock,

Your letter as to handwriting provokes a line following recent letters. I never did hold it, as our statists do, a baseness to write fair (I suppose on the theory that it showed time taken from the sword for the pen). On the contrary I used rather to pride myself on writing legal documents before the times of modern apparatus. Somewhat in this manner, only more elaborate. But as I noticed once in a book that studied design in New Guinea (Haddon, *Evolution in Art*) degeneration in one direction may mean development in another, and rudimentary human hands or frigate birds etc. become beautiful and complex arabesques. So, as the copy book fades personality becomes more distinct and sometimes appearance is improved . . .

To Harold Laski

Beverly Farms, August 24, 1924

Dear Laski,

Your letter, like Hume for Kant, awakens me from my dogmatic slumber. This is not a compliment but a figurative expression of the puddle of repose into which your letter splashes. After I got through *La guerre et la paix* with some admiration and not great pleasure I turned for ease of mind to [Roscoe] Pound's *Law and Morals* which I gobbled up with comfort. But again I was led to agree with your remark that he brings his categories ready made instead of finding them in the *res*. I always blow Pound's horn. I admire and am overwhelmed by his learning, but I rarely find that unexpectedness which as you say is the most attractive thing. It worries me to think that perhaps or probably I don't do him justice but few of his own thoughts about the law seem to me important contributions. I say this in the most private confidence, and ask you to correct me if you can. I often find things I didn't know and am glad to know—but they are old facts not new theories. I beg you to teach me to qualify this impression—I want to admire more. As to your Latin dramas, I wrote to you last winter of the effect of Plautus on me. *The Way of All Flesh* which I am reading now has an amusing essay supposed to be by a Cambridge student, the hero, to the effect that the Greek tragedians are also bores, and that Aristophanes thought and said so. I always am moved by the *Prometheus* and find passages in the others—but I think we hardly realize on what a different plane they are from modern drama. I agree with you about Montesquieu, but think that we must give Rousseau credit for his echoes—I thought I was reading a first sketch of Hegel when I read his *Contrat social*. I was pleased in a lecture of Santayana on the unknowable to see another man now out of fashion, Herbert Spencer, given a certain credit. If I may quote myself we must correct the judgment of posterity by that of the time. He was in fashion once, therefore he filled a need. Our fashion is no more respectable than any other. If a man has his time of being in fashion he has all that anyone has, and has proved his claim to be a force shaping the future.

As to onomatopoeia in poetry—hm—taking onomatopoeia in the strict sense—but I agree to and assert that the main feature of style properly so called is sound—what I have called an undersong in the words. Thackeray has it to a marked degree. I don't see how you can doubt that modern poetry is more subtle, taken in the mass, than any earlier verse. This Butler (*Way of All Flesh*) is a queer chap—over-valued I think by those who discovered him. (I first did for myself in *The New Quarterly*, a short-lived periodical for which I subscribed because I had stayed at the home of the man who kept it going—at Bury St. Edmonds where they had the pageant.) But he was a clever, original-minded man with *aperçus* that I suspect were not quite penetrating enough to give him a coherent view of the world. I have some philosophical books sent me by Cohen which I hope to plunge into tomorrow—after finishing *The Way of All Flesh*. Lord how I like this irresponsible leisure. My love to you both.

February 1, 1925

Dear Laski,

. . . I always say whether it be philosophy or law, or what you like, begin with the latest. The modern book starts from your *milieu*, emotional and intellectual, and of course, whatever they say, has enormous advantages also from the advance of science. I shouldn't tell a law student to begin with Coke, Littleton, or even with Blackstone. I did with Blackstone and had infinite trouble from details and language that I didn't understand, and that no one could understand until he had made some progress in the history and philosophy of law. As I said of Montesquieu, to read the great books of the past with intelligent appreciation is one of the last achievements of a studious life. Oh—I am fierce on that theme. The philosophically least consideration, perhaps, is practically very great. Ideas rarely are difficult to grasp. The difficulties come from the language and emphasis. The language, even if English, and the emphasis, of a different time, to some extent also of a different place, are strange and puzzling to a neophyte. To this day I am troubled as I hear arguments in patents, or mining, or admiralty or railroad cases, by the slang of the specialty. The thoughts behind the words rarely require a colossus. Of course I agree with you as to morality and have uttered my barbaric yawp on the subject from time to time. It is amusing to see in the law how in a century what was thought natural and wholesome may become anathema—like rum and the lottery—but they generally are argued about as if the present view was an eternal truth . . .

Herbert v. Shanley Company
242 U.S. 591 (1917)

These two cases present the same question: whether the performance of a copyrighted musical composition in a restaurant or hotel without charge for admission to hear it infringes the exclusive right of the owner of the copyright to perform the work publicly for profit . . .

If the rights under the copyright are infringed only by a performance where money is taken at the door, they are very imperfectly protected. Performances not different in kind from those of the defendants could be given that might compete with and even destroy the success of the monopoly that the law intends the plaintiffs to have. It is enough to say that there is no need to construe the statute so narrowly. The defendants' performances are not eleemosynary. They are part of a total for which the public pays, and the fact that the price of the whole is attributed to a particular item which those present are expected to order, is not important. It is true that the music is not the sole object, but neither is the food, which probably could be got cheaper elsewhere. The object is a repast in surroundings that to people having limited powers of conversation or disliking the rival noise give a luxurious pleasure not to be had from eating a silent meal. If music did not pay it would be given up. If it pays, it pays out of the public's pocket. Whether it pays or not the purpose of employing it is profit and that is enough.

To Lewis Einstein

Beverly Farms, July 28, 1928

Dear Einstein,

. . . I have just read a book about Villon which seems to give one all there is (by Wyndham Lewis); but I don't like the writer very well. He has a Catholic swagger that seems to me like a literary flavor rather than devotion, he pads, and, while he affects Urquhart's Rabelaisian English, the minute he comes to a straight stout word in Villon that calls a cock a cock he dodges and gives some flat generality instead. I shouldn't mind if he wasn't so damned Rabelaisian when it costs nothing. Also a book by a young American living in Paris (Hemingway), *The Sun Still* [sic] *Rises,* which excites some interest in others and in me. No events greater than going to a bull fight, much conversation without an idea in it, characterizing phrases replaced by damn and hell, no marked character, the chief interest of the parties food and drink with a discreet hint of fornication, and most of them drunk nearly every evening. I think of rereading the book to try to find out why it interests and why I suspect it to be a work of art. I should think that the chances were that the author of such a book living in Paris would go to the devil, but he may leave the swill pail and rise . . .

Bleistein v. Donaldson Lithographing Company
188 U.S. 239 (1903)

This is . . . an action . . . to recover the penalties prescribed for infringements of copyrights. The alleged infringements consisted in the copying in reduced form of three chromolithographs prepared by employes of the plaintiffs for advertisements of a circus owned by one Wallace. Each of the three contained a portrait of Wallace in the corner, and lettering bearing some slight relation to the scheme of decoration, indicating the subject of the design and the fact that the reality was to be seen at the circus. One of the designs was of an ordinary ballet, one of a number of men and women, described as the Stirk family, performing on bicycles, and one of groups of men and women whitened to represent statues. The circuit court directed a verdict for the defendant on the ground that the chromolithographs were not within the protection of the copyright law, and this ruling was sustained by the circuit court of appeals . . .

We shall do no more than mention the suggestion that painting and engraving, unless for a mechanical end, are not among the useful arts, the progress of which Congress is empowered by the Constitution to promote. The Constitution does not limit the useful to that which satisfies immediate bodily needs. It is obvious also that the plaintiffs' case is not affected by the fact, if it be one, that the pictures represent actual groups—visible things. They seem from the testimony to have been composed from hints or description, not from sight of a performance. But even if they had been drawn from the life, that fact would not deprive them of protection. The opposite proposition would mean that a portrait by Velasquez or Whistler was common property because others might try their hand on the same face. Others are free to copy the original. They are not free to copy the copy. The copy is the personal reaction of an individual upon nature. Personality always contains something unique. It expresses its singularity even in handwriting, and a very modest grade of art has in it something irreducible, which is one man's alone. That something he may copyright unless there is a restriction in the words of the act.

If there is a restriction it is not to be found in the limited pretensions of these particular works. The least pretentious picture has more originality in it than directories and the like, which may be copyrighted. The amount of training required for humbler efforts than those before us is well indicated by Ruskin. "If any young person, after being taught what is, in polite circles, called 'drawing,' will try to copy the commonest piece of real work—suppose a lithograph on the title page of a new opera air, or a woodcut in the cheapest illustrated newspaper of the day—they will find themselves entirely beaten." There is no reason to doubt that these prints in their *ensemble* and in all their details, in their design and particular combinations of figures, lines, and colors, are the original work of the plaintiffs' designer. If it be necessary, there is express testimony to that effect. It would be pressing the defendant's right to the verge, if not beyond, to leave the question of originality to the jury upon the evidence in this case . . .

These chromolithographs are "pictorial illustrations." The word "illustrations" does not mean that they must illustrate the text of a book, and that the etchings of Rembrandt or Steinla's engraving of the Madonna di San Sisto could not be protected today if any man were able to produce them. Again, the act, however construed, does not mean that ordinary posters are not good enough to be considered within its scope. The antithesis to "illustrations or works connected with the fine arts" is not works of little merit or of humble degree, or illustrations addressed to the less educated classes; it is "prints or labels designed to be used for any other articles of manufacture." Certainly works are not the less connected with the fine arts because their pictorial quality attracts the crowd, and therefore gives them a real use—if use means to increase trade and to help to make money. A picture is none the less a subject of copyright that it is used for an advertisement. And if pictures may be used to advertise soap, or the theatre, or monthly magazines, as they are, they may be used to advertise a circus. Of course, the ballet is as legitimate a subject for illustration as any other. A rule cannot be laid down that would excommunicate the paintings of Degas . . .

It would be a dangerous undertaking for persons trained only to the law to constitute themselves final judges of the worth of pictorial illustrations, outside of the narrowest and most obvious limits. At the one extreme, some works of genius would be sure to miss appreciation. Their very novelty would make them repulsive until the public had learned the new language in which their author spoke. It may be more than doubted, for instance, whether the etchings of Goya or the paintings of Manet would have been sure of protection when seen for the first time. At the other end, copyright would be denied to pictures which appealed to a public less educated than the judge. Yet if they command the interest of any public, they have a commercial value—it would be bold to say that they have not an aesthetic and educational value—and the taste of any public is not to be treated with contempt. It is an ultimate fact for the moment, whatever may be our hopes for a change. That these pictures had their worth and their success is sufficiently shown by the desire to reproduce them without regard to the plaintiffs' rights. We are of opinion that there was evidence that the plaintiffs have rights entitled to the protection of the law.

To Harold Laski

March 11, 1922

Dear Laski,

. . . I am interested by what you say of Gibbon. I too was vastly impressed by his sweep and mastery and his power of telling a story. I doubt if one can say that Maitland could have made such a picture had he lived at that time. But what struck me was that he told me very little that I cared to hear. The emphasis has changed, as it always does, and apart from the fact that much more is known upon the subjects that we do want to hear about, such as Christianity and the Roman law, he takes time in giving characters that I don't believe and am indifferent to, and a thousand details of wanderings, incursions and alarums that I forget as soon as read, but gives me nothing of the rise and decay of institutions such as I could read about in Fustel de Coulanges. I speak from a memory of about ten years ago. History has to be rewritten because history is the selection of those threads of causes or antecedents that we are interested in—and the interest changes in fifty years. Newman struck me, probably forty or 50 years ago, much as [he] does you—a tender spirit and a born writer arguing like a pettifogger—but I have only read the *Grammar of Assent* I believe. A fine start he makes in pointing out how much we must take for granted if we would talk together. But I said to myself, accepting that premise, if I put it brutally I think him an incompetent old ass—and he would think me an impertinent young monkey. (I was young then.) Adam Smith is about as far back as Newman. His book seemed to me more like a treatise on life than political economy in a narrow sense. I didn't think Karl Marx the size to patronize him as a bourgeois intelligence, as I think he did . . .

To Frederick Pollock

January 23, 1922

Dear Pollock,

The forty-eight hours that have elapsed since I received your letter have changed the tone of my thoughts, since today brings news of Bryce's death. Thus breaks one of the oldest associations that I had with living men. Ah, my dear boy, please make sure that you survive me and don't leave me in the greater solitude. We intimately mixed, rather than chemically combined, but the mixture was so intimate that the loss is great to me as, no doubt, to you. I am glad that we didn't miss a visit from him last summer and had some last familiar talks. I felt a little shy about asking them, thinking that they would be bored with many invitations, but found that they were glad to come as we were glad to have them—many old memories come back but I will say no more.

To Lewis Einstein

December 5, 1913

Dear Einstein,

. . . Last week while we were adjourned and my work being done I read with a great deal of admiration Santayana's *Winds of Doctrine*. Wonderful knowledge and easy criticisms of systems with many *aperçus* that I have shared without owing them to him. I said (considering his possible retention of his membership in the Catholic Church) that he stood on the flat road to heaven and buttered slides to hell for all the rest, so well does he state the fundamental scepticisms without committing himself . . .

To Harold Laski

February 17, 1924

Dear Laski,

. . . Yesterday eve I looked into Shaftesbury's *Characteristics* and read the *Letter on Enthusiasm*. It is a b c to us, but still not to a large part of the world and wonderfully rational, serene, and well written. I suppose he had a good deal of influence at or a little before the time of Hume. But when a man disregards current conventions he must wait for the future. I notice that Allibone evidently regards him as a noxious outsider—as late as 1858. Queer that Allibone and Lea should have been providing works of such massive labor in their several corners in Philadelphia at about the same time. Philadelphia hardly seems the natural home of scholars—but they were world men. I wonder if they had any relations with each other. I think I have A. F.'s *Penguins* and will look for it in a moment. But books except reports will be shut for a month. I must tuck in some odd ends to be ready for tomorrow. So *adieu* for the moment.

Affectionately yours,
O. W. Holmes

Frankfurter sent me a discourse of Santayana's on the Unknowable. It needs reading twice. In a general way his thinking more than that of other philosophers coincides with mine. But he has a patronizing tone—as of one who saw through himself but didn't expect others to.

To Lewis Einstein

Beverly Farms, July 23, 1906

Dear Einstein,

. . . After a sociological riot I read Aristotle's *Ethics* with some pleasure. The eternal, universal, wise, good man. He is much in advance of ordinary Christian morality with its slapdash universals (Never tell a lie. Sell all thou hast and give to the poor etc.). He has the ideals of altruism, and yet understands that life is painting a picture not doing a sum, that specific cases can't be decided by general rules, and that everything is a question of degree . . .

To Frederick Pollock

February 26, 1911

Dear Pollock,

. . . The few odd minutes I have had to spare I have given to Plato, recurring to his *Symposium* after fifty years; with a translation alongside I find the Greek easy. My successive reflections have been these: How natural the talk. But it is the "first intention" common to the classics. They have not a looking glass at each end of their room, and their simplicity is the bark of a dog, not the simplicity of art. But they seem to say things that no human being really would say and think. But that criticism shows how small a part of the field of human possibilities any one man realizes. On the other hand, platitudes. But is not this simply an illustration of the flatness of an original work when it has wrought its effects and been followed by centuries—millennia—of development, so that we take for granted what it took a man of genius to say? More specifically, just as Christianity is taken to have brought a new note of love into the world, was not Plato the first to make articulate the high idealizing that we recognize as the best thing in man? No doubt the divine gossip—Aristophanes hindered from discoursing by the hiccups and Alcibiades more or less drunk describing Socrates—have done much toward floating the dialogue down to us, but is there not a more portentous significance in it, of the kind I mention? I am not quite sure. When I have finished it I may reach conviction . . .

To Harold Laski

March 28, 1924

Dear Laski,

Before another letter comes from you let me emit a little steam. I have had a few days with not much to do and have turned with vacuous mind toward unknown regions in the classics. First, coming on a volume of Seneca that hitherto had escaped me among my books. I spent a very few hours in turning the pages. It seemed to me that a little went a good way, but I picked up an impression. When you see a Roman gentleman praising a younger man for letting his slaves eat with him and suggesting that he should look for the gentleman in them as they may see the slave in him and laying down the maxim, treat your inferiors as you would like your superiors to treat you, you begin to suspect that the lesson of cosmopolitan humanity came to the Christian churches from the Romans rather than to the Romans from the Christians. And when, just after, I read a little Plutarch the impression was confirmed, adding of course Greeks to Romans for the total thought. But I have begun with my exceptions before laying down my rule. The starting point is a blasphemy. The literature of the past is a bore. When it is not so, it is because it is an object of present reflection and scientific study and the interest is in your thought about it, not in it—or because it is presented with illusion as in Gilbert Murray's Euripides—where what pleases the ladies is what is not in Euripides—or because an occasional student has got himself into an artificial attitude by study and preparation. But you can get impressions that are worth while if you don't waste too much time on them. There are passages in Euripides that moved me when a school boy and move me still. The glance into Seneca paid, I then took a play of Plautus—having read that the *précieux* of the time of M. Aurelius affected his speech. The ease of the Latin and the rudimentariness of the emotion made it worth while. There is little to please the sophisticated intellect until modern times. So at least I said as I read Plautus but then never having read—I blush to say—Tacitus I took up his history. I stand by my general proposition, but there is a cove who is alive today as ever. The intensity of his speech is enough—little though you care for Galba or Otho. He is an eternal lesson in writing. I don't spend a great deal of time on him so I have read only one book—but it was worth the price of admission. Before I leave you for the day and drop the subject let me repeat if I have said it before that I think the biggest thing in antiquity is "Father forgive them—they know not what they do." There is the modern transcending of a moral judgment in the most dramatic of settings—and purporting to come from the mouth of one who has been supposed authority for the Athanasian Creed . . .

To Frederick Pollock

Beverly Farms, August 9, 1924

Dear Pollock,

Laski in his letters to me has said nothing about the case after the first stages when he seemed much interested. He never told me what it was. I don't for a moment believe that he is a Communist, but I think his experience with Figgis gave an unfortunate turn to his speculations on government. I doubt if he has much practical experience, and don't feel sure of his judgment on practical matters. But he is a devoted scholar and an independent mind and I am glad to have him go ahead with his books. He will forward thought even if he goes wrong. I have finished my last chore, Thucydides, whom I hitherto have shirked barring the short passages I read in school or college. I read books 1, 2 and 7 in the Greek, for the rest I mainly contented myself with the translation, as I didn't care to spend more time on it. It isn't the kind of thing I like to read—just as I hate to read of our Civil War—and apart from its being the first of its kind, a most important fact, no doubt, I think it is overvalued in England. Of course there are brave and fine things in it, and sayings of eternal truth, but I can get more of them for the same money in modern books. I am struck again as in the Greek choruses by the absence of our notion of manners. They say what they think with no polite veils. Nikias by way of compliment tells his allies that they are distinguished for imitating the Athenians more exactly than any others! I like the absence of the hypocritic Christian unction. They say outright that of course the crowd that has the force means to have the top—and everybody understands it. But I had enough of his for the most part tuppenny skirmishes, and reflected with satisfaction that meantime Socrates was jawing away and that after Athens fell it became the leader of the world in philosophy. I shall bother no more about improving my mind this vacation. I have begun *La Guerre et la Paix* which was interrupted years ago. I am motored an hour or more *per diem* and take naps. All goes well so far. This month I always fear.

To Lewis Einstein

March 8, 1914

Dear Einstein,

. . . Gilbert Murray's *Euripides and His Age,* in the Home University Library series, seems to me charming; more so than his translations regarded as such. People think they are getting Euripides and get Swinburne and water . . .

To Harold Laski

Beverly Farms, September 22, 1922

Dear Laski,

Your letter of the 6th gives me the usual pleasure. Each letter is a literary event for me. Beyond that my only one is that I have finished the Bard—his plays I mean. As Barlow remarked to me the other day in other words, if a man does the trick he remains, and it doesn't matter how much other stuff he pours out! I wound up with *Othello, Lear* and *Macbeth* and one is inclined to be silent about them—they are so stupendous. *Othello* is disagreeable to me because his villain comes down front and tells you he is a villain and what nasty things he means to do, and chance favors him unfairly, but the talk is so tremendous that you forgive that. As to Shakespeare generally, apart from the superlative passages, as I believe I said the other day, he can talk better than Richard II or Macbeth or any of the rest of them, and he gives you his talk without too much regard to whose mouth he uses. It is a transcendent echo of life rather than life. How far is our pleasure in his language a matter of education and convention like that in the language of the Bible or the French delight in snoring tirades in Alexandrine verse which gives me no pleasure at all? . . .

April 14, 1921

My dear Laski,

Another delightful letter from you. I hope you realize what a joy they are to me and with what pleasure I follow you in your picking up of treasures and interviews with interesting people . . . Bryce sent me his book but I haven't had time to examine it since receiving it a few days ago. I can't help fearing what you indicate. He has been too industrious. A man can't have a stream going through his person all the time and send it out highly tinctured with his acids and deposits (not elegant but relevant I think) . . . Did I mention my revelation . . . ? Herman Melville and *Moby Dick*—an account of sperm whaling with a story superadded. Anyhow I have finished it now and can say more certainly than ever that, with *longueurs,* it is, yet, I think, a mighty book. Not Shakespeare had more feeling of the mystery of the world and of life. There are mountain peaks and chasms—and the whole is as thick with life at first hand now as the day it was written—as Hawthorne's *Scarlet Letter* seemed to me thin, 20 years ago. (W. James replied to me when I said so, Because it is an original book.) Incidentally, it pleases me that he takes his fellow-sailors, a cannibal, an Indian, a negro and old Nantucket mates and captain with the same unconscious seriousness that common men would reserve for Presidents and Prime Ministers. And my, but he nobly exalts the Nantucket Whalemen, the Macys, the Coffins and the rest. I don't want to say too much but if you like George Borrow as I do I think this is a bigger man. If I made a shelf of strong impressions of recent years it would be an odd lot. *Moby Dick* beside Pearson's *Grammar of Science* or the best of Santayana or Lotze's *Microcosmos.* Apropos of the obscurity of original ideas in their first appearance, of which no doubt we have talked etc. (I doubt not I told you my experience with Plato's *Symposium*), I have just finished a little volume that Cohen sent me—*The Literature of the Old Testament* which speaks of Hosea as starting the notion that God is Love . . .

To Frederick Pollock

February 10, 1925

Dear Pollock,

It seems long since the winged word has flown between us. Lo, an adjournment for this month and my work is done unless I take over some extras, so for the moment I am a gent. of leisure. I never had read anything of Bradley's so I got his *Essays on Truth & Reality* and perused them. It seems to me that Hegel has been a blight wherever he has passed: if people once have got into that system they continue to swing round and round in his circles and not to get any forrarder. I feel that with Bradley as I have with Haldane. But he is a keen logician and makes a good deal of common writing and thinking seem thin. Whatever the different way of getting there, I am thoroughly with him on the inseparability of the individual from the cosmos. But his cosmos has got its tail in its mouth and is self-supporting as a row of men sitting in each other's laps in a circle, whereas mine is an I know not what, beyond my capacity to predicate (wherein I fear we are not quite at one). Meantime how are you? Is the leg all right now? I have made what to my regret many people here call in´-quĩries but have only inference to go on.

Accident has just led me to reread *Troilus and Cressida*—hardly enough esteemed I should think in popular speech, but illustrating what seems to me very characteristic of the bard, *viz.*, when anything suggests to him his magnificent tall talk about life or the ultimate mysteries he fires it off bang, without the slightest regard to dramatic fitness, and as we would rather hear Shakespeare talk than Richard II or Achilles or Macbeth it goes—we accept it as all right and are grateful. If we can have nectar we don't mind the cup, to talk like an earlier generation.

My messenger waiteth to go home, so with this tweak at my fellow monkey's tail I shut up . . .

To Harold Laski

Beverly Farms, July 21, 1921

Dear Laski,

. . . I forget whether I had finished Hegel's *Logic* when I last wrote. It is hard reading and many sentences displaying the movement of his dialectics I didn't fully understand. But I didn't bother on that as they are merely details of an attempt I don't believe in. Yet the old devil with all his charlatanry felt, if he didn't lead, as perhaps he did, the future of thought, and made a misty world poem in the form of syllogisms . . .

Beverly Farms, August 6, 1917

My dear Laski,

Your man Berth seems to me to have sucked other people's candy—Hegel's, Bergson's, Sorel's, Marx's, Proudhon's—until he drools. Anyone who is contemptuously cocksure warrants a contemptuous retort. Hegel's trilogies when applied to concrete events in time may here and there furnish an amusing or even a suggestive synthesis at the hands of the original master, but applied by Berth, aided by Bergson, to transcending the concept and getting into life they make me puke. Pray what is Berth but an intellectual—a parasite of concepts? Transcending the concept has no meaning to my mind except thinking a little more accurately. If it is getting outside of thought then it has no validity except for the one who experiences it and I hope that for my time the policemen will be able to take care of the transcenders. The way in which Berth talks of the producers, as if only those produced who were in manual contact with the product would be enough to make me sure that I had no use for him. What is production? Man does not produce matter or force, to use popular terms. All that he does is to determine the direction of a force—and every one who has shared in the determining of direction from the time the seed went into the ground to the time when I eat the bread or wear the shirt has shared in producing that which I consume. The architect produces more than the brick layer because he determines motion on a larger scale—and in a hundred years Descartes or Kant produces more than either . . .

To Patrick Sheehan

My dear friend,

Your second letter has just arrived and I hasten to add a postscript to my answer to your former one. By the by, I have doubted whether you received all my letters but to the best of my memory I never have let a week go by without writing when I have heard from you. You doubt if mysticism is in my line—and you are right if mysticism means belief in an ineffable direct intercourse with the higher powers. Yet I used to say, and still might, that every wise man is a mystic at bottom. That is, he recognizes the probability that his ultimates are not cosmic ultimates . . . You put it much too strongly when you say that I had no sympathy with Emerson. When he was breaking and I was still young, I saw him on the other side of the street and ran over and said to him: "If I ever do anything, I shall owe a great deal of it to you," which was true. He was one of those who set one on fire—to impart a [thought] was the gift of genius. My qualification is that I don't regard either him or Carlyle as thinkers. They are at the opposite pole—poets—whose function is not to discern but to make us realize truth. My father once asked me what book I would take to a desert island if I could have but one. I said *The French Revolution.* I should not say so now, but that wish indicated my appreciation of his [Carlyle's] imaginative power and his humor. And I should be inclined to add that he reached the highest point in the language in the magnificence of his prose. I don't care what he thinks—because I don't regard thinking as his job. You make me talk about myself in defence of an ideal that I have passionately followed. Don't talk about me going into other fields, to which I have not given the study of a life. As a fellow once said to me about cigars: Only the first rate lasts. The only thing that charms my fancy is to know a thing as a master and to put into it some fundamental ideas, that the public won't know enough to give you credit for—that you are lucky if you get any credit for but that if your dream is true are first rate and shaping. Then to carry your theory and attitude into detail and practice and thus to submit it to the test of reality is the other half. But is not the big thing to show the infinite in the finite? to take some detail that presents itself as mere arbitrary fact and to show it as a case of the universal? I confess that most of Bryce's [writings] (we have been friends from youth) seems to me diluted with industry. He has poured so constantly that there has been no time for the crystallization of genius. So far as I know Lecky, I should say, moreover the same thing—although I think he had a most aggravating gift for being right when men with more lightning in them are so often wrong.

Dear friend, again understand that I write about other things than yourself only because I hope I may amuse or distract you.

To Frederick Pollock

February 9, 1921

Dear F.P.,

A good letter from you, just after reading *Theodore Roosevelt & His Time,* a class of work that I eschew. Of course I pretty well made up my package about him a good while ago, and I don't think I was too much disturbed by what you admit to and what was formulated by a Senator in his day, thus: "What the boys like about Roosevelt is that he doesn't care a damn for the law." It broke up our incipient friendship, however, as he looked on my dissent to the *Northern Securities* case as a political departure (or, I suspect, more truly, couldn't forgive anyone who stood in his way). We talked freely later but it never was the same after that, and if he had not been restrained by his friends, I am told that he would have made a fool of himself and would have excluded me from the White House—and as in his case about the law, so in mine about that, I never cared a damn whether I went there or not. He was very likeable, a big figure, a rather ordinary intellect, with extraordinary gifts, a shrewd and I think pretty unscrupulous politician. He played all his cards—if not more. *R.i.p.*

Hohfeld was as you surmise an ingenious gent, taking, as I judge from flying glimpses, pretty good and keen distinctions of the kind that are more needed by a lower grade of lawyer than they are by you and me. I think all those systematic schematisms rather bores; and now Kocourek in the *Illinois Law Rev.* and elsewhere adds epicycles—and I regard him civilly but as I have written don't care much for the whole machinery. I even doubt the profit of the terminology of rights (the hypostatis of a prophecy); as Hohfeld used to crack me up naturally I thought well of him, but his industry was not of a kind that I should give much time to. I took another flying glimpse at your man Vinogradoff's new book. It gave me the impression of the Chinaman who ran three miles to jump over a hill—but I just looked, yawned and passed on . . .

To Lewis Einstein

November 24, 1912

Dear Einstein,

It seems uncertain from your letter whether this will reach you, so I cut it short. I am delighted at what you say about the young'un and her prospective, and philosophically disgusted to find you on the side of T.R. I knew him and liked him personally very much, as much as it was possible to like a man that you knew would throw over the friendship he professed the moment one allowed one's own understanding of one's judicial duty to prevail over what he wanted. But as I think I did not say to you, but did say to someone, the Bull Moose Manifestos struck me as exhibiting a strenuous vagueness that produced atmospheric disturbance without transmitting a message. And as I regard the party as only meaning T.R., so far as articulate, and regard him as perhaps unconsciously but wholly cynical in self-seeking, I naturally feel no enthusiasm for it. Even your quotation seems a trifle vague as to what there may be behind the new person. The thing I see most plainly is a vast amount of more or less real social discontent based on economic superstition and ignorance of what is possible. Everything in our literature and speech favors the squashy, and T.R. is the last man to stand up to the crowd and say: "Stop whining. Stop thinking you can have something for nothing. Stop churning the void for cheese. You have got all there is. Now be men or else die like dogs."

However there are a lot of young men who think with you. And although as yet I have not extracted any definite proposition from any of them (except an ignoble fear of something worse from one more intelligent than most of the rest) I admit in words and, so far as humanely may be, in my heart that they may have the message of the future in their belly. I find it dreadfully hard to think there is much chance that they have, thinking as I do that all the strange currents that I see in legislation etc. are wrong to the point of being ridiculous.

To return to what you quote from your unpublished MS, it smacks of a yearning for Socialism, qualified or not. I have read a good many things or rather some leading books on that theme and as yet have found none that did not repose on the confusion between ownership and consumption of which I have written before. I think the great body of our wealth is administered socially now. Of course I have no *a priori* objection to socialism any more than to polygamy. Our public schools and our post office are socialist, and wherever it is thought to pay I have no objection except that it probably is wrongly thought. But on the other hand I have as little enthusiasm for it as I have for teetotalism.

Well, I never wrote so much politics before, but it is a pleasure to let out a little irresponsible slack in the hope of giving pain (as R.L.S. says).

To Harold Laski

December 15, 1917

Dear Laski,

Even on Saturday P.M. I must be brief. I enclose a letter from my N.Y. friend [Franklin Ford]—as to whom I never am sure whether he has a big piece of the future in his belly or only is riding his hobby hard. I have had striking *aperçus* from him but on his main points the wave swells with mighty portent and then so far as I am concerned sinks away without breaking . . .

To Frederick Pollock

May 25, 1906

Dear Pollock,

Your pleasant letter has just come. I have finished my (presumably) last case and am free to answer at once. Brooks Adams sent me the book you mention and [Melville] Bigelow also wrote to me about it. I acknowledged it at once with necessary excuses but read it later and felt the same embarrassment that you do. Bigelow is a good and most creditable creature, but you must have noticed before now that he never hits the first rate and that at times he assumes an air of significance hardly warranted by the facts. I couldn't see that he had anything important to say. Brooks Adams I still find it hard to formulate with confidence of justice. I have known him from boyhood. I have found him more suggestive than almost anyone, generally with propositions which I don't believe, and yet I still don't quite know what to say or think. He will hand you out a statement with an august air, and you can't tell whether it is the result of ten years study or a fellow told it to him just before he met you—or for the matter of that whether you didn't tell it to him yourself within half an hour. Whatever matter he is interested in, generally a question of property, a brief history of the world winds up with his solution. I imagine that dissatisfaction with the treatment of Spokane, where he had land, has stirred him up on the rate bill, and you hear the echo of his grievances in his first chapter. This of course can't be said. I thought his customary picture of a class gradually rising through self protection to knocking the one previously dominant in the head was amusing and not without stimulating power. On the other hand I think his talk about the world being slaves to the man who commands the necessaries of life, rot. If Jim Hill (the great railroad man) does not follow the economically necessary course he comes to grief. I remember what a very able man who made a fortune on the Stock Exchange once said to me. "They talk about our leading the procession— we only *follow it ahead* like little boys. If we turn down a side street it doesn't" . . .

December 31, 1911

Dear F.P.,

A happy New Year to you and yours . . . Your impression as to Ashley on *Contracts* is more favorable than mine. I haven't read it but it seemed to me from casual glances to be a professor's book, without much actuality beyond a certain not very effective sharpness. But I only opened it at random. Just now taking it up to make sure of the name I happened to open on a criticism of a decision of mine that seemed to me not very intelligent—but that had nothing to do with my expression and I stand ready to correct my notions from further knowledge or your more instructed judgment. Harriman in his day struck me as a man of different and very superior timber, and I was confirmed by seeing him last summer. I hope I am not growing dyspeptic in my judgments, but the worthy Bigelow strikes me as appearing in the undisguise of an ass in his later politico-economic lucubrations. It is well enough for Brooks Adams to *pontifier* on matters he doesn't understand, because Brooks after all is an extraordinarily suggestive and interesting man and writer, but he is about the last whose judgment I should follow, and when Bigelow begins to prophesy in his name to my mind he pitiably drools. The two best men that I know of, of the generation or half generation after us, in this country are Wigmore and Roscoe Pound (the latter, I am told, also a distinguished botanist). I was rejoiced that Harvard should have got Pound and wish it had Wigmore as then I should have thought it better equipped than ever. There is a Philadelphian, Bohlen, who is well thought of in Torts. I remember two articles of his—the fact, but not the content, except that he thought he knew more than I did about taking the risk, apropos of a case here, and I thought he didn't. But somehow the Philadelphians while not infrequently having the manners of the great world always have struck me as hopelessly injected with the second rate, when I have seen them in their law, on which they pride themselves—but I would not breathe this aloud . . .

I have been working like the devil almost all the time. Now being finished up to Tuesday next I have taken up *Vita Nuova* with Rossetti's translation alongside. Rossetti justifies to my mind my proposition that everything is dead in 25 years. What seemed to that lot (and very likely to all of us, then) exquisite and passionate speech now produces somewhat the effect of the fashions of the same time—self-conscious and faded and more or less bogus. Only the classic simplicity of the *naïf* who know no better and of Mephistopheles who knows enough, last. The rest is like shaking hands with your elbow up to your chin, which tells your neighbor that you are thinking of yourself and not of him—or told, while it was a fashion. As to Dante, as I was saying to someone else, his discourse seems in equal parts from the heart and through the hat. Out of respect for Kohler I have got a new ed. of Hegel's *Philosophy of Law,* and may reread him, though methinks he has not succeeded in convincing me that the King of Prussia was God, in his day . . .

To Lewis Einstein

Beverly Farms, June 17, 1908

My dear Einstein,

After too long a delay I am at last here to write to you. I was much harassed during the latter part of the term and in no condition to expatiate. Now I am fairly settled here for the summer. My worries and anxieties are over—the last of them disposed of by paying a bill that I thought discreditable with a letter written, as Stevenson says, with the hope of giving pain; but by a paradox, some people have hides that can be penetrated only with a pretty blunt weapon. My only remaining work is to sit tomorrow and possibly the rest of the week in the Circuit Court of Appeals, and to write an opinion or two afterwards.

I am beginning my leisure by reading Balzac, I blush to say in a translation, but we have a lot of translations down here in the cheap library fit for a summer house left unoccupied most of the year. I want to form a critical opinion of the great man, but uncritical pleasures are lifegiving. I delight in melodrama that could move the scorn of the cultured class, and I fear that I get more fun out of the story of the thirteen than from *Eugénie Grandet.*

I think I could write an essay on life-saving devices, including women—*honi soit qui mal y pense.* I mean talk after work, with just a touch of gallantry; it shakes you out of the law and shifts the machinery belt on to a dummy wheel. But I don't have much time for that sort of thing in Washington, and the result is that when the term ends for some days I want to do nothing but eat, drink, sleep, and play solitaire. My only serious interest when I first got here a week ago was to have my work for the term bound up in a little volume as I do each year. Until that is done the term is not closed. Then it becomes history and I can hold eight months of life in my hand and look it over. One can put passion into anything that comes near enough to fundamental propensities. And in my fool's paradise I see a philosophy of law and some little touch of a philosophy of life gradually unrolling itself as I write. I remember reading of a man who had a passion for windmills and committed a murder in the hope that he might be confined in a place from which windmills were visible. He too was a philosopher, but a little careless in his premises.

I heard the other day that you could tell a Bostonian (var. Harvard man) anywhere but you couldn't tell him much. Which pleased me.

I hear occasional echoes of William James's *Pragmatism,* which I regard as an amusing humbug. He has the Irish perception of varieties of human nature, but I don't think him strong in speculation, and may have observed before that his suggestion that prayer is answered in the subliminal consciousness was a true spiritualist's thought: a miracle, if you will turn down the gas. So as to free will. And as to the will to believe: why should he call on me to believe one thing rather than another except on the postulate that I *must* admit the premises, or the good of the end subserved by the belief, or something. But as I have said before all I mean by truth is what I can't help thinking. But my can't helps are outside the scope of exhortation although I suspect they are inside the cosmos, whatever that may be, and therefore not necessarily limits to it. You tell me of politics and world affairs of which I am ignorant; I can only ramble among the generalities as a poor reply.

Beverly Farms, September 27, 1909

Dear Einstein,

. . . As I could not hope to humbug you I am afraid that Cosmic themes must slumber. I may mention however that I was amused by an article by William James on what he thought, or rather for the moment thinks, about the occult (Spiritualistic Manifestations). He concludes that there is something in it, no one knows what. Meantime he adopts a very patronising tone towards the sceptics, talks of "the good Huxley," and as I am one of them I naturally make counter-criticism. It is quite true that you can't safely say *falsus in uno falsus in omnibus;* but when you find a person who is cheating as far as you can see, whose general attitude is fraudulent (and remember how many juggler's tricks you can't explain), the matter becomes quite different. And when it is said that there must be a significant residuum in such a mass of stuff I think it a fair reply that the mass is insignificant compared with the mass of events that give no hint of extra phenomenal causes for phenomena. I can't but note W.J.'s confession of how he helped out a scientific experiment, for I noticed the same thing when the first so-called mind-reading experiment was on, though then it was unconscious, no doubt. I note too that I have known of cases that were pronounced crucial beforehand and said nothing about when they failed. In other words he longs to have the business succeed in the interest of religion. He is eternally trying to get devout conclusions from sceptical premises, which I think very possible; but I think he takes the wrong road. He believes in miracles if you will turn down the lights. Free will and answer to prayer in the subliminal consciousness—a somewhat from a universal consciousness in table-tipping etc. I think scepticism should be humble and be content with saying the universe has consciousness, significance, etc. *inside* of it, for it has *us;* but the chances are that it transcends them in some unimaginable way. All of which no doubt I have said before twenty times . . .

To Harold Laski

Beverly Farms, June 14, 1922

Dear Laski,

. . . I read John Dewey, *Human Nature and Conduct,* a book that I find it hard to characterize. It is like shavings of jade—subtle—sometimes epigrammatic—emancipated—seeing the world and man as fluid—an immense advance upon any book there was when I was younger—yet somehow not quite seeming to arrive anywhere—and not feeling to me quite as new as it is civilised. I seem to have known the fundamentals before. Also he indicates emotional attitudes that do not quite stir my sceptical mind. He talks of the exploitation of man by man—which always rather gets my hair up . . .

To Lewis Einstein

May 19, 1927

My dear Einstein,

. . .[T]oday I have read Lawrence's *Revolt in the Desert,* a vivid book, that leaves me rather wondering why he thought it worth while to take so much trouble, but giving a vivid picture of the Arabs and of tremendous hardship borne without special emphasis because they were his. They say he is now a private in the English army. A devil of a fellow. It reminds me of Clarence Day's *This Simian World,* which says that being super-monkies when we get through fighting we have to do a lot of chattering. Had we been super-cats we simply should have stopped and walked away. Lawrence, although he was collared for a book, seems simply to have stopped and walked away.

Also I have read most of a little volume by Laski on Communism which seems to state the pros and cons in an interesting way, although he seems to believe in the fundamental thesis that the rich exploit the poor and the ideal of equality, both of which (with some slight explanation) I believe to be drool. Indeed they provoke me out of intellectual indifference into a fiercely contemptuous wrath. But perhaps I don't know enough to be entitled to it.

I believe *Elmer Gantry* is outlawed in Boston on some fool action. I suppose really because it pitched into the clergy. I haven't read it, but am tempted to. *Arrowsmith* began by boring me and ended by leaving the impression of a great book. I think *great* is not too strong though I could not recite now. I am told that Boston also is down on Mencken, and when we add the row that has been kicked up, Frankfurter potently abetting, over the trial of Sacco & Vanzetti some years ago, I feel as if I was going to a perturbed teapot when I turn North in June . . .

To Franklin Ford

Beverly Farms, August 30, 1917

Dear Mr. Ford,

A second copy of your letter to Mr. Smith suggests that perhaps you expect an acknowledgment. You always make me think that perhaps you have a vision that extends beyond what the rest of us see. But as you very frankly patronize us all you warrant the expression of a doubt how far you mistake your personal realizations for discoveries. For realization even of the obvious always seems to me discovery. I never have succeeded in getting your views into a whole. Partly no doubt because of my ignorance of many things that I ought to know, but I think not wholly so. I have not read any of Veblen's later books. His *Leisure Class* struck me many years ago as either failing to see, or purposely excluding, a large and to my mind most important side of the facts and as taking 300 pages to say what could have been said in 30. Ross's *Social Control* on the other hand struck me as very stimulating, but I could not recite on it now. I don't believe that any one man or even the News Office has the universe in its belly—et superest agar—so I like all sorts of stimuli—even philosophies like Bergson's that I don't believe. Your *aperçus* certainly stimulate and let in rays of light. If you have the sun under your waistcoat I wish you would unbutton it a little more.

I am much obliged to you for remembering me.

4 • THE LIFE STRUGGLE

The Fraternity of Arms

Remarks at a Meeting of the 20th Regimental Association,
December 11, 1897

OS 100

Fellow Soldiers of the 20th:

I made no preparations for a set speech to you. It would not be natural if I did. We have heard each other cursing as we stumbled through the long night marches—we have worked together in dreadful silence through the summer dust when we could only see the bayonet of the man ahead—we have stood side by side in line—we have charged and swept the enemy—and we have run away like rabbits—all together. And when men have seen each other inside out it is too late for one of them to stand up and make orations to the rest. As I once heard a man say: You can't fool your own brother. So all that I shall say is that I am glad to see you once more. Time has passed since those days, the memory of which brings us together. We are getting to be old fellows and already feel rather complimented still to be called middle-aged men. When I look at it one way it seems to me to have passed as you see a juggler twitch off a table cloth and have everything that was on it standing just as before. But things have not stood still. The list of ghosts grows long. The roster of men grows short. My memory of those stirring days has faded to a blurred dream. Only one thing has not changed. As I look into your eyes I feel as I always do that a great trial in your youth made you different—made all of us different from what we could have been without it. It made us feel the brotherhood of man. It made us citizens of the world and not of a little town. And best of all it made us believe in something else besides doing the best for ourselves and getting all the loaves and fishes we could. I hate to hear old soldiers telling what heroes they were. We did just what any other Americans— what the last generation would have done, what the next generation would if put in our place. But we had the good luck to learn a lesson early which has given a different feeling to life. We learned to believe that doing one's duty is better than the loaves and fishes and that honor is better than a whole skin. To know that puts a kind of fire into a man's heart, and there is nowhere a man learns it as he does in battle. Those who died there died, as a soldier said hundreds of years ago, with a bird singing in their breast. Those of us who survive have heard the same music and through all the hard work of later years have remembered that once we listened to strains from a higher world.

Address at Ipswich

At the Unveiling of Memorial Tablets,
July 31, 1902.

S 92

We are told by scholars that the Greeks and Romans built up their cities and their civilization on the worship of their ancestors and care for the shadowy needs of the dead. That ancient religion has vanished, but the reverence for venerable traditions remains. I feel it to my finger tips, but with just the change from personal and family story to the larger, vaguer, but not less inspiring belief that we tread a sacred soil. I have been too busy trying to account for myself to stop to account for my ancestors. I have the poems of Ann Bradstreet, that pale passion flower of our first spring, but I do not read them often, and I cannot say much more of Governor Dudley than that what I once wrongly thought his portrait, in modest form, hangs in my house. But I love every brick and shingle of the old Massachusetts towns where once they worked and prayed, and I think it a noble and pious thing to do whatever we may by written word and moulded bronze and sculptured stone to keep our memories, our reverence and our love alive and to hand them on to new generations all too ready to forget.

It may be that we are to be replaced by other races that come here with other traditions and to whom at first the great past of Massachusetts seems, as they sometimes proclaim it, but the doings in a corner of a little band of provincial heretics. But I am bold to hope that the mighty leaven that swelled the hearts of the founders of this Commonwealth still works and will work even under altered forms—that their successors will keep the state what the founders made it, a hearthstone for sacred fire.

We all, the most unbelieving of us, walk by faith. We do our work and live our lives not merely to vent and realize our inner force, but with a blind and trembling hope that somehow the world will be a little better for our striving. Our faith must not be limited to our personal task; to the present, or even to the future. It must include the past and bring all, past, present and future, into the unity of a single continuous life. We consecrate these memorials of what has been with the intent and expectation that centuries from now those who read the simple words will find their lives richer, their purposes stronger, against the background of that different past.

From early days there have been built in the ports of Essex County, or drawn to them from neighboring towns, boats that were to seek from them new harbors across the barren sea. So, in altered guise, long may it be with us. Long may it be true, as it still is, that not only we, descendants of the stern old builders, but many others from afar who come here to launch their craft, may send to all the havens of the world new thoughts and the impulses of great deeds. To the accomplishment of that prayer it is no slight help to feel that we have a past, to remember that many generations of men have stored the earth—yes, this very spot—with electric example. Modest as they are, the monuments now unveiled seem to me trumpets which two hundred years from now may blow the great battle calls of life, as two hundred years ago those whom they commemorate heard them in their hearts. And to many a gallant spirit, two hundred years from now as two hundred years ago, the white sands of Ipswich, terrible as engulfing graves, lovely as the opal flash of fairy walls, will gleam in the horizon, the image of man's mysterious goal.

To Lewis Einstein's Daughter

May 6, 1925

My dear Marchioness,

It is short and, as you say, long since a direct word has passed between us, and I am truly rejoiced that the silence is broken. In the meantime you have married and have children whom I never have seen and I have become an old man. An anonymous letter a day or two ago said superannuated, but, as it embraced the whole Court except perhaps two dissenting judges because of a judgment that probably made the writer pay more taxes, I do not take it as a serious warning.

Turning to what you write about, of course you have to take a hand, and I think it futile to ask what does it all amount to. One may ask that about all human activities; and to one who thinks as I do, there is no answer except that it is not our business to enquire. It is a question of the significance of the universe, when we do not know even whether that is only a human ultimate quite inadequate to the I-know-not-what of which we are a part. It is enough for us that it has intelligence and significance inside of it, for it has produced us, and that our manifest destiny is to do our damnedest because we want to and because we have to let off our superfluous energy just as the puppies you speak of have to chase their tails. It satisfies our superlatives and it seems to me unnecessary to demand of the Cosmos an assurance that to it also our best is superlative. It is so in our world and that is as far as we can go. So I accept the motives of vanity, ambition, altruism, or whatever moves us as fact, only reserving the right to smile on half-holidays at the obvious *dureté* of nature to get our work out of us. One of my old formulas is to be an enthusiast in the front part of your heart and ironical in the back. It is true that many people can't do their best, or think they can't, unless they are cocksure.

As long ago as when I was in the Army I realized the power that prejudice gives a man; but I don't think it necessary to believe that the enemy is a knave in order to do one's best to kill him. However, I am now a spectator in everything except my judicial duties. I don't read the papers and am not what the reporters call abreast of the time. I read and try to enrich my mind when I am not turning out stuff that other people have to read; but in the main I read books not periodicals; though I pick up some things from my wife's reading while I play solitaire of an evening. I read a little of the old, but one can't read the old with much profit until one is mature. What the old can tell us is better said and more clearly understood in modern books. An idea becomes part of the common stock in twenty years (the common stock of the civilized that is, for the humbugs that Malthus killed a hundred years ago are alive and kicking today). So when I read the classics or anything of that sort it is more to enlarge my historical understanding than for themselves, bar, of course, the aesthetic pleasures one can laboriously pick out here and there.

My work for this term is mainly done and so I have spent a part of this forenoon in driving in Rock Creek Park (Do you remember it?) by the side of the stream through all manner of tender greens with the white of the dogwood blossoms flashing out on one. It always makes me remember "to haunt, to startle and waylay"—which seems written for it as much as for a woman. Also agreeable zoological possibilities roundabout one from wolves and lions to a swan setting on her nest between the road and the creek laughing regardless of automobiles.

If now I could have a talk with you it would put the *comble* to my felicity. But indeed I have vivid thoughts and affectionate recollections of you, and am delighted that you have remembered me enough to write.

To Harold Laski

Beverly Farms, August 20, 1926

My dear Laski,

. . . Well, I have finished Höffding, and thank you as much for recommending that as I damned you for putting me on to Declareuil. The book is already a little old, but really excellent, and his brief criticisms are pungent. He has the best short account of Kant that I remember. Eminent persons who have counted and have disappeared I (unlike you) forget as fast as I read about them, but I get the movement. One thing that bothers them all, I suppose from theological presuppositions, strikes me as twaddle—the "problem of evil." Of course the universe is a mystery—and its manifestation of life in seemingly isolated fractions—but, given that, evil is simply death—the end of a transitory manifestation. The withering of a leaf, the sickness of man, the struggle for life, all are normal sequences of the datum—as are frauds and murders. The philosophers seem to me to put their mystery in the wrong place, as spiritualists and Catholics do their miracles . . .

December 15, 1926

My dear Laski,

. . . The army taught me some great lessons—to be prepared for catastrophe—to endure being bored—and to know that however fine [a] fellow I thought myself in my usual routine there were other situations alongside and many more in which I was inferior to men that I might have looked down upon had not experience taught me to look up.

Speech

At a Dinner Given to Chief Justice Holmes by the Bar Association of Boston, March 7, 1900.

S 82

Gentlemen of the Suffolk Bar:

The kindness of this reception almost unmans me, and it shakes me the more when taken with a kind of seriousness which the moment has for me. As with a drowning man, the past is telescoped into a minute, and the stages are all here at once in my mind. The day before yesterday I was at the law school, fresh from the army, arguing cases in a little club with Goulding and Beaman and Peter Olney, and laying the dust of pleading by certain sprinklings which Huntington Jackson, another ex-soldier, and I managed to contrive together. A little later in the day, in Bob Morse's office, I saw a real writ, acquired a practical conviction of the difference between assumpsit and trover, and marvelled openmouthed at the swift certainty with which a master of his business turned it off.

Yesterday I was at the law school again, in the chair instead of on the benches, when my dear partner, Shattuck, came out and told me that in one hour the Governor would submit my name to the council for a judgeship, if notified of my assent. It was a stroke of lightning which changed the whole course of my life.

And the day before yesterday, gentlemen, was thirty-five years, and yesterday was more than eighteen years, ago. I have gone on feeling young, but I have noticed that I met fewer of the old to whom to show my deference, and recently I was startled by being told that ours is an old bench. Well, I accept the fact, although I find it hard to realize, and I ask myself, what is there to show for this half lifetime that has passed? I look into my book in which I keep a docket of the decisions of the full court which fall to me to write, and find about a thousand cases. A thousand cases, many of them upon trifling or transitory matters, to represent nearly half a lifetime! A thousand cases, when one would have liked to study to the bottom and to say his say on every question which the law ever has presented, and then to go on and invent new problems which should be the test of doctrine, and then to generalize it all and write it in continuous, logical, philosophic exposition, setting forth the whole corpus with its roots in history and its justifications of expedience real or supposed!

Alas, gentlemen, that is life. I often imagine Shakespeare or Napoleon summing himself up and thinking: "Yes, I have written five thousand lines of solid gold and a good deal of padding—I, who would have covered the milky way with words which outshone the stars!" "Yes, I beat the Austrians in Italy and elsewhere: I made a few brilliant campaigns, and I ended in middle life in a *cul-de-sac*—I, who had dreamed of a world monarchy and Asiatic power." We cannot live our dreams. We are lucky enough if we can give a sample of our best, and if in our hearts we can feel that it has been nobly done.

Some changes come about in the process, changes not necessarily so much in the nature as in the emphasis of our interest. I do not mean in our wish to make a living and to succeed—of course, we all want those things—but I mean in our ulterior intellectual or spiritual interest, in the ideal part, without which we are but snails or tigers.

One begins with a search for a general point of view. After a time he finds one, and then for a while he is absorbed in testing it, in trying to satisfy himself whether it is true. But after many experiments or investigations all have come out one way, and his theory is confirmed and settled in his mind, he knows in advance that the next case will be but another verification, and the stimulus of anxious curiosity is gone. He realizes that his branch of knowledge only presents more illustrations of the universal principle; he sees it all as another case of the same old ennui, or the same sublime mystery—for it does not matter what epithets you apply to the whole of things, they are merely judgments of yourself. At this stage the pleasure is no less, perhaps, but it is the pure pleasure of doing the work, irrespective of further aims, and when you reach that stage you reach, as it seems to me, the triune formula of the joy, the duty, and the end of life.

It was of this that Malebranche was thinking when he said that, if God held in one hand truth, and in the other the pursuit of truth, he would say: "Lord, the truth is for thee alone; give me the pursuit." The joy of life is to put out one's power in some natural and useful or harmless way. There is no other. And the real misery is not to do this. The hell of the old world's literature is to be taxed beyond one's powers. This country has expressed in story—I suppose because it has experienced it in life—a deeper abyss, of intellectual asphyxia or vital ennui, when powers conscious of themselves are denied their chance.

The rule of joy and the law of duty seem to me all one. I confess that altruistic and cynically selfish talk seem to me about equally unreal. With all humility, I think "Whatsoever thy hand findeth to do, do it with thy might," infinitely more important than the vain attempt to love one's neighbor as one's self. If you want to hit a bird on the wing, you must have all your will in a focus, you must not be thinking about yourself, and, equally, you must not be thinking about your neighbor; you must be living in your eye on that bird. Every achievement is a bird on the wing.

The joy, the duty, and, I venture to add, the end of life. I speak only of this world, of course, and of the teachings of this world. I do not seek to trench upon the province of spiritual guides. But from the point of view of the world the end of life is life. Life is action, the use of one's powers. As to use them to their height is our joy and duty, so it is the one end that justifies itself. Until lately the best thing that I was able to think of in favor of civilization, apart from blind acceptance of the order of the universe, was that it made possible the artist, the poet, the philosopher, and the man of science. But I think that is not the greatest thing. Now I believe that the greatest thing is a matter that comes directly home to us all. When it is said that we are too much occupied with the means of living to live, I answer that the chief worth of civilization is just that it makes the means of living more complex; that it calls for great and combined intellectual efforts, instead of simple, uncoördinated ones, in order that the crowd may be fed and clothed and housed and moved from place to place. Because more complex and intense intellectual efforts mean a fuller and richer life. They mean more life. Life is an end in itself, and the only question as to whether it is worth living is whether you have enough of it.

I will add but a word. We all are very near despair. The sheathing that floats us over its waves is compounded of hope, faith in the unexplainable worth and sure issue of effort, and the deep, sub-conscious content which comes from the exercise of our powers. In the words of a touching negro song—

> Sometimes I's up, sometimes I's down,
> Sometimes I's almost to the groun';

but these thoughts have carried me, as I hope they will carry the young men who hear me, through long years of doubt, self-distrust, and solitude. They do now, for, although it might seem that the day of trial was over, in fact it is renewed each day. The kindness which you have shown me makes me bold in happy moments to believe that the long and passionate struggle has not been quite in vain.

Memorial Day

An Address Delivered May 30, 1884, at Keene, N. H., before John Sedgwick Post No. 4, Grand Army of the Republic.

S 1

NOT long ago I heard a young man ask why people still kept up Memorial Day, and it set me thinking of the answer. Not the answer that you and I should give to each other—not the expression of those feelings that, so long as you and I live, will make this day sacred to memories of love and grief and heroic youth—but an answer which should command the assent of those who do not share our memories, and in which we of the North and our brethren of the South could join in perfect accord.

So far as this last is concerned, to be sure, there is no trouble. The soldiers who were doing their best to kill one another felt less of personal hostility, I am very certain, than some who were not imperilled by their mutual endeavors. I have heard more than one of those who had been gallant and distinguished officers on the Confederate side say that they had had no such feeling. I know that I and those whom I knew best had not. We believed that it was most desirable that the North should win; we believed in the principle that the Union is indissoluble; we, or many of us at least, also believed that the conflict was inevitable, and that slavery had lasted long enough. But we equally believed that those who stood against us held just as sacred convictions that were the opposite of ours, and we respected them as every man with a heart must respect those who give all for their belief. The experience of battle soon taught its lesson even to those who came into the field more bitterly disposed. You could not stand up day after day in those indecisive contests where overwhelming victory was impossible because neither side would run as they ought when beaten, without getting at last something of the same brotherhood for the enemy that the north pole of a magnet has for the south—each working in an opposite sense to the other, but each unable to get along without the other. As it was then, it is now. The soldiers of the war need no explanations; they can join in commemorating a soldier's death with feelings not different in kind, whether he fell toward them or by their side.

But Memorial Day may and ought to have a meaning also for those who do not share our memories. When men have instinctively agreed to celebrate an anniversary, it will be found that there is some thought or feeling behind it which is too large to be dependent upon associations alone. The Fourth of July, for instance, has still its serious aspect, although we no longer should think of rejoicing like children that we have escaped from an outgrown control, although we have achieved not only our national but our moral independence and know it far too profoundly to make a talk about it, and although an Englishman can join in the celebration without a scruple. For, stripped of the temporary associations which gave rise to it, it is now the moment when by common consent we pause to become conscious of our national life and to rejoice in it, to recall what our country has done for each of us, and to ask ourselves what we can do for our country in return.

So to the indifferent inquirer who asks why Memorial Day is still kept up we may answer, It celebrates and solemnly reaffirms from year to year a national act of enthusiasm and faith. It embodies in the most impressive form our belief that to act with enthusiasm and faith is the condition of acting greatly. To fight out a war, you must believe something and want something with all your might. So must you do to carry anything else to an end worth reaching. More than that, you must be willing to commit yourself to a course, perhaps a long and hard one, without being able to foresee exactly where you will come out. All that is required of you is that you should go somewhither as hard as ever you can. The rest belongs to fate. One may fall—at the beginning of the charge or at the top of the earthworks; but in no other way can he reach the rewards of victory.

When it was felt so deeply as it was on both sides that a man ought to take part in the war unless some conscientious scruple or strong practical reason made it impossible, was that feeling simply the requirement of a local majority that their neighbors should agree with them? I think not: I think the feeling was right—in the South as in the North. I think that, as life is action and passion, it is required of a man that he should share the passion and action of his time at peril of being judged not to have lived.

If this be so, the use of this day is obvious. It is true that I cannot argue a man into a desire. If he says to me, Why should I wish to know the secrets of philosophy? Why seek to decipher the hidden laws of creation that are graven upon the tablets of the rocks, or to unravel the history of civilization that is woven in the tissue of our jurisprudence, or to do any great work, either of speculation or of practical affairs? I cannot answer him; or at least my answer is as little worth making for any effect it will have upon his wishes as if he asked why should I eat this, or drink that. You must begin by wanting to. But although desire cannot be imparted by argument, it can be by contagion. Feeling begets feeling, and great feeling begets great feeling. We can hardly share the emotions that make this day to us the most sacred day of the year, and embody them in ceremonial pomp, without in some degree imparting them to those who come after us. I believe from the bottom of my heart that our memorial halls and statues and tablets, the tattered flags of our regiments gathered in the Statehouses, and this day with its funeral march and decorated graves, are worth more to our young men by way of chastening and inspiration than the monuments of another hundred years of peaceful life could be.

But even if I am wrong, even if those who come after us are to forget all that we hold dear, and the future is to teach and kindle its children in ways as yet unrevealed, it is enough for us that to us this day is dear and sacred.

Accidents may call up the events of the war. You see a battery of guns go by at a trot, and for a moment you are back at White Oak Swamp, or Antietam, or on the Jerusalem Road. You hear a few shots fired in the distance, and for an instant your heart stops as you say to yourself, The skirmishers are at it, and listen for the long roll of fire from the main line. You meet an old comrade after many years of absence; he recalls the moment when you were nearly surrounded by the enemy, and again there comes up to you that swift and cunning thinking on which once hung life or freedom—Shall I stand the best chance if I try the pistol or the sabre on that man who means to stop me? Will he get his carbine free before I reach him, or can I kill him first? These and the thousand other events we have known are called up, I say, by accident, and, apart from accident, they lie forgotten.

But as surely as this day comes round we are in the presence of the dead. For one hour, twice a year at least—at the regimental dinner, where the ghosts sit at table more numerous than the living, and on this day when we decorate their graves—the dead come back and live with us.

I see them now, more than I can number, as once I saw them on this earth. They are the same bright figures, or their counterparts, that come also before your eyes; and when I speak of those who were my brothers, the same words describe yours.

I see a fair-haired lad, a lieutenant, and a captain on whom life had begun somewhat to tell, but still young, sitting by the long mess-table in camp before the regiment left the State, and wondering how many of those who gathered in our tent could hope to see the end of what was then beginning. For neither of them was that destiny reserved. I remember, as I awoke from my first long stupor in the hospital after the battle of Ball's Bluff, I heard the doctor say, "He was a beautiful boy," and I knew that one of those two speakers was no more. The other, after passing harmless through all the previous battles, went into Fredericksburg with strange premonition of the end, and there met his fate.

I see another youthful lieutenant as I saw him in the Seven Days, when I looked down the line at Glendale. The officers were at the head of their companies. The advance was beginning. We caught each other's eye and saluted. When next I looked, he was gone.

I see the brother of the last—the flame of genius and daring in his face—as he rode before us into the wood of Antietam, out of which came only dead and deadly wounded men. So, a little later, he rode to his death at the head of his cavalry in the Valley.

In the portraits of some of those who fell in the civil wars of England, Vandyke has fixed on canvas the type of those who stand before my memory. Young and gracious figures, somewhat remote and proud, but with a melancholy and sweet kindness. There is upon their faces the shadow of approaching fate, and the glory of generous acceptance of it. I may say of them, as I once heard it said of two Frenchmen, relics of the *ancien régime*, "They were very gentle. They cared nothing for their lives." High breeding, romantic chivalry—we who have seen these men can never believe that the power of money or the enervation of pleasure has put an end to them. We know that life may still be lifted into poetry and lit with spiritual charm.

But the men not less, perhaps even more, characteristic of New England, were the Puritans of our day. For the Puritan still lives in New England, thank God! and will live there so long as New England lives and keeps her old renown. New England is not dead yet. She still is mother of a race of conquerors—stern men, little given to the expression of their feelings, sometimes careless of the graces, but fertile, tenacious, and knowing only duty. Each of you, as I do, thinks of a hundred such that he has known. I see one—grandson of a hard rider of the Revolution and bearer of his historic name—who was with us at Fair Oaks, and afterwards for five days and nights in front of the enemy the only sleep that he would take was what he could snatch sitting erect in his uniform and resting his back against a hut. He fell at Gettysburg.

His brother, a surgeon, who rode, as our surgeons so often did, wherever the troops would go, I saw kneeling in ministration to a wounded man just in rear of our line at Antietam, his horse's bridle round his arm—the next moment his ministrations were ended. His senior associate survived all the wounds and perils of the war, but, not yet through with duty as he understood it, fell in helping the helpless poor who were dying of cholera in a Western city.

I see another quiet figure, of virtuous life and silent ways, not much heard of until our left was turned at Petersburg. He was in command of the regiment as he saw our comrades driven in. He threw back his left wing, and the advancing tide of defeat was shattered against his iron wall. He saved an army corps from disaster, and then a round shot ended all for him.

There is one who on this day is always present to my mind. He entered the army at nineteen, a second lieutenant. In the Wilderness, already at the head of his regiment, he fell, using the moment that was left him of life to give all his little fortune to his soldiers. I saw him in camp, on the march, in action. I crossed debatable land with him when we were rejoining the army together. I observed him in every kind of duty, and never in all the time that I knew him did I see him fail to choose that alternative of conduct which was most disagreeable to himself. He was indeed a Puritan in all his virtues, without the Puritan austerity; for, when duty was at an end, he who had been the master and leader became the chosen companion in every pleasure that a man might honestly enjoy. In action he was sublime. His few surviving companions will never forget the awful spectacle of his advance alone with his company in the streets of Fredericksburg. In less than sixty seconds he would become the focus of a hidden and annihilating fire from a semicircle of houses. His first platoon had vanished under it in an instant, ten men falling dead by his side. He had quietly turned back to where the other half of his company was waiting, had given the order, "Second platoon, forward!" and was again moving on, in obedience to superior command, to certain and useless death, when the order he was obeying was countermanded. The end was distant only a few seconds; but if you had seen him with his indifferent carriage, and sword swinging from his finger like a cane, you never would have suspected that he was doing more than conducting a company drill on the camp parade ground. He was little more than a boy, but the grizzled corps commanders knew and admired him; and for us, who not only admired, but loved, his death seemed to end a portion of our life also.

There is one grave and commanding presence that you all would recognize, for his life has become a part of our common history. Who does not remember the leader of the assault at the mine of Petersburg? The solitary horseman in front of Port Hudson, whom a foeman worthy of him bade his soldiers spare, from love and admiration of such gallant bearing? Who does not still hear the echo of those eloquent lips after the war, teaching reconciliation and peace? I may not do more than allude to his death, fit ending of his life. All that the world has a right to know has been told by a beloved friend in a book wherein friendship has found no need to exaggerate facts that speak for themselves. I knew him, and I may even say I knew him well; yet, until that book appeared, I had not known the governing motive of his soul. I had admired him as a hero. When I read, I learned to revere him as a saint. His strength was not in honor alone, but in religion; and those who do not share his creed must see that it was on the wings of religious faith that he mounted above even valiant deeds into an empyrean of ideal life.

I have spoken of some of the men who were near to me among others very near and dear, not because their lives have become historic, but because their lives are the type of what every soldier has known and seen in his own company. In the great democracy of self-devotion private and general stand side by side. Unmarshalled save by their own deeds, the armies of the dead sweep before us, "wearing their wounds like stars." It is not because the men whom I have mentioned were my friends that I have spoken of them, but, I repeat, because they are types. I speak of those whom I have seen. But you all have known such; you, too, remember!

It is not of the dead alone that we think on this day. There are those still living whose sex forbade them to offer their lives, but who gave instead their happiness. Which of us has not been lifted above himself by the sight of one of those lovely, lonely women, around whom the wand of sorrow has traced its excluding circle—set apart, even when surrounded by loving friends who would fain bring back joy to their lives? I think of one whom the poor of a great city know as their benefactress and friend. I think of one who has lived not less greatly in the midst of her children, to whom she has taught such lessons as may not be heard elsewhere from mortal lips. The story of these and of their sisters we must pass in reverent silence. All that may be said has been said by one of their own sex—

> But when the days of golden dreams had perished,
> And even despair was powerless to destroy,
> Then did I learn how existence could be cherished,
> Strengthened, and fed without the aid of joy.
>
> Then did I check the tears of useless passion,
> Weaned my young soul from yearning after thine
> Sternly denied its burning wish to hasten
> Down to that tomb already more than mine.

Comrades, some of the associations of this day are not only triumphant, but joyful. Not all of those with whom we once stood shoulder to shoulder—not all of those whom we once loved and revered—are gone. On this day we still meet our companions in the freezing winter bivouacs and in those dreadful summer marches where every faculty of the soul seemed to depart one after another, leaving only a dumb animal power to set the teeth and to persist—a blind belief that somewhere and at last there was rest and water. On this day, at least, we still meet and rejoice in the closest tie which is possible between men—a tie which suffering has made indissoluble for better, for worse.

When we meet thus, when we do honor to the dead in terms that must sometimes embrace the living, we do not deceive ourselves. We attribute no special merit to a man for having served when all were serving. We know that, if the armies of our war did anything worth remembering, the credit belongs not mainly to the individuals who did it, but to average human nature. We also know very well that we cannot live in associations with the past alone, and we admit that, if we would be worthy of the past, we must find new fields for action or thought, and make for ourselves new careers.

But, nevertheless, the generation that carried on the war has been set apart by its experience. Through our great good fortune, in our youth our hearts were touched with fire. It was given to us to learn at the outset that life is a profound and passionate thing. While we are permitted to scorn nothing but indifference, and do not pretend to undervalue the worldly rewards of ambition, we have seen with our own eyes, beyond and above the gold fields, the snowy heights of honor, and it is for us to bear the report to those who come after us. But, above all, we have learned that whether a man accepts from Fortune her spade, and will look downward and dig, or from Aspiration her axe and cord, and will scale the ice, the one and only success which it is his to command is to bring to his work a mighty heart.

Such hearts—ah me, how many!—were stilled twenty years ago; and to us who remain behind is left this day of memories. Every year—in the full tide of spring, at the height of the symphony of flowers and love and life—there comes a pause, and through the silence we hear the lonely pipe of death. Year after year lovers wandering under the apple boughs and through the clover and deep grass are surprised with sudden tears as they see black veiled figures stealing through the morning to a soldier's grave. Year after year the comrades of the dead follow, with public honor, procession and commemorative flags and funeral march—honor and grief from us who stand almost alone, and have seen the best and noblest of our generation pass away.

But grief is not the end of all. I seem to hear the funeral march become a pæan. I see beyond the forest the moving banners of a hidden column. Our dead brothers still live for us, and bid us think of life, not death—of life to which in their youth they lent the passion and glory of the spring. As I listen, the great chorus of life and joy begins again, and amid the awful orchestra of seen and unseen powers and destinies of good and evil our trumpets sound once more a note of daring, hope, and will.

The Soldier's Faith.

An Address Delivered on Memorial Day, May 30, 1895, at a Meeting Called by the Graduating Class of Harvard University.

S 56

Any day in Washington Street, when the throng is greatest and busiest, you may see a blind man playing a flute. I suppose that some one hears him. Perhaps also my pipe may reach the heart of some passer in the crowd.

I once heard a man say, "Where Vanderbilt sits, there is the head of the table. I teach my son to be rich." He said what many think. For although the generation born about 1840, and now governing the world, has fought two at least of the greatest wars in history, and has witnessed others, war is out of fashion, and the man who commands the attention of his fellows is the man of wealth. Commerce is the great power. The aspirations of the world are those of commerce. Moralists and philosophers, following its lead, declare that war is wicked, foolish, and soon to disappear.

The society for which many philanthropists, labor reformers, and men of fashion unite in longing is one in which they may be comfortable and may shine without much trouble or any danger. The unfortunately growing hatred of the poor for the rich seems to me to rest on the belief that money is the main thing (a belief in which the poor have been encouraged by the rich), more than on any grievance. Most of my hearers would rather that their daughters or their sisters should marry a son of one of the great rich families than a regular army officer, were he as beautiful, brave, and gifted as Sir William Napier. I have heard the question asked whether our war was worth fighting, after all. There are many, poor and rich, who think that love of country is an old wife's tale, to be replaced by interest in a labor union, or, under the name of cosmopolitanism, by a rootless self-seeking search for a place where the most enjoyment may be had at the least cost.

Meantime we have learned the doctrine that evil means pain, and the revolt against pain in all its forms has grown more and more marked. From societies for the prevention of cruelty to animals up to socialism, we express in numberless ways the notion that suffering is a wrong which can be and ought to be prevented, and a whole literature of sympathy has sprung into being which points out in story and in verse how hard it is to be wounded in the battle of life, how terrible, how unjust it is that any one should fail.

Even science has had its part in the tendencies which we observe. It has shaken established religion in the minds of very many. It has pursued analysis until at last this thrilling world of colors and sounds and passions has seemed fatally to resolve itself into one vast network of vibrations endlessly weaving an aimless web, and the rainbow flush of cathedral windows, which once to enraptured eyes appeared the very smile of God, fades slowly out into the pale irony of the void.

And yet from vast orchestras still comes the music of mighty symphonies. Our painters even now are spreading along the walls of our Library glowing symbols of mysteries still real, and the hardly silenced cannon of the East proclaim once more that combat and pain still are the portion of man. For my own part, I believe that the struggle for life is the order of the world, at which it is vain to repine. I can imagine the burden changed in the way in which it is to be borne, but I cannot imagine that it ever will be lifted from men's backs. I can imagine a future in which science shall have passed from the combative to the dogmatic stage, and shall have gained such catholic acceptance that it shall take control of life, and condemn at once with instant execution what now is left for nature to destroy. But we are far from such a future, and we cannot stop to amuse or to terrify ourselves with dreams. Now, at least, and perhaps as long as man dwells upon the globe, his destiny is battle, and he has to take the chances of war. If it is our business to fight, the book for the army is a war-song, not a hospital-sketch. It is not well for soldiers to think much about wounds. Sooner or later we shall fall; but meantime it is for us to fix our eyes upon the point to be stormed, and to get there if we can.

Behind every scheme to make the world over, lies the question, What kind of a world do you want? The ideals of the past for men have been drawn from war, as those for women have been drawn from motherhood. For all our prophecies, I doubt if we are ready to give up our inheritance. Who is there who would not like to be thought a gentleman? Yet what has that name been built on but the soldier's choice of honor rather than life? To be a soldier or descended from soldiers, in time of peace to be ready to give one's life rather than to suffer disgrace, that is what the word has meant; and if we try to claim it at less cost than a splendid carelessness for life, we are trying to steal the good will without the responsibilities of the place. We will not dispute about tastes. The man of the future may want something different. But who of us could endure a world, although cut up into five-acre lots and having no man upon it who was not well fed and well housed, without the divine folly of honor, without the senseless passion for knowledge outreaching the flaming bounds of the possible, without ideals the essence of which is that they never can be achieved? I do not know what is true. I do not know the meaning of the universe. But in the midst of doubt, in the collapse of creeds, there is one thing I do not doubt, that no man who lives in the same world with most of us can doubt, and that is that the faith is true and adorable which leads a soldier to throw away his life in obedience to a blindly accepted duty, in a cause which he little understands, in a plan of campaign of which he has no notion, under tactics of which he does not see the use.

Most men who know battle know the cynic force with which the thoughts of common sense will assail them in times of stress; but they know that in their greatest moments faith has trampled those thoughts under foot. If you have been in line, suppose on Tremont Street Mall, ordered simply to wait and to do nothing, and have watched the enemy bring their guns to bear upon you down a gentle slope like that from Beacon Street, have seen the puff of the firing, have felt the burst of the spherical case-shot as it came toward you, have heard and seen the shrieking fragments go tearing through your company, and have known that the next or the next shot carries your fate; if you have advanced in line and have seen ahead of you the spot which you must pass where the rifle bullets are striking; if you have ridden by night at a walk toward the blue line of fire at the dead angle of Spottsylvania, where for twenty-four hours the soldiers were fighting on the two sides of an earthwork, and in the morning the dead and dying lay piled in a row six deep, and as you rode have heard the bullets splashing in the mud and earth about you; if you have been on the picket-line at night in a black and unknown wood, have heard the spat of the bullets upon the trees, and as you moved have felt your foot slip upon a dead man's body; if you have had a blind fierce gallop against the enemy, with your blood up and a pace that left no time for fear—if, in short, as some, I hope many, who hear me, have known, you have known the vicissitudes of terror and of triumph in war, you know that there is such a thing as the faith I spoke of. You know your own weakness and are modest; but you know that man has in him that unspeakable somewhat which makes him capable of miracle, able to lift himself by the might of his own soul, unaided, able to face annihilation for a blind belief.

From the beginning, to us, children of the North, life has seemed a place hung about by dark mists, out of which come the pale shine of dragon's scales, and the cry of fighting men, and the sound of swords. Beowulf, Milton, Dürer, Rembrandt, Schopenhauer, Turner, Tennyson, from the first war-song of our race to the stall-fed poetry of modern English drawing-rooms, all have had the same vision, and all have had a glimpse of a light to be followed. "The end of worldly life awaits us all. Let him who may, gain honor ere death. That is best for a warrior when he is dead." So spoke Beowulf a thousand years ago.

> Not of the sunlight,
> Not of the moonlight,
> Not of the starlight!
> O young Mariner,
> Down to the haven,
> Call your companions,
> Launch your vessel,
> And crowd your canvas,
> And, ere it vanishes
> Over the margin,
> After it, follow it,
> Follow The Gleam.

So sang Tennyson in the voice of the dying Merlin.

When I went to the war I thought that soldiers were old men. I remembered a picture of the revolutionary soldier which some of you may have seen, representing a white-haired man with his flint-lock slung across his back. I remembered one or two living examples of revolutionary soldiers whom I had met, and I took no account of the lapse of time. It was not until long after, in winter quarters, as I was listening to some of the sentimental songs in vogue, such as—

> Farewell, Mother, you may never
> See your darling boy again,

that it came over me that the army was made up of what I now should call very young men. I dare say that my illusion has been shared by some of those now present, as they have looked at us upon whose heads the white shadows have begun to fall. But the truth is that war is the business of youth and early middle age. You who called this assemblage together, not we, would be the soldiers of another war, if we should have one, and we speak to you as the dying Merlin did in the verse which I just quoted. Would that the blind man's pipe might be transfigured by Merlin's magic, to make you hear the bugles as once we heard them beneath the morning stars! For you it is that now is sung the Song of the Sword:—

> The War-Thing, the Comrade,
> Father of honor
> And giver of kingship,
> The fame-smith, the song master.
> . . .
> *Priest* (saith the Lord)
> *Of his marriage with victory.*
> . . .
> Clear singing, clean slicing;
> Sweet spoken, soft finishing;
> Making death beautiful
> Life but a coin
> To be staked in the pastime
> Whose playing is more
> Than the transfer of being;
> Arch-anarch, chief builder,
> Prince and evangelist,
> I am the Will of God:
> I am the Sword.

War, when you are at it, is horrible and dull. It is only when time has passed that you see that its message was divine. I hope it may be long before we are called again to sit at that master's feet. But some teacher of the kind we all need. In this snug, over-safe corner of the world we need it, that we may realize that our comfortable routine is no eternal necessity of things, but merely a little space of calm in the midst of the tempestuous untamed streaming of the world, and in order that we may be ready for danger. We need it in this time of individualist negations, with its literature of French and American humor, revolting at discipline, loving flesh-pots, and denying that anything is worthy of reverence—in order that we may remember all that buffoons forget.

We need it everywhere and at all times. For high and dangerous action teaches us to believe as right beyond dispute things for which our doubting minds are slow to find words of proof. Out of heroism grows faith in the worth of heroism. The proof comes later, and even may never come. Therefore I rejoice at every dangerous sport which I see pursued. The students at Heidelberg, with their sword-slashed faces, inspire me with sincere respect. I gaze with delight upon our polo-players. If once in a while in our rough riding a neck is broken, I regard it, not as a waste, but as a price well paid for the breeding of a race fit for headship and command.

We do not save our traditions, in this country. The regiments whose battle-flags were not large enough to hold the names of the battles they had fought vanished with the surrender of Lee, although their memories inherited would have made heroes for a century. It is the more necessary to learn the lesson afresh from perils newly sought, and perhaps it is not vain for us to tell the new generation what we learned in our day, and what we still believe. That the joy of life is living, is to put out all one's powers as far as they will go; that the measure of power is obstacles overcome; to ride boldly at what is in front of you, be it fence or enemy; to pray, not for comfort, but for combat; to keep the soldier's faith against the doubts of civil life, more besetting and harder to overcome than all the misgivings of the battle-field, and to remember that duty is not to be proved in the evil day, but then to be obeyed unquestioning; to love glory more than the temptations of wallowing ease, but to know that one's final judge and only rival is oneself: with all our failures in act and thought, these things we learned from noble enemies in Virginia or Georgia or on the Mississippi, thirty years ago; these things we believe to be true.

> "Life is not lost," said she, "for which is bought
> Endlesse renown."

We learned also, and we still believe, that love of country is not yet an idle name.

> Deare countrey! O how dearely deare
> Ought thy remembraunce, and perpetuall band
> Be to thy foster-child, that from thy hand
> Did commun breath and nouriture receave!
> How brutish is it not to understand
> How much to her we owe, that all us gave;
> That gave unto us all, whatever good we have!

As for us, our days of combat are over. Our swords are rust. Our guns will thunder no more. The vultures that once wheeled over our heads are buried with their prey. Whatever of glory yet remains for us to win must be won in the council or the closet, never again in the field. I do not repine. We have shared the incommunicable experience of war; we have felt, we still feel, the passion of life to its top.

Three years ago died the old colonel of my regiment, the Twentieth Massachusetts. He gave our regiment its soul. No man could falter who heard his "Forward, Twentieth!" I went to his funeral. From a side door of the church a body of little choir-boys came in like a flight of careless doves. At the same time the doors opened at the front, and up the main aisle advanced his coffin, followed by the few gray heads who stood for the men of the Twentieth, the rank and file whom he had loved, and whom he led for the last time. The church was empty. No one remembered the old man whom we were burying, no one save those next to him, and us. And I said to myself, The Twentieth has shrunk to a skeleton, a ghost, a memory, a forgotten name which we other old men alone keep in our hearts. And then I thought: It is right. It is as the colonel would have had it. This also is part of the soldier's faith: Having known great things, to be content with silence. Just then there fell into my hands a little song sung by a warlike people on the Danube, which seemed to me fit for a soldier's last word, another song of the sword, but a song of the sword in its scabbard, a song of oblivion and peace.

A soldier has been buried on the battle-field.

> And when the wind in the tree-tops roared,
> The soldier asked from the deep dark grave:
>   "Did the banner flutter then?"
> "Not so, my hero," the wind replied,
> "The fight is done, but the banner won,
> Thy comrades of old have borne it hence,
>   Have borne it in triumph hence."
> Then the soldier spake from the deep dark grave:
>   "I am content."
>
> Then he heareth the lovers laughing pass,
>   And the soldier asks once more:
> "Are these not the voices of them that love,
>   That love—and remember me?"
> "Not so, my hero," the lovers say,
> "We are those that remember not;
> For the spring has come and the earth has smiled,
>   And the dead must be forgot."
> Then the soldier spake from the deep dark grave:
>   "I am content."

The Class of '61

At the Fiftieth Anniversary of Graduation, June 28, 1911

S 95

Mr. President and Brethren of the Alumni:

One of the recurring sights of Alaska, I believe, is when a section of a great glacier cracks and drops into the sea. The last time that I remember witnessing the periodic semi-centennial plunge of a college class was when I heard Longfellow say "Morituri salutamus." If I should repeat that phrase of the gladiators soon to die, it would be from knowledge and reason, not from feeling, for I own that I am apt to wonder whether I do not dream that I have lived, and may not wake to find that all that I thought done is still to be accomplished and that life is all ahead. But we have had our warning. Even within the last three months Henry Bowditch, the world-known physiologist, and Frank Emmons, the world-known geologist, have dropped from the class, leaving only the shadow of great names.

I like to think that they were types of '61, not only in their deeds, but in their noble silence. It has been my fortune to belong to two bodies that seemed to me somewhat alike—the 20th Massachusetts Regiment and the class of '61. The 20th never wrote about itself to the newspapers, but for its killed and wounded in battle it stood in the first half-dozen of all the regiments of the north. This little class never talked much about itself, but graduating just as the war of secession began, out of its eighty-one members it had fifty-one under arms, the largest proportion that any class sent to that war.

One learns from time an amiable latitude with regard to beliefs and tastes. Life is painting a picture, not doing a sum. As twenty men of genius looking out of the same window will paint twenty canvases, each unlike all the others, and every one great, so, one comes to think, men may be pardoned for the defects of their qualities if they have the qualities of their defects. But, after all, we all of us have our notions of what is best. I learned in the regiment and in the class the conclusion, at least, of what I think the best service that we can do for our country and for ourselves: To see so far as one may, and to feel, the great forces that are behind every detail—for that makes all the difference between philosophy and gossip, between great action and small; the least wavelet of the Atlantic Ocean is mightier than one of Buzzard's Bay—to hammer out as compact and solid a piece of work as one can, to try to make it first-rate, and to leave it unadvertised.

It was a good thing for us in our college days . . . that we were all poor. At least we lived as if we were. It seems to me that the training at

West Point is better fitted to make a man than for a youth to have all the luxuries of life poured into a trough for him at twenty. We had something of that discipline, and before it was over many of us were in barracks learning the school of the soldier. Man is born a predestined idealist, for he is born to act. To act is to affirm the worth of an end, and to persist in affirming the worth of an end is to make an ideal. The stern experience of our youth helped to accomplish the destiny of fate. It left us feeling through life that pleasures do not make happiness and that the root of joy as of duty is to put out all one's powers toward some great end.

When one listens from above to the roar of a great city, there comes to one's ears—almost indistinguishable, but there—the sound of church bells, chiming the hours, or offering a pause in the rush, a moment for withdrawal and prayer. Commerce has outsoared the steeples that once looked down upon the marts, but still their note makes music of the din. For those of us who are not churchmen the symbol still lives. Life is a roar of bargain and battle, but in the very heart of it there rises a mystic spiritual tone that gives meaning to the whole. It transmutes the dull details into romance. It reminds us that our only but wholly adequate significance is as parts of the unimaginable whole. It suggests that even while we think that we are egotists we are living to ends outside ourselves.

On Receiving the Degree of Doctor of Laws
Yale University Commencement, June 30, 1886.
S 26

Mr. President and Gentlemen:
I know of no mark of honor which this country has to offer that I should value so highly as this which you have conferred upon me. I accept it proudly as an accolade, like the little blow upon the shoulder from the sword of a master of war which in ancient days adjudged that a soldier had won his spurs and pledged his life to decline no combat in the future.

The power of honor to bind men's lives is not less now than it was in the Middle Ages. Now as then it is the breath of our nostrils; it is that for which we live, for which, if need be, we are willing to die. It is that which makes the man whose gift is the power to gain riches sacrifice health and even life to the pursuit. It is that which makes the scholar feel that he cannot afford to be rich.

One would sometimes think, from the speech of young men, that things had changed recently, and that indifference was now the virtue to be cultivated. I never heard any one profess indifference to a boat race. Why should you row a boat race? Why endure long months of pain in preparation for a fierce half-hour that will leave you all but dead? Does any one ask the question? Is there any one who would not go through all it costs, and more, for the moment when anguish breaks into triumph—or even for the glory of having nobly lost? Is life less than a boat race? If a man will give all the blood in his body to win the one, will he not spend all the might of his soul to prevail in the other?

I know, Mr. President, that there is a motive above even honor which may govern men's lives. I know that there are some rare spirits who find the inspiration of every moment, the aim of every act, in holiness. I am enough of a Puritan, I think, to conceive the exalted joy of those who look upon themselves only as instruments in the hands of a higher power to work out its designs. But I think that most men do and must reach the same result under the illusion of self-seeking. If the love of honor is a form of that illusion, it is no ignoble one. If it does not lift a man on wings to the sky, at least it carries him above the earth and teaches him those high and secret pathways across the branches of the forest the travellers on which are only less than winged.

Not the least service of this great University and its sister from which I come is that by their separate teaching and by their mutual rivalry they have fostered that lofty feeling among their graduates. You have done all that a university can do to fan the spark in me. I will try to maintain the honor you have bestowed.

To Harold Laski

November 13, 1921

Dear Laski,

. . . Well, we have been having doings here that somewhat disturbed the even current. First came the unknown soldier. I had been disgusted by the vulgarities of the bogus sentiment, the odious emptiness of reporters' talk that seems an echo of the popular mind. But when I saw the coffin borne into the great rotunda of the Capitol, which became beautiful and impressive in the dim twilight, and afterwards saw the miles of people marching through, three abreast, from early morning into the next day, I realized that a feeling may be great notwithstanding its inability to get itself expressed . . . To return to the unknown soldier I couldn't help thinking how on the one side was a little life, probably like thousands of others, and on the other the passion of a people striving to meet, and stretching away into the infinite, eternally drawing nearer, but like parabola and asymptote never quite meeting—for he will never know and we shall never know . . .

George Otis Shattuck (1897)
S 70

. . . People often speak of correcting the judgment of the time by that of posterity. It think it is quite as true to say that we must correct the judgment of posterity by that of the time. A small man may be remembered for some little felicity which enabled him to write a successful lyric, or in some way to charm the senses or emotions of a world always readier with its rewards for pleasures than for great thoughts or deeds. But I know of no true measure of men except the total of human energy which they embody—counting everything, with due allowance for quality, from Nansen's power to digest blubber or to resist cold, up to his courage, or to Wordsworth's power to express the unutterable, or to Kant's speculative reach. The final test of this energy is battle in some form—actual war—the crush of Arctic ice—the fight for mastery in the market or the court. Many of those who are remembered have spared themselves this supreme trial, and have fostered a faculty at the expense of their total life. It is one thing to utter a happy phrase from a protected cloister; another to think under fire—to think for action upon which great interests depend. The most powerful men are apt to go into the melee and fall or come out generals. The great problems are questions of here and now. Questions of here and now occupy nine hundred and ninety-nine thousandths of the ability of the world; and when the now has passed and has given place to another now, the heads and hands that built the organic structure of society are forgotten from the speech of their fellows, and live only in the tissue of their work.

Such may be the fate of the man whom today we remember and honor. But remembered or forgotten, few indeed, I believe, of those whom I have seen have counted for as much in the hardest work of the day. I do not regret that it should be known by few. What is any remembrance of men to our high ambition? Sooner or later the race of men will die; but we demand an eternal record. We have it. What we have done is woven forever into the great vibrating web of the world. The eye that can read the import of its motion can decipher the story of all our deeds, of all our thoughts. To that eye I am content to leave the recognition and the memory of this great head and heart.

Address of Chief Justice Holmes

At the Dedication of the Northwestern University Law School Building, Chicago, October 20, 1902.

CLP 272

Mr. President and Gentlemen:

Nature has but one judgment on wrong conduct—if you can call that a judgment which seemingly has no reference to conduct as such—the judgment of death. That is the judgment or the consequence which follows uneconomical expenditure if carried far enough. If you waste too much food you starve; too much fuel, you freeze; too much nerve tissue, you collapse. And so it might seem that the law of life is the law of the herd; that man should produce food and raiment in order that he might produce yet other food and other raiment to the end of time. Yet who does not rebel at that conclusion? Accepting the premises, I nevertheless almost am prepared to say that every joy that gives to life its inspiration consists in an excursion toward death, although wisely stopping short of its goal. Art, philosophy, charity, the search for the north pole, the delirium of every great moment in man's experience—all alike mean uneconomic expenditure—mean waste—mean a step toward death. The justification of art is not that it offers prizes to those who succeed in the economic struggle, to those who in an economic sense have produced the most, and that thus by indirection it increases the supply of wine and oil. The justification is in art itself, whatever its economic effect. It gratifies an appetite which in some noble spirits is stronger than the appetite for food. The principle might be pressed even further and be found to furnish art with one of its laws. For it might be said, as I often have said, and as I have been gratified to find elaborated by that true poet Coventry Patmore, that one of the grounds of aesthetic pleasure is waste. I need not refer to Charles Lamb's well-known comments on the fallacy that enough is as good as a feast. Who does not know how his delight has been increased to find some treasure of carving upon a mediaeval cathedral in a back alley—to see that the artist has been generous as well as great, and has not confined his best to the places where it could be seen to most advantage? Who does not recognize the superior charm of a square-hewed beam over a joist set on edge which would be enough for the work? To leave art, who does not feel that Nansen's account of his search for the pole rather loses than gains in ideal satisfaction by the pretense of a few trifling acquisitions for science? If I wished to make you smile I might even ask whether life did not gain an enrichment from neglected opportunities which would be missed in the snug filling out of every chance. But I am not here to press a paradox. I only mean to insist on the importance of the un-economic to man as he actually feels today. You may philosophize about the honors of leisure as a survival; you may, if you like, describe in the same way, as I have heard them described, the ideals which burn in the center of our hearts. Nonetheless they are there. They are categorical imperatives. They hold their own against hunger and thirst; they scorn to be classed as mere indirect supports of our bodily needs, which rather they defy; and our friends the economists would do well to take account of them . . . if they are to deal with man as he is. No doubt already you have perceived the reason why I have insisted upon this double view of life. The special value of a university is that it moves in the twofold direction of man's desires which I have described. I have listened with interest to able business men when they argued and testified that a university training made men fitter to succeed in their practical struggles. I am far from denying it. No doubt such a training gives men a larger mastery of the laws of nature under which they must work, a wider outlook over the world of science and of fact. If it could give to every student a scientific point of view, if education could make men realize that you cannot produce something out of nothing and make them promptly detect the pretense of doing so with which at present the talk of every day is filled, I should think it had more than paid for itself. Still more should I think so if it could send men into the world with a good rudimentary knowledge of the laws of their environment. I cannot believe that anything else would be so likely to secure prosperity as the universal acceptance of scientific premises in every department of thought. But beside prosperity there is to be considered happiness, which is not the same thing. The chance of a university to enlarge men's power of happiness is at least not less than its chance to enlarge their capacity for gain. I own that with regard to this, as with regard to every other aspiration of man, the most important question seems to me to be, what are his inborn qualities?

Mr. Ruskin's first rule for learning to draw, you will remember, was, Be born with genius. It is the first rule for everything else. If a man is adequate in native force, he probably will be happy in the deepest sense, whatever his fate. But we must not undervalue effort, even if it is the lesser half. And the opening which a university is sure to offer to all the idealizing tendencies—which, I am not afraid to say, it ought to offer to the romantic side of life—makes it above all other institutions the conservator of the vestal fire. Our tastes are finalities, and it has been recognized since the days of Rome that there is not much use in disputing about them. If some professor should proclaim that what he wanted was a strictly economic world, I should see no more use in debating with him than I do in arguing with those who despise the ideals which we owe to war. But most men at present are on the university side. They want to be told stories and to go to the play. They want to understand and, if they can, to paint pictures, and to write poems, whether the food product is greater in the long run because of them or not. They want to press philosophy to the uttermost edge of the articulate, and to try forever after some spiritual ray outside the spectrum that will bring a message to them from behind phenomena. They love the gallant adventure which yields no visible return. I think it the glory of that university which I know best, that under whatever reserves of manner they may hide it, its graduates have the romantic passion in their hearts.

But gentlemen, there is one department of your institution to which I must be permitted specially to refer—the department to which I am nearest by profession, and to which I owe the honor of being here. I mean, of course, the department of law. Let me say one word about that before I sit down. It was affirmed, I believe, by a man not without deserved honor in his generation—the late Chief Justice Cooley—that the law was and ought to be commonplace. No doubt the remark has its truth. It is better that the law should be commonplace than that it should be eccentric. No doubt, too, in any aspect it would seem commonplace to a mind that understood everything. But that is the weakness of all truth. If instead of the joy of eternal pursuit you imagine yourself to have mastered it as a complete whole, you would find yourself reduced to the alternative either of finding the remotest achievement of quaternions or ontology—the whole frame of the universe, in short—a bore, or of dilating with undying joy over the proposition that twice two is four. It seems to me that for men as they are, the law may keep its everyday character and yet be an object of understanding wonder and a field for the lightning of genius. One reason why it gives me pleasure to be here today and to express my good wishes for the future and my appreciation of the past of your law school is that it is here and in places like it that such wonder is kindled and that from it may fly sparks that shall set free in some genius his explosive message.

I am not dealing in generalities. I mean more than good will to a law school, simply because it is a law school. Indeed, I almost fear that the intellectual ferment of the better schools may be too potent an attraction to young men and seduce into the profession many who would be better elsewhere. But I am thinking of this law school and no other. I never have had an opportunity to give public expression to my sense of the value of the work of your accomplished dean [John H. Wigmore]. I have come in for my share of criticism from him, as also I have had from him words which have given me new courage on a lonely road. But my appreciation of what I have seen from his hands is untouched by personal relations. It is solely because I think that it is the duty of those who know to recognize the unadvertised first rate, that I wish now to express my respect for his great learning and originality and for the volume and delicacy of his production, which seem to me to deserve more distinct and public notice than, so far as I am aware, they have received. I feel quite sure, from his printed work that his teaching will satisfy the twofold desire of man; that it will be enlightened with intelligent economic views and give men what they want to know when they go out to fight, but that also it will send them forth with a pennon as well as with a sword, to keep before their eyes in the long battle the little flutter that means ideals, honor, yes, even romance, in all the dull details.

To Lewis Einstein

October 12, 1914

Dear Einstein,

If one could forget the war for a moment in the beginning of our term today your letter would be enough to bring back one's feelings in the most poignant form. I grieve for you all, and have a heartache underneath even when I am thinking of other things. Poor, dear, little Midge, if I may borrow the name in talking to you. I hate to think of suffering beginning so early for her.

As to the bearing of German success upon us, I don't know enough to feel convinced that it will be worse than the possible effects of Russian ascendancy. My sympathies are determined without regard to a calculation of relative advantages or disadvantages, although in national matters it may be that they should come first. At least I am so uncertain on that point that I leave it out of my account. I believe in "my country right or wrong," and next to my country my crowd, and England is my crowd. I earnestly long to see her keep on top, and yet I shall grieve if, as I hope, Germany is crushed. I suppose the war was inevitable, and yet whatever the event, it fills me with sorrow, disinterested sorrow, apart from its effect upon us and from my personal sympathy with England. But it shows us that classes as well as nations that mean to be in the saddle have got to be ready to kill to keep their seat; and that the notion that all that remained for the civilized world was to sit still, converse, and be comfortable was humbug. It even makes one wonder whether Flinders Petrie's rather inadequately backed up conception of cycles, say of a thousand years, for civilization to rise and fall, is going to come true for now. I don't mean that I believe it. While the trouble is on we always exaggerate its magnitude and import, as, indeed, I suspect you exaggerate the bloodiness of the fighting. My impression has been that, although a good many men have been killed and wounded because of the great number engaged, tested by the proportion of regimental losses (killed and wounded, by official reports) it has not been very severe. But my knowledge is nothing, only a conjecture from occasional figures.

I had to stop here to go to Court, see McReynolds sworn in *vice* Lurton, deceased, and make an annual call on the President. I have the impression that he has gained with the country. The war withdrew attention from Mexico, the death of his wife brought him sympathy when he kept on at his work, and I suppose that even the drooling business of suggesting prayers for peace meant votes from Methodists and Baptists. As I was saying to someone, prayers are like nettlerash— anything from heat to champagne may bring them out.

I was pleased to be told by a man who had seen the German Ambassador that he had changed his note very much and was nearer to talking peace than of going to Paris. But I should think that this would have to be fought nearer a finish than it is now. It seems as if Russia was going to be more of a factor than at least I realize it to have been so far.

If you know of a regiment that authentically has lost in killed and wounded (missing not counted) a quarter of its number, I should like to know it. If one has lost a half it is entitled to speak of a very bloody fight. Except in exceptional circumstances I think the improved weapons mean smaller losses. The great ones used to come when troops stood within a few paces letting into one another. To some of my English friends I can write on other themes, but with your letter before me it seems impossible.

Dear me, from the time of the Civil War to now it seems to me that some great anxiety has hung over life.

Affectionate remembrances to your two.

To Frederick Pollock

February 1, 1920

Dear Pollock,

. . . I am not an admiral or a general. I loathe war—which I described when at home with a wound in our Civil War as an organized bore—to the scandal of the young women of the day who thought that Captain Holmes was wanting in patriotism. But I do think that man at present is a predatory animal. I think that the sacredness of human life is a purely municipal ideal of no validity outside the jurisdiction. I believe that force, mitigated so far as may be by good manners, is the *ultima ratio,* and between two groups that want to make inconsistent kinds of world I see no remedy except force. I may add what I no doubt have said often enough, that it seems to me that every society rests on the death of men—as does also the romantic interest of long inhabited lands. I should be glad, to speak Hibernianly, if it could be arranged that the death should precede life by provisions for a selected race, but we shall not live to see that. However, I dare say that all this is in the air and that you may say that on these or any other principles it is a good thing if we can unite forces to put down avoidable displays of force. I find it somewhat hard to believe that we can come to such intimate understanding with the East that future slaughters can be avoided. But I am very nearly an old man and must content myself with my job and leave this business to you young chaps . . .

Buck v. Bell
274 U.S. 200 (1927)

. . . Carrie Buck is a feeble minded white woman who was committed to the State Colony in due form. She is the daughter of a feeble minded mother in the same institution, and the mother of an illegitimate feeble minded child. She was eighteen years old at the time of the trial of her case in the circuit court in the latter part of 1924. An Act of Virginia approved March 20, 1924, recites that the health of the patient and the welfare of society may be promoted in certain cases by the sterilization of mental defectives, under careful safeguard, etc.; that the sterilization may be effected in males by vasectomy and in females by salpingectomy, without serious pain or substantial danger to life; that the Commonwealth is supporting in various institutions many defective persons who if now discharged would become a menace but if incapable of procreating might be discharged with safety and become self-supporting with benefit to themselves and to society; and that experience has shown that heredity plays an important part in the transmission of insanity, imbecility, etc. The statute then enacts that whenever the superintendent of certain institutions including the above named State Colony shall be of opinion that it is for the best interests of the patients and of society that an inmate under his care should be sexually sterilized, he may have the operation performed upon any patient afflicted with hereditary forms of insanity, imbecility, etc., on complying with the very careful provisions by which the act protects the patients from possible abuse.

The superintendent first presents a petition to the special board of

directors of his hospital or colony, stating the facts and the grounds for
his opinion, verified by affidavit. Notice of the petition and of the time
and place of the hearing in the institution is to be served upon the inmate, and also upon his guardian, and if there is no guardian the superintendent is to apply to the circuit court of the county to appoint one. If
the inmate is a minor, notice also is to be given to his parents if any with
a copy of the petition. The board is to see to it that the inmate may attend the hearings if desired by him or his guardian. The evidence is all
to be reduced to writing, and after the board has made its order for or
against the operation, the superintendent, or the inmate, or his guardian may appeal to the circuit court of the county. The circuit court may
consider the record of the board and the evidence before it and such
other admissible evidence as may be offered, and may affirm, revise, or
reverse the order of the board and enter such order as it deems just.
Finally any party may apply to the supreme court of appeals, which, if it
grants the appeal, is to hear the case upon the record of the trial in the
circuit court and may enter such order as it thinks the circuit court
should have entered. There can be no doubt that so far as procedure is
concerned the rights of the patient are most carefully considered, and
as every step in this case was taken in scrupulous compliance with the
statute and after months of observation, there is no doubt that in that
respect the plaintiff in error has had due process of law.

   The attack is not upon the procedure but upon the substantive law. It
seems to be contended that in no circumstances could such an order be
justified. It certainly is contended that the order cannot be justified
upon the existing grounds. The judgment finds the facts that have been
recited and that Carrie Buck "is the probable potential parent of socially inadequate offspring, likewise afflicted, that she may be sexually
sterilized without detriment to her general health and that her welfare
and that of society will be promoted by her sterilization," and thereupon makes the order. In view of the general declarations of the legislature and the specific findings of the court obviously we cannot say as
matter of law that the grounds do not exist, and if they exist they justify
the result. We have seen more than once that the public welfare may call
upon the best citizens for their lives. It would be strange if it could not
call upon those who already sap the strength of the State for these
lesser sacrifices, often not felt to be such by those concerned, in order to
prevent our being swamped with incompetence. It is better for all the
world, if instead of waiting to execute degenerate offspring for crime,
or to let them starve for their imbecility, society can prevent those who
are manifestly unfit from continuing their kind. The principle that sustains compulsory vaccination is broad enough to cover cutting the Fallo-
pian tubes. Three generations of imbeciles are enough.

But, it is said, however it might be if this reasoning were applied generally, it fails when it is confined to the small number who are in the institutions named and is not applied to the multitudes outside. It is the usual last resort of constitutional arguments to point out shortcomings of this sort. But the answer is that the law does all that is needed when it does all that it can, indicates a policy, applies it to all within the lines, and seeks to bring within the lines all similarly situated so far and so fast as its means allow. Of course so far as the operations enable those who otherwise must be kept confined to be returned to the world, and thus open the asylum to others, the equality aimed at will be more nearly reached.

To Morris Cohen

September 6, 1920

My dear Cohen,

. . . Man is like a strawberry plant, the shoots that he throws out take root and become independent centres. And one illustration of the tendency is the transformation of means into ends. A man begins a pursuit as a means of keeping alive—he ends by following it at the cost of life. A miser is an example—but so is the man who makes righteousness his end. Morality is simply another means of living but the saints make it an end in itself. Until just now it never occurred to me I think that the same is true of philosophy or art. Philosophy as a fellow once said to me is only thinking. Thinking is an instrument of adjustment to the conditions of life—but it becomes an end in itself. So that we can see how man is inevitably an idealist of some sort, but whatever his ideal and however ultimate to himself, all that he can say to anyone else is—*Je suis comme ça*. But he can admit that a person who lives a certain emotional sphere should be indifferent to intellectual justifications although he reserves to himself his advantage of believing that he can explain the other and that this other can't explain him.

That is all that I wanted to say but I will add apropos of the acquired superiority of means to ends that we think the statesman better than the man who simply eats his dinner, travels to and fro and begets—yet the statesman is only a means to his doing so. Also an anecdote of when I was young—a man who called himself a juridical traveller said: We speak of the Remorse of Conscience—a thousand years ago more or less we said The Agen Bite of Inwit. The image is the same—biting back on oneself—and is equally intelligible to you or me. But the introduction of a dead language has made it unintelligible to the man in the street. And so by the mere force of language (he concluded) we are creating a spiritual aristocracy. The answer again is that the derivation has got new roots—that we no more think of the image than does the man in the street, and that he knows what remorse means as well as we do.

I think the best image for man is an electric light—the spark feels isolated and independent but really is only a moment in a current.

Have I talked banalities or what is worth saying?

5 • METAPHYSICS

To Harold Laski

January 27, 1929

My dear Laski,

. . . I think I mentioned a book on behaviourism once. [The author] seems to think that consciousness is shown to be a futile conception by the fact that no one tells or, he would say, can tell what it is. That seems to me silly. When I was a small boy my father taught me a philosophical lesson by asking me to tell him how salt tasted. You can't—and you can't tell a blind person how colors look. There are many questions to which you must know the answer at first hand or you can't know it. You don't disprove an ultimate by showing that I can't go beyond it. This detached reflection I interject for no particular reason—except my desire to mark my disrespect for what the writer thought a sockdolager.

January 11, 1929

My dear Laski,

. . . As to your Berkeleian idealism I suppose you know my short formulas—I have repeated them often enough in talk and print. I begin by an act of faith. I assume that I am [not] dreaming, although I can't prove it—that you exist in the same sense that I do—and that gives me an outside world of some sort (and I think the *Ding an sich*)—so I assume that I am in the world not it in me. Next when I say that a thing is true I only mean that I can't help believing it—but I have no grounds for assuming that my can't helps are cosmic can't helps and some reasons for thinking otherwise. I therefore define the truth as the system of my intellectual limitations—there being a tacit reference to what I bet is or will be the prevailing can't help of the majority of that part of the world that I count. The ultimate, even humanly speaking, is a mystery. I don't see that it matters whether you call it motion or thought or X—all we know of it is that it is capable when tied in a certain knot of producing you and me and all the rest of the show. Absolute truth is a mirage. Thus I am indifferent to the Berkeley business. Also as I see no reasons for attributing cosmic importance to man, other than that attaching to whatever is, I regard him as I do the other species (except that my private interests are with his) having for his main business to live and propagate, and for his main interest food and sex. A few get a little further along and get pleasure in it, but are fools if they are proud . . .

To Frederick Pollock

Beverly Farms, August 30, 1929

My dear Pollock,

. . . I don't understand your seeming inclination to controvert my *can't helps.* I see nothing behind the force of reason except that *ich kann nicht anders*—and I don't know whether the cosmos can or not. I do not see what more there is in your law of contradiction, except to assert that the universe can't make nonsense sense. Even to that I should simply say I don't know. I can't imagine it—but I hardly think that a measure of the possible.

If there is anything that has been supposed to be compulsory upon us short of not affirming nonsense I should think it was that every phenomenon must have a cause. Yet I find scientific men suggesting nowadays (*e.g.* Eddington) that there are phenomena for which no causes can be discovered and seemingly believing that they are outside the category of cause and effect. I am far from believing with them, but I am entirely ready to believe it on proof. Chauncey Wright, a nearly forgotten philosopher of real merit, taught me when young that I must not say *necessary* about the universe, that we don't know whether anything is necessary or not. So I describe myself as a *bet*tabilitarian. I believe that we can *bet* on the behavior of the universe in its contact with us. We bet we can know what it will be. That leaves a loophole for free will—in the miraculous sense—the creation of a new atom of force, although I don't in the least believe in it. I guess (strict sense) that you think man a more important manifestation than I do. I suppose that such differences depend a good deal on the ultimate make-up of different men and hardly can be argued about. Of course from the human point of view he is important; he hardly would live if he didn't think so. Also I hasten to admit that I don't dare pronounce any fact unimportant that the Cosmos has produced. I only mean that when one thinks coldly I see no reason for attributing to man a significance different in kind from that which belongs to a baboon or to a grain of sand. But the time approaches when I must go down stairs and play solitaire I fear. I have just finished *Political Thought in the Sixteenth Century* (J. W. Allen), a mighty good book. It is amusing to see what used to strike me with the abolitionists before our war, as an eternally recurring phenomenon. The abolitionists had a stock phrase that man was either a knave or a fool who did not act as they (the abolitionists) *knew* to be right. So Calvin thought of the Catholics and the Catholics of Calvin. So I don't doubt do the more convinced prohibitionists think of their opponents today. When you know that you know persecution comes easy. It is as well that some of us don't know that we know anything. One month more here, and then back to work. I shall hold on until nature or man gives me a hint that the end has come. Meantime I get a quiet pleasure out of this day. My love to the Lady.

To Harold Laski

June 1, 1919

Dear Laski,

. . . The Chief [Justice] has suggested that I write a case of his and has done it in such a kind hesitating way that even if I could [have] hesitated otherwise, which I shouldn't have done, I can't now. Hence I shan't be happy till I get at it—but your letter just arrived imperatively demands a word of agreement right off. It is apropos of Oriental insights. What I have been in the habit of saying is this. For fifty years it has been my business to know the movement of thought in one of its great expressions—the law—and my pleasure to try to know something of its movement in philosophy, and if anything is plain it is that during the period that counts—from Pericles to now—there has been a gradual advance and that our view of life today is more manifold and more profound than it ever has been before. When the Europe and Asia man said Europe has given us the steam engine, Asia every religion that ever commanded the reverence of mankind—I answered I bet on the steam engine. For the steam engine means science and science is the root from which comes the flower of our thought. When I have seen clever women who have read all their lives go off into enthusiasm over some oriental, pseudo-oriental, or spiritualistic fad it has struck me that all their reading seems to have given them no point of view—no *praejudicia*—or preliminary bets as to the probability that the sign turn to the left will lead to a *cul de sac*. If I follow Brandeis's suggestion I shall have little time for other things—but as my bet, on the strength of what I do know, is with Archer—bar reservations for the Taj Mahal, etc. that will keep.

I turn to another matter. I had a dear little letter from Pound expressing satisfaction at what I wrote to Grinnell but also saying that people there want to push Frankfurter out of the school. He says nothing about himself but I have been led to fear that the push extends to Pound. Two days ago I asked Brandeis if he thought it would be well for me to write to Lowell—he rather inclined yes. I still hesitate but probably should be writing to him were I not writing to you. If the school should lose Pound and Frankfurter it would lose its soul, it seems to me. I hesitate because I know no details, but my conviction is strong. So far as Pound is concerned it is also disinterested, for I don't know his opinions except through his writings and so far as I know I never have come in for much credit in them. But there can be no doubt that he is a real focus of spiritual energy—and even if his presence has prevented subscriptions to the Law School I can't but believe that the spark of inspiration is worth more than dollars. By Jove, I think I'll say that to Lowell. I am worried—and all the more that without my foreknowledge I was put in as President of the Law School Association—of course merely as a figurehead—but I hate to feel King Log. With which I shut up as the barber is due to cut my hair. Does the movement threaten you? I am full of helpless anxiety.

To Morris Cohen

February 5, 1919

Dear Mr. Cohen,

Oh no—it was not Voltaire—it was the influence of the scientific way of looking at the world—that made the change [from the way of thinking of my father's generation] to which I referred. My father was brought up scientifically—i.e. he studied medicine in France—and I was not. Yet there was with him as with the rest of his generation a certain softness of attitude toward the interstitial miracle—the phenomenon without phenomenal antecedents, that I did not feel. The difference was in the air, although perhaps only the few of my time felt it. *The Origin of Species* I think came out while I was in college. H. Spencer had announced his intention to put the universe into our pockets—I hadn't read either of them to be sure, but as I say it was in the air. I did read Buckle—now almost forgotten—but making a noise in his day, but I could refer to no book as the specific cause—I never have read much of Voltaire and probably at that time had read nothing. Emerson and Ruskin were the men that set me on fire. Probably a sceptical temperament that I got from my mother had something to do with my way of thinking. Then I was in with the abolitionists, some or many of whom were sceptics as well as dogmatists. But I think science was at the bottom. Of course my father was by no means orthodox, but like other even lax Unitarians there were questions that he didn't like to have asked—and he always spoke of keeping his mind open on matters like spiritualism or whether Bacon wrote Shakespeare—so that when I wanted to be disagreeable I told him that he straddled, in order to be able to say, whatever might be accepted, well I always have recognized etc., which was not just on my part . . .

To Alice Stopford Green

October 1, 1901

My dear Mrs. Green,

It is impossible not to reply at once to such a challenging confession of faith. It sounds to me a trifle *voulu*—an attitude that pleases your fancy—but hardly a complete expression of deliberate conviction. I am neither optimist nor pessimist. There are half a dozen futures (I mean for our civilization) that seem to me equally probable and among them is the possibility of civilization cutting its own throat or of one going down hill in some way. But I can't see how one can doubt as a fact of history that our reasoned view of life is more organized and profound than it ever was before. Then again as to another factor in the belief in evolution—viz. the increased sense of the continuity of the universe. I grant it is a faith, like Newman's, or W. James's assertion of the contrary. It is not completely proved—but the faith that there is a little more continuity than already established has been at the bottom of every advance in science. I mean by continuity quantitatively fixed relations of every phenomenon to antecedent phenomena. I admit that the growth of a new belief shakes various sacrednesses of the past and by one who does not take a somewhat bird's-eye view is judged bad morally—but that seems to me like workingmen talking about the oppression of masters when prices are shaken by the increased organization of the world and new nations coming in as competitors. A moral view is a dangerous means of judging. [In?] judging the past at least, it seems to me that all great or general facts should be looked at only as cosmical changes. Good and bad are of real significance only for the future where our effort is one of the instrumentalities that bring the inevitable to pass . . . If there is a world it seems to me that one may surmise that our judgments of significance and worth have no meaning for it. Indeed I think it adds a poignancy to the passion of life to doubt its seriousness— Blasphemy as Heine saw is one of the joys of the devout. Then why so savage about our poor time? I should have supposed we had seen a good many thinkers—I even am bold enough to believe that both you and I have done some work in that way . . . I referred to the law when I boasted a little above and I hardly should ask you to follow me into that field and judge for yourself. Of course thinking grows more specialized because we have got too far along with science for men to be encyclopaedic with success—but still the law, although by no means to my mind a vast subject, is a considerable one and was happily devoid of general views when I began so that it gave one a chance to theorize a bit. In that field I could name a number of men still living and others recently dead who seem to me to bear to have been thinkers. Also in philosophy. The English irritate you, and I understand it, having had an Irish great grandmother luckily for me, but still you think better of them than you admit, I guess. After all, one may like or dislike as a Celt (pronounce Kelt to be aesthetic) or a Briton but one must think as a rational being. The worth of the process I leave undecided. Perhaps there is not such a thing as worth. All I mean by truth is the path I have to travel. Whether that compulsion has any more universal meaning than the compulsion that draws me to one woman and repels me from another I don't know. It is final for me but I go no further. This seems to have turned out a sort of counter-confession of faith and to need apology—but I shall send it and hope you will be remembering me kindly enough to be interested.

To Harold Laski

February 26, 1918

Dear Laski,

. . . The eternal demand for the superlative degree—the unwillingness to accept less than being in on the ground floor with God—don't impress me much, except as a fact in psychology. Why should we not be humble—why not willing to admit that the primordial wiggle of the first churning of chaos came before our time? Not that I shouldn't like to have an angel about a span long light on the top of my inkstand here and say, "God directs me to tell you that it's you and He, that He made the rest but you made yourself and He desires your friendship"—or other encouraging message—that was warmer than the tepid concession of life as it is . . .

April 13, 1929

My dear Laski,

Your page written from solitude comes on top of an unanswered longer letter and I begin my reply when about to go to a conference. Your companions at the funeral who took part in prayer they didn't believe in merely illustrate what I am eternally repeating: that man is like all other growing things and when he has grown in a certain crevice for say twenty years you can't straighten him out without attacking his life. That is what gives the power to churches that no rational man would deem worthy of thought if he were growing free and had no past. You know my oft repeated formula that property, friendship and truth have a common root in time. I am not entirely insensible to the effect of church ceremonies even now—though neither they nor the patent fallacies in what they read from St. Paul interest me very much—but I let time run over me till the show is over. But if, as is unusual, the service is well done, and you are in a crowd moved by emotion, there is a contagion about it.

Now I have returned from the conference pretty well tired with it, though afterwards Brandeis and I drove over to Georgetown and home by a *circumbendibus* around the Cathedral, to see the white and pink dogwood and wisteria that lined a part of our road. The sights here are fleeting but they are superlative while they last. What damned fools people are who believe things. A case* has gone over for further consideration, of a woman wanting to become a citizen, but who, being as she says, more of a pacifist than Jane Ad[d]ams, has to explain that she would not fight for the Constitution (or, as her counsel said, wouldn't do what the law wouldn't let her do) and so opens to the Government a discourse on the foundation of the Constitution being in readiness to defend itself by force, etc., etc. All 'isms seem to me silly—but this hyperaethereal respect for human life seems perhaps the silliest of all.

But I almost fear that I am impolite—for you are not without your creed—to my regret. I haven't read much since my dash of philosophy but I am engaged in Lewis Mumford's *Life of Herman Melville*—which interests me much as a careful study of a man whom the writer believes great—but hardly less from the tone and attitude of the author . . .

September 27, 1921

Dear Laski,

. . . He surprised me also by seeming bothered over the question of the future life. He asked me if I believed in it and if I was a Christian—two questions that astonished me—and when I said I saw no ground for believing in a future life thought that then we were the victims of a cruel joke. I told him he retained a remnant of theology and thought of himself as a little God over against the universe instead of a cosmic ganglion—that any one was free to say I don't like it, but that it was like damning the weather—simply a declaration that one was not adapted to the environment—a criticism of self not of the universe—all of which commonplaces it seemed odd to find myself repeating . . .

*United States v. Schwimmer (see ch. 10).—Ed.

To Lewis Einstein

May 21, 1914

Dear Einstein,

. . . I am all on the Greek side in their rationality as to what Christians call sin and they call error. I daresay I have made to you a remark that I have thought of in these later days, that morals are imperfect social generalizations expressed in terms of feeling, and that to make the generalization perfect we must wash out the emotion and get a cold head. The retail dealers in thought will do the emotionalizing of whatever happens to be accepted doctrine of the day. *Nous autres* will permit them that. In fact, if we have got to hate anything, I don't see why we mightn't as well invert the Christian saying and hate the sinner but not the sin. Hate being a personal emotion naturally falls on the obstacles to our making the kind of world we like. It imports no judgement. Disgust is ultimate and therefore as irrational as reason itself—a dogmatic datum. The world has produced the rattlesnake as well as me; but I kill it if I get a chance, as also mosquitos, cockroaches, murderers, and flies. My only judgment is that they are incongruous with the world I want; the kind of world we all try to make according to our power.

I am afraid I also should find it hard to get on with the Greeks. We want the infinite, which Livingstone says they disliked. We want the reflection of the reflection, the looking-glass at both ends of the room. We are thankful to be corrupt, if not to be first intentioned is to be so; and I would rather read Livingstone (though I fear he is a Christian and hates sin) than Plato. But I prefer Socrates to the prophets even with the very great gain they got by being translated into English by people who only partly understood them, but, being convinced that they meant something pretty tall, achieved effect transcending the simple inspiration of Jehovah . . .

To Franklin Ford

December 29, 1917

Dear Mr. Ford,

. . . Man's "resistiveness" to experience has struck me much of late years. Man believes what he wants to, and is moved only a little by reason. But reason means facts, and if neglected is likely or liable to knock a hole in his boat, but usually it is not big enough to swamp it and he sticks in an old hat and goes on. I was writing to Laski a while ago that when I read Malthus I thought he had ripped the guts out of some humbugs—but humbugs have not guts and are living happily without them a century later . . .

To Harold Laski

December 9, 1921

Dear Laski,

Your letter of "23 xi 21" (wondrous) came yesterday and as always I go off bang when you pull the trigger. Of course the first thing is the suggestion that you stand for parliament! It may be that I am too timid and cautious, but I greatly rejoice that you did not yield to the temptation. Of course I don't know the conditions but it seems to me that, for the present at least, you are in the right place now, and that the big book is better both as a contribution to the world and as a form of self-expression. I put self-expression last out of deference to popular speech, but I think it first. As you know, I think nature takes care of our altruism for us, and that a man who thinks he has been an egotist all his life, if he has been a true jobbist, will find on the Day of Judgment that he has been a better altruist than those who thought more about it. I read your article on Christian Socialism with the pleasure I always get from your writing, but with a touch of regret at the tone that you hint from time to time that the existing order is wicked. The inevitable is not wicked. If you can improve upon it all right, but it is not necessary to damn the stem because you are the flower. As it seems to me that all society has rested on the death of men and must rest on that or on the prevention of the lives of a good many, I naturally shrink from the moral tone. In short I believe in Malthus—in the broad—not bothering about details . . .

April 6, 1920

Dear Laski,

We talk about the truth and yet another man will say that he can see nothing in reasoning that seems to you conclusive. Truth is the unanimous consent of mankind to a system of propositions. It is an ideal and as such postulates itself as a thing to be attained, but like other good ideals it is unattainable and therefore may be called absurd. Some ideals, like morality, a system of specific conduct for every situation, would be detestable if attained and therefore the postulate must be conditioned—that it is a thing to be striven for on the tacit understanding that it will not be reached . . .

To Alice Stopford Green

Beverly Farms, August 20, 1909

Dear Mrs. Green,

This is just a word of affectionate reminder—to say nothing in particular. Fred. Pollock and his son Jack are with us until Sunday and the air has hummed with culture talk. That brings up London, if it needed bringing up. Otherwise I am living most quietly—I read a legal history and wrote a notice of it for F.P.'s Law Quarterly and since then have dozed over philosophy and belles lettres. But most of my authors seem to believe in some form of the absolute and make me wonder whether I live on a lower plane than is attainable by man, or whether, as of course I maintain, they are churning the void in the hope of making cheese. When a man begins to think outside of space and time, using all the time words that seem to me to get all their meaning inside of those forms, I wait for better days. For instance, what is a will outside of time? I should think that will implied time—persistence—if it meant anything. Even in belles lettres I feel in H. James's *Ambassadors* an attitude of absoluteness—excluding from the heights all who do not share his scale of values. As against that, I think that values like truth are largely personal. There is enough community for us to talk, not enough for anyone to command. How has a man who lives in the domain of taste and among the spices of moral vacillation a right to bully you—another who is wrapt in the spectacle of the growth and struggle for life of ideas? I don't see that either can say more than that one likes one thing, another another . . .

To Harold Laski

June 24, 1926

My dear Laski,
 . . . A new untruth is better than an old truth . . .

Beverly Farms, September 15, 1929

My dear Laski,
 Your remark about the "oughts" and system of values in political science leaves me rather cold. If, as I think, the values are simply generalizations emotionally expressed, the generalizations are matters for the same science as other observations of fact. If, as I sometimes suspect, you believe in some transcendental sanction, I don't. Of course different people, and especially different races, differ in their values—but those differences are matters of fact and I have no respect for them except my general respect for what exists. Man is an idealizing animal— and expresses his ideals (values) in the conventions of his time. I have very little respect for the conventions in themselves, but respect and generally try to observe those of my own environment as the transitory expression of an eternal fact . . .

April 18, 1930

My dear Laski,

A wonderfully interesting account of your jaw with the mussoos about classicism and romanticism, etc. Of course they seem to me as to you ridiculous. But that we must discount, for it means that you and I tacitly assume *our* aesthetic ultimates to be valid against theirs. I think they are because I think them founded on a wider view—but if the Frenchmen think not, we can't patronize them before a dispassionate tribunal, although of course we do between ourselves. I often think of the way our side shrieked during the late war at various things done by the Germans such as the use of gas. We said gentlemen don't do such things—to which the Germans: "Who the hell are you? *We* do them." There was no superior tribunal to decide—so logically the Germans stood as well as we did. That case reminded me of a *cause célèbre* in a yearly collection that used to be put out by Albert Bataille from the *Figaro*. A duellist was tried on the ground that he had done a forbidden thing—grasped his adversary's weapon—and a lot of experts testified that that couldn't be done. Then a lot of duellists went on the stand and said that is a fencing school rule—when you go on the ground you go there to kill the other man and may do what you can. Probably I have told you of this a dozen times before, as it is a stock illustration of mine. But to use another stock phrase inverted—you must deal with friends as you do with great men and let them bore you if you want to get the themness of them . . .

Ideals and Doubts

10 *Illinois Law Review* I (1915)

. . . [To the Neo-Kantian idealist, experience] takes place and is organized in consciousness, by its machinery and according to its laws, such as the category of cause and effect. Therefore consciousness constructs the universe and as the fundamental fact is entitled to fundamental reverence. From this it is easy to proceed to the Kantian injunction to regard every human being as an end in himself and not as a means.

I confess that I rebel at once. If we want conscripts, we march them up to the front with bayonets in their rear to die for a cause in which perhaps they do not believe. The enemy we treat not even as a means but as an obstacle to be abolished, if so it may be. I feel no pangs of conscience over either step, and naturally am slow to accept a theory that seems to be contradicted by practices that I approve. In fact, it seems to me that the idealists give away their case when they write books. For it shows that they have done the great act of faith and decided that they are not God. If the world were my dream, I should be God in the only universe I know. But although I cannot prove that I am awake, I believe that my neighbors exist in the same sense that I do, and if I admit that, it is easy to admit also that I am in the universe, not it in me.

When I say that a thing is true, I mean that I cannot help believing it. I am stating an experience as to which there is no choice. But as there are many things that I cannot help doing that the universe can, I do not venture to assume that my inabilities in the way of thought are inabilities of the universe. I therefore define the truth as the system of my limitations, and leave absolute truth for those who are better equipped. With absolute truth I leave absolute ideals of conduct equally on one side.

But although one believes in what commonly, with some equivocation, is called necessity; that phenomena always are found to stand in quantitatively fixed relations to earlier phenomena; it does not follow that without such absolute ideals we have nothing to do but to sit still and let time run over us. As I wrote many years ago, the mode in which the inevitable comes to pass is through effort. Consciously or unconsciously we all strive to make the kind of a world that we like. And although with Spinoza we may regard criticism of the past as futile, there is every reason for doing all that we can to make a future such as we desire.

There is every reason also for trying to make our desires intelligent. The trouble is that our ideals for the most part are inarticulate, and that even if we have made them definite we have very little experimental knowledge of the way to bring them about. The social reformers of today seem to me so far to forget that we no more can get something for nothing by legislation than we can by mechanics as to be satisfied if the bill to be paid for their improvements is not presented in a lump sum. Interstitial detriments that may far outweigh the benefit promised are not bothered about. Probably I am too skeptical as to our ability to do more than shift disagreeable burdens from the shoulders of the stronger to those of the weaker. But I hold to a few articles of a creed that I do not expect to see popular in my day. I believe that the wholesale social regeneration which so many now seem to expect, if it can be helped by conscious, coordinated human effort, cannot be affected appreciably by tinkering with the institution of property, but only by taking in hand life and trying to build a race. That would be my starting point for an ideal for the law. The notion that with socialized property we should have women free and a piano for everybody seems to me an empty humbug.

To get a little nearer to the practical, our current ethics and our current satisfaction with conventional legal rules, it seems to me, can be purged to a certain extent without reference to what our final ideal may be. To rest upon a formula is a slumber that, prolonged, means death. Our system of morality is a body of imperfect social generalizations expressed in terms of emotion. To get at its truth, it is useful to omit the emotion and ask ourselves what those generalizations are and how far they are confirmed by fact accurately ascertained. So in regard to the formulas of the law, I have found it very instructive to consider what may be the postulates implied. They are generically two: that such and such a condition or result is desirable and that such and such means are appropriate to bring it about. In all debatable matters there are conflicting desires to be accomplished by inconsistent means, and the further question arises, which is entitled to prevail in the specific case? Upon such issues logic does not carry us far, and the practical solution sometimes may assume a somewhat cynical shape. But I have found it a help to clear thinking to try to get behind my conventional assumptions as a judge whose first business is to see that the game is played according to the rules whether I like them or not. To have doubted one's own first principles is the mark of a civilized man. To know what you want and why you think that such a measure will help it is the first but by no means the last step towards intelligent legal reform. The other and more difficult one is to realize what you must give up to get it, and to consider whether you are ready to pay the price.

It is fashionable nowadays to emphasize the criterion of social welfare as against the individualistic eighteenth century bills of rights . . . The trouble with some of those who hold to that modest platitude is that they are apt to take the general premise as a sufficient justification for specific measures. One may accept the premise in good faith and yet disbelieve all the popular conceptions of socialism, or even doubt whether there is a panacea in giving women votes. Personally I like to know what the bill is going to be before I order a luxury. But it is a pleasure to see more faith and enthusiasm in the young men; and I thought that one of them made a good answer to some of my skeptical talk when he said, "You would base legislation upon regrets rather than upon hopes."

6 • THE SOCIAL STRUGGLE

The Gas-Stokers' Strike
7 American Law Review 582 (1873)

The famous strike of the gas-stokers in December last, by which all London was plunged for several nights into partial darkness, at last found its way into the courts. The company prosecuted five men for conspiracy. The trial lasted only one day; the facts were simple and undisputed, substantially as follows: The stokers are hired by the company under special contracts, which require a certain notice to be given of an intention to leave work; the time of this notice varies in the contracts of different classes of workmen, ranging from one week to thirty days. Most of the stokers were combined together into a trade-union association. One of them, a member of the association, was discharged by the company, for what cause did not appear; but it was not claimed that the discharge was in violation of the contract. His fellow members of the association demanded his reinstatement, but in vain. They thereupon, on the 2d December, refused altogether to go to work unless their demand was complied with. There was no violence towards officers of the company; but there was some violence, accompanied by a good deal of threatening, towards members of the association who had not been advised of the intention of the conspirators, and who at first hesitated to fall in with the design. The court charged the jury that the defendants had a perfect right to form a trade-union, and that the fact that their action was in restraint of trade, which would have made it an offence at common law, could not be considered in this action; but that the company alleged that the defendants "either agreed to do an unlawful act or to do a lawful act by unlawful means; and he asked the jury whether there was a combination between the defendants either to hinder or prevent the company from carrying on their business by means of the men simultaneously breaking the contract of service they had entered into with the company. This was an illegal act, and, what was more, a criminal act. If they did agree to interfere with their employers' business, by simultaneously breaking such contracts, they were then agreeing to do that which would bring them within the definition of conspiracy."

The jury were out only twenty minutes, and then brought in a verdict of guilty, but with a recommendation to mercy. This, however, the court disregarded, and sentenced the accused to imprisonment for one year. In imposing the sentence the judge said that he had told the jury that "on the question whether they were to find the defendants guilty or not, they ought not to be influenced by the suggestion that what they were attempting to do would be dangerous to the public. But it did seem to him now, when he was called on to consider what kind of conspiracy they had been guilty of, that he could not throw aside what was one of the obvious results of the conspiracy into which they entered, and what must have been in their minds; and he could not doubt that the obvious result was great danger to the public of this metropolis; that that danger was present to their minds; and it was by the acting on that knowledge and on the effect they thought it would have upon their masters' minds, and trading upon their knowledge of the danger, that they entered into this conspiracy, in order to force their masters to follow their will . . .

"The prisoners were the principals—the chief actors; two of them were delegates chosen by the men, and therefore evidently men to whom they looked up. They took a leading part in the conspiracy. Therefore, notwithstanding their good character they had unfortunately put themselves into the position of being properly convicted of a dangerous and wicked conspiracy. The time had come when a serious punishment, and not a nominal or a light one, must be inflicted—a punishment that would teach men in their position that, although without offence they might be members of a trade-union, or might agree to go into an employment, or to leave it without committing any offence, yet that they must take care when they agreed together that they must not agree to do it by illegal means. If they did that they were guilty of conspiracy, and if they misled others they were guilty of a wicked conspiracy."

. . . It has always seemed to us a singular anomaly that believers in the theory of evolution and in the natural development of institutions by successive adaptations to the environment should be found laying down a theory of government intended to establish its limits once for all by a logical deduction from axioms. But the objection which we wish to express at the present time is that this presupposes an identity of interest between the different parts of a community which does not exist in fact. Consistently with his views, however, Mr. [Herbert] Spencer is forever putting cases to show that the reaction of legislation is equal to its action. By changing the law, he argues, you do not get rid of any burden, but only change the mode of bearing it; and if the change does not make it easier to bear for society, considered as a whole, legislation is inexpedient. This tacit assumption of the solidarity of the interests of society is very common, but seems to us to be false. The struggle for life, undoubtedly, is constantly putting the interests of men at variance with those of the lower animals. And the struggle does not stop in the ascending scale with the monkeys, but is equally the law of human existence. Outside of legislation this is undeniable. It is mitigated by sympathy, prudence, and all the social and moral qualities. But in the last resort a man rightly prefers his own interest to that of his neighbors. And this is as true in legislation as in any other form of corporate action. All that can be expected from modern improvements is that legislation should easily and quickly, yet not too quickly, modify itself in accordance with the will of the de facto supreme power in the community, and that the spread of an educated sympathy should reduce the sacrifice of minorities to a minimum. But whatever body may possess the supreme power for the moment is certain to have interests inconsistent with others which have competed unsuccessfully. The more powerful interests must be more or less reflected in legislation, which, like every other device of man or beast, must tend in the long run to aid the survival of the fittest. The objection to class legislation is not that it favors a class, but either that it fails to benefit the legislators, or that it is dangerous to them because a competing class has gained in power, or that it transcends the limits of self-preference which are imposed by sympathy. Interference with contracts by usury laws and the like is open to the first objection, that it only makes the burden of borrowers heavier. The law brought to bear upon the gas-stokers is perhaps open to the second, that it requires to be backed by a more unquestioned power than is now possessed by the favored class; and some English statutes are also very probably open to the third. But it is no sufficient condemnation of legislation that it favors one class at the expense of another; for much or all legislation does that; and nonetheless when the bona fide object is the greatest good of the greatest number. Why should the greatest number be preferred? Why not the greatest good of the most intelligent and most highly developed? The greatest good of a minority of our generation may be the greatest good of the greatest number in the long run. But if the welfare of all future ages is to be considered, legislation may as well be abandoned for the present. If the welfare of the living majority is paramount, it can only be on the ground that the majority have the power in their hands. The fact is that legislation in this country, as well as elsewhere, is empirical. It is necessarily made a means by which a body, having the power, put burdens which are disagreeable to them on the shoulders of somebody else. Communism would no more get rid of the difficulty than any other system, unless it limited or put a stop to the propagation of the species. And it may be doubted whether that solution would not be as disagreeable as any other . . .

Commonwealth v. Perry
155 Mass. 117, 28 N.E. 1126 (1891)
(Dissent)

I have the misfortune to disagree with my brethren. I have submitted my views to them at length, and, considering the importance of the question, feel bound to make public a brief statement, notwithstanding the respect and deference I feel for the judgment of those with whom I disagree.

In the first place, if the statute [forbidding an employer to withhold an employee's wages as a penalty for imperfect work] is unconstitutional as construed by the majority, I think it would be construed more narrowly and literally, so as to save it. Taking it literally, it is not infringed, and there is no withholding of wages, when the employer only promises to pay a reasonable price for imperfect work, or a price less than the price paid for perfect work, and does pay that price in fact. But I agree that the act should be construed more broadly, and should be taken to prohibit palpable evasions, because I am of opinion that even so construed it is constitutional, so far as any argument goes which I have heard. The prohibition, if any, must be found in the words of the Constitution, either expressed or implied upon a fair and historical construction. What words of the United States or state constitutions are relied on? The statute cannot be said to impair the obligation of contracts made after it went into effect. So far as has been pointed out to me, I do not see that it interferes with the right of acquiring, possessing, and protecting property any more than the laws against usury or gaming. In truth, I do not think that that clause of the Bill of Rights has any application. It might be urged, perhaps, that the power to make reasonable laws impliedly prohibits the making of unreasonable ones, and that this law is unreasonable. If I assume that this construction of the Constitution is correct, and that, speaking as a political economist, I should agree in condemning the law, still I should not be willing or think myself authorized to overturn legislation on that ground, unless I thought that an honest difference of opinion was impossible, or pretty nearly so.

But if the statute did no more than to abolish in certain cases contracts for a quantum meruit, and recoupment for defective quality not amounting to a failure of consideration, I suppose that it only would put an end to what are, relatively speaking, innovations in the common law, and I know of nothing to hinder it. This, however, is not all. I do not confine myself to technical considerations. I suppose that this act was passed because the operatives, or some of them, thought that they were often cheated out of a part of their wages under a false pretense that the work done by them was imperfect, and persuaded the legislature that their view was true. If their view was true, I cannot doubt that the legislature had the right to deprive the employers of an honest tool which they were using for a dishonest purpose, and I cannot pronounce the legislation void, as based on a false assumption, since I know nothing about the matter one way or the other. The statute, however construed, leaves the employers their remedy for imperfect work by action. I doubt if we are at liberty to consider the objection that this remedy is practically worthless; but if we are, then the same objection is equally true, although for different reasons, if the workmen are left to their remedy against their employers for wages wrongfully withheld.

Vegelahn v. Guntner

167 Mass. 92, 44 N.E. 1077 (1896)

(Dissent)

In a case like the present, it seems to me that, whatever the true result may be, it will be of advantage to sound thinking to have the less popular view of the law stated, and therefore, although when I have been unable to bring my brethren to share my convictions my almost invariable practice is to defer to them in silence, I depart from that practice in this case [in which the majority upheld an injunction against labor picketing], notwithstanding my unwillingness to do so in support of an already rendered judgment of my own . . .

I agree, whatever may be the law in the case of a single defendant, that when a plaintiff proves that several persons have combined and conspired to injure his business, and have done acts producing that effect, he shows temporal damage and a cause of action, unless the facts disclose, or the defendants prove, some ground of excuse or justification. And I take it to be settled, and rightly settled, that doing that damage by combined persuasion is actionable, as well as doing it by falsehood or by force.

Nevertheless, in numberless instances the law warrants the intentional infliction of temporal damage because it regards it as justified. It is on the question of what shall amount to a justification, and more especially on the nature of the considerations which really determine or ought to determine the answer to that question, that judicial reasoning seems to me often to be inadequate. The true grounds of decision are considerations of policy and of social advantage, and it is vain to suppose that solutions can be attained merely by logic and the general propositions of law which nobody disputes. Propositions as to public policy rarely are unanimously accepted, and still more rarely, if ever, are capable of unanswerable proof. They require a special training to enable anyone even to form an intelligent opinion about them. In the early stages of law, at least, they generally are acted on rather as inarticulate instincts than as definite ideas for which a rational defense is ready.

To illustrate what I have said in the last paragraph, it has been the law for centuries that a man may set up a business in a country town too small to support more than one, although he expects and intends thereby to ruin someone already there, and succeeds in his intent. In such a case he is not held to act "unlawfully and without justifiable cause." The reason, of course, is that the doctrine generally has been accepted that free competition is worth more to society than it costs, and that on this ground the infliction of the damage is privileged. Yet even this proposition nowadays is disputed by a considerable body of persons, including many whose intelligence is not to be denied, little as we may agree with them.

I have chosen this illustration partly with reference to what I have to say next. It shows without the need of further authority that the policy of allowing free competition justifies the intentional inflicting of temporal damage, including the damage of interference with a man's business by some means, when the damage is done not for its own sake but as an instrumentality in reaching the end of victory in the battle of trade. In such a case it cannot matter whether the plaintiff is the only rival of the defendant, and so is aimed at specifically, or is one of a class of all of whom are hit. The only debatable ground is the nature of the means by which such damage may be inflicted. We all agree that it cannot be done by force or threats of force. We all agree, I presume, that it may be done by persuasion to leave a rival's shop and come to the defendant's. It may be done by the refusal or withdrawal of various pecuniary advantages which, apart from this consequence, are within the defendant's lawful control. It may be done by the withdrawal, or threat to withdraw, such advantages from third persons who have a right to deal or not to deal with the plaintiff, as a means of inducing them not to deal with him either as customers or servants.

I pause here to remark that the word "threats" often is used as if, when it appeared that threats had been made, it appeared that unlawful conduct had begun. But it depends on what you threaten. As a general rule, even if subject to some exceptions, what you may do in a certain event you may threaten to do, that is, give warning of your intention to do in that event, and thus allow the other person the chance of avoiding the consequences . . .

I have seen the suggestion made that the conflict between employers and employed is not competition. But I venture to assume that none of my brethren would rely on that suggestion. If the policy on which our law is founded is too narrowly expressed in the term "free competition," we may substitute "free struggle for life." Certainly the policy is not limited to struggles between persons of the same class competing for the same end. It applies to all conflicts of temporal interests.

So far, I suppose, we are agreed. But there is a notion which latterly has been insisted on a good deal, that a combination of persons to do what any one of them lawfully might do by himself will make the otherwise lawful conduct unlawful. It would be rash to say that some as yet unformulated truth may not be hidden under this proposition. But in the general form in which it has been presented and accepted by many courts, I think it plainly untrue, both on authority and on principle . . . It is plain from the slightest consideration of practical affairs, or the most superficial reading of industrial history, that free competition means combination, and that the organization of the world, now going on so fast, means an ever-increasing might and scope of combination. It seems to me futile to set our faces against this tendency. Whether beneficial on the whole, as I think it, or detrimental, it is inevitable, unless the fundamental axioms of society, and even the fundamental conditions of life, are to be changed.

One of the eternal conflicts out of which life is made up is that between the effort of every man to get the most he can for his services, and that of society, disguised under the name of capital, to get his services for the least possible return. Combination on the one side is patent and powerful. Combination on the other is the necessary and desirable counterpart, if the battle is to be carried on in a fair and equal way.

If it be true that workingmen may combine with a view, among other things, to getting as much as they can for their labor, just as capital may combine with a view to getting the greatest possible return, it must be true that when combined they have the same liberty that combined capital has to support their interests by argument, persuasion, and the bestowal or refusal of those advantages which they otherwise lawfully control. I can remember when many people thought that, apart from violence or breach of contract, strikes were wicked, as organized refusals to work. I suppose that intelligent economists and legislators have given up that notion today. I feel pretty confident that they equally will abandon the idea that an organized refusal by workmen of social intercourse with a man who shall enter their antagonist's employ is wrong, if it is dissociated from any threat of violence, and is made for the sole object of prevailing, if possible, in a contest with their employer about the rate of wages. The fact that the immediate object of the act by which the benefit to themselves is to be gained is to injure their antagonist does not necessarily make it unlawful, any more than when a great house lowers the price of goods for the purpose and with the effect of driving a smaller antagonist from the business.

Plant v. Woods
176 Mass. 492, 57 N.E. 1011 (1900)
(Dissent)

. . . Although this is not the place for extended economic discussion, and although the law may not always reach ultimate economic conceptions, I think it well to add that I cherish no illusions as to the meaning and effect of strikes. While I think the strike a lawful instrument in the universal struggle of life, I think it pure phantasy to suppose that there is a body of capital of which labor as a whole secures a larger share by that means. The annual product, subject to an infinitesimal deduction for the luxuries of the few, is directed to consumption by the multitude, and is consumed by the multitude, always. Organization and strikes may get a larger share for the members of an organization, but, if they do, they get it at the expense of the less organized and less powerful portion of the laboring mass. They do not create something out of nothing. It is only by divesting our minds of questions of ownership and other machinery of distribution, and by looking solely at the question of consumption—asking ourselves what is the annual product, who consumes it, and what changes would or could we make—that we can keep in the world of realities. But, subject to the qualifications which I have expressed, I think it lawful for a body of workmen to try by combination to get more than they now are getting, although they do it at the expense of their fellows, and to that end to strengthen their union by the boycott and the strike . . .

Economic Elements (1904)*

CLP 279

I entertain some opinions concerning the issues raised by your questions, and though not strictly responsive, I will state them.

The real problem is not who owns, but who consumes, the annual product. The identification of these two very different questions is the source of many fallacies, and misleads many workingmen. The real evil of fifty-thousand-dollar balls and other manifestations of private splendor is that they tend to confirm this confusion in the minds of the ignorant by an appeal to their imagination, and make them think that the Vanderbilts and Rockefellers swallow their incomes like Cleopatra's dissolved pearl. The same conception is at the bottom of Henry George's *Progress and Poverty.* He thinks he has finished the discussion when he shows the tendency of wealth to be owned by the landlords. He does not consider what the landlords do with it.

I conceive that economically it does not matter whether you call Rockefeller or the United States owner of all the wheat in the United States if that wheat is annually consumed by the body of the people; except that Rockefeller, under the illusion of self-seeking or in the conscious pursuit of power, will be likely to bring to bear a more poignant scrutiny of the future in order to get a greater return for the next year.

If then, as I believe, the ability of the ablest men under the present régime is directed to getting the largest markets and the largest returns, such ability is directed to the economically desirable end.

I have vainly urged our various statisticians to exhibit in the well-known form the proportions of the products consumed by the many and those consumed by the few, expressed in labor hours or in any other convenient way. This would show whether private ownership was abused for the production of an undue proportion of luxuries for the few. I do not believe the luxuries would be one per cent.

It follows from what I have said that the objections to unlimited private ownership are sentimental or political, not economic. Of course, as the size of a private fortune increases, the interest of the public in the administration of it increases. If a man owned one-half of the wheat in the country and announced his intention to burn it, such abuse of ownership would not be permitted. The crowd would kill him sooner than stand it.

But it seems to me that if every desirable object were in the hands of a

*A letter written in response to a series of questions put to prominent men, first published in 40 *Cosmopolitan Magazine* 397 (1906).—Ed.

monopolist, intent on getting all he could for it (subject to the limitation that it must be consumed, and that it might not be wantonly destroyed, as, of course, it would not be), the value of the several objects would be settled by the intensity of the desires for them respectively, and they would be consumed by those who were able to get them and that would be the ideal result.

The first question put,* if I may be permitted to say so, seems to me rather fanciful. I see no way of answering it intelligently, and if I am right, it appears to imply an acceptance of what I have already tried to show to be a fallacy or confusion.

So far as I can answer it, what I should say would be this: All that any man contributes to the world is the intelligence which directs a change in the place of matter. A man does not create the thing he handles or the force he exerts. The force could be got cheaper if the directing intelligence were not needed. The whole progress of the world in a material way is to put the need of intelligence further back. It is obvious that the intelligence of an architect contributes more to the change of form which takes place in a house than that of all the laboring hands. How can any one measure the scope and value of remote causes of change? How can I compare the present effect on the lives of men of the speculations of Kant and of the empire of Napoleon? I should not think it absurd to assert that the former counted for the more, though, of course, it is impossible to prove it. My practical answer is that a great fortune does not mean a corresponding consumption, but a power of command; that some one must exercise that command, and that I know of no way of finding the fit man so good as the fact of winning it in the competition of the market.

I already have intimated my opinion that the owner of a great fortune has public functions, and therefore, subject to legal questions which I am not considering, should be subject to some negative restraint. Among others, I should like to see him prohibited from giving great sums to charities which could not be clearly justified as long-sighted public investments.

The only other question on which I desire to say a word is the nature of taxes in this connection. Taxes, when thought out in things and results, mean an abstraction of a part of the annual product for government purposes, and cannot mean anything else. Whatever form they take in their imposition they must be borne by the consumer, that is, mainly by the working-men and fighting-men of the community. It is

---

*Whether a man can render services entitling him to a fortune as great as some of ours in America.

well that they should have this fact brought home to them, and not too much disguised by the form in which the taxes are imposed.

Northern Securities Company v. United States
193 U.S. 197 (1904)
(Dissent)

I am unable to agree with the judgment of the majority of the court, and although I think it useless and undesirable, as a rule, to express dissent, I feel bound to do so in this case and to give my reasons for it.

Great cases like hard cases make bad law. For great cases are called great, not by reason of their real importance in shaping the law of the future, but because of some accident of immediate overwhelming interest which appeals to the feelings and distorts the judgment. These immediate interests exercise a kind of hydraulic pressure which makes what previously was clear seem doubtful, and before which even well settled principles of law will bend. What we have to do in this case is to find the meaning of some not very difficult words. We must try, I have tried, to do it with the same freedom of natural and spontaneous interpretation that one would be sure of if the same question arose upon an indictment for a similar act which excited no public attention, and was of importance only to a prisoner before the court. Furthermore, while at times judges need for their work the training of economists or statesmen, and must act in view of their foresight of consequences, yet when their task is to interpret and apply the words of a statute, their function is merely academic to begin with—to read English intelligently—and a consideration of consequences comes into play, if at all, only when the meaning of the words used is open to reasonable doubt.

The question to be decided is whether, under the [Sherman Act], it is unlawful, at any stage of the process, if several men unite to form a corporation for the purpose of buying more than half the stock of each of two competing interstate railroad companies, if they form the corporation, and the corporation buys the stock. I will suppose further that every step is taken, from the beginning, with the single intent of ending competition between the companies. I make this addition not because it may not be and is not disputed but because, as I shall try to show, it is totally unimportant under any part of the statute with which we have to deal.

The statute of which we have to find the meaning is a criminal statute. The two sections on which the government relies both make certain acts crimes. That is their immediate purpose and that is what they say. It is vain to insist that this is not a criminal proceeding. The words cannot be read one way in a suit which is to end in fine and imprisonment and another way in one which seeks an injunction. The construction which is adopted in this case must be adopted in one of the other sort. I am no friend of artificial interpretations because a statute is of one kind rather than another, but all agree that before a statute is to be taken to punish that which always has been lawful it must express its intent in clear words. So I say we must read the words before us as if the question were whether two small exporting grocers should go to jail.

Again the statute is of a very sweeping and general character. It hits "every" contract or combination of the prohibited sort, great or small, and "every" person who shall monopolize or attempt to monopolize, in the sense of the act, "any part" of the trade or commerce among the several states. There is a natural inclination to assume that it was directed against certain great combinations and to read it in that light. It does not say so. On the contrary, it says "every," and "any part." Still less was it directed specially against railroads. There even was a reasonable doubt whether it included railroads until the point was decided by this court.

Finally, the statute must be construed in such a way as not merely to save its constitutionality but, so far as is consistent with a fair interpretation, not to raise grave doubts on that score. I assume, for the purposes of discussion, although it would be a great and serious step to take, that in some case that seemed to it to need heroic measures, Congress might regulate not only commerce, but instruments of commerce, or contracts the bearing of which upon commerce would be only indirect. But it is clear that the mere fact of an indirect effect upon commerce not shown to be certain and very great would not justify such a law. The point decided in *United States v. E. C. Knight Co.* was that "the fact . . . that trade or commerce might be indirectly affected was not enough to entitle complainants to a decree." Commerce depends upon population, but Congress could not, on that ground, undertake to regulate marriage and divorce. If the act before us is to be carried out according to what seems to me the logic of the argument for the government, which I do not believe that it will be, I can see no part of the conduct of life with which on similar principles Congress might not interfere.

This act is construed by the government to affect the purchasers of shares in two railroad companies because of the effect it may have, or, if you like, is certain to have, upon the competition of these roads. If such a remote result of the exercise of an ordinary incident of property and personal freedom is enough to make that exercise unlawful, there is hardly any transaction concerning commerce between the states that may not be made a crime by the finding of a jury or a court. The personal ascendency of one man may be such that it would give to his advice the effect of a command, if he owned but a single share in each road. The tendency of his presence in the stockholders' meetings might be certain to prevent competition, and thus his advice, if not his mere existence, become a crime.

I state these general considerations as matters which I should have to take into account before I could agree to affirm the decree appealed from, but I do not need them for my own opinion, because when I read the act I cannot feel sufficient doubt as to the meaning of the words to need to fortify my conclusion by any generalities. Their meaning seems to me plain on their face.

The first section makes "Every contract, combination in the form of trust or otherwise, or conspiracy in restraint of trade or commerce among the several States, or with foreign nations" a misdemeanor, punishable by fine, imprisonment or both. Much trouble is made by substituting other phrases assumed to be equivalent, which then are reasoned from as if they were in the act. The court below argued as if maintaining competition were the expressed object of the act. The act says nothing about competition. I stick to the exact words used. The words hit two classes of cases, and only two—contracts in restraint of trade and combinations or conspiracies in restraint of trade, and we have to consider what these respectively are. Contracts in restraint of trade are dealt with and defined by the common law. They are contracts with a stranger to the contractor's business (although in some cases carrying on a similar one), which wholly or partially restrict the freedom of the contractor in carrying on that business as otherwise he would. The objection of the common law to them was primarily on the contractor's own account. The notion of monopoly did not come in unless the contract covered the whole of England. Of course this objection did not apply to partnerships or other forms, if there were any, of substituting a community of interest where there had been competition. There was no objection to such combinations merely as in restraint of trade, or otherwise unless they amounted to a monopoly. Contracts in restraint of trade, I repeat, were contracts with strangers to the contractor's business, and the trade restrained was the contractor's own.

Combinations or conspiracies in restraint of trade, on the other hand, were combinations to keep strangers to the agreement out of the business. The objection to them was not an objection to their effect upon the parties making the contract, the members of the combination or firm, but an objection to their intended effect upon strangers to the firm and their supposed consequent effect upon the public at large. In other words, they were regarded as contrary to public policy because they monopolized or attempted to monopolize some portion of the trade or commerce of the realm. All that is added to the first section by §2 is that like penalties are imposed upon every single person who, without combination, monopolizes or attempts to monopolize commerce among the states; and that the liability is extended to attempting to monopolize any part of such trade or commerce. It is more important as an aid to the construction of §1 than it is on its own account. It shows that whatever is criminal when done by way of combination is equally criminal if done by a single man. That I am right in my interpretation of the words of §1 is shown by the words "in the form of trust or otherwise." The prohibition was suggested by the trusts, the objection to which, as every one knows, was not the union of former competitors, but the sinister power exercised or supposed to be exercised by the combination in keeping rivals out of the business and ruining those who already were in. It was the ferocious extreme of competition with others, not the cessation of competition among the partners, that was the evil feared. Further proof is to be found in §7, giving an action to any person injured in his business or property by the forbidden conduct. This cannot refer to the parties to the agreement and plainly means that outsiders who are injured in their attempt to compete with a trust or other similar combination may recover for it. How effective the section may be or how far it goes is not material to my point. My general summary of the two classes of cases which the act affects is confirmed by the title, which is "An Act to Protect Trade and Commerce Against Unlawful Restraints and Monopolies."

What I now ask is under which of the foregoing classes this case is supposed to come, and that question must be answered as definitely and precisely as if we were dealing with the indictments which logically ought to follow this decision. The provision of the statute against contracts in restraint of trade has been held to apply to contracts between railroads, otherwise remaining independent, by which they restricted their respective freedom as to rates. This restriction by contract with a stranger to the contractor's business is the ground of the decision in *United States v. Joint Traffic Association,* following and affirming *United States v. Trans-Missouri Freight Association.* I accept those decisions absolutely, not only as binding upon me, but as decisions which I have no desire to criticise or abridge. But the provision has not been decided, and, it seems to me, could not be decided without perversion of plain language, to apply to an arrangement by which competition is ended through community of interest—an arrangement which leaves the parties without external restriction. That provision, taken alone, does not require that all existing competitions shall be maintained. It does not look primarily, if at all, to competition. It simply requires that a party's freedom in trade between the states shall not be cut down by contract with a stranger. So far as that phrase goes, it is lawful to abolish competition by any form of union. It would seem to me impossible to say that the words "every contract in restraint of trade is a crime punishable with imprisonment," would send the members of a partnership between, or a consolidation of, two trading corporations to prison—still more impossible to say that it forbade one man or corporation to purchase as much stock as he liked in both. Yet those words would have that effect if this clause of §1 applies to the defendants here. For it cannot be too carefully remembered that that clause applies to "every" contract of the forbidden kind—a consideration which was the turning point of the *Trans-Missouri Freight Association* case.

If the statute applies to this case it must be because the parties, or some of them, have formed, or because the Northern Securities Company is, a combination in restraint of trade among the states, or, what comes to the same thing in my opinion, because the defendants, or some or one of them, are monopolizing or attempting to monopolize some part of the commerce between the states. But the mere reading of those words shows that they are used in a limited and accurate sense. According to popular speech, every concern monopolizes whatever business it does, and if that business is trade between two states it monopolizes a part of the trade among the states. Of course the statute does not forbid that. It does not mean that all business must cease. A single railroad down a narrow valley or through a mountain gorge monopolizes all the railroad transportation through that valley or gorge. Indeed every railroad monopolizes, in a popular sense, the trade of some area. Yet I suppose no one would say that the statute forbids a combination of men into a corporation to build and run such a railroad between the states.

I assume that the Minnesota charter of the Great Northern and the Wisconsin charter of the Northern Pacific both are valid. Suppose that, before either road was built, Minnesota, as part of a system of transportation between the states, had created a railroad company authorized singly to build all the lines in the states now actually built, owned or controlled by either of the two existing companies. I take it that the charter would have been just as good as the present one, even if the statutes which we are considering had been in force. In whatever sense it would have created a monopoly the present charter does. It would have been a large one, but the act of Congress makes no discrimination according to size. Size has nothing to do with the matter. A monopoly of "any part" of commerce among the states is unlawful. The supposed company would have owned lines that might have been competing—probably the present one does. But the act of Congress will not be construed to mean the universal disintegration of society into single men, each at war with all the rest, or even the prevention of all further combinations for a common end.

There is a natural feeling that somehow or other the statute meant to strike at combinations great enough to cause just anxiety on the part of those who love their country more than money, while it viewed such little ones as I have supposed with just indifference. This notion, it may be said, somehow breathes from the pores of the act, although it seems to be contradicted in every way by the words in detail. And it has occurred to me that it might be that when a combination reached a certain size it might have attributed to it more of the character of a monopoly merely by virtue of its size than would be attributed to a smaller one. I am quite clear that it is only in connection with monopolies that size could play any part. But my answer has been indicated already. In the first place size in the case of railroads is an inevitable incident and if it were an objection under the act, the Great Northern and the Northern Pacific already were too great and encountered the law. In the next place in the case of railroads it is evident that the size of the combination is reached for other ends than those which would make them monopolies. The combinations are not formed for the purpose of excluding others from the field. Finally, even a small railroad will have the same tendency to exclude others from its narrow area that great ones have to exclude others from a greater one, and the statute attacks the small monopolies as well as the great. The very words of the act make such a distinction impossible in this case and it has not been attempted in express terms.

If the charter which I have imagined above would have been good notwithstanding the monopoly, in a popular sense, which it created, one next is led to ask whether and why a combination or consolidation of existing roads, although in actual competition, into one company of exactly the same powers and extent, would be any more obnoxious to the law. Although it was decided in *Louisville & Nashville Railroad Co. v. Kentucky* that since the statute, as before, the states have the power to regulate the matter, it was said, in the argument, that such a consolidation would be unlawful, and it seems to me that the Attorney General was compelled to say so in order to maintain his case. But I think that logic would not let him stop there, or short of denying the power of a state at the present time to authorize one company to construct and own two parallel lines that might compete. The monopoly would be the same as if the roads were consolidated after they had begun to compete—and it is on the footing of monopoly that I now am supposing the objection made. But to meet the objection to the prevention of competition at the same time, I will suppose that three parties apply to a state for charters; one for each of two new and possibly competing lines respectively, and one for both of these lines, and that the charter is granted to the last. I think that charter would be good, and I think the whole argument to the contrary rests on a popular instead of an accurate and legal conception of what the word "monopolize" in the statute means. I repeat, that in my opinion there is no attempt to monopolize, and what, as I have said, in my judgment amounts to the same thing, that there is no combination in restraint of trade until something is done with the intent to exclude strangers to the combination from competing with it in some part of the business which it carries on.

Unless I am entirely wrong in my understanding of what a "combination in restraint of trade" means, then the same monopoly may be attempted and effected by an individual and is made equally illegal in that case by §2. But I do not expect to hear it maintained that Mr. Morgan could be sent to prison for buying as many shares as he liked of the Great Northern and the Northern Pacific, even if he bought them both at the same time and got more than half the stock of each road.

There is much that was mentioned in argument which I pass by. But in view of the great importance attached by both sides to the supposed attempt to suppress competition, I must say a word more about that. I said at the outset that I should assume, and I do assume, that one purpose of the purchase was to suppress competition between the two roads. I appreciate the force of the argument that there are independent stockholders in each; that it cannot be presumed that the respective boards of directors will propose any illegal act, that if they should they could be restrained, and that all that has been done as yet is too remote from the illegal result to be classed even as an attempt. Not every act done in furtherance of an unlawful end is an attempt or contrary to the law. There must be a certain nearness to the result. It is a question of proximity and degree. So, as I have said, is the amenability of acts in furtherance of interference with commerce among the states to legislation by Congress. So, according to the intimation of this court, is the question of liability under the present statute. But I assume further, for the purposes of discussion, that what has been done is near enough to the result to fall under the law, if the law prohibits that result, although that assumption very nearly if not quite contradicts the decision in *United States v. E. C. Knight Co.* But I say that the law does not prohibit the result. If it does it must be because there is some further meaning than I have yet discovered in the words "combinations in restraint of trade." I think that I have exhausted the meaning of those words in what I already have said. But they certainly do not require all existing competitions to be kept on foot, and, on the principle of the *Trans-Missouri Freight Association* case, invalidate the continuance of old contracts by which former competitors united in the past.

A partnership is not a contract or combination in restraint of trade between the partners unless the well known words are to be given a new meaning invented for the purposes of this act. It is true that the suppression of competition was referred to in *United States v. Trans-Missouri Freight Association,* but, as I have said, that was in connection with a contract with a stranger to the defendant's business—a true contract in restraint of trade. To suppress competition in that way is one thing, to suppress it by fusion is another. The law, I repeat, says nothing about competition, and only prevents its suppression by contracts or combinations in restraint of trade and such contracts or combinations derive their character as restraining trade from other features than the suppression of competition alone. To see whether I am wrong, the illustrations put in the argument are of use. If I am, then a partnership between two stage drivers who had been competitors in driving across a state line, or two merchants once engaged in rival commerce among the states whether made after or before the act, if now continued, is a crime. For, again I repeat, if the restraint on the freedom of the members of a combination caused by their entering into partnership is a restraint of trade, every such combination, as well the small as the great, is within the act.

In view of my interpretation of the statute I do not go further into the question of the power of Congress. That has been dealt with by my brother White and I concur in the main with his views. I am happy to know that only a minority of my brethren adopt an interpretation of the law which in my opinion would make eternal the *bellum omnium contra omnes* and disintegrate society so far as it could into individual atoms. If that were its intent I should regard calling such a law a regulation of commerce as a mere pretense. It would be an attempt to reconstruct society. I am not concerned with the wisdom of such an attempt, but I believe that Congress was not entrusted by the Constitution with the power to make it and I am deeply persuaded that it has not tried.

I am authorized to say that the Chief Justice, Mr. Justice White and Mr. Justice Peckham concur in this dissent.

To Franklin Ford

April 6, 1911

Dear Mr. Ford,

I largely, if not wholly agree with you. The points of possible difference don't need mention now. The thing I had articulately in mind was
that if unification were complete—call it socialism or no-ism, descen-
dant of the military power of independent industrial organization, or
what you like—the problem would remain of adjusting production to
the equilibrium of social desires; and, as I said long ago, that if every
desideratum were in the hands of a separate monopolist bent on getting all he could for it, you would get an ideal result, if each monopolist
knew his business, as he would have to to keep his place.

I confess that the present passion for disorganization seems to me, I
won't say amazing, but certainly foolish. Of course what I say and said
has nothing to do with what I shall say or do in the famous cases now
under consideration; there my duty is to deal with a statute, and what I
think of its wisdom is totally immaterial.

I always say that I regard legislation like buying a ticket to the theatre; if you are sure that you want to go to the show and have the money
to pay for it there is an end of the matter. I may think you foolish to
want to go, but that has nothing to do with my duty.

Years ago the Russian Ambassador said to me that we ought to build
a statue of Rockefeller instead of damning him, and gave his reasons.
The head of such a concern keeps his headship by seeing further into
the economic necessities than others, and those to whom such necessities are disagreeable hold him responsible for the whole business, and
they say damn Rockefeller when they would not dare to damn God, or
the order of the universe.

Dr. Miles Medical Co. v. John D. Park & Sons Co.
220 U.S. 373 (1911)

(Dissent)

. . . The second contract is that of the retail agents, so called, being
really the first purchasers, fixing the price below which they will not sell
to the public. There is no attempt to attach a contract or condition to
the goods, or in any way to restrict dealings with them after they leave
the hands of the retail men. The sale to the retailers is made by the
plaintiff, and the only question is whether the law forbids a purchaser
to contract with his vendor that he will not sell below a certain price.
This is the important question in this case. I suppose that in the case of a

single object such as a painting or a statue the right of the artist to make such a stipulation hardly would be denied. In other words, I suppose that the reason why the contract is held bad is that it is part of a scheme embracing other similar contracts each of which applies to a number of similar things, with the object of fixing a general market price. This reason seems to me inadequate in the case before the court. In the first place, by a slight change in the form of the contract the plaintiff can accomplish the result in a way that would be beyond successful attack. If it should make the retail dealers also agents in law as well as in name and retain the title until the goods left their hands I cannot conceive that even the present enthusiasm for regulating the prices to be charged by other people would deny that the owner was acting within his rights. It seems to me that this consideration by itself ought to give us pause.

But I go farther. There is no statute covering the case; there is no body of precedent that by ineluctable logic requires the conclusion to which the court has come. The conclusion is reached by extending a certain conception of public policy to a new sphere. On such matters we are in perilous country. I think that at least it is safe to say that the most enlightened judicial policy is to let people manage their own business in their own way, unless the ground for interference is very clear. What then is the ground upon which we interfere in the present case? Of course, it is not the interest of the producer. No one, I judge, cares for that. It hardly can be the interest of subordinate vendors, as there seems to be no particular reason for preferring them to the originator and first vendor of the product. Perhaps it may be assumed to be the interest of the consumers and the public. On that point I confess that I am in a minority as to larger issues than are concerned here. I think that we greatly exaggerate the value and importance to the public of competition in the production or distribution of an article (here it is only distribution) as fixing a fair price. What really fixes that is the competition of conflicting desires. We, none of us, can have as much as we want of all the things that we want. Therefore, we have to choose. As soon as the price of something that we want goes above the point at which we are willing to give up other things to have that, we cease to buy it and buy something else. Of course, I am speaking of things that we can get along without. There may be necessaries that sooner or later must be dealt with like short rations in a shipwreck, but they are not Dr. Miles's medicines. With regard to things like the latter it seems to me that the point of most profitable returns marks the equilibrium of social desires and determines the fair price in the only sense in which I can find meaning in those words. The Dr. Miles Medical Company knows better than we do what will enable it to do the best business. We must assume its retail price to be reasonable, for it is so alleged and the case is here on demurrer; so I see nothing to warrant my assuming that the public will not be served best by the company being allowed to carry out its plan. I cannot believe that in the long run the public will profit by this court permitting knaves to cut reasonable prices for some ulterior purpose of their own and thus to impair, if not to destroy, the production and the sale of articles which it is assumed to be desirable that the public should be able to get.

The conduct of the defendant falls within a general prohibition of the law. It is fraudulent and has no merits of its own to recommend it to the favor of the court. An injunction against a defendant's dealing in nontransferable round-trip reduced-rate tickets has been granted to a railroad company upon the general principles of the law protecting contracts, and the demoralization of rates has been referred to as a special circumstance in addition to the general grounds. The general and special considerations equally apply here, and we ought not to disregard them, unless the evil effect of the contract is very plain. The analogy relied upon to establish that evil effect is that of combinations in restraint of trade. I believe that we have some superstitions on that head, as I have said; but those combinations are entered into with intent to exclude others from a business naturally open to them, and we unhappily have become familiar with the methods by which they are carried out. I venture to say that there is no likeness between them and this case. I think also that the importance of the question and the popularity of what I deem mistaken notions makes it my duty to express my view in this dissent.

To Harold Laski

July 23, 1925

Dear Laski,

. . . As you will have expected I don't sympathize very greatly with your dream. You think more nobly of man than I do—and of course, you may be right. But I look at men through Malthus's glasses—as like flies—here swept away by a pestilence—there multiplying unduly and paying for it. I think your morals (I am struck by the delicacy of your feeling) are not the last word but only a check for varying intensity upon force, which seems to me likely to remain the ultimate as far as I can look ahead. I was hearing only a day or two ago a traveler's report that every French boy was brought up to think of licking Germany and every German to look forward to revenge upon France. I think I perceive at critical moments a tacit assumption that papa Laski, or those who think like him, are to regulate paternally the popular desires. If a man makes a great fortune by selling some patent medicine to the crowd, that shows that in those circumstances the crowd wants it—and I can see no justification in a government's undertaking to rectify social desires—except upon an aristocratic assumption that you know what is good for them better than they (which no doubt you do) . . . As to the *right* of citizens to support and education I don't see it. It may be a desirable ideal to aim at, but I see no right in my neighbor to share my bread. I mean moral right of course—there is no pretense of any other, except so far as he in combination has power to take it. I always have said that the rights of a given crowd are what they will fight for . . .

To Lewis Einstein

October 28, 1912

Dear Einstein,

. . . You are wrong in thinking that I am even an unbelieving Rooseveltian. I agree with Mr. Dooley that the country in the main will pursue its destinies no matter who is president; but even presidents can do harm. And I think the most harmful thing that can be done is done by such of the Rooseveltian manifestos as I have seen. For they touch and irritate the sensitive points of the social consciousness and suggest in a vague and shocking way that something would happen if only they got in; whereas I should like to see the truth told, that legislation can't cure things, that the crowd now has substantially all there is, that the sooner they make up their mind to it the better, and that the fights against capital are simply fights between the different bands of producers only properly to be settled by the equilibrium of social desires. But I won't repeat all the commonplaces I have bored you with before now. If I had a vote I should vote for Taft in spite of the fact that he like the rest of them seems to believe in the present legislative tendencies, anti-trust etc. etc. that I believe to be noxious humbug. Perhaps I told you of a conversation with him in which I said that of course I carried out in good faith these damned laws (perhaps I didn't say damned), and that if they could make a case for putting Rockefeller in prison I should do my part; but if they left it to me I should put up a bronze statue of him. All this *entre nous* of course.

We are in full blast now and I am stealing time from duty to write even this short letter. My blood is up and I am out for slaughter. Things seem more satisfactory than they did at the end of last term. My own opinions have cleared up at least a number of important matters. Hesitation and doubt are the most uncomfortable feelings of the mind and though *au fond* I believe almost nothing I generally can settle my conclusions as to a practical course, I mean in my own job. If my wife should consult me as to the household I should be an imbecile. My function there is that of God, a terrific idol to be appealed to on condition that it remains dumb.

To Harold Laski,

Beverly Farms, August 1, 1925

Dear Laski,

. . . I am worried by this letter—because I have read your book and it does not command my sympathy and I hate to have any words but praise for you. Of course I recognize that it may mean that I am finished—an old fogey no longer able to keep the pace—all the more that I appreciate the ability and great knowledge with which you write. I never read so penetrating a socialist book—but I told you the other day that I don't believe your premises and I must add that the elaborate construction of an imaginary society seems to me premature and like the constitution makers of the 18th century. Yet here again I recognize that what you say may have a more practical significance for England than it has for me. But just as I said the other day that I take no stock in abstract rights, I equally fail to respect the passion for equality. I think it an ignoble aspiration which only culminates in the statement of one of your Frenchmen that inequality of talents was an injustice. I do not presume to think that even if I am right your book may not be a benefit to the world—but, in its immediate effect to encourage what I think mistaken views and desires, I feel sorry. If, as you say, the alternative is the ruin of civilization I think that more likely to come—but I do not accept any prophecy with confidence. The unforeseen is generally what happens. There—I have done my duty—and I hope I have not hurt my friend . . .

May 24, 1919

Dear Laski,

. . . For a quarter of a century I have said that the real foundations of discontent were emotional not economic, and that if the socialists would face the facts and put the case on that ground I should listen to them with respect. I used to tell my wife or she used to tell me, it was a joint opinion, that the manner of the Beacon Street women toward their servants and employees did more than the women were worth to upset the existing order. My opinion, however, is based on the effort to think quantitatively not dramatically. I won't go over the old ground, but to my mind the notion that any rearrangement of property, while any part of the world propagates freely, will prevent civilization from killing its weaker members, is absurd. I think that the crowd now has substantially all there is—and that every mitigation of the lot of any body of men has to be paid for by some other or the same body of men—and I don't think that cutting off the luxuries of the few would make an appreciable difference in the situation . . .

February 28, 1919

Γε Λασχε:*

. . . I reread Mill on *Liberty*—fine old sportsman—Mill, and just now from a different way of thinking, but with somewhat similar atmosphere, T. H. Green's *Essay on Liberal Legislation* and *Liberty of Contract* and some other things of his. What strikes me in that one as in so many of the discourses of you who believe is that while he talks about what I would not waste breath upon—the possible moral disadvantages of compelling a man to be better than he is ready to be—he never bothers about the bill, the real, hard, concrete bill. If you require guards to machinery you say the detriment of increased cost to the public is less than that caused by the loss of certain fingers etc. If you say minimum wage you say those who can't get it must starve or be supported, and in the latter case those who get the wages must do the supporting. The only attempt to estimate the proportions of advantage and disadvantage that I remember reading is in Woodbury's *Social Insurance* that I read last summer. His general conclusion being, I don't know but I think it worth trying. Civilization is the reduction of the infinite to the finite. The realizing that there is so much forest, coal, etc. so much even atmosphere—and no more. I wonder if it might not be possible that those who are withdrawing nitrogen from the latter might in time be found to be doing a deadly thing . . .

May 21, 1927

My dear Laski,

Another day has come—I have finished your book and I don't feel quite so seedy as I did yesterday—wherefore this p.s. Of course I appreciate what you and Keynes say, that the Russian Communism is a

*Γε (γε) is a Greek particle with the approximate force of "at least." Λασχε is a transliteration of "Laski" into Greek; a more exact transliteration would be Λασκι.—Ed.

religion and therefore cannot be expected to be just. But I don't see why sympathetic understanding should be confined to one side. Capitalism may not be a religion but it commands a fighting belief on its side and I don't at all agree to describing its tyrannies with resentment, as coming from bad men when you gloss those on the other side. I think that most of the so-called tyrannies of capital express the economic necessities created by the pressure of population—a pressure for which capitalism is not responsible and for which communism has offered no remedy. If I praised or blamed (which I don't) either one, I should blame the communists as consciously and voluntarily contemplating their despotism whereas on the other side it is largely unconscious and the automatic result of the situation. I may add that class for class I think the one that communism would abolish is more valuable—contributes more, a great deal more, than those whom communism exalts. For as I said the other day, the only contribution that any man makes that can't be got more cheaply from the water and the sky is ideas—the immediate or remote direction of energy which man does not produce, whether it comes from his muscles or a machine. Ideas come from the despised *bourgeoisie* not from labor. With which I shut up and go for a capitalistic drive from which I hope some little joy.

We look at our fellow men with sympathy but nature looks at them as she looks at flies—and some of her dealings are hard but should not be attributed to those who from the accident of position happen to be her instruments.

Beverly Farms, July 8, 1928

My dear Laski,

. . . I have partly read an account of *Russia after Ten Years*—report of the American Trade Union Delegates to the Soviet Union—optimistic, but intended to be fair. Perhaps it comes down to the question, as so many things do—of what kind of world you want. Personally I do not prefer a world with a hundred million bores in it to one with ten. The fewer the people who do not contribute beauty or thought, the better to my fancy. I perfectly realize that the other fellers feel otherwise and very likely would prefer to get rid of me and all my kind. Perhaps they will, and if they do I have nothing to say except that our tastes differ. That is the justification of war—if people vehemently want to make different kinds of worlds I don't see what there is to do except for the most powerful to kill the others—as I suppose they did in Russia. I believe Kropotkin points out the mistake of the French Revolution in not doing so . . .

Law and the Court

Speech at a Dinner of the Harvard Law School Association
of New York, February 15, 1913

S 98

Mr. Chairman and Gentlemen:

Vanity is the most philosophical of those feelings that we are taught to despise. For vanity recognizes that if a man is in a minority of one we lock him up, and therefore longs for an assurance from others that one's work has not been in vain. If a man's ambition is the thirst for a power that comes not from office but from within, he never can be sure that any happiness is not a fool's paradise—he never can be sure that he sits on that other bench reserved for the masters of those who know. Then too, at least until one draws near to seventy, one is less likely to hear the trumpets than the rolling fire of the front. I have passed that age, but I still am on the firing line, and it is only in rare moments like this that there comes a pause and for half an hour one feels a trembling hope. They are the rewards of a lifetime's work.

But let me turn to more palpable realities—to that other visible Court to which for ten now accomplished years it has been my opportunity to belong. We are very quiet there, but it is the quiet of a storm centre, as we all know. Science has taught the world scepticism and has made it legitimate to put everything to the test of proof. Many beautiful and noble reverences are impaired, but in these days no one can complain if any institution, system, or belief is called on to justify its continuance in life. Of course we are not excepted and have not escaped. Doubts are expressed that go to our very being. Not only are we told that when Marshall pronounced an Act of Congress unconstitutional he usurped a power that the Constitution did not give, but we are told that we are the representatives of a class—a tool of the money power. I get letters, not always anonymous, intimating that we are corrupt. Well, gentlemen, I admit that it makes my heart ache. It is very painful, when one spends all the energies of one's soul in trying to do good work, with no thought but that of solving a problem according to the rules by which one is bound, to know that many see sinister motives and would be glad of evidence that one was consciously bad. But we must take such things philosophically and try to see what we can learn from hatred and distrust and whether behind them there may not be some germ of in-articulate truth.

The attacks upon the Court are merely an expression of the unrest that seems to wonder vaguely whether law and order pay. When the ignorant are taught to doubt they do not know what they safely may believe. And it seems to me that at this time we need education in the obvious more than investigation of the obscure. I do not see so much immediate use in committees on the high cost of living and inquiries how far it is due to the increased production of gold, how far to the narrowing of cattle ranges and the growth of population, how far to the bugaboo, as I do in bringing home to people a few social and economic truths. Most men think dramatically, not quantitatively, a fact that the rich would be wise to remember more than they do. We are apt to con-trast the palace with the hovel, the dinner at Sherry's with the working man's pail, and never ask how much or realize how little is withdrawn to make the prizes of success (subordinate prizes—since the only prize much cared for by the powerful is power. The prize of the general is not a bigger tent, but command). We are apt to think of ownership as a ter-minus, not as a gateway, and not to realize that except the tax levied for personal consumption large ownership means investment, and invest-ment means the direction of labor towards the production of the great-est returns—returns that so far as they are great show by that very fact that they are consumed by the many, not alone by the few. If I may ride a hobby for an instant, I should say we need to think things instead of words—to drop ownership, money, etc., and to think of the stream of products; of wheat and cloth and railway travel. When we do it is obvi-ous that the many consume them; that they now as truly have substan-tially all there is, as if the title were in the United States; that the great body of property is socially administered now, and that the function of private ownership is to divine in advance the equilibrium of social desires—which socialism equally would have to divine, but which, un-der the illusion of self-seeking, is more poignantly and shrewdly fore-seen.

I should like to see it brought home to the public that the question of fair prices is due to the fact that none of us can have as much as we want of all the things we want; that as less will be produced than the public wants, the question is how much of each product it will have and how much go without; that thus the final competition is between the objects of desire, and therefore between the producers of those objects; that when we oppose labor and capital, labor means the group that is selling its product and capital all the other groups that are buying it. The hated capitalist is simply the mediator, the prophet, the adjuster according to his divination of the future desire. If you could get that believed, the body of the people would have no doubt as to the worth of law.

That is my outside thought on the present discontents. As to the truth embodied in them, in part it cannot be helped. It cannot be helped, it is as it should be, that the law is behind the times. I told a labor leader once that what they asked was favor, and if a decision was against them they called it wicked. The same might be said of their opponents. It means that the law is growing. As law embodies beliefs that have triumphed in the battle of ideas and then have translated themselves into action, while there still is doubt, while opposite convictions still keep a battle front against each other, the time for law has not come; the notion destined to prevail is not yet entitled to the field. It is a misfortune if a judge reads his conscious or unconscious sympathy with one side or the other prematurely into the law, and forgets that what seem to him to be first principles are believed by half his fellow men to be wrong. I think that we have suffered from this misfortune, in state courts at least, and that this is another and very important truth to be extracted from the popular discontent. When twenty years ago a vague terror went over the earth and the word socialism began to be heard, I thought and still think that fear was translated into doctrines that had no proper place in the Constitution or the common law. Judges are apt to be naif, simple-minded men, and they need something of Mephistopheles. We too need education in the obvious—to learn to transcend our own convictions and to leave room for much that we hold dear to be done away with short of revolution by the orderly change of law.

I have no belief in panaceas and almost none in sudden ruin. I believe with Montesquieu that if the chance of a battle—I may add, the passage of a law—has ruined a state, there was a general cause at work that made the state ready to perish by a single battle or law. Hence I am not much interested one way or the other in the nostrums now so strenuously urged. I do not think the United States would come to an end if we lost our power to declare an Act of Congress void. I do think the Union would be imperiled if we could not make that declaration as to the laws of the several states. For one in my place sees how often a local policy prevails with those who are not trained to national views and how often action is taken that embodies what the Commerce Clause was meant to end. But I am not aware that there is any serious desire to limit the Court's power in this regard. For most of the things that properly can be called evils in the present state of the law I think the main remedy, as for the evils of public opinion, is for us to grow more civilized.

If I am right it will be a slow business for our people to reach rational views, assuming that we are allowed to work peaceably to that end. But as I grow older I grow calm. If I feel what are perhaps an old man's apprehensions, that competition from new races will cut deeper than working men's disputes and will test whether we can hang together and can fight; if I fear that we are running through the world's resources at a pace that we cannot keep; I do not lose my hopes. I do not pin my dreams for the future to my country or even to my race. I think it probable that civilization somehow will last as long as I care to look ahead—perhaps with smaller numbers, but perhaps also bred to greatness and splendor by science. I think it not improbable that man, like the grub that prepares a chamber for the winged thing it never has seen but is to be—that man may have cosmic destinies that he does not understand. And so beyond the vision of battling races and an impoverished earth I catch a dreaming glimpse of peace.

The other day my dream was pictured to my mind. It was evening. I was walking homeward on Pennsylvania Avenue near the Treasury, and as I looked beyond Sherman's Statue to the west the sky was aflame with scarlet and crimson from the setting sun. But, like the note of downfall in Wagner's opera, below the sky line there came from little globes the pallid discord of the electric lights. And I thought to myself the Götterdämmerung will end, and from those globes clustered like evil eggs will come the new masters of the sky. It is like the time in which we live. But then I remembered the faith that I partly have expressed, faith in a universe not measured by our fears, a universe that has thought and more than thought inside of it, and as I gazed, after the sunset and above the electric lights there shone the stars.

7 • THE ACTIVITY OF LAW

Despondency and Hope
Remarks at a Dinner of the Chicago Bar Association, October 21, 1902
OS 146

Mr. Chairman and Gentlemen:

Only twice before in my life have I had a glimpse of your wonderful city. Once in 1867, with Mr. Cabot Lodge, not then a senator of the United States, on our way to try to shoot prairie chickens. We had met a perfidious friend who hoped we had thick boots, on account of the rattlesnakes. So we rose early, before even Chicago was awake, in the hope of buying some, and jumped a yard on the prairie every time a cricket stirred in the grass. But we were temperate and saw no snakes. The other time was in the course of a journey across the continent, when our beloved friend Huntington Jackson showed me the courts and introduced me to Mr. Fuller, then just nominated by the President for Chief Justice of the United States. Now, after hope deferred and under altered circumstances, I am here again. Under altered circumstances—for if the senate should be of the same mind as the President, this meeting marks for me the turn to the home stretch of the race. Some sad thoughts will come up at the moment. One feels as if the second stage of life—one's twenty years of work as a state judge—were up for judgment in its turn, and that there must be few who will take the trouble or find it worth the trouble to consider it with discrimination or to discover one's aims. Then, of course, most of us find it easy to despond. When a man is satisfied with himself it means that he has ceased to struggle and therefore has ceased to achieve. He is dead, and may be allowed the thin delight of reading his own obituary. But this occasion drowns out all the rats that gnaw at one within. In this place, in the midst of so much force and life and success, one would indeed be morbid if he did not hope, and were not ready to tell the younger men who hear him that the race is worth the running. A man is pretty sure to get his due share of appreciation, for, whether he speaks or is silent, the world generally finds him out. But while it is a delight to get praise that one deserves, the fiercest joy is in the doing. Those who run hardest probably have the least satisfaction with themselves, but they find, I am sure, that they know most of the joy of life when at top speed.

Some of you probably have read the story of Calumet K. There is a little love in it as an obligatory concession to what is expected in a novel, but the whole romance of the tale is in the getting an elevator built in time to break a corner in wheat. That is the universal romance of man—to face obstacles and to measure his force by the number that he overcomes. Force *in vacuo* is Hegel's pure being—it is pure nothing. I was struck by the distinction of a remark in a letter to me the other day, that the true path is the line of most resistance. Following a similar train of thought, I sometimes have amused myself with the imagination of a society for the preservation of abuses, with closed seasons and fixed times within which alone one was authorized to make the crooked straight. For nature always is self-defeating, and if you imagine a time when our ideal was achieved, and there was nothing left to be set right, what would become of man? The faculties which are his life, finding no place for their exercise, would dwindle and decay, and the joy of life, as we know it, would be at an end.

A judge in our day need not fear such an atrophy of his powers. He has his share of obstacles to overcome, and none the less if his decision is beyond appeal. If he aims at the highest, he must take risks. He must be superior to class prejudices and to his own prejudices. He must not stop at consecrated phrases, which in their day were a revelation, but which in time from their very felicity tend to stop the endless necessary process of further analysis and advance. He must throw down his naked thought, unswaddled in pompous commonplaces, to take its chance for life. He must try to realize the paradox that it is not necessary to be heavy in order to have weight.

Gentlemen, I might go on, but you all know these things better than I can say them to you. Who dares flatter himself that he fills the requirements which I imagine for a great judge? All that I venture to say for myself is that I have done my best with delight for twenty years, that I think my standards are cosmopolitan, and that by those standards some of the aids to immediate success must be condemned. As I said at the beginning, it is very easy to despond. But the unexpected honor which you have done me, the more than cordiality and good will, the generous and delicate hospitality with which I have been received, made me dream for a moment that it is even easier to succeed, and that perhaps after all I have not failed. At all events, and to the end, succeed or fail, the fight is joy, and I shall long hear in it the trumpet of your cheer.

Twenty Years in Retrospect

Speech at a Banquet of the Middlesex Bar Association,
December 3, 1902

OS 154

. . . At this moment, too, the work of twenty years comes up for judgment, and that also is not without its sadness. You are the judges, and even you are more likely to take your views from the accident of your professional needs than from a consideration of any general aspect of a man's work.

I have tried to see the law as an organic whole. I also have tried to see it as a reaction between tradition on the one side and the changing desires and needs of a community on the other. I have studied tradition in order that I might understand how it came to be what it is, and to estimate its worth with regard to our present needs; and my references to the Year Books often have had a skeptical end. I have considered the present tendencies and desires of society and have tried to realize that its different portions want different things, and that my business was to express not my personal wish, but the resultant, as nearly as I could guess, of the pressure of the past and the conflicting wills of the present. I have considered the social and economic postulates on which we frame the conception of our needs, and I have to see them in a dry light. It has seemed to me that certainty is an illusion, that we have few scientific data on which to affirm that one rule rather than another has the sanction of the universe, that we rarely could be sure that one tends more distinctly than its opposite to the survival and welfare of the society where it is practiced, and that the wisest are but blind guides.

But we have a great body of law which has at least this sanction that it exists. If one does not affirm that it is intrinsically better than a different body of principles which one could imagine, one can see an advantage which, if not the greatest, at least, is very great—that we know what it is. For this reason I am slow to assent to overruling a decision. Precisely my skepticism, my doubt as to the absolute worth of a large part of the system we administer, or of any other system, makes me very unwilling to increase the doubt as to what the court will do. I have noticed the opposite tendency in minds that regarded our corpus juris as an image, however faint, of the eternal law. Well, gentlemen, I will avoid the longwindedness which I have deplored in others, and will leave my case in your hands, not trying to state it, but knowing that when one's work is done, generally there is someone, sooner or later, who sees the aim and judges the success . . .

Giles v. Harris

189 U.S. 475 (1903)

This is a bill in equity brought by a colored man, on behalf of himself "and on behalf of more than five thousand negroes, citizens of the county of Montgomery, Alabama, similarly situated and circumstanced as himself," against the board of registrars of that county. The prayer of the bill is in substance that the defendants may be required to enroll upon the voting lists the name of the plaintiff and of all other qualified members of his race who applied for registration before August 1, 1902, and were refused, and that certain sections of the constitution of Alabama may be declared contrary to the Fourteenth and Fifteenth Amendments of the Constitution of the United States, and void.

The allegations of the bill may be summed up as follows: The plaintiff is subject to none of the disqualifications set forth in the constitution of Alabama and is entitled to vote—entitled, as the bill plainly means, under the constitution as it is. He applied in March, 1902, for registration as a voter, and was refused arbitrarily on the ground of his color, together with large numbers of other duly qualified negroes, while all white men were registered. The same thing was done all over the state. Under §187 of article 8 of the Alabama constitution, persons registered before January 1, 1903, remain electors for life unless they become disqualified by certain crimes, etc., while after that date severer tests come into play which would exclude, perhaps, a large part of the black race. Therefore by the refusal the plaintiff and the other negroes excluded were deprived, not only of their vote at an election which has taken place since the bill was filed, but of the permanent advantage incident to registration before 1903. The white men generally are registered for good under the easy test, and the black men are likely to be kept out in the future as in the past. This refusal to register the blacks was part of the general scheme to disfranchise them, to which the defendants and the state itself, according to the bill, were parties. The defendants accepted their office for the purpose of carrying out the scheme. The part taken by the state, that is, by the white population which framed the constitution, consisted in shaping that instrument so as to give opportunity and effect to the wholesale fraud which has been practised . . .

Perhaps it should be added that the bill was filed in September, 1902, and alleged the plaintiff's desire to vote at an election coming off in November. This election has gone by, so that it is impossible to give specific relief with regard to that. But we are not prepared to dismiss the bill or the appeal on that ground, because to be enabled to cast a vote in

that election is not the whole object of the bill. It is not even the principal object of the relief sought by the plaintiff. The principal object of
that is to obtain the permanent advantages of registration as of a date
before 1903 . . .

It seems to us impossible to grant the equitable relief which is asked.
It will be observed in the first place that the language of §1979 does not
extend the sphere of equitable jurisdiction in respect of what shall be
held an appropriate subject-matter for that kind of relief. The words
are, "shall be liable to the party injured in an action at law, suit in equity,
or other proper proceeding for redress." They allow a suit in equity
only when that is the proper proceeding for redress, and they refer to
existing standards to determine what is a proper proceeding. The traditional limits of proceedings in equity have not embraced a remedy for
political wrongs. But we cannot forget that we are dealing with a new
and extraordinary situation, and we are unwilling to stop short of the
final considerations which seem to us to dispose of the case.

The difficulties which we cannot overcome are two, and the first is
this: The plaintiff alleges that the whole registration scheme of the
Alabama constitution is a fraud upon the Constitution of the United
States, and asks us to declare it void. But, of course, he could not maintain a bill for a mere declaration in the air. He does not try to do so, but
asks to be registered as a party qualified under the void instrument. If,
then, we accept the conclusion which it is the chief purpose of the bill to
maintain, how can we make the court a party to the unlawful scheme by
accepting it and adding another voter to its fraudulent lists? If a white
man came here on the same general allegations, admitting his sympathy with the plan, but alleging some special prejudice that had kept him
off the list, we hardly should think it necessary to meet him with a
reasoned answer. But the relief cannot be varied because we think that
in the future the particular plaintiff is likely to try to overthrow the
scheme. If we accept the plaintiff's allegations for the purposes of his
case, he cannot complain. We must accept or reject them. It is impossible
simply to shut our eyes, put the plaintiff on the lists, be they honest or
fraudulent, and leave the determination of the fundamental question
for the future. If we have an opinion that the bill is right on its face, or if
we are undecided; we are not at liberty to assume it to be wrong for the
purposes of decision. It seems to us that unless we are prepared to say
that it is wrong, that all its principal allegations are immaterial, and that
the registration plan of the Alabama constitution is valid, we cannot order the plaintiff's name to be registered. It is not an answer to say that if
all the blacks who are qualified according to the letter of the instrument
were registered, the fraud would be cured. In the first place, there is no

probability that any way now is open by which more than a few could be registered; but, if all could be, the difficulty would not be overcome. If the sections of the constitution concerning registration were illegal in their inception, it would be a new doctrine in constitutional law that the original invalidity could be cured by an administration which defeated their intent. We express no opinion as to the alleged fact of their unconstitutionality beyond saying that we are not willing to assume that they are valid, in the face of the allegations and main object of the bill, for the purpose of granting the relief which it was necessary to pray in order that the object should be secured.

The other difficulty is of a different sort, and strikingly reinforces the argument that equity cannot undertake now, any more than it has in the past, to enforce political rights, and also the suggestion that state constitutions were not left unmentioned in §1979 by accident. In determining whether a court of equity can take jurisdiction, one of the first questions is what it can do to enforce any order that it may make. This is alleged to be the conspiracy of a state, although the state is not and could not be made a party to the bill. The circuit court has no constitution power to control its action by any direct means. And if we leave the state out of consideration, the court has as little practical power to deal with the people of the state in a body. The bill imports that the great mass of the white population intends to keep the blacks from voting. To meet such an intent something more than ordering the plaintiff's name to be inscribed upon the lists of 1902 will be needed. If the conspiracy and the intent exist, a name on a piece of paper will not defeat them. Unless we are prepared to supervise the voting in that state by officers of the court, it seems to us that all that the plaintiff could get from equity would be an empty form. Apart from damages to the individual, relief from a great political wrong, if done, as alleged by the people of a state and the state itself, must be given by them or by the legislative and political department of the government of the United States.

American Banana Co. v. United Fruit Co.
213 U.S. 347 (1909)

This is an action brought to recover threefold damages under the act to protect trade against monopolies. The circuit court dismissed the complaint upon motion, as not setting forth a cause of action. This judgment was affirmed by the circuit court of appeals, and the case then was brought to this court by writ of error.

The allegations of the complaint may be summed up as follows: The plaintiff is an Alabama corporation, organized in 1904. The defendant is a New Jersey corporation, organized in 1899. Long before the plaintiff was formed, the defendant, with intent to prevent competition and to control and monopolize the banana trade, bought the property and business of several of its previous competitors, with provision against their resuming the trade, made contracts with others, including a majority of the most important, regulating the quantity to be purchased and the price to be paid, and acquired a controlling amount of stock in still others. For the same purpose it organized a selling company, of which it held the stock, that by agreement sold at fixed prices all the bananas of the combining parties. By this and other means it did monopolize and restrain the trade and maintained unreasonable prices. The defendant being in this ominous attitude, one McConnell, in 1903, started a banana plantation in Panama, then part of the United States of Columbia, and began to build a railway (which would afford his only means of export), both in accordance with the laws of the United States of Columbia. He was notified by the defendant that he must either combine or stop. Two months later, it is believed at the defendant's instigation, the governor of Panama recommended to his national government that Costa Rica be allowed to administer the territory through which the railroad was to run, and this although that territory had been awarded to Colombia under an arbitration agreed to by treaty. The defendant, and afterwards, in September, the government of Costa Rica, it is believed by the inducement of the defendant, interfered with McConnell. In November, 1903, Panama revolted and became an independent republic, declaring its boundary to be that settled by the award. In June, 1904, the plaintiff bought out McConnell and went on with the work, as it had a right to do under the laws of Panama. But in July, Costa Rican soldiers and officials, instigated by the defendant, seized a part of the plantation and a cargo of supplies and have held them ever since, and stopped the construction and operation of the plantation and railway. In August one Astua, by *ex parte* proceedings, got a judgment from a Costa Rican court, declaring the plantation to be his, although, it is alleged, the proceedings were not within the jurisdiction of Costa Rica, and were contrary to its laws and void. Agents of the defendant then bought the lands from Astua. The plaintiff has tried to induce the government of Costa Rica to withdraw its soldiers, and also has tried to persuade the United States to interfere, but has been thwarted in both by the defendant and has failed. The government of Costa Rica remained in possession down to the bringing of the suit.

As a result of the defendant's acts the plaintiff has been deprived of the use of the plantation, and the railway, the plantation, and supplies have been injured. The defendant also, by outbidding, has driven purchasers out of the market and has compelled producers to come to its terms, and it has prevented the plaintiff from buying for export and sale. This is the substantial damage alleged. There is thrown in a further allegation that the defendant has "sought to injure" the plaintiff's business by offering positions to its employees, and by discharging and threatening to discharge persons in its own employ who were stockholders of the plaintiff. But no particular point is made of this. It is contended, however, that, even if the main argument fails and the defendant is held not to be answerable for acts depending on the cooperation of the government of Costa Rica for their effect, a wrongful conspiracy resulting in driving the plaintiff out of business is to be gathered from the complaint, and that it was entitled to go to trial upon that.

It is obvious that, however stated, the plaintiff's case depends on several rather startling propositions. In the first place, the acts causing the damage were done, so far as appears, outside the jurisdiction of the United States, and within that of other states. It is surprising to hear it argued that they were governed by the act of Congress.

No doubt in regions subject to no sovereign, like the high seas, or to no law that civilized countries would recognize as adequate, such countries may treat some relations between their citizens as governed by their own law, and keep, to some extent, the old notion of personal sovereignty alive. They go further, at times, and declare that they will punish anyone, subject or not, who shall do certain things, if they can catch him, as in the case of pirates on the high seas. In cases immediately affecting national interests they may go further still and may make, and, if they get the chance, execute, similar threats as to acts done within another recognized jurisdiction. An illustration from our statutes is found with regard to criminal correspondence with foreign governments. And the notion that English statutes bind British subjects everywhere has found expression in modern times and has had some startling applications. But the general and almost universal rule is that the character of an act as lawful or unlawful must be determined wholly by the law of the country where the act is done . . . For another jurisdiction, if it should happen to lay hold of the actor, to treat him according to its own notions rather than those of the place where he did the acts, not only would be unjust, but would be an interference with the authority of another sovereign, contrary to the comity of nations, which the other state concerned justly might resent.

Law is a statement of circumstances in which the public force will be brought to bear upon men through the courts. But the word commonly is confined to such prophecies or threats when addressed to persons living within the power of the courts. A threat that depends upon the choice of the party affected to bring himself within that power hardly would be called law in the ordinary sense. We do not speak of blockade running by neutrals as unlawful. And the usages of speech correspond to the limit of the attempts of the lawmaker, except in extraordinary cases. It is true that domestic corporations remain always within the power of the domestic law; but, in the present case, at least, there is no ground for distinguishing between corporations and men.

The foregoing considerations would lead, in case of doubt, to a construction of any statute as intended to be confined in its operation and effect to the territorial limits over which the lawmaker has general and legitimate power. "All legislation is prima facie territorial." Words having universal scope, such as "every contract in restraint of trade," "every person who shall monopolize," etc., will be taken, as a matter of course, to mean only everyone subject to such legislation, not all that the legislator subsequently may be able to catch. In the case of the present statute, the improbability of the United States attempting to make acts done in Panama or Costa Rica criminal is obvious, yet the law begins by making criminal the acts for which it gives a right to sue. We think it entirely plain that what the defendant did in Panama or Costa Rica is not within the scope of the statute so far as the present suit is concerned. Other objections of a serious nature are urged, but need not be discussed.

For again, not only were the acts of the defendant in Panama or Costa Rica not within the Sherman act, but they were not torts by the law of the place, and therefore were not torts at all, however contrary to the ethical and economic postulates of that statute. The substance of the complaint is that, the plantation being within the *de facto* jurisdiction of Costa Rica, that state took and keeps possession of it by virtue of its sovereign power. But a seizure by a state is not a thing that can be complained of elsewhere in the courts. The fact, if it be one, that *de jure* the estate is in Panama, does not matter in the least; sovereignty is pure fact. The fact has been recognized by the United States, and, by the implication of the bill, is assented to by Panama.

The fundamental reason why persuading a sovereign power to do this or that cannot be a tort is not that the sovereign cannot be joined as a defendant or because it must be assumed to be acting lawfully. The intervention of parties who had a right knowingly to produce the harmful result between the defendant and the harm has been thought to be a nonconductor and to bar responsibility, but it is not clear that this is always true; for instance, in the case of the privileged repetition of a slander, or the malicious and unjustified persuasion to discharge from employment. The fundamental reason is that it is a contradiction in terms to say that, within its jurisdiction, it is unlawful to persuade a sovereign power to bring about a result that it declares by its conduct to be desirable and proper. It does not, and foreign courts cannot, admit that the influences were improper or the results bad. It makes the persuasion lawful by its own act. The very meaning of sovereignty is that the decree of the sovereign makes law. In the case of private persons, it consistently may assert the freedom of the immediate parties to an injury and yet declare that certain persuasions addressed to them are wrong.

The plaintiff relied a good deal on *Rafael v. Verelst.* But in that case, although the nabob who imprisoned the plaintiff was called a sovereign for certain purposes, he was found to be the mere tool of the defendant, an English governor. That hardly could be listened to concerning a really independent state. But of course it is not alleged that Costa Rica stands in that relation to the United Fruit company.

The acts of the soldiers and officials of Costa Rica are not alleged to have been without the consent of the government, and must be taken to have been done by its order. It ratified them, at all events, and adopted and keeps the possession taken by them. The injuries to the plantation and supplies seem to have been the direct effect of the acts of the Costa Rican government, which is holding them under an adverse claim of right. The claim for them must fall with the claim for being deprived of the use and profits of the place. As to the buying at a high price, etc., it is enough to say that we have no ground for supposing that it was unlawful in the countries where the purchases were made. Giving to this complaint every reasonable latitude of interpretation we are of opinion that it alleges no case under the act of Congress, and discloses nothing that we can suppose to have been a tort where it was done. A conspiracy in this country to do acts in another jurisdiction does not draw to itself those acts and make them unlawful, if they are permitted by the local law.

Further reasons might be given why this complaint should not be upheld, but we have said enough to dispose of it and to indicate our general point of view.

Olmstead v. United States
277 U.S. 438 (1928)

(Dissent)

My brother Brandeis has given this case* so exhaustive an examination that I desire to add but a few words. While I do not deny it, I am not

---

*The majority held that evidence obtained by illegal wiretapping was nevertheless admissible in evidence against the defendant in a federal criminal proceeding.—Ed.

prepared to say that the penumbra of the Fourth and Fifth Amendments covers the defendant, although I fully agree that courts are apt to err by sticking too closely to the words of a law where those words import a policy that goes beyond them. But I think, as Mr. Justice Brandeis says, that apart from the Constitution the government ought not to use evidence obtained and only obtainable by a criminal act. There is no body of precedents by which we are bound, and which confines us to logical deduction from established rules. Therefore we must consider the two objects of desire, both of which we cannot have, and make up our minds which to choose. It is desirable that criminals should be detected, and to that end that all available evidence should be used. It also is desirable that the government should not itself foster and pay for other crimes, when they are the means by which the evidence is to be obtained. If it pays its officers for having got evidence by crime I do not see why it may not as well pay them for getting it in the same way, and I can attach no importance to protestations of disapproval if it knowingly accepts and pays and announces that in future it will pay for the fruits. We have to choose, and for my part I think it a less evil that some criminals should escape than that the government should play an ignoble part.

For those who agree with me, no distinction can be taken between the government as prosecutor and the government as judge. If the existing code does not permit district attorneys to have a hand in such dirty business it does not permit the judge to allow such iniquities to succeed. And if all that I have said so far be accepted it makes no difference that in this case wire tapping is made a crime by the law of the state, not by the law of the United States. It is true that a state cannot make rules of evidence for courts of the United States, but the state has authority over the conduct in question, and I hardly think that the United States would appear to greater advantage when paying for an odious crime against state law than when inciting to the disregard of its own. I am aware of the often repeated statement that in a criminal proceeding the court will not take notice of the manner in which papers offered in evidence have been obtained. But that somewhat rudimentary mode of disposing of the question has been overthrown by *Weeks v. United States* and the cases that have followed it. I have said that we are free to choose between two principles of policy. But if we are to confine ourselves to precedent and logic the reason for excluding evidence obtained by violating the Constitution seems to me logically to lead to excluding evidence obtained by a crime of the officers of the law.

The Path of the Law
10 *Harvard Law Review* 457 (1897)

When we study law we are not studying a mystery but a well known profession. We are studying what we shall want in order to appear before judges, or to advise people in such a way as to keep them out of court. The reason why it is a profession, why people will pay lawyers to argue for them or to advise them, is that in societies like ours the command of the public force is intrusted to the judges in certain cases, and the whole power of the state will be put forth, if necessary, to carry out their judgments and decrees. People want to know under what circumstances and how far they will run the risk of coming against what is so much stronger than themselves, and hence it becomes a business to find out when this danger is to be feared. The object of our study, then, is prediction, the prediction of the incidence of the public force through the instrumentality of the courts.

The means of the study are a body of reports, of treatises, and of statutes, in this country and in England, extending back for six hundred years, and now increasing annually by hundreds. In these sibylline leaves are gathered the scattered prophecies of the past upon the cases in which the axe will fall. These are what properly have been called the oracles of the law. Far the most important and pretty nearly the whole meaning of every new effort of legal thought is to make these prophecies more precise, and to generalize them into a thoroughly connected system. The process is one, from a lawyer's statement of a case, eliminating as it does all the dramatic elements with which his client's story has clothed it, and retaining only the facts of legal import, up to the final analyses and abstract universals of theoretic jurisprudence. The reason why a lawyer does not mention that his client wore a white hat when he made a contract, while Mrs. Quickly would be sure to dwell upon it along with the parcel gilt goblet and the sea-coal fire, is that he foresees that the public force will act in the same way whatever his client had upon his head. It is to make the prophecies easier to be remembered and to be understood that the teachings of the decisions of the past are put into general propositions and gathered into text-books, or that statutes are passed in a general form. The primary rights and duties with which jurisprudence busies itself again are nothing but prophecies. One of the many evil effects of the confusion between legal and moral ideas, about which I shall have something to say in a moment, is that theory is apt to get the cart before the horse, and to consider the right or the duty as something existing apart from and independent of the consequences of its breach, to which certain sanctions are added afterward. But, as I shall try to show, a legal duty so called is nothing but a prediction that if a man does or omits certain things he will be made to suffer in this or that way by judgment of the court—and so of a legal right.

The number of our predictions when generalized and reduced to a system is not unmanageably large. They present themselves as a finite body of dogma which may be mastered within a reasonable time. It is a great mistake to be frightened by the ever-increasing number of reports. The reports of a given jurisdiction in the course of a generation take up pretty much the whole body of the law, and restate it from the present point of view. We could reconstruct the corpus from them if all that went before were burned. The use of the earlier reports is mainly historical, a use about which I shall have something to say before I have finished.

I wish, if I can, to lay down some first principles for the study of this body of dogma or systematized prediction which we call the law, for men who want to use it as the instrument of their business to enable them to prophesy in their turn, and, as bearing upon the study, I wish to point out an ideal which as yet our law has not attained.

The first thing for a businesslike understanding of the matter is to understand its limits, and therefore I think it desirable at once to point out and dispel a confusion between morality and law, which sometimes rises to the height of conscious theory, and more often and indeed constantly is making trouble in detail without reaching the point of consciousness. You can see very plainly that a bad man has as much reason as a good one for wishing to avoid an encounter with the public force, and therefore you can see the practical importance of the distinction between morality and law. A man who cares nothing for an ethical rule which is believed and practised by his neighbors is likely nevertheless to care a good deal to avoid being made to pay money, and will want to keep out of jail if he can.

I take it for granted that no hearer of mine will misinterpret what I have to say as the language of cynicism. The law is the witness and external deposit of our moral life. Its history is the history of the moral development of the race. The practice of it, in spite of popular jests, tends to make good citizens and good men. When I emphasize the difference between law and morals I do so with reference to a single end, that of learning and understanding the law. For that purpose you must definitely master its specific marks, and it is for that that I ask you for the moment to imagine yourselves indifferent to other and greater things.

I do not say that there is not a wider point of view from which the distinction between law and morals becomes of secondary or no importance, as all mathematical distinctions vanish in presence of the infinite. But I do say that that distinction is of the first importance for the object which we are here to consider—a right study and mastery of the law as a business with well understood limits, a body of dogma enclosed within definite lines. I have just shown the practical reason for saying so. If you want to know the law and nothing else, you must look at it as a bad man, who cares only for the material consequences which such knowledge enables him to predict, not as a good one, who finds his reasons for conduct, whether inside the law or outside of it, in the vaguer sanctions of conscience. The theoretical importance of the distinction is no less, if you would reason on your subject aright. The law is full of phraseology drawn from morals, and by the mere force of language continually invites us to pass from one domain to the other without perceiving it, as we are sure to do unless we have the boundary constantly before our minds. The law talks about rights, and duties, and malice, and intent, and negligence, and so forth, and nothing is easier, or, I may say, more common in legal reasoning, than to take these words in their moral sense, at some stage of the argument, and so to drop into fallacy. For instance, when we speak of the rights of man in a moral sense, we mean to mark the limits of interference with individual freedom which we think are prescribed by conscience, or by our ideal, however reached. Yet it is certain that many laws have been enforced in the past, and it is likely that some are enforced now, which are condemned by the most enlightened opinion of the time or which at all events pass the limit of interference as many consciences would draw it. Manifestly, therefore, nothing but confusion of thought can result from assuming that the rights of man in a moral sense are equally rights in the sense of the Constitution and the law. No doubt simple and extreme cases can be put of imaginable laws which the statute-making power would not dare to enact, even in the absence of written constitutional prohibitions, because the community would rise in rebellion and fight; and this gives some plausibility to the proposition that the law, if not a part of morality, is limited by it. But this limit of power is not coextensive with any system of morals. For the most part it falls far within the lines of any such system, and in some cases may extend beyond them, for reasons drawn from the habits of a particular people at a particular time. I once heard the late Professor Agassiz say that a German population would rise if you added two cents to the price of a glass of beer. A statute in such a case would be empty words not because it was wrong, but because it could not be enforced. No one will deny that wrong statutes can be and are enforced, and we should not all agree as to which were the wrong ones.

The confusion with which I am dealing besets confessedly legal conceptions. Take the fundamental question, What constitutes the law? You will find some text writers telling you that it is something different from what is decided by the courts of Massachusetts or England, that it is a system of reason, that it is a deduction from principles of ethics or admitted axioms or what not, which may or may not coincide with the decisions. But if we take the view of our friend the bad man we shall find that he does not care two straws for the axioms or deductions, but that he does want to know what the Massachusetts or English courts are likely to do in fact. I am much of his mind. The prophecies of what the courts will do in fact, and nothing more pretentious, are what I mean by the law.

Take again a notion which as popularly understood is the widest conception which the law contains—the notion of legal duty, to which already I have referred. We fill the word with all the content which we draw from morals. But what does it mean to a bad man? Mainly, and in the first place, a prophecy that if he does certain things he will be subjected to disagreeable consequences by way of imprisonment or compulsory payment of money. But from his point of view, what is the difference between being fined and being taxed a certain sum for doing a certain thing? That his point of view is the test of legal principles is shown by the many discussions which have arisen in the courts on the very question whether a given statutory liability is a penalty or a tax. On the answer to this question depends the decision whether conduct is legally wrong or right, and also whether a man is under compulsion or free. Leaving the criminal law on one side, what is the difference between the liability under the mill acts or statutes authorizing a taking by eminent domain and the liability for what we call a wrongful conversion of property where restoration is out of the question? In both cases the party taking another man's property has to pay its fair value as assessed by a jury, and no more. What significance is there in calling one taking right and another wrong from the point of view of the law? It does not matter, so far as the given consequence, the compulsory payment, is concerned, whether the act to which it is attached is described in terms of praise or in terms of blame, or whether the law purports to prohibit it or to allow it. If it matters at all, still speaking from the bad man's point of view, it must be because in one case and not in the other some further disadvantages, or at least some further consequences, are attached to the act by the law. The only other disadvantages thus attached to it which I ever have been able to think of are to be found in two somewhat insignificant legal doctrines, both of which might be abolished without much disturbance. One is, that a contract to do a prohibited act is unlawful, and the other, that, if one of two or more joint wrongdoers has to pay all the damages, he cannot recover contribution from his fellows. And that I believe is all. You see how the vague circumference of the notion of duty shrinks and at the same time grows more precise when we wash it with cynical acid and expel everything except the object of our study, the operations of the law.

Nowhere is the confusion between legal and moral ideas more manifest than in the law of contract. Among other things, here again the so-called primary rights and duties are invested with a mystic significance beyond what can be assigned and explained. The duty to keep a contract at common law means a prediction that you must pay damages if you do not keep it—and nothing else. If you commit a tort, you are liable to pay a compensatory sum. If you commit a contract, you are liable to pay a compensatory sum unless the promised event comes to pass, and that is all the difference. But such a mode of looking at the matter stinks in the nostrils of those who think it advantageous to get as much ethics into the law as they can . . .

I have spoken only of the common law, because there are some cases in which a logical justification can be found for speaking of civil liabilities as imposing duties in an intelligible sense. These are the relatively few in which equity will grant an injunction, and will enforce it by putting the defendant in prison or otherwise punishing him unless he complies with the order of the court. But I hardly think it advisable to shape general theory from the exception, and I think it would be better to cease troubling ourselves about primary rights and sanctions altogether than to describe our prophecies concerning the liabilities commonly imposed by the law in those inappropriate terms.

I mentioned, as other examples of the use by the law of words drawn from morals, malice, intent, and negligence. It is enough to take malice as it is used in the law of civil liability for wrongs—what we lawyers call the law of torts—to show you that it means something different in law from what it means in morals, and also to show how the difference has been obscured by giving to principles which have little or nothing to do with each other the same name. Three hundred years ago a parson preached a sermon and told a story out of Fox's *Book of Martyrs* of a man who had assisted at the torture of one of the saints, and afterward died, suffering compensatory inward torment. It happened that Fox was wrong. The man was alive and chanced to hear the sermon, and thereupon he sued the parson. Chief Justice Wray instructed the jury that the defendant was not liable, because the story was told innocently, without malice. He took malice in the moral sense, as importing a malevolent motive. But nowadays no one doubts that a man may be liable, without any malevolent motive at all, for false statements manifestly calculated to inflict temporal damage. In stating the case in pleading, we still should call the defendant's conduct malicious; but, in my opinion at least, the word means nothing about motives, or even about the defendant's attitude toward the future, but only signifies that the tendency of his conduct under the known circumstances was very plainly to cause the plaintiff temporal harm.

In the law of contract the use of moral phraseology has led to equal confusion, as I have shown in part already, but only in part. Morals deal with the actual internal state of the individual's mind, what he actually intends. From the time of the Romans down to now, this mode of dealing has affected the language of the law as to contract, and the language used has reacted upon the thought. We talk about a contract as a meeting of the minds of the parties, and thence it is inferred in various cases that there is no contract because their minds have not met; that is, because they have intended different things or because one party has not known of the assent of the other. Yet nothing is more certain than that parties may be bound by a contract to things which neither of them intended, and when one does not know of the other's assent. Suppose a contract is executed in due form and in writing to deliver a lecture, mentioning no time. One of the parties thinks that the promise will be construed to mean at once, within a week. The other thinks that it means when he is ready. The court says that it means within a reasonable time. The parties are bound by the contract as it is interpreted by the court, yet neither of them meant what the court declares that they have said. In my opinion no one will understand the true theory of contract or be able even to discuss some fundamental questions intelligently until he has understood that all contracts are formal, that the making of a contract depends not on the agreement of two minds in one intention, but on the agreement of two sets of external signs—not on the parties' having *meant* the same thing but on their having *said* the same thing. Furthermore, as the signs may be addressed to one sense or another—to sight or to hearing—on the nature of the sign will depend the moment when the contract is made. If the sign is tangible, for instance, a letter, the contract is made when the letter of acceptance is delivered. If it is necessary that the minds of the parties meet, there will be no contract until the acceptance can be read—none, for example, if the acceptance be snatched from the hand of the offerer by a third person.

This is not the time to work out a theory in detail, or to answer many obvious doubts and questions which are suggested by these general views. I know of none which are not easy to answer, but what I am trying to do now is only by a series of hints to throw some light on the narrow path of legal doctrine, and upon two pitfalls which, as it seems to me, lie perilously near to it. Of the first of these I have said enough. I hope that my illustrations have shown the danger, both to speculation and to practice, of confounding morality with law, and the trap which legal language lays for us on that side of our way. For my own part, I often doubt whether it would not be a gain if every word of moral significance could be banished from the law altogether, and other words adopted which should convey legal ideas uncolored by anything outside the law. We should lose the fossil records of a good deal of history and the majesty got from ethical associations, but by ridding ourselves of an unnecessary confusion we should gain very much in the clearness of our thought.

So much for the limits of the law. The next thing which I wish to consider is what are the forces which determine its content and its growth. You may assume, with Hobbes and Bentham and Austin, that all law emanates from the sovereign, even when the first human beings to enunciate it are the judges, or you may think that law is the voice of the Zeitgeist, or what you like. It is all one to my present purpose. Even if every decision required the sanction of an emperor with despotic power and a whimsical turn of mind, we should be interested nonetheless, still with a view to prediction, in discovering some order, some rational explanation, and some principle of growth for the rules which he laid down. In every system there are such explanations and principles to be found. It is with regard to them that a second fallacy comes in, which I think it important to expose.

The fallacy to which I refer is the notion that the only force at work in the development of the law is logic. In the broadest sense, indeed, that notion would be true. The postulate on which we think about the universe is that there is a fixed quantitative relation between every phenomenon and its antecedents and consequents. If there is such a thing as a phenomenon without these fixed quantitative relations, it is a miracle. It is outside the law of cause and effect, and as such transcends our power of thought, or at least is something to or from which we cannot reason. The condition of our thinking about the universe is that it is capable of being thought about rationally, or, in other words, that every part of it is effect and cause in the same sense in which those parts are with which we are most familiar. So in the broadest sense it is true that the law is a logical development, like everything else. The danger of which I speak is not the admission that the principles governing other phenomena also govern the law, but the notion that a given system, ours, for instance, can be worked out like mathematics from some general axioms of conduct. This is the natural error of the schools, but it is not confined to them. I once heard a very eminent judge say that he never let a decision go until he was absolutely sure that it was right. So judicial dissent often is blamed, as if it meant simply that one side or the other were not doing their sums right, and, if they would take more trouble, agreement inevitably would come.

This mode of thinking is entirely natural. The training of lawyers is a training in logic. The processes of analogy, discrimination, and deduction are those in which they are most at home. The language of judicial decision is mainly the language of logic. And the logical method and form flatter that longing for certainty and for repose which is in every human mind. But certainty generally is illusion, and repose is not the destiny of man. Behind the logical form lies a judgment as to the relative worth and importance of competing legislative grounds, often an inarticulate and unconscious judgment, it is true, and yet the very root and nerve of the whole proceeding. You can give any conclusion a logical form. You always can imply a condition in a contract. But why do you imply it? It is because of some belief as to the practice of the community or of a class, or because of some opinion as to policy, or, in short, because of some attitude of yours upon a matter not capable of exact quantitative measurement, and therefore not capable of founding exact logical conclusions. Such matters really are battlegrounds where the means do not exist for determinations that shall be good for all time, and where the decision can do no more than embody the preference of a given body in a given time and place. We do not realize how large a part of our law is open to reconsideration upon a slight change in the habit of the public mind. No concrete proposition is self-evident, no matter how ready we may be to accept it, not even Mr. Herbert Spencer's Every man has a right to do what he wills, provided he interferes not with a like right on the part of his neighbors.

Why is a false and injurious statement privileged, if it is made honestly in giving information about a servant? It is because it has been thought more important that information should be given freely, than that a man should be protected from what under other circumstances would be an actionable wrong. Why is a man at liberty to set up a business which he knows will ruin his neighbor? It is because the public good is supposed to be best subserved by free competition. Obviously such judgments of relative importance may vary in different times and places. Why does a judge instruct a jury that an employer is not liable to an employee for an injury received in the course of his employment unless he is negligent, and why does the jury generally find for the plaintiff if the case is allowed to go to them? It is because the traditional policy of our law is to confine liability to cases where a prudent man might have foreseen the injury or at least the danger, while the inclination of a very large part of the community is to make certain classes of persons insure the safety of those with whom they deal. Since the last words were written, I have seen the requirement of such insurance put forth as part of the programme of one of the best known labor organizations. There is a concealed, half-conscious battle on the question of legislative policy, and if anyone thinks that it can be settled deductively, or once for all, I only can say that I think he is theoretically wrong, and that I am certain that his conclusion will not be accepted in practice *semper ubique et ab omnibus*.

Indeed, I think that even now our theory upon this matter is open to reconsideration, although I am not prepared to say how I should decide if a reconsideration were proposed. Our law of torts comes from the old days of isolated, ungeneralized wrongs, assaults, slanders, and the like, where the damages might be taken to lie where they fell by legal judgment. But the torts with which our courts are kept busy today are mainly the incidents of certain well known businesses. They are injuries to person or property by railroads, factories, and the like. The liability for them is estimated, and sooner or later goes into the price paid by the public. The public really pays the damages, and the question of liability, if pressed far enough, is really the question how far it is desirable that the public should insure the safety of those whose work it uses. It might be said that in such cases the chance of a jury finding for the defendant is merely a chance, once in a while rather arbitrarily interrupting the regular course of recovery, most likely in the case of an unusually conscientious plaintiff, and therefore better done away with. On the other hand, the economic value even of a life to the community can be estimated, and no recovery, it may be said, ought to go beyond that amount. It is conceivable that some day in certain cases we may find ourselves imitating, on a higher plane, the tariff for life and limb which we see in the Leges Barbarorum.

I think that the judges themselves have failed adequately to recognize their duty of weighing considerations of social advantage. The duty is inevitable, and the result of the often proclaimed judicial aversion to deal with such considerations is simply to leave the very ground and foundation of judgments inarticulate, and often unconscious, as I have said. When socialism first began to be talked about, the comfortable classes of the community were a good deal frightened. I suspect that this fear has influenced judicial action both here and in England, yet it is certain that it is not a conscious factor in the decisions to which I refer. I think that something similar has led people who no longer hope to control the legislatures to look to the courts as expounders of the constitutions, and that in some courts new principles have been discovered outside the bodies of those instruments, which may be generalized into acceptance of the economic doctrines which prevailed about fifty years ago, and a wholesale prohibition of what a tribunal of lawyers does not think about right. I cannot but believe that if the training of lawyers led them habitually to consider more definitely and explicitly the social advantage on which the rule they lay down must be justified, they sometimes would hesitate where now they are confident, and see that really they were taking sides upon debatable and often burning questions.

So much for the fallacy of logical form. Now let us consider the present condition of the law as a subject for study, and the ideal toward which it tends. We still are far from the point of view which I desire to see reached. No one has reached it or can reach it as yet. We are only at the beginning of a philosophical reaction, and of a reconsideration of the worth of doctrines which for the most part still are taken for granted without any deliberate, conscious, and systematic questioning of their grounds. The development of our law has gone on for nearly a thousand years, like the development of a plant, each generation taking the inevitable next step, mind, like matter, simply obeying a law of spontaneous growth. It is perfectly natural and right that it should have been so. Imitation is a necessity of human nature . . . Most of the things we do, we do for no better reason than that our fathers have done them or that our neighbors do them, and the same is true of a larger part than we suspect of what we think. The reason is a good one, because our short life gives us no time for a better, but it is not the best. It does not follow, because we all are compelled to take on faith at second hand most of the rules on which we base our action and our thought, that each of us may not try to set some corner of his world in the order of reason, or that all of us collectively should not aspire to carry reason as far as it will go throughout the whole domain. In regard to the law, it is true, no doubt, that an evolutionist will hesitate to affirm universal validity for his social ideals, or for the principles which he thinks should be embodied in legislation. He is content if he can prove them best for here and now. He may be ready to admit that he knows nothing about an absolute best in the cosmos, and even that he knows next to nothing about a permanent best for men. Still it is true that a body of law is more rational and more civilized when every rule it contains is referred articulately and definitely to an end which it subserves, and when the grounds for desiring that end are stated or are ready to be stated in words.

At present, in very many cases, if we want to know why a rule of law has taken its particular shape, and more or less if we want to know why it exists at all, we go to tradition. We follow it into the Year Books, and perhaps beyond them to the customs of the Salian Franks, and somewhere in the past, in the German forests, in the needs of Norman kings, in the assumptions of a dominant class, in the absence of generalized ideas, we find out the practical motive for what now best is justified by the mere fact of its acceptance and that men are accustomed to it. The rational study of law is still to a large extent the study of history. History must be a part of the study, because without it we cannot know the precise scope of rules which it is our business to know. It is a part of the rational study, because it is the first step toward an enlightened scepticism, that is, toward a deliberate reconsideration of the worth of those rules. When you get the dragon out of his cave on to the plain and in the daylight, you can count his teeth and claws, and see just what is his strength. But to get him out is only the first step. The next is either to kill him, or to tame him and make him a useful animal. For the rational study of the law the black-letter man may be the man of the present, but the man of the future is the man of statistics and the master of economics. It is revolting to have no better reason for a rule of law than that so it was laid down in the time of Henry IV. It is still more revolting if the grounds upon which it was laid down have vanished long since, and the rule simply persists from blind imitation of the past . . .

Let me take an illustration, which can be stated in a few words, to show how the social end which is aimed at by a rule of law is obscured and only partially attained in consequence of the fact that the rule owes its form to a gradual historical development, instead of being reshaped as a whole, with conscious articulate reference to the end in view. We think it desirable to prevent one man's property being misappropriated by another, and so we make larceny a crime. The evil is the same whether the misappropriation is made by a man into whose hands the owner has put the property, or by one who wrongfully takes it away. But primitive law in its weakness did not get much beyond an effort to prevent violence, and very naturally made a wrongful taking, a trespass, part of its definition of the crime. In modern times the judges enlarged the definition a little by holding that, if the wrongdoer gets possession by a trick or device, the crime is committed. This really was giving up the requirement of a trespass, and it would have been more logical, as well as truer to the present object of the law, to abandon the requirement altogether. That, however, would have seemed too bold, and was left to statute. Statutes were passed making embezzlement a crime. But the force of tradition caused the crime of embezzlement to be regarded as so far distinct from larceny that to this day, in some jurisdictions at least, a slip corner is kept open for thieves to contend, if indicted for larceny, that they should have been indicted for embezzlement, and if indicted for embezzlement, that they should have been indicted for larceny, and to escape on that ground.

Far more fundamental questions still await a better answer than that we do as our fathers have done. What have we better than a blind guess to show that the criminal law in its present form does more good than harm? I do not stop to refer to the effect which it has had in degrading prisoners and in plunging them further into crime, or to the question whether fine and imprisonment do not fall more heavily on a criminal's wife and children than on himself. I have in mind more far-reaching questions. Does punishment deter? Do we deal with criminals on proper principles? A modern school of Continental criminalists plumes itself on the formula . . . that we must consider the criminal rather than the crime. The formula does not carry us very far, but the inquiries which have been started look toward an answer of my questions based on science for the first time. If the typical criminal is a degenerate, bound to swindle or to murder by as deep seated an organic necessity as that which makes the rattlesnake bite, it is idle to talk of deterring him by the classical method of imprisonment. He must be got rid of; he cannot be improved, or frightened out of his structural reaction. If, on the other hand, crime, like normal human conduct, is mainly a matter of imitation, punishment fairly may be expected to help to keep it out of fashion. The study of criminals has been thought by some well known men of science to sustain the former hypothesis. The statistics of the relative increase of crime in crowded places like large cities, where example has the greatest chance to work, and in less populated parts, where the contagion spreads more slowly, have been used with great force in favor of the latter view. But there is weighty authority for the belief that, however this may be, "not the nature of the crime, but the dangerousness of the criminal, constitutes the only reasonable legal criterion to guide the inevitable social reaction against the criminal."

The impediments to rational generalization, which I illustrated from the law of larceny, are shown in the other branches of the law, as well as in that of crime. Take the law of tort or civil liability for damages apart from contract and the like. Is there any general theory of such liability, or are the cases in which it exists simply to be enumerated, and to be explained each on its special ground, as is easy to believe from the fact that the right of action for certain well known classes of wrongs like trespass or slander has its special history for each class? I think that there is a general theory to be discovered, although resting in tendency rather than established and accepted. I think that the law regards the infliction of temporal damage by a responsible person as actionable, if under the circumstances known to him the danger of his act is manifest according to common experience, or according to his own experience if it is more than common, except in cases where upon special grounds of policy the law refuses to protect the plaintiff or grants a privilege to the defendant. I think that commonly malice, intent, and negligence mean only that the danger was manifest to a greater or less degree, under the circumstances known to the actor, although in some cases of privilege malice may mean an actual malevolent motive, and such a motive may take away a permission knowingly to inflict harm, which otherwise would be granted on this or that ground of dominant public good. But when I stated my view to a very eminent English judge the other day, he said: "You are discussing what the law ought to be; as the law is, you must show a right. A man is not liable for negligence unless he is subject to a duty." If our difference was more than a difference in words, or with regard to the proportion between the exceptions and the rule, then, in his opinion, liability for an act cannot be referred to the manifest tendency of the act to cause temporal damage in general as a sufficient explanation, but must be referred to the special nature of the damage, or must be derived from some special circumstances outside of the tendency of the act, for which no generalized explanation exists. I think that such a view is wrong, but it is familiar, and I dare say generally is accepted in England.

Everywhere the basis of principle is tradition, to such an extent that we even are in danger of making the role of history more important than it is . . . The classification of certain obligations to pay money, imposed by the law irrespective of any bargain as quasi contracts, is merely historical. The doctrine of consideration is merely historical. The effect given to a seal is to be explained by history alone. Consideration is a mere form. Is it a useful form? If so, why should it not be required in all contracts? A seal is a mere form, and is vanishing in the scroll and in enactments that a consideration must be given, seal or no seal. Why should any merely historical distinction be allowed to affect the rights and obligations of business men?

Since I wrote this discourse I have come on a very good example of the way in which tradition not only overrides rational policy, but overrides it after first having been misunderstood and having been given a new and broader scope than it had when it had a meaning. It is the settled law of England that a material alteration of a written contract by a party avoids it as against him. The doctrine is contrary to the general tendency of the law. We do not tell a jury that if a man ever has lied in one particular he is to be presumed to lie in all. Even if a man has tried to defraud, it seems no sufficient reason for preventing him from proving the truth. Objections of like nature in general go to the weight, not to the admissibility, of evidence. Moreover, this rule is irrespective of fraud, and is not confined to evidence. It is not merely that you cannot use the writing, but that the contract is at an end. What does this mean? The existence of a written contract depends on the fact that the offeror and offeree have interchanged their written expressions, not on the continued existence of those expressions. But in the case of a bond the primitive notion was different. The contract was inseparable from the parchment. If a stranger destroyed it, or tore off the seal, or altered it, the obligee could not recover, however free from fault, because the defendant's contract, that is, the actual tangible bond which he had sealed, could not be produced in the form in which it bound him. About a hundred years ago Lord Kenyon undertook to use his reason on this tradition, as he sometimes did to the detriment of the law, and, not understanding it, said he could see no reason why what was true of a bond should not be true of other contracts. His decision happened to be right, as it concerned a promissory note, where again the common law regarded the contract as inseparable from the paper on which it was written, but the reasoning was general, and soon was extended to other written contracts, and various absurd and unreal grounds of policy were invented to account for the enlarged rule.

I trust that no one will understand me to be speaking with disrespect of the law, because I criticise it so freely. I venerate the law, and especially our system of law, as one of the vastest products of the human mind. No one knows better than I do the countless number of great intellects that have spent themselves in making some addition or improvement, the greatest of which is trifling when compared with the mighty whole. It has the final title to respect that it exists, that it is not a Hegelian dream, but a part of the lives of men. But one may criticise even what one reveres. Law is the business to which my life is devoted, and I should show less than devotion if I did not do what in me lies to improve it, and, when I perceive what seems to me the ideal of its future, if I hesitated to point it out and to press toward it with all my heart.

Perhaps I have said enough to show the part which the study of history necessarily plays in the intelligent study of the law as it is today. In the teaching of this school and at Cambridge* it is in no danger of being undervalued. Mr. Bigelow here and Mr. Ames and Mr. Thayer there have made important contributions which will not be forgotten, and in

---

*The references are to Boston University School of Law, where "The Path of the Law" was given as an address on a commemorative occasion, and to Harvard Law School, respectively.

England the recent history of early English law by Sir Frederick Pollock and Mr. Maitland has lent the subject an almost deceptive charm. We must beware of the pitfall of antiquarianism, and must remember that for our purposes our only interest in the past is for the light it throws upon the present. I look forward to a time when the part played by history in the explanation of dogma shall be very small, and instead of ingenious research we shall spend our energy on a study of the ends sought to be attained and the reasons for desiring them. As a step toward that ideal it seems to me that every lawyer ought to seek an understanding of economics. The present divorce between the schools of political economy and law seems to me an evidence of how much progress in philosophical study still remains to be made. In the present state of political economy, indeed, we come again upon history on a larger scale, but there we are called on to consider and weigh the ends of legislation, the means of attaining them, and the cost. We learn that for everything we have to give up something else, and we are taught to set the advantage we gain against the other advantage we lose, and to know what we are doing when we elect.

There is another study which sometimes is undervalued by the practical minded, for which I wish to say a good word, although I think a good deal of pretty poor stuff goes under that name. I mean the study of what is called jurisprudence. Jurisprudence, as I look at it, is simply law in its most generalized part. Every effort to reduce a case to a rule is an effort of jurisprudence, although the name as used in English is confined to the broadest rules and most fundamental conceptions. One mark of a great lawyer is that he sees the application of the broadest rules. There is a story of a Vermont justice of the peace before whom a suit was brought by one farmer against another for breaking a churn. The justice took time to consider, and then said that he had looked through the statues and could find nothing about churns, and gave judgment for the defendant. The same state of mind is shown in all our common digests and textbooks. Applications of rudimentary rules of contract or tort are tucked away under the head of Railroads or Telegraphs or go to swell treatises on historical subdivisions, such as Shipping or Equity, or are gathered under an arbitrary title which is thought likely to appeal to the practical mind, such as Mercantile law. If a man goes into law it pays to be a master of it, and to be a master of it means to look straight through all the dramatic incidents and to discern the true basis for prophecy. Therefore, it is well to have an accurate notion of what you mean by law, by a right, by a duty, by malice, intent, and negligence, by ownership, by possession, and so forth . . .

The advice of the elders to young men is very apt to be as unreal as a list of the hundred best books. At least in my day I had my share of such counsels, and high among the unrealities I place the recommendation to study the Roman law. I assume that such advice means more than collecting a few Latin maxims with which to ornament the discourse— the purpose for which Lord Coke recommended Bracton. If that is all that is wanted, the title *De Regulis Juris Antiqui* can be read in an hour. I assume that, if it is well to study the Roman law, it is well to study it as a working system. That means mastering a set of technicalities more difficult and less understood than our own, and studying another course of history by which even more than our own the Roman law must be explained . . . No. The way to gain a liberal view of your subject is not to read something else, but to get to the bottom of the subject itself. The means of doing that are, in the first place, to follow the existing body of dogma into its highest generalizations by the help of jurisprudence; next, to discover from history how it has come to be what it is; and, finally, so far as you can, to consider the ends which the several rules seek to accomplish, the reasons why those ends are desired, what is given up to gain them, and whether they are worth the price.

We have too little theory in the law rather than too much, especially on this final branch of study. When I was speaking of history, I mentioned larceny as an example to show how the law suffered from not having embodied in a clear form a rule which will accomplish its manifest purpose. In that case the trouble was due to the survival of forms coming from a time when a more limited purpose was entertained. Let me now give an example to show the practical importance, for the decision of actual cases, of understanding the reasons of the law, by taking an example from rules which, so far as I know, never have been explained or theorized about in any adequate way. I refer to statutes of limitation and the law of prescription. The end of such rules is obvious, but what is the justification for depriving a man of his rights, a pure evil as far as it goes, in consequence of the lapse of time? Sometimes the loss of evidence is referred to, but that is a secondary matter. Sometimes the desirability of peace, but why is peace more desirable after twenty years than before? It is increasingly likely to come without the aid of legislation. Sometimes it is said that, if a man neglects to enforce his rights, he cannot complain if, after a while, the law follows his example. Now if this is all that can be said about it, you probably will decide a case I am going to put, for the plaintiff; if you take the view which I shall suggest, you possibly will decide it for the defendant. A man is sued for trespass upon land, and justifies under a right of way. He proves that he has used the way openly and adversely for twenty years, but it turns out that the plaintiff had granted a license to a person whom he reasonably supposed to be the defendant's agent, although not so in fact, and therefore had assumed that the use of the way was permissive, in which case no right would be gained. Has the defendant gained a right or not? If his gaining it stands on the fault and neglect of the landowner in the ordinary sense, as seems commonly to be supposed, there has been no such neglect, and the right of way has not been acquired. But if I were the defendant's counsel, I should suggest that the foundation of the acquisition of rights by lapse of time is to be looked for in the position of the person who gains them, not in that of the loser. Sir Henry Maine has made it fashionable to connect the archaic notion of property with prescription. But the connection is further back than the first recorded history. It is in the nature of man's mind. A thing which you have enjoyed and used as your own for a long time, whether property or an opinion, takes root in your being and cannot be torn away without your resenting the act and trying to defend yourself, however you came by it. The law can ask no better justification than the deepest instincts of man. It is only by way of reply to the suggestion that you are disappointing the former owner, that you refer to his neglect having allowed the gradual dissociation between himself and what he claims, and the gradual association of it with another. If he knows that another is doing acts which on their face show that he is on the way toward establishing such an association, I should argue that in justice to that other he was bound at his peril to find out whether the other was acting under his permission, to see that he was warned, and, if necessary, stopped.

I have been speaking about the study of the law, and I have said next to nothing of what commonly is talked about in that connection—textbooks and the case system, and all the machinery with which a student comes most immediately in contact. Nor shall I say anything about them. Theory is my subject, not practical details. The modes of teaching have been improved since my time, no doubt, but ability and industry will master the raw material with any mode. Theory is the most important part of the dogma of the law, as the architect is the most important man who takes part in the building of a house. The most important improvements of the last twenty-five years are improvements in theory. It is not to be feared as unpractical, for, to the competent, it simply means going to the bottom of the subject. For the incompetent, it sometimes is true, as has been said, that an interest in general ideas means an absence of particular knowledge. I remember in army days reading of a youth, who, being examined for the lowest grade and being asked a question about squadron drill, answered that he never had considered the evolutions of less than ten thousand men. But the weak and foolish must be left to their folly. The danger is that the able and practical minded should look with indifference or distrust upon ideas the connection of which with their business is remote. I heard a story, the other day, of a man who had a valet to whom he paid high wages, subject to deduction for faults. One of his deductions was, "For lack of imagination, five dollars." The lack is not confined to valets. The object of ambition, power, generally presents itself nowadays in the form of money alone. Money is the most immediate form, and is a proper object of desire. "The fortune," said Rachel, "is the measure of the intelligence." That is a good text to waken people out of a fool's paradise. But, as Hegel says, "It is in the end not the appetite, but the opinion, which has to be satisfied." To an imagination of any scope the most far-reaching form of power is not money, it is the command of ideas. If you want great examples read Mr. Leslie Stephen's *History of English Thought in the Eighteenth Century*, and see how a hundred years after his death the abstract speculations of Descartes had become a practical force controlling the conduct of men. Read the works of the great German jurists, and see how much more the world is governed today by Kant than by Bonaparte. We cannot all be Descartes or Kant, but we all want happiness. And happiness, I am sure from having known many successful men, cannot be won simply by being counsel for great corporations and having an income of fifty thousand dollars. An intellect great enough to win the prize needs other food beside success. The remoter and more general aspects of the law are those which give it universal interest. It is through them that you not only become a great master in your calling, but connect your subject with the universe and catch an echo of the infinite, a glimpse of its unfathomable process, a hint of the universal law.

Dunbar v. Boston & Providence Railroad
181 Mass. 383, 63 N.E. 916 (1902)

This is a petition for the assessment of damages to land of the petitioner on Dartmouth Street in Boston caused by raising the grade of that street under the terminal company act. The petition was filed under §23 of the act, and therefore we may assume that the claim was subject to the limitation of one year imposed by that section, although no land of the petitioner was taken. The section contains a general provision giving a jury to parties who have suffered damage to be compensated under the act, and the limitation no doubt was intended to be coextensive with the grant. Upon this construction it is admitted that the petition was not filed within the year, and indeed the opposite view was not much pressed on any ground. The answer relied upon is that on May 23, 1899, "the time within which any party suffering damages whose land is not taken may file his petition in the Superior Court for damages accruing from a change of grade occasioned by the location and construction of any railroad by any railroad company other than the terminal company" under the above §23 was extended to January 1, 1900. The respondent [i.e., the defendant railroad that was forced to pay damages to the petitioner, Dunbar] contends that this statute is unconstitutional . . .

The statute assailed is of general operation, and if valid applies as well to the petitioner, who had unquestioned notice of the change of grade by the actual completion of the work before the year expired, as to possible cases of persons who might have found their remedy gone before they knew that anything affecting their rights had been done. In such a case, apart from the authorities, it is impossible not to feel the greatest difficulty in sustaining the act. However much you may disguise or palliate the change by saying that the statute deals only with the remedy, or that a party has no vested right to a merely technical defence, or by adopting any other cloudy phrase that keeps the light from the fact, such legislation does enact that the property of a person previously free from legal liability shall be given to another who before the statute had no legal claim. It is not merely as it was put by the counsel for the respondent, following the cases, that the defence is as valuable and as much entitled to protection as the claim, if that be true, but the effect of the statute by enabling the barred claim to be collected is to allow property of the respondent to be appropriated which before was free. It is true that the property is not identified until it is seized on execution, but when it is identified by seizure it is taken as truly as land would be if it were allowed to be recovered in a real action notwithstanding the lapse of twenty years.

In the present case there is not the excuse apparent that the statute cured an earlier injustice, as might be the case where a petitioner had had no actual notice of the loss of any rights until he was too late. It cannot be said in more general terms that a statute of limitations as such embodies an arbitrary or merely technical rule. Prescription and limitation are based on one of the deepest principles of human nature, the working of association with what one actually enjoys for a long time, whatever one's defects of title may be, and of dissociation from that of which one is deprived, whatever may be one's rights. The mind like any other organism gradually shapes itself to what surrounds it, and resents disturbance in the form which its life has assumed. In cases like the present, when the period of limitations is short, no doubt other but also important elements are predominant—the desirableness for business reasons of getting a quasi-public transaction finished—but whatever the details, the principle involved is as worthy of respect as any known to the law.

Nevertheless . . . the constitutional provisions allow a certain limited degree of latitude in dealing with cases where remedies have been extinguished by lapse of time when the seeming infraction of right is not very great and when justice requires relief. Where the original time allowed after actual notice was very short and may have seemed to the legislature inadequate, where the extension was granted within little more than two months of the time when it could have been granted without question and not improbably before the transaction as a whole had been finished, where the plaintiff's claim is held to be barred only by a somewhat doubtful inference, and where in short we cannot say that the legislature with its larger view of the facts may not have been satisfied that substantial justice required its action, we are not prepared to pronounce the statute unconstitutional in the face of the most authoritative decisions. We regard this case as distinguishable from a wholesale attempt to relieve from the effect of open and adverse possession of land for twenty years . . .

To Frederick Pollock

January 19, 1928

My dear Pollock,

. . . As to hypostasis—I don't remember ever using it but once; at first as an intentionally magniloquent and pedagogical answer to Pound's question: What is a right? And then in an article, as a real reduction of a right to its rudiments. It starts from my definition of law (in the sense in which it is used by the modern lawyer) as a statement of the circumstances in which the public force will be brought to bear upon men through the courts: that is the prophecy in general terms. Of course the prophecy becomes more specific to define a right. So we prophesy that the earth and sun will act towards each other in a certain way. Then as we pretend to account for that mode of action by the hypothetical cause, the force of gravitation, which is merely the hypostasis of the prophesied fact and an empty phrase. So we get up the empty substratum, a *right,* to pretend to account for the fact that the courts will act in a certain way. We have got accustomed to our phraseology and might find it hard for a time to do without it; but in that as in other cases I think our morally tinted words have caused a great deal of confused thinking. I should like to write a first book of the law keeping to hard fact and using no images.

To Franklin Ford

January 13, 1911

Dear Mr. Ford:

I am much obliged to you for sending me clippings from time to time. I am a wretch who does not read the newspapers, and, for instance, never should have seen the articles on the bank guaranty cases, but for you. *Of course,* when I said "and thus, 'it is believed,' to prevent panics," I did not mean it is believed by me or by the Court, but it is believed by the body that determines the policy of the State so far as legislation can determine it. I don't disguise that I am disposed to be very cautious and slow in reading my own economic views or anybody else's into the general words of a Constitution. Between ourselves, I think that the tendency to do so is one of the great dangers of the American plan of giving the judges the last word.

Natural Law

32 *Harvard Law Review* 40 (1918)

It is not enough for the knight of romance that you agree that his lady is a very nice girl—if you do not admit that she is the best that God ever made or will make, you must fight. There is in all men a demand for the superlative, so much so that the poor devil who has no other way of reaching it attains it by getting drunk. It seems to me that this demand is at the bottom of the philosopher's effort to prove that truth is absolute and of the jurist's search for criteria of universal validity which he collects under the head of natural law.

I used to say when I was young, that truth was the majority vote of that nation that could lick all others. Certainly we may expect that the received opinion about the present war will depend a good deal upon which side wins (I hope with all my soul it will be mine), and I think that the statement was correct insofar as it implied that our test of truth is a reference to either a present or an imagined future majority in favor of our view. If . . . the truth may be defined as the system of my (intellectual) limitations, what gives it objectivity is the fact that I find my fellow man to a greater or less extent (never wholly) subject to the same *Can't Helps.* If I think that I am sitting at a table I find that the other persons present agree with me; so if I say that the sum of the angles of a triangle is equal to two right angles. If I am in a minority of one they send for a doctor or lock me up; and I am so far able to transcend the to me convincing testimony of my sense or my reason as to recognize that if I am alone probably something is wrong with my works.

Certitude is not the test of certainty. We have been cocksure of many things that were not so. If I may quote myself again, property, friendship, and truth have a common root in time. One cannot be wrenched from the rocky crevices into which one has grown for many years without feeling that one is attacked in one's life. What we most love and revere generally is determined by early associations. I love granite rocks and barberry bushes, no doubt because with them were my earliest joys that reach back through the past eternity of my life. But while one's experience thus makes certain preferences dogmatic for oneself, recognition of how they came to be so leaves one able to see that others, poor souls, may be equally dogmatic about something else. And this again means scepticism. Not that one's belief or love does not remain. Not that we would not fight and die for it if important—we all, whether we know it or not, are fighting to make the kind of a world that we should like—but that we have learned to recognize that others will fight and die to make a different world, with equal sincerity or belief. Deep-seated preferences cannot be argued about—you cannot argue a man into liking a glass of beer—and therefore, when differences are sufficiently far reaching, we try to kill the other man rather than let him have his way. But that is perfectly consistent with admitting that, so far as appears, his grounds are just as good as ours.

The jurists who believe in natural law seem to me to be in that naïve state of mind that accepts what has been familiar and accepted by all men everywhere. No doubt it is true that, so far as we can see ahead, some arrangements and the rudiments of familiar institutions seem to be necessary elements in any society that may spring from our own and that would seem to us to be civilized—some form of permanent association between the sexes—some residue of property individually owned—some mode of binding oneself to specified future conduct—at the bottom of all, some protection for the person. But without speculating whether a group is imaginable in which all but the last of these might disappear and the last be subject to qualifications that most of us would abhor, the question remains as to the *Ought* of natural law.

It is true that beliefs and wishes have a transcendental basis in the sense that their foundation is arbitrary. You cannot help entertaining and feeling them, and there is an end of it. As an arbitrary fact people wish to live, and we say with various degrees of certainty that they can do so only on certain conditions. To do it they must eat and drink. That necessity is absolute. It is a necessity of less degree but practically general that they should live in society. If they live in society, so far as we can see, there are further conditions. Reason working on experience does tell us, no doubt, that if our wish to live continues, we can do it only on those terms. But that seems to me the whole of the matter. I see no *a priori* duty to live with others and in that way, but simply a statement of what I must do if I wish to remain alive. If I do live with others they tell me that I must do and abstain from doing various things or they will put the screws on to me. I believe that they will, and being of the same mind as to their conduct I not only accept the rules but come in time to accept them with sympathy and emotional affirmation and begin to talk about duties and rights. But for legal purposes a right is only the hypostasis of a prophecy—the imagination of a substance supporting the fact that the public force will be brought to bear upon those who do things said to contravene it—just as we talk of the force of gravitation accounting for the conduct of bodies in space. One phrase adds no more than the other to what we know without it. No doubt behind these legal rights is the fighting will of the subject to maintain them, and the spread of his emotions to the general rules by which they are maintained; but that does not seem to me the same thing as the supposed *a priori* discernment of a duty or the assertion of a preexisting right. A dog will fight for his bone.

The most fundamental of the supposed preexisting rights—the right to life—is sacrificed without a scruple not only in war, but whenever the interest of society, that is, of the predominant power in the community, is thought to demand it. Whether that interest is the interest of mankind in the long run no one can tell, and as, in any event, to those who do not think with Kant and Hegel it is only an interest, the sanctity disappears. I remember a very tender-hearted judge being of opinion that closing a hatch to stop a fire and the destruction of a cargo was justified even if it was known that doing so would stifle a man below. It is idle to illustrate further, because to those who agree with me I am uttering commonplaces and to those who disagree I am ignoring the necessary foundations of thought. The *a priori* men generally call the dissentients superficial. But I do agree with them in believing that one's attitude on these matters is closely connected with one's general attitude toward the universe. Proximately, as has been suggested, it is determined largely by early associations and temperament, coupled with the desire to have an absolute guide. Men to a great extent believe what they want to—although I see in that no basis for a philosophy that tells us what we should want to want.

Now when we come to our attitude toward the universe I do not see any rational ground for demanding the superlative—for being dissatisfied unless we are assured that our truth is cosmic truth, if there is such a thing—that the ultimates of a little creature on this little earth are the last word of the unimaginable whole. If a man sees no reason for believing that significance, consciousness and ideals are more than marks of the finite, that does not justify what has been familiar in French sceptics; getting upon a pedestal and professing to look with haughty scorn upon a world in ruins. The real conclusion is that the part cannot swallow the whole—that our categories are not, or may not be, adequate to formulate what we cannot know. If we believe that we come out of the universe, not it out of us, we must admit that we do not know what we are talking about when we speak of brute matter. We do know that a certain complex of energies can wag its tail and another can make syllogisms. These are among the powers of the unknown, and if, as may be, it has still greater powers that we cannot understand, as Fabre in his studies of instinct would have us believe, studies that gave Bergson one of the strongest strands for his philosophy and enabled Maeterlinck to make us fancy for a moment that we heard a clang from behind phenomena—if this be true, why should we not be content? Why should we employ the energy that is furnished to us by the cosmos to defy it and shake our fist at the sky? It seems to me silly.

That the universe has in it more than we understand, that the private soldiers have not been told the plan of campaign, or even that there is one, rather than some vaster unthinkable to which every predicate is an impertinence, has no bearing upon our conduct. We still shall fight— all of us because we want to live, some, at least, because we want to realize our spontaneity and prove our powers, for the joy of it, and we may leave to the unknown the supposed final valuation of that which in any event has value to us. It is enough for us that the universe has produced us and has within it, as less than it, all that we believe and love. If we think of our existence not as that of a little god outside, but as that of a ganglion within, we have the infinite behind us. It gives us our only but our adequate significance. A grain of sand has the same, but what competent person supposes that he understands a grain of sand? That is as much beyond our grasp as man. If our imagination is strong enough to accept the vision of ourselves as parts inseverable from the rest, and to extend our final interest beyond the boundary of our skins, it justifies the sacrifice even of our lives for ends outside of ourselves. The motive, to be sure, is the common wants and ideals that we find in man. Philosophy does not furnish motives, but it shows men that they are not fools for doing what they already want to do. It opens to the forlorn hopes on which we throw ourselves away, the vista of the farthest stretch of human thought, the chords of a harmony that breathes from the unknown.

Learning and Science.

Speech at a Dinner of the Harvard Law School Association
in Honor of Professor C. C. Langdell, June 25, 1895.

S 67

Mr. President and Gentlemen of the Association:

As most of those here have graduated from the Law School within the last twenty-five years, I know that I am in the presence of very learned men. For my own part, lately my thoughts have been turned to

> old, unhappy, far-off things,
> And battles long ago;

and when once the ghosts of the dead fifers of thirty years since begin to play in my head, the laws are silent. And yet as I look around me, I think to myself, like Correggio, "I too am or at least have been, a pedagogue." And as such I will venture a reflection.

Learning, my learned brethren, is a very good thing. I should be the last to undervalue it, having done my share of quotation from the Year Books. But it is liable to lead us astray. The law, so far as it depends on learning, is indeed, as it has been called, the government of the living by the dead. To a very considerable extent no doubt it is inevitable that the living should be so governed. The past gives us our vocabulary and fixes the limits of our imagination; we cannot get away from it. There is, too, a peculiar logical pleasure in making manifest the continuity between what we are doing and what has been done before. But the present has a right to govern itself so far as it can; and it ought always to be remembered that historic continuity with the past is not a duty, it is only a necessity.

I hope that the time is coming when this thought will bear fruit. An ideal system of law should draw its postulates and its legislative justification from science. As it is now, we rely upon tradition, or vague sentiment, or the fact that we never thought of any other way of doing things, as our only warrant for rules which we enforce with as much confidence as if they embodied revealed wisdom. Who here can give reasons of any different kind for believing that half the criminal law does not do more harm than good? Our forms of contract, instead of being made once for all, like a yacht, on lines of least resistance, are accidental relics of early notions, concerning which the learned dispute. How much has reason had to do in deciding how far, if at all, it is expedient for the state to meddle with the domestic relations? And so I might go on through the whole law.

The Italians have begun to work upon the notion that the foundations of the law ought to be scientific, and, if our civilization does not collapse, I feel pretty sure that the regiment or division that follows us will carry that flag. Our own word seems the last always; yet the change of emphasis from an argument in Plowden to one in the time of Lord Ellenborough, or even from that to one in our own day, is as marked as the difference between Cowley's poetry and Shelley's. Other changes as great will happen. And so the eternal procession moves on, we in the front for the moment; and, stretching away against the unattainable sky, the black spearheads of the army that has been passing in unbroken line already for near a thousand years.

Law in Science and Science in Law
12 *Harvard Law Review* 443 (1899)

The law of fashion is a law of life. The crest of the wave of human interest is always moving, and it is enough to know that the depth was greatest in respect of a certain feature or style in literature or music or painting a hundred years ago to be sure that at that point it no longer is so profound. I should draw the conclusion that artists and poets, instead of troubling themselves about the eternal, had better be satisfied if they can stir the feelings of a generation, but that is not my theme. It is more to my point to mention that what I have said about art is true within the limits of the possible in matters of the intellect. What do we mean when we talk about explaining a thing? A hundred years ago men explained any part of the universe by showing its fitness for certain ends, and demonstrating what they conceived to be its final cause according to a providential scheme. In our less theological and more scientific day, we explain an object by tracing the order and process of its growth and development from a starting point assumed as given.

This process of historical explanation has been applied to the matter of our profession, especially of recent years, with great success, and with so much eagerness, and with such a feeling that when you had the true historic dogma you had the last word not only in the present but for the immediate future, that I have felt warranted heretofore in throwing out the caution that continuity with the past is only a necessity and not a duty. As soon as a legislature is able to imagine abolishing the requirement of a consideration for a simple contract, it is at perfect liberty to abolish it, if it thinks it wise to do so, without the slightest regard to continuity with the past. The continuity simply limits the possibilities of our imagination, and settles the terms in which we shall be compelled to think.

Historical explanation has two directions or aspects, one practical and the other abstractly scientific. I by no means share that morality which finds in a remoter practice the justification of philosophy and science. I do not believe that we must justify our pursuits by the motive of social well-being. If we have satisfied ourselves that our pursuits are good for society, or at least not bad for it, I think that science, like art, may be pursued for the pleasure of the pursuit and of its fruits, as an end in itself. I somewhat sympathize with the Cambridge mathematician's praise of his theorem, "The best of it all is that it can never by any possibility be made of the slightest use to anybody for anything." I think it one of the glories of man that he does not sow seed, and weave cloth, and produce all the other economic means simply to sustain and multiply other sowers and weavers that they in their turn may multiply, and so *ad infinitum,* but that on the contrary he devotes a certain part of his economic means to uneconomic ends—ends, too, which he finds in himself and not elsewhere. After the production of food and cloth has gone on a certain time, he stops producing and goes to the play, or he paints a picture, or asks unanswerable questions about the universe, and thus delightfully consumes a part of the world's food and clothing while he idles away the only hours that fully account for themselves.

Thinking in this way, you readily will understand that I do not consider the student of the history of legal doctrine bound to have a practical end in view. It is perfectly proper to regard and study the law simply as a great anthropological document. It is proper to resort to it to discover what ideals of society have been strong enough to reach that final form of expression, or what have been the changes in dominant ideals from century to century. It is proper to study it as an exercise in the morphology and transformation of human ideas. The study pursued for such ends becomes science in the strictest sense. Who could fail to be interested in the transition through the priest's test of truth, the miracle of the ordeal, and the soldier's, the battle of the duel, to the democratic verdict of the jury! Perhaps I might add, in view of the great increase of jury-waived cases, a later transition yet—to the commercial and rational test of the judgment of a man trained to decide.

It is still only the minority who recognize how the change of emphasis which I have called the law of fashion has prevailed even in the realm of morals. The other day I was looking over Bradford's history . . . and I was struck to see recounted the execution of a man with horrible solemnities for an offence which still, to be sure, stands on the statute book as a serious crime, but which no longer is often heard of in court, which many would regard as best punished simply by the disgust of normal men, and which a few would think of only as a physiological aberration, of interest mainly to the pathologist. I found in the same volume the ministers consulted as the final expounders of the law, and learnedly demonstrating that what now we should consider as needing no other repression than a doctor's advice was a crime punishable with death and to be ferreted out by searching the conscience of the accused, although after discussion it was thought that torture should be reserved for state occasions.

To take a less odious as well as less violent contrast, when we read in old books that it is the duty of one exercising a common calling to do his work upon demand and to do it with reasonable skill, we see that the gentleman is in the saddle and means to have the common people kept up to the mark for his convenience. We recognize the imperative tone which in our day has changed sides, and is oftener to be heard from the hotel clerk than from the guest.

I spoke of the scientific study of the morphology and transformation of human ideas in the law, and perhaps the notion did not strike all of you as familiar. I am not aware that the study ever has been systematically pursued, but I have given some examples as I have come upon them in my work, and perhaps I may mention some now by way of illustration, which, so far as I know, have not been followed out by other writers. In the Lex Salica—the law of the Salian Franks—you find going back to the fifth century a very mysterious person, later named the salmannus—the sale man—a third person who was called in to aid in completing the transfer of property in certain cases. The donor handed to him a symbolic staff which he in due season handed over in solemn form to the donee. If we may trust M. Dareste, and take our information at second hand, a copious source of error, it would look as if a similar use of a third person was known to the Egyptians and other early peoples. But what is certain is that we see the same form used down to modern times in England for the transfer of copyhold.* I dare say that many of you were puzzled, as I was when I was a law student, at the strange handing over of a staff to the lord or steward of the manor as a first step toward conveying copyhold land to somebody else. It really is nothing but a survival of the old form of the Salic law . . . There you have the Salic device in its original shape. But it is the transformations which it has undergone to which I wish to call your attention. The surrender to the steward is expressed to be to the use of the purchaser or donee . . . I have shown heretofore that the saleman became in England the better known feoffee to uses,**and thus that

*An interest in real estate.—Ed.
**What we would call a trustee.—Ed.

the connection between him and the steward of the manor when he receives the surrender of copyhold is clear. But the executor originally was nothing but a feoffee to uses. The heir was the man who paid his ancestor's debts and took his property. The executor did not step into the heir's shoes, and come fully to represent the person of the testator as to personal property and liabilities until after Bracton wrote his great treatise on the laws of England. Surely a flower is not more unlike a leaf, or a segment of a skull more unlike a vertebra, than the executor as we know him is remote from his prototype, the saleman of the Salic law. I confess that such a development as that fills me with interest, not only for itself, but as an illustration of what you see all through the law—the paucity of original ideas in man, and the slow, coasting way in which he works along from rudimentary beginnings to the complex and artificial conceptions of civilized life. It is like the niggardly uninventiveness of nature in its other manifestations, with its few smells or colors or types, its short list of elements, working along in the same slow way from compound to compound until the dramatic impressiveness of the most intricate compositions, which we call organic life, makes them seem different in kind from the elements out of which they are made, when set opposite to them in direct contrast . . .

Examples like these lead us beyond the transformations of an idea to the broader field of the development of our more general legal conceptions. We have evolution in this sphere of conscious thought and action no less than in lower organic stages, but an evolution which must be studied in its own field. I venture to think that the study is not yet finished. Take for instance the origin of contract . . . Sohm, following a thought first suggested, I believe, by Savigny, and made familiar by Maine in his *Ancient Law,* sees the beginning of contract in an interrupted sale. This is expressed in later law by our common law Debt, founded upon a *quid pro quo* received by the debtor from the creditor. Out of this, by a process differently conceived by different writers, arises the formal contract, the *fides facta* of the Salic law, the covenant familiar to us. And this dichotomy exhausts the matter. I do not say that this may not be proved to be the final and correct account, but there are some considerations which I should like to suggest in a summary way. We are not bound to assume with Sohm that his Frankish ancestors had a theory in their heads which, even if a trifle inarticulate, was the majestic peer of all that was done at Rome. The result of that assumption is to lead to the further one, tacitly made, but felt to be there, that there must have been some theory of contract from the beginning, if only you can find what it was. It seems to me well to remember that men begin with no theory at all, and with no such generalization as contract. They begin with particular cases, and even when they have generalized they are often a long way from the final generalizations of a later time . . .

Well, I have called attention elsewhere to the fact that giving hostages may be followed back to the beginning of our legal history, as far back as sales, that is, and that out of the hostage grew the surety, quite independently of the development of debt or formal contract. If the obligation of the surety, who, by a paradox explained by his origin, appears often in early law without a principal contractor, as the only party bound, had furnished the analogy for other undertakings, we never should have had the doctrine of consideration. If other undertakings were to be governed by the analogy of the law developed out of sales, sureties must either have received a *quid pro quo* or have made a covenant. There was a clash between the competing ideas, and just as commerce was prevailing over war the children of the sale drove the child of the hostage from the field. In the time of Edward III it was decided that a surety was not bound without a covenant, except in certain cities where local custom maintained the ancient law. Warranty of land came to require, and thus to be, a covenant in the same way, although the warranty of title upon a sale of chattels still retains its old characteristics, except that it now is thought of as a contract.

But the hostage was not the only competitor for domination. The oath also goes back as far as the history of our race. It started from a different point, and, leaving the possible difference of sanction on one side, it might have been made to cover the whole field of promises. The breach of their promissory oath by witnesses still is punished as perjury, and formerly there were severe penalties for the jury if convicted of a similar offence by attaint. The solemnity was used for many other purposes, and, if the church had had its way, the oath, helped by its cousin the plighting of troth, would have been very likely to succeed. In the time of Henry III, faith, oath, and writing, that is, the covenant, were the popular familiar forms of promise. The plighting of a man's faith or troth, still known to us in the marriage ceremony, was in common use, and the courts of the church claimed jurisdiction over it as well as over the oath. I have called attention elsewhere to a hint of inclination on the part of the early clerical chancellors to continue the clerical jurisdiction in another court, and to enforce the ancient form of obligation . . . Down to later times we still find the ecclesiastical tribunals punishing breach of faith or of promissory oaths with spiritual penalties. When we know that a certain form of undertaking was in general use, and that it was enforced by the clergy in their own courts, a very little evidence is enough to make us believe that in a new court, also presided over by a clergyman and with no substantive law of its own, the idea of enforcing it well might have been entertained, especially in view of the restrictions which the civil power put upon the church. But oath and plighting of troth did not survive in the secular forum except as an occasional solemnity, and I have mentioned them only to show a lively example of the struggle for life among competing ideas, and of the ultimate victory and survival of the strongest . . .

Another important matter is the way in which the various obligations were made binding after they were recognized. A breach of oath of course brought with it the displeasure of the gods. In other cases, as might be expected, we find hints that liabilities of a more primitive sort were extended to the new candidates for legal recognition. In the Roman law a failure to pay the price of a purchase seems to have suggested the analogy of theft. All over the world slavery for debt is found, and this seems not to have stood on the purely practical considerations which first would occur to us, but upon a notion akin to the noxal surrender of the offending body for a tort. There is a mass of evidence that various early contracts in the systems of law from which our own is descended carried with them the notion of pledging the person of the contracting party—a notion which we see in its extreme form in the seizure or division of the dead body of the debtor . . .

I am not going to trace the development of every branch of our law in succession, but if we turn to the law of torts we find there, perhaps even more noticeably than in the law of contracts, another evolutionary process which Mr. Herbert Spencer has made familiar to us by the name of Integration. The first stage of torts embraces little if anything beyond those simple acts of violence where the appeals of death, of wounding or maiming, of arson and the like had taken the place of self-help, to be succeeded by the modification known as the action of trespass. But when the action on the case let libel and slander and all the other wrongs which are known to the modern law into the civil courts, for centuries each of the recognized torts had its special history, its own precedents, and no one dreamed, so far as I know, that the different cases of liability were, or ought to be, governed by the same principles throughout. As is said in the preface to Mr. Jaggard's book, "the use of a book on Torts, as a distinct subject, was a few years ago a matter of ridicule." You may see the change which has taken place by comparing Hilliard on Torts, which proceeds by enumeration in successive chapters through assault and battery, libel and slander, nuisance, trespass, conversion, etc., with Sir Frederick Pollock's Introduction, in which he says that the purpose of his book "is to show that there really is a Law of Torts, not merely a number of rules of law about various kinds of torts—that this is a true living branch of the Common Law, not a collection of heterogeneous instances" . . .

Anyone who thinks about the world as I do does not need proof that the scientific study of any part of it has an interest which is the same in kind as that of any other part. If the examples which I have given fail to make the interest plain, there is no use in my adding to them, and so I shall pass to another part of my subject. But first let me add a word. The man of science in the law is not merely a bookworm. To a microscopic eye for detail he must unite an insight which tells him what details are significant. Not every maker of exact investigation counts, but only he who directs his investigation to a crucial point. But I doubt if there is any more exalted form of life than that of a great abstract thinker, wrapt in the successful study of problems to which he devotes himself, for an end which is neither unselfish nor selfish in the common sense of those words, but is simply to feed the deepest hunger and to use the greatest gifts of his soul.

But after all the place for a man who is complete in all his powers is in the fight. The professor, the man of letters, gives up one-half of life that his protected talent may grow and flower in peace. But to make up your mind at your peril upon a living question, for purposes of action, calls upon your whole nature. I trust that I have shown that I appreciate what I thus far have spoken of as if it were the only form of the scientific study of law, but of course I think, as other people do, that the main ends of the subject are practical, and from a practical point of view, history, with which I have been dealing thus far, is only a means, and one of the least of the means, of mastering a tool. From a practical point of view . . . its use is mainly negative and skeptical. It may help us to know the true limit of a doctrine, but its chief good is to burst inflated explanations. Everyone instinctively recognizes that in these days the justification of a law for us cannot be found in the fact that our fathers always have followed it. It must be found in some help which the law brings toward reaching a social end which the governing power of the community has made up its mind that it wants. And when a lawyer sees a rule of law in force he is very apt to invent, if he does not find, some ground of policy for its base. But in fact some rules are mere survivals. Many might as well be different, and history is the means by which we measure the power which the past has had to govern the present in spite of ourselves, so to speak, by imposing traditions which no longer meet their original end. History sets us free and enables us to make up our minds dispassionately whether the survival which we are enforcing answers any new purpose when it has ceased to answer the old. Notwithstanding the contrasts which I have been making, the practical study of the law ought also to be scientific. The true science of the law does not consist mainly in a theological working out of dogma or a logical development as in mathematics, or only in a study of it as an anthropological document from the outside; an even more important part consists in the establishment of its postulates from within upon accurately measured social desires instead of tradition. It is this latter part to which I now am turning, and I begin with one or two instances of the help of history in clearing away rubbish—instances of detail from my own experience.

Last autumn our court had to consider the grounds upon which evidence of fresh complaint by a ravished woman is admitted as part of the government's case in an indictment for rape. All agree that it is an exception to the ordinary rules of evidence to allow a witness to be corroborated by proof that he has said the same thing elsewhere when not under oath, except possibly by way of rebuttal under extraordinary circumstances. But there is the exception, almost as well settled as the rule, and courts and lawyers finding the law to be established proceed to account for it by consulting their wits. We are told that the outrage is so great that there is a natural presumption that a virtuous woman would disclose it at the first suitable opportunity. I confess that I should think this was about the last crime in which such a presumption could be made, and that it was far more likely that a man who had had his pocket picked or who had been the victim of an attempt to murder would speak of it, than that a sensitive woman would disclose such a horror. If we look into history no further than Hale's *Pleas of the Crown,* where we first find the doctrine, we get the real reason and the simple truth. In an appeal of rape the first step was for the woman to raise hue and cry. Lord Hale, after stating that fact, goes on to say that upon an indictment for the same offence the woman can testify, and that her testimony will be corroborated if she made fresh complaint and pursued the offender. That is the hue and cry over again. At that time there were few rules of evidence. Later our laws of evidence were systematized and developed. But the authority of Lord Hale has caused his dictum to survive as law in the particular case, while the principle upon which it would have to be justified has been destroyed. The exception in other words is a pure survival, having nothing or very little to back it except that the practice is established . . .

In *Brower v. Fisher,* the defendant, a deaf and dumb person, had conveyed to the plaintiff real and personal property, and had got a judgment against the plaintiff for the price. The plaintiff brought a bill to find out whether the conveyance was legal, and got an injunction *pendente lite* to stay execution on the judgment. On the plaintiff's petition a commission of lunacy was issued to inquire whether the defendant was *compos mentis.* It was found that he was so unless the fact that he was born deaf and dumb made him otherwise. Thereupon Chancellor

Kent dismissed the bill but held the inquiry so reasonable that he imposed no costs. The old books of England fully justified his view; and why? History again gives us the true reason. The Roman law held very properly that the dumb, and by extension the deaf, could not make the contract called *stipulatio* because the essence of that contract was a formal question and answer which the dumb could not utter and the deaf could not hear. Bracton copies the Roman law and repeats the true reason, that they could not express assent, *consentire;* but shows that he had missed the meaning of *stipulari* by suggesting that perhaps it might be done by gestures or writing. Fleta copied Bracton, but seemed to think that the trouble was inability to bring the consenting mind, and whereas the Roman law explained that the rule did not apply to one who was only hard of hearing . . . Fleta seems to have supposed that this pointed to a difference between a man born deaf and dumb and one who became so later in life. In Perkins's *Profitable Book,* this is improved upon by requiring that the man should be born blind, deaf, and dumb, and then the reason is developed that "a man that is born blind, deaf, and dumb can have no understanding, so that he cannot make a gift or a grant." In a case before Vice-Chancellor Wood good sense prevailed, and it was laid down that there is no exception to the presumption of sanity in the case of a deaf and dumb person.

Other cases of what I have called inflated and unreal explanations, which collapse at the touch of history, are the liability of a master for the torts of his servant in the course of his employment . . . which thus far never, in my opinion, has been put upon a rational footing; and the liability of a common carrier, which, as I conceive, is another distorted survival from the absolute responsibility of bailees* in early law, crossed with the liability of those exercising a common calling . . . These examples are sufficient, I hope, to illustrate my meaning and to point out the danger of inventing reasons offhand for whatever we find established in the law. They lead me to some other general considerations in which history plays no part, or a minor part, but in which my object is to show the true process of law-making, and the real meaning of decision upon a doubtful case and thus, as in what I have said before, to help in substituting a scientific foundation for empty words.

I pass from unreal explanations to unreal formulas and inadequate generalizations, and I will take up one or two with especial reference to the problems with which we have to deal at the present time. The first illustration which occurs to me, especially in view of what I have been

---

*A bailee is someone to whom another entrusts goods for transportation or storage.—Ed.

saying, is suggested by another example of the power of fashion. I am immensely struck with the blind imitativeness of man when I see how a doctrine, a discrimination, even a phrase, will run in a year or two over the whole English-speaking world . . . Do we not hear every day of taking the risk—an expression which we never heard used as it now is until within a very few years? Do we not hear constantly of invitation and trap—which came into vogue within the memory of many, if not most of those who are here? Heaven forbid that I should find fault with an expression because it is new, or with the last mentioned expressions on any ground! Judges commonly are elderly men, and are more likely to hate at sight any analysis to which they are not accustomed, and which disturbs repose of mind, than to fall in love with novelties. Every living sentence which shows a mind at work for itself is to be welcomed. It is not the first use but the tiresome repetition of inadequate catch words upon which I am observing—phrases which originally were contributions, but which, by their very felicity, delay further analysis for fifty years. That comes from the same source as dislike of novelty—intellectual indolence or weakness—a slackening in the eternal pursuit of the more exact.

The growth of education is an increase in the knowledge of measure. To use words familiar to logic and to science, it is a substitution of quantitative for qualitative judgments. The difference between the criticism of a work of art by a man of perception without technical training and that by a critic of the studio will illustrate what I mean. The first, on seeing a statue, will say, "It is grotesque," a judgment of quality merely; the second will say, "That statue is so many heads high, instead of the normal so many heads." His judgment is one of quantity. On hearing a passage of Beethoven's Ninth Symphony the first will say, "What a gorgeous sudden outburst of sunshine!"—the second, "Yes, great idea to bring in his major third just there, wasn't it?" Well, in the law we only occasionally can reach an absolutely final and quantitative determination, because the worth of the competing social ends which respectively solicit a judgment for the plaintiff or the defendant cannot be reduced to number and accurately fixed. The worth, that is, the intensity of the competing desires, varies with the varying ideals of the times, and, if the desires were constant, we could not get beyond a relative decision that one was greater and one was less. But it is of the essence of improvement that we should be as accurate as we can. Now to recur to such expressions as taking the risk, . . . which are very well for once in the sprightly mouth which first applies them, the objection to the repetition of them as accepted legal formulas is that they do not represent a final analysis, but dodge difficulty and responsibility with a rhetorical phrase. When we say that a workman takes a certain risk as incident to his employment, we mean that on some general grounds of policy blindly felt or articulately present to our mind, we read into his contract a term of which he never thought; and the real question in every case is, What are the grounds, and how far do they extend? The question put in that form becomes at once and plainly a question for scientific determination, that is, for quantitative comparison by means of whatever measure we command. When we speak of taking the risk apart from contract, I believe that we merely are expressing what the law means by negligence, when for some reason or other we wish to express it in a conciliatory form.

In our approach towards exactness we constantly tend to work out definite lines or equators to mark distinctions which we first notice as a difference of poles. It is evident in the beginning that there must be differences in the legal position of infants and adults. In the end we establish twenty-one as the dividing point. There is a difference manifest at the outset between night and day. The statutes of Massachusetts fix the dividing points at one hour after sunset and one hour before sunrise, ascertained according to mean time. When he has discovered that a difference is a difference of degree, that distinguished extremes have between them a penumbra in which one gradually shades into the other, a tyro thinks to puzzle you by asking where you are going to draw the line, and an advocate of more experience will show the arbitrariness of the line proposed by putting cases very near to it on one side or the other. But the theory of the law is that such lines exist, because the theory of the law as to any possible conduct is that it is either lawful or unlawful. As that difference has no gradation about it, when applied to shades of conduct that are very near each other it has an arbitrary look. We like to disguise the arbitrariness, we like to save ourselves the trouble of nice and doubtful discriminations. In some regions of conduct of a special sort we have to be informed of facts which we do not know before we can draw our lies intelligently, and so, as we get near the dividing point we call in the jury. From saying that we will leave a question to the jury to saying that it is a question of fact is but a step, and the result is that at this day it has come to be widespread doctrine that negligence not only is a question for the jury but is a question of fact. I have heard it urged with great vehemence by counsel, and calmly maintained by professors that, in addition to their wrongs to labor, courts were encroaching upon the province of the jury when they directed a verdict in a negligence case, even in the unobtrusive form of a ruling that there was no evidence of neglect.

I venture to think, on the other hand, now, as I thought twenty years ago, before I went upon the bench, that every time that a judge declines to rule whether certain conduct is negligent or not he avows his inability to state the law, and that the meaning of leaving nice questions to the jury is that while if a question of law is pretty clear we can decide it, as it is our duty to do, if it is difficult it can be decided better by twelve men taken at random from the street. If a man fires a gun over a prairie that looks empty to the horizon, or crosses a railroad which he can see is clear for a thousand yards each way, he is not negligent, that is, he is free from legal liability in the first case, he has not prevented his recovery by his own conduct, if he is run over, in the second, as matter of law. If he fires a gun into a crowded street, or tries to cross a track ten feet in front of an express train in full sight running sixty miles an hour, he is liable, or he cannot recover, again as matter of law, supposing these to be all the facts in the case. What new question of fact is introduced if the place of firing is something half way between a prairie and a crowded street, or if the express train is two hundred, one hundred, or fifty yards away? I do not wish to repeat arguments which I published long ago, and which have been more or less quoted in leading textbooks. I only wish to insist that false reasons and false analogies shall not be relied upon for daily practice. It is so easy to accept the phrase "there is no evidence of negligence," and thence to infer . . . that the question is the same in kind as any other question whether there is evidence of a fact.

When we rule on evidence of negligence we are ruling on a standard of conduct, a standard which we hold the parties bound to know beforehand, and which in theory is always the same upon the same facts and not a matter dependent upon the whim of the particular jury or the eloquence of the particular advocate. And I may be permitted to observe that, referring once more to history, similar questions originally were, and to some extent still are, dealt with as question of law. It was and is so on the question of probable cause in malicious prosecution. It was so on the question of necessaries for an infant. It was so in question of what is reasonable, as—a reasonable fine, convenient time, seasonable time, reasonable time, reasonable notice of dishonor. It is so in regard to the remoteness of damage in an action of contract. Originally in malicious prosecution, probable cause, instead of being negatived in the declaration, was pleaded by the defendant, and the court passed upon the sufficiency of the cause alleged. In the famous case of *Weaver v. Ward*, the same course was suggested as proper for negligence. I quote: "as if the defendant had said that the plaintiff ran across his piece when it was discharging, or had set forth the case with the circumstances, so as it had appeared to the court that it had been inevitable, and that the defendant had committed no negligence to give occasion to the hurt." But about the middle of the last century, when the rule of conduct was complicated with practical details the court began to leave some of these questions to the jury . . . When the circumstances are too special and complicated for a general rule to be laid down the jury may be called in. But it is obvious that a standard of conduct does not cease to be a law because the facts to which that standard applies are not likely to be repeated.

I do not believe that the jury have any historic or *a priori* right to decide any standard of conduct. I think that the logic of the contrary view would be that every decision upon such a question by the court is an invasion of their province and that all the law properly is in their breasts. I refer to the subject, however, merely as another matter in which phrases have taken the place of real reasons, and to do my part toward asserting a certain freedom of approach in dealing with negligence cases, not because I wish to quarrel with the existing and settled practice . . . There are many cases where no one could lay down a standard of conduct intelligently without hearing evidence upon that, as well as concerning what the conduct was. And though it does not follow that such evidence is for the jury, any more than the question of fact whether a legislature passed a certain statute, still they are a convenient tribunal, and if the evidence to establish a rule of law is to be left to them, it seems natural to leave the conclusion from the evidence to them as well. I confess that in my experience I have not found juries especially inspired for the discovery of truth. I have not noticed that they could see further into things or form a saner judgment than a sensible and well trained judge. I have not found them freer from prejudice than an ordinary judge would be. Indeed one reason why I believe in our practice of leaving questions of negligence to them is what is precisely one of their gravest defects from the point of view of their theoretical function: that they will introduce into their verdict a certain amount—a very large amount, so far as I have observed—of popular prejudice, and thus keep the administration of the law in accord with the wishes and feelings of the community. Possibly such a justification is a little like that which an eminent English barrister gave me many years ago for the distinction between barristers and solicitors. It was in substance that if law was to be practised somebody had to be damned, and he preferred that it should be somebody else.

My object is not so much to point out what seem to me to be fallacies in particular cases as to enforce by various examples and in various applications the need of scrutinizing the reasons for the rules which we follow, and of not being contented with hollow forms of words merely because they have been used very often and have been repeated from one end of the union to the other. We must think things not words, or at least we must constantly translate our words into the facts for which they stand, if we are to keep to the real and the true. I sometimes tell students that the law schools pursue an inspirational combined with a logical method, that is, the postulates are taken for granted upon authority without inquiry into their worth, and then logic is used as the only tool to develop the results. It is a necessary method for the purpose of teaching dogma. But inasmuch as the real justification of a rule of law, if there be one, is that it helps to bring about a social end which we desire, it is no less necessary that those who make and develop the law should have those ends articulately in their minds. I do not expect or think it desirable that the judges should undertake to renovate the law. That is not their province. Indeed precisely because I believe that the world would be just as well off if it lived under laws that differed from ours in many ways, and because I believe that the claim of our especial code to respect is simply that it exists, that it is the one to which we have become accustomed, and not that it represents an eternal principle, I am slow to consent to overruling a precedent, and think that our most important duty is to see that the judicial duel shall be fought out in the accustomed way. But I think it most important to remember whenever a doubtful case arises, with certain analogies on one side and other analogies on the other, that what really is before us is a conflict between two social desires, each of which seeks to extend its dominion over the case, and which cannot both have their way. The social question is which desire is strongest at the point of conflict. The judicial one may be narrower, because one or the other desire may have been expressed in previous decisions to such an extent that logic requires us to assume it to preponderate in the one before us. But if that be clearly so, the case is not a doubtful one. Where there is doubt the simple tool of logic does not suffice, and even if it is disguised and unconscious the judges are called on to exercise the sovereign prerogative of choice.

I have given an example of what seems to me the uninstructive and indolent use of phrases to save the trouble of thinking closely, in the expression "taking the risk," and of what I think a misleading use in calling every question left to the jury a question of fact. Let me give one of overgeneralization, or rather of the danger of reasoning from generalizations unless you have the particulars which they embrace in mind. A generalization is empty so far as it is general. Its value depends on the number of particulars which it calls up to the speaker and the hearer. Hence the futility of arguments on economic questions by anyone whose memory is not stored with economic facts. *Allen v. Flood* was decided lately by the English House of Lords upon a case of maliciously inducing workmen to leave the plaintiff's employ . . . I infer that [the jury] were instructed . . . in such a way that their finding meant little more than that the defendant had acted with knowledge and under- standing of the harm which he would inflict if successful. Or if I should add an intent to harm the plaintiff without reference to any immediate advantage to the defendant, still I do not understand that finding meant that the defendant's act was done from disinterestedly malev- olent motives, and not from a wish to better the defendant's union in a battle of the market. Taking the point decided to be what I suppose it to be, this case confirms opinions which I have had occasion to express judicially, and commands my hearty assent. But in the elaborate, al- though to my notion inadequate, discussion which took place, eminent judges intimated that anything which a man has a right to do he has a right to do whatever his motives, and this has been hailed as a triumph of the principle of external standards in the law, a principle which I have done my best to advocate as well as to name. Now here the reason- ing starts from the vague generalization Right, and one asks himself at once whether it is definite enough to stand the strain. If the scope of the right is already determined as absolute and irrespective of mo- tive, . . . there is nothing to argue about. So if all rights have that scope. But if different rights are of different extent, if they stand on different grounds of policy and have different histories, it does not follow that because one right is absolute another is—and if you simply say all rights shall be so, that is only a pontifical or imperial way of forbidding discus- sion. The right to sell property is about as absolute as any I can think of, although, under statutes at least, even that may be affected by motive, as in the case of an intent to prefer creditors. But the privilege of a master [employer] to state his servant's [employee's] character to one who is thinking of employing him is also a right within its limits. Is it equally extensive? I suppose it would extend to mistaken statements volunteered in good faith out of love for the possible employer. Would it extend to such statements volunteered simply out of hate for the man? To my mind here, again, generalities are worse than useless, and the only way to solve the problem presented is to weigh the reasons for the particular right claimed and those for the competing right to be free from slander as well as one can, and to decide which set preponde- rates. Any solution in general terms seems to me to mark a want of ana- lytic power.

Gentlemen, I have tried to show by examples something of the inter- est of science as applied to the law, and to point out some possible im- provement in our way of approaching practical questions in the same sphere. To the latter attempt, no doubt, many will hardly be ready to yield me their assent. But in that field, as in the other, I have had in mind an ultimate dependence upon science because it is finally for science to determine, so far as it can, the relative worth of our different social ends, and, as I have tried to hint, it is our estimate of the proportion between these, now often blind and unconscious, that leads us to insist upon and to enlarge the sphere of one principle and to allow another gradually to dwindle into atrophy. Very likely it may be that with all the help that statistics and every modern appliance can bring us there never will be a commonwealth in which science is everywhere supreme. But it is an ideal, and without ideals what is life worth? They furnish us our perspectives and open glimpses of the infinite. It often is a merit of an ideal to be unattainable. Its being so keeps forever before us something more to be done, and saves us from the ennui of a monotonous perfection. At the least it glorifies dull details, and uplifts and sustains weary years of toil with George Herbert's often quoted but ever inspiring verse:

> Who sweeps a room as in Thy cause,
> Makes that and the action fine.*

To Franklin Ford

February 8, 1908

Dear Sir:

. . . I do not quite see what you are driving at in your demand for a new theory of law—naturally, perhaps, as you are asking for something that you assume not to exist. I am hampered by not being a business man or familiar with any business details. No one can know more than a part of what he deals with, and I have done the best I could with my time, and venture to think that I have done my share of originating.

Certainly one thing I have always had in mind [is] to suggest scepticism as to the finality of existing legal dogma. But I should think that what was wanted from lawyers was not so much what I should call a new theory of law as a more enlightened understanding of economic facts, for instance (a hobby of mine) that ownership does not mean consumption, but that the real question in that matter is not who owns, but who consumes the annual product; obviously the crowd does, more than ever before . . .

*Shortly after the publication of this article, Holmes realized he had misquoted Herbert—the line is "Who sweeps a room as for Thy laws"—and wrote the law review a letter of correction, printed at 12 *Harvard Law Review* 556 (1899).—Ed.

I have every sympathy with your wish to make the social body the subject of exact observation. Long ago I put the question in a speech to lawyers: Who has any reason for believing that half our criminal law does more good than harm, better than tradition, vague sentiment, and the fact that we never thought of any other way of doing things? And similar questions as to other great branches of the law. It was thought of doubtful propriety then.

Thus far I have seen but few data that would warrant the scientific conclusion that I desire. It well may be that your field of knowledge, in which I am wholly ignorant, will furnish us means of taking the next step with relative intelligence, however far we may be from a final conclusion—perhaps there is no final conclusion. At all events the next step is the important matter for us, and if we could substitute conscious and relatively intelligent choice for blind instinct, it would be a great advance. Believe me, I have no reluctance to accept your conclusions so far as I understand them—and indeed, as you recognize, long have accepted them in their more general aspects.

The trouble I find is that I don't get far beyond the starting point. Agreed that we want to put law like other things on a scientific basis. Give me the scientifically ascertained facts that should meet on any specific doctrine, and I should be only too glad to apply them so far as I have authority and power. As I said to the President a little while ago, I regard Montague and Capulet with equal detachment, for legal purposes. But as yet I have heard little that gives me any light when I sit upon the bench. Even within the limits of my present enlightenment I am hampered by the duty to enforce statutes that I did not make or to follow precedents that seem to me inadequate. After all, one of the first things for a court to remember is that people care more to know that the rules of the game will be stuck to, than to have the best possible rules.

I should be glad if I could prophesy whether the great wave of prejudice against the very rich, having in its belly as the more important fact, a prejudice against economic necessities and organization, is going to spend its force without destruction and putting back the inevitable concomitant of advance; and how the future competition of the yellow races is going to react on our whole self-satisfied civilization.

But this letter is only a general outburst in one of my rare moments of leisure. Most of my time is spent in doing as well as I can the work immediately at hand. One hopes that by doing quietly and without parade as solid work as one can in the time when one is occupied, one makes the best contribution possible to one's country.

Jackman v. Rosenbaum Company
260 U.S. 22 (1922)

The plaintiff . . . owned a theater building in Pittsburgh, Pennsylvania, a wall of which went to the edge of his line. Proceeding under a statute of Pennsylvania, the defendant, owner of the adjoining land, began to build a party wall, intending to incorporate the plaintiff's wall. The city authorities decided that the latter was not safe and ordered it to be removed, which was done by the contractor employed by the defendant. The plaintiff later brought this suit. The declaration did not set up that the entry upon the plaintiff's land was unlawful, but alleged wrongful delay in completing the wall and the use of improper methods. It claimed damages for the failure to restore the plaintiff's building to the equivalent of its former condition, and for the delay, which, it was alleged, caused the plaintiff to lose the rental for a theatrical season. At the trial the plaintiff asked for a ruling that the statute relating to party walls, if interpreted to exclude the recovery of damages without proof of negligence, was contrary to the Fourteenth Amendment. This was refused, the court ruling that the defendant was not liable for damages necessarily resulting from the exercise of the right given by the statute to build a party wall upon the line, and, more specifically, was not liable for the removal of the plaintiff's old wall . . .

In the state court the judgment was justified by reference to the power of the state to impose burdens upon property or to cut down its value in various ways without compensation, as a branch of what is called the police power. The exercise of this has been held warranted in some cases by what we may call the average reciprocity of advantage, although the advantages may not be equal in the particular case. The supreme court of the state adverted also to increased safety against fire and traced the origin to the great fire in London in 1666. It is unnecessary to decide upon the adequacy of these grounds. It is enough to refer to the fact, also brought out and relied upon in the opinion below, that the custom of party walls was introduced by the first settlers in Philadelphia under William Penn and has prevailed in the state ever since . . .

The Fourteenth Amendment, itself a historical product, did not destroy history for the states and substitute mechanical compartments of law all exactly alike. If a thing has been practised for two hundred years by common consent, it will need a strong case for the Fourteenth Amendment to affect it. Such words as "right" are a constant solicitation to fallacy. We say a man has a right to the land that he has bought and that to subject a strip six inches or a foot wide to liability to use for a party wall therefore takes his right to that extent. It might be so and we might be driven to the economic and social considerations that we have mentioned if the law were an innovation, now heard of for the first time. But if, from what we may call time immemorial, it has been the understanding that the burden exists, the land owner does not have the right to that part of his land except as so qualified and the statute that embodies that understanding does not need to invoke the police power.

Of course a case could be imagined where the modest mutualities of simple townspeople might become something very different when extended to buildings like those of modern New York. There was a suggestion of such a difference in this case. But, although the foundations spread wide, the wall above the surface of the ground was only thirteen inches thick, or six and half on the plaintiff's land, and as the damage complained of was a necessary incident to any such building, the question how far the liability might be extended does not arise. It follows, as stated by the supreme court of Pennsylvania, that "when either lot-owner builds upon his own property up to the division line, he does so with the knowledge that, in case of the erection of a party wall, that part of his building which encroaches upon the portion of the land subject to the easement will have to come down, if not suitable for incorporation into the new wall." In a case involving local history, as this does, we should be slow to overrule the decision of courts steeped in the local tradition, even if we saw reasons for doubting it, which in this case we do not.

Stack v. New York, New Haven & Hartford Railroad Company ·
177 Mass. 155, 58 N.E. 686 (1900)

This is an action for personal injuries. The defendant denied the injuries, and, two days before a second trial, was permitted to send two doctors, who made a thorough examination of the plaintiff in company with the doctors employed by the plaintiff. After the plaintiff had closed his case and after the defendant had called its two doctors as witnesses, it asked the court to order the plaintiff to submit to an examination by another doctor named by it. The plaintiff objected, on the ground that his relations with that doctor were unfriendly, but offered to allow an examination by any other physician whom the defendant might select. The defendant declined the offer, and thereupon the court refused to make the order, ruling that it had no power or right to make it under the circumstances. The defendant excepted.

Perhaps the words "under the circumstances" so far cut down the seemingly absolute denial of power in the first part of the ruling that it meant only to state emphatically the plain injustice and outrage which it would have been to make the order proposed. Other language used has somewhat that look. The judge probably was justified in assuming the truth of the plaintiff's statement that his relations with the doctor were hostile. He certainly was justified in assuming that the plaintiff had personal objections to him. When the plaintiff coupled with his objection an offer to accept any other doctor whom the defendant might choose to send, bearing in mind the large possibilities that were open by telegraph and rail, he had a plain right to have his personality respected to the small extent that he asked. If that is all that the ruling meant, as it certainly was all that was needed to dispose of the matter, in our opinion it was right.

But if the ruling requires the decision of a broader question, we agree with the Supreme Court of the United States, the New York court of appeals, and some other able courts, that the power does not exist . . . The need of the power easily may be exaggerated, because if, contrary to usual experience, a plaintiff should dare to refuse a reasonable examination, it would be the subject of just comment to the jury. But if the power should be deemed needful to a more perfect administration of justice, the remedy should be furnished by the legislature, which as yet has not gone so far. The statutes compel the answer to interrogatories and the exhibition of documents under the penalty of a nonsuit* or default. They also empower the court to order a view of a place in question, or of "any property, matter, or thing relating to the controversy between the parties." But these words do not extend to the ordering of an interference with the person of a party by someone out of court, in order to enable him to qualify himself to be called as a witness by the opposing party if the latter sees fit.

We cannot doubt that as matter of history the power which we are asked to assert was of a kind rarely claimed or exercised by common law courts . . .

We agree that, in view of the great increase of actions for personal injuries, it may be desirable that the courts should have the power in dispute. We appreciate the ease with which, if we were careless or ignorant of precedent, we might deem it enlightened to assume that power. We do not forget the continuous process of developing the law that goes on through the courts, in the form of deduction, or deny that in a clear case it might be possible even to break away from a line of decisions

*Dismissal.—Ed.

in favor of some rule generally admitted to be based upon a deeper insight into the present wants of society. But the improvements made by the courts are made, almost invariably, by very slow degrees and by very short steps. Their general duty is not to change but to work out the principles already sanctioned by the practice of the past. No one supposes that a judge is at liberty to decide with sole reference even to his strongest convictions of policy and right. His duty in general is to develop the principles which he finds, with such consistency as he may be able to attain. No one supposes that this court might have anticipated the legislature by declaring parties to be competent witnesses, any more than today it could abolish the requirement of consideration for a simple contract. In the present case we perceive no such pressing need of our anticipating the legislature as to justify our departure from what we cannot doubt is the settled tradition of the common law to a point beyond that which we believe to have been reached by equity, and beyond any to which our statutes dealing with kindred subjects ever have seen fit to go. It will be seen that we put our decision not upon the impolicy of admitting such a power, but on the ground that it would be too great a step of judicial legislation to be justified by the necessities of the case . . .

Holdsworth's English Law

25 *Law Quarterly Review* 412 (1909)

. . . If the development of ideas and their struggle for life are the interests of the day, the interest of the future, the final and most important question in the law is that of their worth. I mean their worth in a more far-reaching sense than that of expressing the *de facto* will of the community for the time. On this as yet no one has much to say. To answer it we should have in the first place to establish the ideals upon which our judgments of worth depend; and the statement of such ideals by different classes would differ, at least in form. But suppose that we had agreed that the end of law was, for instance, the survival of a certain type of man, still we should have made very little way toward the founding of a scientific code. Statistics would leave the effect of the criminal law open to doubt. Who can prove that the doctrine of master and servant, or the theory of consideration, helps to attain the ideal assumed? The attitude of the state toward marriage and divorce is governed more by church and tradition than by facts. Wherever we turn we find that what are called good laws are apt to be called so because men see that they promote a result that they fancy desirable, and do not see the bill that has to be paid in reactions that are relatively obscure. One fancies that one could invent a different code under which men would have been as well off as they are now, if they had happened to adopt it. But that *if* is a very great one. The tree has grown as we know it. The practical question is what is to be the next organic step. No doubt the history of the law encourages scepticism when one sees how a rule or a doctrine has grown up, or when one notices the *naïveté* with which social prejudices are taken for eternal principles. But it also leads to an unconvinced conservatism. For it points out that almost the only thing that can be assumed as certainly to be wished is that men should know the rules by which the game will be played. Doubt as to the value of some of those rules is no sufficient reason why they should not be followed by the courts. Legislation gives notice at least if it makes a change. And after all, those of us who believe with Mr. Lester Ward, the sociologist, in the superiority of the artificial to the natural may see in what has been done some ground for believing that mankind yet may take its own destiny consciously and intelligently in hand.

Mr. Holdsworth is telling us a profoundly interesting story. It is one of the most important chapters in the greatest human document—the tale of what men have most believed and most wanted. It is told with learning and scientific instinct, and the book is to be recommended equally to philosophers who can understand it and to practical students of the law. Readers of M. Tarde* will see that author's laws of imitation illustrated by the most striking example, and if they doubt how far it can be said that the principles of any system are eternal, will realize that imitation of the past, until we have a clear reason for change, no more needs justification than appetite. It is a form of the inevitable to be accepted until we have a clear vision of what different thing we want.

John Marshall

In Answer to a Motion That the Court Adjourn, on February 4, 1901, the One Hundredth Anniversary of the Day on Which Marshall Took His Seat as Chief Justice.

S 87

As we walk down Court Street [Boston] in the midst of a jostling crowd, intent like us upon today and its affairs, our eyes are like to fall upon the small, dark building that stands at the head of State Street, and, like an ominous reef, divides the stream of business in its course to the gray cliffs that tower beyond. And, whoever we may be, we may chance to

*Gabriel de Tarde, nineteenth-century French sociologist.—Ed.

pause and forget our hurry for a moment, as we remember that the first waves that foretold the coming storm of the Revolution broke around that reef. But, if we are lawyers, our memories and our reverence grow more profound. In the old State House, we remember, James Otis argued the case of the writs of assistance, and in that argument laid one of the foundations for American constitutional law. Just as that little building is not diminished, but rather is enhanced and glorified, by the vast structures which somehow it turns into a background, so the beginnings of our national life, whether in battle or in law, lose none of their greatness by contrast with all the mighty things of later date, beside which, by every law of number and measure, they ought to seem so small. To us who took part in the Civil War, the greatest battle of the Revolution seems little more than a reconnoissance in force, and Lexington and Concord were mere skirmishes that would not find mention in the newspapers. Yet veterans who have known battle on a modern scale are not less aware of the spiritual significance of those little fights, I venture to say, than the enlightened children of commerce who tell us that soon war is to be no more.

If I were to think of John Marshall simply by number and measure in the abstract, I might hesitate in my superlatives, just as I should hesitate over the battle of the Brandywine if I thought of it apart from its place in the line of historic cause. But such thinking is empty in the same proportion that it is abstract. It is most idle to take a man apart from the circumstances which, in fact, were his. To be sure, it is easier in fancy to separate a person from his riches than from his character. But it is just as futile. Remove a square inch of mucous membrane, and the tenor will sing no more. Remove a little cube from the brain, and the orator will be speechless; or another, and the brave, generous and profound spirit becomes a timid and querulous trifler. A great man represents a great ganglion in the nerves of society, or, to vary the figure, a strategic point in the campaign of history, and part of his greatness consists in his being *there*. I no more can separate John Marshall from the fortunate circumstance that the appointment of Chief Justice fell to John Adams, instead of to Jefferson a month later, and so gave it to a Federalist and loose constructionist to start the working of the Constitution, than I can separate the black line through which he sent his electric fire at Fort Wagner from Colonel Shaw. When we celebrate Marshall we celebrate at the same time and indivisibly the inevitable fact that the oneness of the nation and the supremacy of the national Constitution were declared to govern the dealings of man with man by the judgments and decrees of the most august of courts.

I do not mean, of course, that personal estimates are useless or teach us nothing. No doubt today there will be heard from able and competent persons such estimates of Marshall. But I will not trench upon their field of work. It would be out of place when I am called on only to express the answer to a motion addressed to the court and when many of those who are here are to listen this afternoon to the accomplished teacher who has had every occasion to make a personal study of the judge, and again this evening to a gentleman who shares by birth the traditions of the man. My own impressions are only those that I have gathered in the common course of legal education and practice. In them I am conscious, perhaps, of some little revolt from our purely local or national estimates, and of a wish to see things and people judged by more cosmopolitan standards. A man is bound to be parochial in his practice—to give his life, and if necessary his death, for the place where he has his roots. But his thinking should be cosmopolitan and detached. He should be able to criticise what he reveres and loves.

The Federalist, when I read it many years ago, seemed to me a truly original and wonderful production for the time. I do not trust even that judgment unrevised when I remember that the Federalist and its authors struck a distinguished English friend of mine as finite; and I should feel a greater doubt whether, after Hamilton and the Constitution itself, Marshall's work proved more than a strong intellect, a good style, personal ascendancy in his court, courage, justice and the convictions of his party. My keenest interest is excited, not by what are called great questions and great cases, but by little decisions which the common run of selectors would pass by because they did not deal with the Constitution or a telephone company, yet which have in them the germ of some wider theory, and therefore of some profound interstitial change in the very tissue of the law. The men whom I should be tempted to commemorate would be the originators of transforming thought. They often are half obscure, because what the world pays for is judgment, not the original mind.

But what I have said does not mean that I shall join in this celebration or in granting the motion before the court in any half-hearted way. Not only do I recur to what I said in the beginning, and remembering that you cannot separate a man from his place, remember also that there fell to Marshall perhaps the greatest place that ever was filled by a judge; but when I consider his might, his justice, and his wisdom, I do fully believe that if American law were to be represented by a single figure, sceptic and worshipper alike would agree without dispute that the figure could be but one alone, and that one John Marshall.

A few words more and I have done. We live by symbols, and what shall be symbolized by any image of the sight depends upon the mind of him who sees it. The setting aside of this day in honor of a great judge may stand to a Virginian for the glory of his glorious state; to a patriot for the fact that time has been on Marshall's side, and that the theory for which Hamilton argued, and he decided, and Webster spoke, and Grant fought, and Lincoln died, is now our cornerstone. To the more abstract but farther-reaching contemplation of the lawyer, it stands for the rise of a new body of jurisprudence, by which guiding principles are raised above the reach of statute and state, and judges are entrusted with a solemn and hitherto unheard-of authority and duty. To one who lives in what may seem to him a solitude of thought, this day—as it marks the triumph of a man whom some Presidents of his time bade carry out his judgments as he could—this day marks the fact that all thought is social, is on its way to action; that, to borrow the expression of a French writer, every idea tends to become first a catechism and then a code; and that according to its worth his unhelped meditation may one day mount a throne, and without armies, or even with them, may shoot across the world the electric despotism of an unresisted power. It is all a symbol, if you like, but so is the flag. The flag is but a bit of bunting to one who insists on prose. Yet, thanks to Marshall and to the men of his generation—and for this above all we celebrate him and them—its red is our life-blood, its stars our world, its blue our heaven. It owns our land. At will it throws away our lives.

Walbridge Abner Field

Chief Justice of the Supreme Judicial Court of Massachusetts.

Answer to Resolutions of the Bar, Boston, November 25, 1899.

S 75

Gentlemen of the Bar:

It is not easy to speak for the bench upon an event like that for which we meet. We judges are brought together so closely, I sat by the side of the late Chief Justice so long—it was nearly seventeen years—that separation has in it something too intimate for speech. Long association makes friendship, as it makes property and belief, a part of our being. When it is wrenched from us, roots are torn and broken that bleed like veins. Nevertheless we must not be silent when we are called to honor the memory of a remarkable man, although he was a brother. We must sink the private in the public loss.

Chief Justice Field was remarkable and was remarked from a very early age. His extraordinary reputation in his college was a prophecy of his later career. It may happen that a man is first scholar in his class, or

whatever may be the modern equivalent of that now vanished distinction, solely by memory, powers of acquisition, and a certain docility of
mind that too readily submits to direction and leadership. It may be,
although I doubt it, that the chances are that some one in the field will
outrun the favorite in the long race. It sometimes occurs that young
men discount their future and exhaust their life in what, after all, is
only preparation and not an end. But the presence of one great faculty
does not argue the absence of others. The chances are that a man who
leads in college will be a leader in after life. The chances are that the
powers which carry a man to the front upon the prepared track will be
accompanied by what is needed to give him at least an honorable place
in the great gallop across the world. The usual happened with Chief
Justice Field. He was always an important man, at the bar as well as later
on the bench. It is a pleasure to me to remember that the first case
which I ever had of my own was tried in the Superior Court before
Judge Lord, whom afterwards I succeeded on this bench, and was argued before this court on the other side by Mr. Field. It is a pleasure to
remember kind words and pleasant relations at that time. But of course
those recollections are more or less swamped in those of a long intercourse here.

His mind was a very peculiar one. In the earlier days of my listening
to him in consultation he seemed to me to think aloud, perhaps too
much so, and to be unable to pass without mention the side suggestions
which pressed in upon him in exuberant abundance. This very abundance made his work much harder to him. It was hard for him to neglect the possibilities of a side alley, however likely it might be to turn
out a *cul-de-sac*. He wanted to know where it led before he passed it by. If
we had eternity ahead this would be right and even necessary. But as life
has but a short number of working hours, we have to choose at our peril; we have to act on the presumptions afforded by our present knowledge as to what paths are most likely to lead to desired goals. If we
investigate Mohammedanism, or Spiritualism, or whether Bacon wrote
Shakespeare, we have so much less time for philosophy, or church, or
literature at large. So in deciding a question of law, one has to consider
this element of time. One has to try to strike the jugular and let the rest
go. I think that the Chief Justice did a vast deal of work which never
appeared, in thus satisfying his conscience and in his unwillingness to
risk leaving something out. You see the same characteristic in the statements of fact in his judgments. There is an elaborateness of detail about
them which illustrates the tendency of his mind. If this exuberance was
a fault, it was diminished as time went on. Without abating his care he
gradually learned to omit.

Outside the law his fertility of mind made him a most interesting and delightful companion. He talked little about people, and never maliciously, but in the field of general ideas he roamed with freedom. He was discursive, humorous, sceptical by temperament, yet having convictions which gave steadiness to his thought. He had an extraordinary gift of repartee, and I used to delight in giving him opportunities to exercise it at my expense, for his answers were sure to be amusing and they never stung . . .

I have said that, although of sceptical temperament, he had convictions. The fact led to a curious result in his way of regarding the authority of decided cases. I am not sure how he would have expressed it, or indeed whether the notion was articulate in his mind, but he seemed to me to conceive of the law as ideally, at least, embodying absolute right. If a case appeared to him to run against some general principle which he thought was or ought to be a part of the law, the fact that it was decided seemed to make but little impression on his mind. He did not hesitate to throw doubt upon it or to disregard it. I do not think that he would have been content to regard the law as an empirical product of history, the particular forms of which are venerable mainly because they are—because in fact these and not something else which would seem to be as good or better if only the world were accustomed to it are what our part of the world has come out on. Perhaps it was the same point of view that made him more ready than some judges to hold rather a tight rein upon the actual practices of the community. If a contract struck him as aiming at a gambling result, he would not enforce it, however much his refusal might encounter the daily practice of a whole board of brokers. He had his views of policy, and he did not doubt that the law agreed with him.

It was part of the same general habit of mind that he should be free to the point of innovation in applying convenient analogies to new cases. He sometimes seemed to me to go not only beyond but against tradition in his wish to render more perfect justice. He was less interested in the embryology of the law as an object of abstract speculation, or in the logical outcome of precedent, than he was in making sure that every interest should be represented before the court, and in extending useful remedies—a good fault, if it be a fault at all. He had an accomplished knowledge of the present state of the law, and a good deal of curious and useful information about our local history, for which I have envied him often . . .

The personal characteristics which I have mentioned went no further than to mark a person. They were no more than what every strong man has and must have. They were governed by excellent sense, moderation, and insight. He sometimes was so possessed by an idea, or special aspect of a case, as to be for a time inaccessible to suggestion until the fire had burned itself out; but in a little while, in two or three days if not the same day, he fully grasped and did justice to the other view. As a rule he was very quick and took an idea in a flash.

Men carry their signatures upon their persons, although they may not always be visible at the first glance. If you had looked casually at the Chief Justice you might not have seen more than a strong man like others. But to a more attentive watch there came out a high intellectual radiance that was all his own. I have caught myself over and over again staring with delight upon his profile as I sat beside him, and admiring the fine keenness of his thought-absorbed gaze.

He had the heroic temper. This is the last, the greatest, thing that I can say. I used to notice, even in little matters, that he always looked his own conduct in the face and did not equivocate, apologize, or disguise. I could not notice, because it was too hidden, but I know, that he did his work in the same great way. It is hard to realize or believe what sufferings he went through long before the end. But if he had walked the floor all night in poignant pain, when he appeared in the morning he gave no sign of it unless it may be by silence. He took his work hard, as I have intimated, but he never said so, and he went down fighting, like a brave man as he was.

Gentlemen, for all of us this is a solemn moment. For me it is almost oppressively solemn. It would be serious enough were I only to remember the line of great, gifted, and good men whose place I have been called on to fill. But it is sadly, yes, awfully solemn, when I remember that with our beloved chief vanishes the last of those who were upon the bench when I took my seat, and so realize the swift, monotonous iteration of death. We sometimes wonder at the interest of mankind in platitudes. It is because truths realized are truths rediscovered, and each of us with advancing years realizes in his own experience what he always has admitted but never before has felt. The careless boy admits that life is short, but he feels that a term in college, a summer vacation, a day, is long. We gray-haired men hear in our ears the roar of the cataract and know that we are very near. The cry of personal anguish is almost drowned by the resounding echo of universal fate. It has become easier for us to imagine even the time when the cataract will be still, the race of men will be no more, and the great silence shall be supreme. What then may be the value of our judgments of significance and worth I know not. But I do firmly believe that if those judgments are not, as they may be, themselves the *flammantia moenia mundi,* bounds and governance of all being, it is only because they are swallowed up and dissolved in something unimaginable and greater out of which they emerged. Our last word about the unfathomable universe must be in terms of thought. If we believe that anything is, we must believe in that, because we can go no further. We may accept its canons even while we admit that we do not know that we know the truth of truth. Accepting them, we accept our destiny to work, to fight, to die for ideal aims. At the grave of a hero who has done these things we end not with sorrow at the inevitable loss, but with the contagion of his courage; and with a kind of desperate joy we go back to the fight.

William Allen

Associate Justice of the Supreme Judicial Court of Massachusetts.
Answer to Resolutions of the Bar, Greenfield, September 15, 1891.
S 52

. . . He seemed to me a typical New Englander, both in character and in ways of thinking; a characteristic product of one of those inland towns which have been our glory—centers large enough to have a society and a culture of their own, and, formerly at least, remote enough to have local traditions, and local rather than cosmopolitan standards and responsibilities. As with others whom I have known that were brought up in similar surroundings, his Yankee caution and sound judgment were leavened with a touch of enthusiasm capable of becoming radical at moments, and his cultivation had destroyed rather than fostered his respect for the old merely as such. He was very kind. He was always perfectly considerate and reasonable, as well as warm of feeling. In ill health as in good he took his share of work without a word or hint of what it cost him until he died. He had the subtlety of a Calvinist theologian, and as sound a training in the common law as was to be found in Massachusetts; but he was saved from becoming over technical by his good sense, his humanitarian turn, and the occasional slight touch of radicalism which I have noted. I never felt quite sure that nothing had been overlooked in a statement of facts, until his eye had scrutinized it. In discussion, if you did not agree with him, you always reached an exact issue, and escape in generalities was impossible. I know few qualities which seem to me more desirable in a judge of a court of last resort than this accuracy of thought, and the habit of keeping one's eye on the things for which words stand. Many men, especially as they grow older, resent attempts to push analysis beyond consecrated phrases, or to formulate anew. Such attempts disturb the intellectual rest for which we long. Our ideal is repose, perhaps because our destiny is effort, just as the eye sees green after gazing at the sun. Judge Allen had none of this weakness, but went on without rest to the end.

Great places make great men. The electric current of large affairs turns even common mould to diamond, and traditions of ancient honor impart something of their dignity to those who inherit them. No man of any loftiness of soul could be long a Justice of this court without rising to his full height. But our dead brother seemed to me too modest to be ambitious for reputation, and to regard his place mainly as an opportunity and a duty. He would have been most pleased, too, I dare say, to slip from it and from life, when his hour came, without remark. He would have preferred not to be celebrated with guns and bells and pealing requiems, the flutter of flags and gleam of steel in the streets, and all the pomp which properly is spent on those who have held power in their right hand . . . I too am content for him that it should be so, if this neglect of outward show means, even for a chosen few, that their eyes have taken a wider sweep, and have seen that such symbols do not express the vast and shadowy command which a thinker holds. Our prevailing ideals are somewhat coarse. Comparatively few imaginations are educated to aspire beyond money and the immediate forms of power. I have no doubt that vulgar conceptions of life at the top are one of the causes of discontent at the bottom of society. Unless we are to accept decadence as the necessary end of civilization, we should be grateful to all men like William Allen, whose ambition, if it can be called so, looks only to remote and mediated command; who do not ask to say to any one, Go, and he goeth, so long as in truthful imagination they wield, according to their degree, that most subtle and intoxicating authority which controls the future from within by shaping the thoughts and speech of a later time.

Such men are to be honored, not by regiments moving with high heads to martial music, but by a few others, lonely as themselves, walking apart in meditative silence, and dreaming in their turn the dream of spiritual reign.

To Frederick Pollock

August 27, 1883

Dear Pollock,

I have been so hard at work that I have neglected correspondence and everything but business until I got to this languid spot where I am apt to spend my vacations by the sound of the polyphloesbian,* the

*Poluphloisbos is a Homeric epithet for the sea, meaning "very noisy." The usual Anglicization is "polyphloesboean."—Ed.

mosquito and the crow. Here I have been for a month however and it is high time that I should remind you of myself. A week from today I shall again be in the whirl. Well, I like my work far more than I dreamed beforehand. The experience is most varied—very different from that one gets at the bar—and I am satisfied most valuable for an all round view of the law. I have written a lot of opinions of the full court, sat alone for some time in equity, disposed of a long divorce list and shall hold *nisi prius** soon after I leave here.

One sees too a good deal of human nature, and I find that I am interested all the time. We are very hard worked and some of the older judges affirm that no one can do all the work without breaking down. I have not yet made up my mind—at all events it is more interesting than if we had less to do. The legislature has just given equity jurisdiction to the superior court which we hope will relieve us somewhat by throwing a good many things into that court in the first instance subject to an appeal to us. I hope you will keep me informed of what is occupying your active mind. You do so many things that I never know whether next to expect a drama, a lawbook, a symphony or a system of philosophy. I hope and believe that you are happy in your new place. It must, I know by experience, be delightful and stimulating to expound to a lot of intelligent young men old enough to have serious opinions . . .

To Harold Laski

June 4, 1920

Dear Laski,

Your letter comes to me just as I return from a wearing conference of the judges—a moment when one is cynical as to one's fellow men. I had last Monday the recrudescence of an old problem. Whether to dissent as to the judge's salaries being included in the income tax was the occasion and the problem whether to allow other considerations than those of the detached intellect to count. The subject didn't interest me particularly—I wasn't at all in love with what I had written and I hadn't got the blood of controversy in my neck. In fact I thought that Vandevanter put his side rather nobly. So when another (not he) suggested that I helped to make the position of the majority embarrassing—as deciding in their own interest, I hesitated. But I reflected that if my opinion were the unpopular one I should be but a poor creature if I held back—and that philosophically the reasons were the same when I was on the other side. And anyhow you get lost in morasses if you think of anything except the question, the answer, and whether the public interest is that both sides should be stated . . .

*I.e., shall be sitting as a trial judge.—Ed.

December 17, 1925

My dear Laski,

. . . As to your doctors and judges on uncontrollable impulse I think the short answer is that the law establishes certain minima of social conduct that a man must conform to at his peril. Of course as I said in my book [*The Common Law*] it bears most hardly on those least prepared for it, but that is what it is for. I am entirely impatient of any but broad distinctions. Otherwise we are lost in the maze of determinism. If I were having a philosophical talk with a man I was going to have hanged (or electrocuted) I should say, I don't doubt that your act was inevitable for you but to make it more avoidable by others we propose to sacrifice you to the common good. You may regard yourself as a soldier dying for your country if you like. But the law must keep its promises. I fear that the touch of sentiment that I notice in your political writing will be revolted at this, but personally I feel neither doubt nor scruple . . .

We adjourned on Monday for two or three weeks and my work is done except some further study on a postponed case. I have had real intellectual pleasure with my cases this term. They have been sufficiently interesting and to write them shortly and compactly with a hint at general theory when possible is good sport. The Chief called me up by telephone to know if a case that he proposed to assign to me would be too troublesome. I told him that if he spared me in that way I ought to leave. He gave me the case and I polished it off in short metre. I always say, and probably have said to you, there is no such thing as a hard case. There may be bothers from complex facts but when you have mastered them one question of law is much like another . . .

To Frederick Pollock

February 24, 1923

Dear Pollock,

Wonderful man to know what is mail day. I have lived steadily on the pre-war tradition that a mail boat sails on Saturday. Whether it does or not I have no information since about 1914 . . . I am just back from a conference. We now have a full court again with Sutherland, Butler, and Sanford *vice* Clarke, Day and Pitney. I am not sure that it should not be Pitney & Day. Mrs. Pitney telephoned to me to call on her husband tomorrow. I dread it, as I believe he is emotional and does not realize how seriously ill he is. When he first came on the bench he used to get on my nerves, as he talked too much from the bench and in conference, but he improved in that and I came to appreciate his great faithfulness to duty, his industry and his candor. He had not wings and was not a thunderbolt, but he was a very honest hard working judge and a useful critic. The new men all impress me favorably though I don't expect to be astonished. The meetings are perhaps pleasanter than I ever have known them—thanks largely to the C.J. [William Howard Taft] but also to the disappearance of men with the habit of some of our older generation, that regarded a difference of opinion as a cockfight and often left a good deal to be desired in point of manners.

I think Pound's book *Interpretations of Legal History* the best thing I have read of his—a larger masterly panoramic view of the whole show. I thought at first that he overticketed and pigeonholed, but it helps clearness and remembering and I am inclined only to praise. The eminent in the law have been gathering here, yearning for the upward and onward—specifically the restatement of the law, I presume by members of their body.* On earnest exhortation I showed up for a few minutes yesterday to the extent of looking in while Root was delivering a somewhat flamboyant address; but I am an aged sceptic and was pleased at Brandeis's remark, "Why I am restating the law every day."

In a few minutes I expect two or three of the pundits to look in on me—Wigmore with Kocourek, Learned Hand, J. (a good U.S. District Judge, whom I should like to see on our bench), and I know not if anyone else. I think of nothing else of momentary interest except that I have been listening in the evenings to two or three thrillers, the last, *Bull Dog Drummond.* Wilkie Collins was right that what men want is a story. Also on Sunday I read, I believe for the first time (bar abridgments for boys), *Gulliver's Travels.* I think that there, as in *Polite Conversation,* you see incipient insanity in the intensity of his insistence on the baseness as on the banality of man.

To Harold Laski

November 10, 1923

Dear Laski,

Another ripper from you. Would that I had matters of equal interest to tell. But I have only a few items. After all I succumbed and have written a short dissent in a case which still hangs fire. I do not expect to convince anyone as it is rather a statement of my convictions than an argument, although it indicate my grounds. Brandeis is with me, but I had written a note to him saying that I did not intend to write when the opinion came and stirred my fighting blood. Not of course that I refer

*The American Law Institute, a prestigious legal society still in existence, promulgated a series of "restatements," in effect unofficial codifications, of common law subjects such as torts and contracts.—Ed.

to that, which I think is the worst possible form—but I think it will be gathered that I don't agree with it. I dislike even the traditional "Holmes *Dissenting.*" We are giving our views on a question of law, not fighting with another cock . . .

January 16, 1918

Dear Laski,

. . . What you say about the form of Brandeis's opinions had been remarked on by me to him before you wrote, if you refer to the form in a strict sense—the putting in of headings and footnotes—and on one occasion I told him that I thought he was letting partisanship disturb his judicial attitude. I am frank with him because I value him and think he brings many admirable qualifications to his work. In one case when he wrote a long essay on the development of employers' liability I told him that I thought it out of place and irrelevant to the only question: whether Congress had dealt with the matter so far as to exclude state action . . .

The Profession of the Law

Conclusion of a Lecture Delivered to Undergraduates of Harvard University, February 17, 1886.

S 22

And now, perhaps, I ought to have done. But I know that some spirit of fire will feel that his main question has not been answered. He will ask, What is all this to my soul? You do not bid me sell my birthright for a mess of pottage; what have you said to show that I can reach my own spiritual possibilities through such a door as this? How can the laborious study of a dry and technical system, the greedy watch for clients and practice of shopkeepers' arts, the mannerless conflicts over often sordid interests, make out a life? Gentlemen, I admit at once that these questions are not futile, that they may prove unanswerble, that they have often seemed to me unanswerable. And yet I believe there is an answer. They are the same questions that meet you in any form of practical life. If a man has the soul of Sancho Panza, the world to him will be Sancho Panza's world; but if he has the soul of an idealist, he will make—I do not say find—his world ideal. Of course, the law is not the place for the artist or the poet. The law is the calling of thinkers. But to those who believe with me that not the least godlike of man's activities is

the large survey of causes, that to know is not less than to feel, I say—
and I say no longer with any doubt—that a man may live greatly in the
law as well as elsewhere; that there as well as elsewhere his thought may
find its unity in an infinite perspective; that there as well as elsewhere
he may wreak himself upon life, may drink the bitter cup of heroism,
may wear his heart out after the unattainable. All that life offers any
man from which to start his thinking or his striving is a fact. And if this
universe is one universe, if it is so far thinkable that you can pass in reason from one part of it to another, it does not matter very much what
that fact is. For every fact leads to every other by the path of the air.
Only men do not yet see how, always. And your business as thinkers is to
make plainer the way from some thing to the whole of things; to show
the rational connection between your fact and the frame of the universe. If your subject is law, the roads are plain to anthropology, the
science of man, to political economy, the theory of legislation, ethics,
and thus by several paths to your final view of life. It would be equally
true of any subject. The only difference is in the ease of seeing the way.
To be master of any branch of knowledge, you must master those which
lie next to it; and thus to know anything you must know all.

Perhaps I speak too much the language of intellectual ambition. I
cannot but think that the scope for intellectual, as for physical adventure, is narrowing. I look for a future in which the ideal will be content
and dignified acceptance of life, rather than aspiration and the passion
for achievement. I see already that surveys and railroads have set limits
to our intellectual wildernesses—that the lion and the bison are disap-
pearing from them, as from Africa and the no longer boundless West.
But that undelightful day which I anticipate has not yet come. The human race has not changed, I imagine, so much between my generation
and yours but that you still have the barbaric thirst for conquest, and
there is still something left to conquer. There are fields still open for
occupation in the law, and there are roads from them that will lead you
where you will.

But do not think I am pointing you to flowery paths and beds of
roses—to a place where brilliant results attend your work, which shall
be at once easy and new. No result is easy which is worth having. Your
education begins when what is called your education is over—when
you no longer are stringing together the pregnant thoughts, the "jewels
five words long," which great men have given their lives to cut from the
raw material, but have begun yourselves to work upon the raw material
for results which you do not see, cannot predict, and which may be long
in coming—when you take the fact which life offers you for your appointed task. No man has earned the right to intellectual ambition until

he has learned to lay his course by a star which he has never seen—to dig by the divining rod for springs which he may never reach. In saying this, I point to that which will make your study heroic. For I say to you in all sadness of conviction that to think great thoughts you must be heroes as well as idealists. Only when you have worked alone—when you have felt around you a black gulf of solitude more isolating than that which surrounds the dying man, and in hope and in despair have trusted to your own unshaken will—then only will you have achieved. Thus only can you gain the secret isolated joy of the thinker, who knows that, a hundred years after he is dead and forgotten, men who never heard of him will be moving to the measure of his thought—the subtle rapture of a postponed power, which the world knows not because it has no external trappings, but which to his prophetic vision is more real than that which commands an army. And if this joy should not be yours, still it is only thus that you can know that you have done what it lay in you to do—can say that you have lived, and be ready for the end.

Sidney Bartlett

Answer to Resolutions of the Bar, Boston, March 23, 1889

S 41

Gentlemen of the Bar:

. . . I do not share the regrets which some are inclined to feel that Mr. Bartlett confined himself strictly to his profession. I think that he was wise in his ambition, and that his life served public ends. It seems to me that we are apt to take short-sighted views of what constitutes power, and of how a man may serve his fellows. The external and immediate result of an advocate's work is but to win or lose a case. But remotely what the lawyer does is to establish, develop, or illuminate rules which are to govern the conduct of men for centuries; to set in motion principles and influences which shape the thought and action of generations which know not by whose command they move. The man of action has the present, but the thinker controls the future; his is the most subtle, the most far-reaching power. His ambition is the vastest as it is the most ideal.

It seems to me further that the rule for serving our fellow men, and, so far as we may speculate or hope upon that awful theme, the rule for fulfilling the mysterious ends of the universe—it seems to me that the beginning of self-sacrifice and of holiness—is to do one's task with one's might. If we do that, I think we find that our motives take care of themselves. We find that what may have been begun as a means becomes an end in itself; that self-seeking is forgotten in labors which are the best contribution that we can make to mankind; that our personality is swallowed up in working to ends outside ourselves. I, for one, am glad that our famous leader never sought the more obvious forms of power or public service, and was content to remain to the close Mr. Bartlett of the Suffolk Bar.

When a great tree falls, we are surprised to see how meagre the landscape seems without it. So when a great man dies. We may not have been intimate with him; it is enough that he was within our view; when he is gone, life seems thinner and less interesting. More than that, just as, when the fire swept the ground of our city to the water's edge, we were surprised to see close at hand the ocean, which before was hidden from our vision and our thoughts, the death of this powerful bulwark against time lays open for a moment to our gaze the horizon into which we are to sail so soon. We are another generation. Our tasks are new. We shall carry different freight. The happiest of us hardly can hope for a destiny so complete and fortunate as that which has just been fulfilled. We shall be fortunate enough if we shall have learned to look into the face of fate and the unknown with a smile like his.

The Law

Suffolk Bar Association Dinner, February 5, 1885

S 16

. . . If we are to speak of the law as our mistress, we who are here know that she is a mistress only to be wooed with sustained and lonely passion—only to be won by straining all the faculties by which man is likest to a god. Those who, having begun the pursuit, turn away uncharmed, do so either because they have not been vouchsafed the sight of her divine figure, or because they have not the heart for so great a struggle. To the lover of the law, how small a thing seem the novelist's tales of the loves and fates of Daphnis and Chloë! How pale a phantom even the Circe of poetry, transforming mankind with intoxicating dreams of fiery ether, and the foam of summer seas, and glowing greensward, and the white arms of women! For him no less a history will suffice than that of the moral life of his race. For him every text that he deciphers, every doubt that he resolves, adds a new feature to the unfolding panorama of man's destiny upon this earth. Nor will his task be done until, by the farthest stretch of human imagination, he has seen as with his eyes the birth and growth of society, and by the farthest stretch of reason he has understood the philosophy of its being. When I think thus of the law, I see a princess mightier than she who once wrought at Bayeux, eternally weaving into her web dim figures of the ever-lengthening past—figures too dim to be noticed by the idle, too symbolic to be interpreted except by her pupils, but to the discerning eye disclosing every painful step and every world-shaking contest by which mankind has worked and fought its way from savage isolation to organic social life.

But we who are here know the Law even better in another aspect. We see her daily, not as anthropologists, not as students and philosophers, but as actors in a drama of which she is the providence and overruling power. When I think of the Law as we know her in the courthouse and the market, she seems to me a woman sitting by the wayside, beneath whose overshadowing hood every man shall see the countenance of his deserts or needs. The timid and overborne gain heart from her protecting smile. Fair combatants, manfully standing to their rights, see her keeping the lists with the stern and discriminating eye of even justice. The wretch who has defied her most sacred commands, and has thought to creep through ways where she was not, finds that his path ends with her, and beholds beneath her hood the inexorable face of death.

Gentlemen, I shall say no more. This is not the moment for disquisitions. But when for the first time I was called to speak on such an occasion as this, the only thought that could come into my mind, the only feeling that could fill my heart, the only words that could spring to my lips, were a hymn to her in whose name we are met here tonight—to our mistress, the Law.

It long has seemed to me a striking circumstance, that the ablest of the agitators for codification, Sir James [Fitzjames] Stephen, and the originator of the present mode of teaching, Mr. Langdell,* start from the same premises to reach seemingly opposite conclusions. The number of legal principles is small, says in effect Sir James Stephen, therefore codify them; the number of legal principles is small, says Mr. Langdell, therefore they may be taught through the cases which have developed and established them. Well, I think there is much force in Sir James' Stephen's argument, if you can find competent men and get them to undertake the task; and at any rate I am not now going to express an opinion that he is wrong. But I am certain from my own experience that Mr. Langdell is right; I am certain that when your object is not to make a bouquet of the law for the public, nor to prune and graft it by legislation, but to plant its roots where they will grow, in minds devoted henceforth to that one end, there is no way to be compared to Mr.

*Dean Christopher Columbus Langdell of the Harvard Law School.—Ed.

Langdell's way. Why, look at it simply in the light of human nature. Does not a man remember a concrete instance more vividly than a general principle? And is not a principle more exactly and intimately grasped as the unexpressed major premise of the half-dozen examples which mark its extent and its limits than it can be in any abstract form of words? Expressed or unexpressed, is it not better known when you have studied its embryology and the lines of its growth than when you merely see it lying dead before you on the printed page? . . .

I sometimes hear a wish expressed by the impatient, that the teaching here should be more practical. I remember that a very wise and able man said to a friend of mine when he was beginning his professional life, "Don't know too much law," and I think we all can imagine cases where the warning would be useful. But a far more useful thing is what was said to me as a student by one no less wise and able—afterwards my partner and always my friend—when I was talking as young men do about seeing practice, and all the other things which seemed practical to my inexperience, "The business of a lawyer is to know law." The Professors of this Law School [Harvard] mean to make their students know law. They think the most practical teaching is that which takes their students to the bottom of what they seek to know. They therefore mean to make them master the common law and equity as working systems, and think that when that is accomplished they will have no trouble with the improvements of the last half-century. I believe they are entirely right, not only in the end they aim at, but in the way they take to reach that end.

Yes, this School has been, is, and I hope long will be, a centre where great lawyers perfect their achievements, and from which young men, even more inspired by their example than instructed by their teaching, go forth in their turn, not to imitate what their masters have done, but to live their own lives more freely for the ferment imparted to them here. The men trained in this School may not always be the most knowing in the ways of getting on. The noblest of them must often feel that they are committed to lives of proud dependence—the dependence of men who command no factitious aids to success, but rely upon unadvertised knowledge and silent devotion; dependence upon finding an appreciation which they cannot seek, but dependence proud in the conviction that the knowledge to which their lives are consecrated is of things which it concerns the world to know. It is the dependence of abstract thought, of science, of beauty, of poetry and art, of every flower of civilization, upon finding a soil generous enough to support it. If it does not, it must die. But the world needs the flower more than the flower needs life.

I said that a law school ought to teach law in the grand manner; that it had something more to do than simply to teach law. I think we may claim for our School that it has not been wanting in greatness. I once heard a Russian say that in the middle class of Russia there were many specialists; in the upper class there were civilized men. Perhaps in America, for reasons which I have mentioned, we need specialists even more than we do civilized men. Civilized men who are nothing else are a little apt to think that they cannot breathe the American atmosphere. But if a man is a specialist, it is most desirable that he should also be civilized; that he should have laid in the outline of the other sciences, as well as the light and shade of his own; that he should be reasonable, and see things in their proportion. Nay, more, that he should be passionate, as well as reasonable—that he should be able not only to explain, but to feel; that the ardors of intellectual pursuit should be relieved by the charms of art, should be succeeded by the joy of life become an end in itself.

At Harvard College is realized in some degree the palpitating manifoldness of a truly civilized life. Its aspirations are concealed because they are chastened and instructed; but I believe in my soul that they are not the less noble that they are silent. The golden light of the University is not confined to the undergraduate department; it is shed over all the schools. He who has once seen it becomes other than he was, forevermore. I have said that the best part of our education is moral. It is the crowning glory of this Law School that it has kindled in many a heart an inextinguishable fire.

The Use of Law Schools.

Oration Before the Harvard Law School Association,
at Cambridge, November 5, 1886, on the 250th Anniversary
of Harvard University

S 29

. . . A law school does not undertake to teach success. That combination of tact and will which gives a man immediate prominence among his fellows comes from nature, not from instruction; and if it can be helped at all by advice, such advice is not offered here. It might be expected that I should say, by way of natural antithesis, that what a law school does undertake to teach is law. But I am not ready to say even that, without a qualification. It seems to me that nearly all the education which men can get from others is moral, not intellectual. The main part of intellectual education is not the acquisition of facts, but learning how to make facts live. Culture, in the sense of fruitless knowledge, I for one abhor. The mark of a master is that facts which before lay scattered in an inorganic mass, when he shoots through them the magnetic current of his thought, leap into an organic order, and live and bear fruit. But you cannot make a master by teaching. He makes himself by aid of his natural gifts.

Education, other than self-education, lies mainly in the shaping of men's interests and aims. If you convince a man that another way of looking at things is more profound, another form of pleasure more subtile than that to which he has been accustomed—if you make him really see it—the very nature of man is such that he will desire the profounder thought and the subtiler joy. So I say business of a law school is not sufficiently described when you merely say that it is to teach law, or to make lawyers. It is to teach law in the grand manner, and to make great lawyers.

Our country needs such teaching very much. I think we should all agree that the passion for equality has passed far beyond the political or even the social sphere. We are not only unwilling to admit that any class or society is better than that in which we move, but our customary attitude towards every one in authority of any kind is that he is only the lucky recipient of honor or salary above the average, which any average man might as well receive as he. When the effervescence of democratic negation extends its workings beyond the abolition of external distinctions of rank to spiritual things—when the passion for equality is not content with founding social intercourse upon universal human sympathy, and a community of interests in which all may share, but attacks the lines of Nature which establish orders and degrees among the souls of men—they are not only wrong, but ignobly wrong. Modesty and reverence are no less virtues of freemen than the democratic feeling which will submit neither to arrogance nor to servility.

To inculcate those virtues, to correct the ignoble excess of a noble feeling to which I have referred, I know of no teachers so powerful and persuasive as the little army of specialists. They carry no banners, they beat no drums; but where they are, men learn that bustle and push are not the equals of quiet genius and serene mastery. They compel others who need their help or who are enlightened by their teaching, to obedience and respect. They set the example themselves; for they furnish in the intellectual world a perfect type of the union of democracy with discipline. They bow to no one who seeks to impose his authority by foreign aid; they hold that science like courage is never beyond the necessity of proof, but must always be ready to prove itself against all challengers. But to one who has shown himself a master, they pay the proud reverence of men who know what valiant combat means, and who reserve the right of combat against their leader even, if he should seem to waver in the service of Truth, their only queen.

In the army of which I speak, the lawyers are not the least important corps. For all lawyers are specialists. Not in the narrow sense in which we sometimes use the word in the profession—of persons who confine themselves to a particular branch of practice, such as conveyancing or patents—but specialists who have taken all law to be their province; specialists because they have undertaken to master a special branch of human knowledge—a branch, I may add, which is more immediately connected with all the highest interests of man than any other which deals with practical affairs.

Lawyers, too, were among the first specialists to be needed and to appear in America. And I believe it would be hard to exaggerate the goodness of their influence in favor of sane and orderly thinking. But lawyers feel the spirit of the times like other people. They, like others, are forever trying to discover cheap and agreeable substitutes for real things. I fear that the bar has done its full share to exalt that most hateful of American words and ideals, "smartness," as against dignity of moral feeling and profundity of knowledge. It is from within the bar, not from outside, that I have heard the new gospel that learning is out of date, and that the man for the times is no longer the thinker and the scholar, but the smart man, unencumbered with other artillery than the latest edition of the Digest and the latest revision of the Statutes.

The aim of a law school should be, the aim of the Harvard Law School has been, not to make men smart, but to make them wise in their calling—to start them on a road which will lead them to the abode of the masters. A law school should be at once the workshop and the nursery of specialists in the sense which I have explained. It should obtain for teachers men in each generation who are producing the best work of that generation. Teaching should not stop, but rather should foster, production. The "enthusiasm of the lecture-room," the contagious interest of companionship, should make the students partners in their teachers' work. The ferment of genius in its creative moment is quickly imparted. If a man is great, he makes others believe in greatness; he makes them incapable of mean ideals and easy self-satisfaction. His pupils will accept no substitute for realities; but at the same time they learn that the only coin with which realities can be bought is Life.

Our School has been such a workshop and such a nursery as I describe. What men it has turned out I have hinted already, and do not need to say; what works it has produced is known to all the world . . . There are plenty of men nowadays of not a hundredth part of Story's power who could write as good statements of the law as his, or better.* And when some mediocre fluent book has been printed, how often have we heard it proclaimed, "Lo, here is a greater than Story!" But if you consider the state of legal literature when Story began to write, and from what wells of learning the discursive streams of his speech were fed, I think you will be inclined to agree with me that he has done more than any other English-speaking man in this century to make the law luminous and easy to understand.

But Story's simple philosophizing has ceased to satisfy men's minds. I think it might be said with safety, that no man of his or of the succeeding generation could have stated the law in a form that deserved to abide, because neither his nor the succeeding generation possessed or could have possessed the historical knowledge, had made or could have made the analyses of principles, which are necessary before the cardinal doctrines of the law can be known and understood in their precise contours and in their innermost meanings.

The new work is now being done. Under the influence of Germany, science is gradually drawing legal history into its sphere. The facts are being scrutinized by eyes microscopic in intensity and panoramic in scope. At the same time, under the influence of our revived interest in philosophical speculation, a thousand heads are analyzing and generalizing the rules of law and the grounds on which they stand . . .

Corresponding to the change which I say is taking place, there has been another change in the mode of teaching. How far the correspondence is conscious, I do not stop to inquire. For whatever reason, the Professors of this School have said to themselves more definitely than ever before, We will not be contented to send forth students with nothing but a rag-bag full of general principles—a throng of glittering generalities, like a swarm of little bodiless cherubs fluttering at the top of one of Coreggio's pictures. They have said that to make a general principle worth anything you must give it a body; you must show in what way and how far it would be applied actually in an actual system; you must show how it has gradually emerged as the felt reconciliation of concrete instances no one of which established it in terms. Finally, you must show its historic relations to other principles, often of very different date and origin, and thus set it in the perspective without which its proportions will never be truly judged.

In pursuance of these views there have been substituted for text-

*Joseph Story, Supreme Court Justice and Harvard Law School Professor in the pre–Civil War era.—Ed.

books more and more, so far as practicable, those books of cases which were received at first by many with a somewhat contemptuous smile and pitying contrast of the good old days, but which now, after fifteen years, bid fair to revolutionize the teaching both of this country and of England . . .

Southern Pacific Co. v. Jensen
244 U.S. 205 (1917)
(Dissent)

The Southern Pacific Company has been held liable under the statutes of New York for an accidental injury happening upon a gangplank between a pier and the company's vessel and causing the death of one of its employees. The company not having insured as permitted, the statute may be taken as if it simply imposed a limited but absolute liability in such a case. The short question is whether the power of the state to regulate the liability in that place and to enforce it in the state's own courts is taken away by the conferring of exclusive jurisdiction of all civil causes of admiralty and maritime jurisdiction upon the courts of the United States.

There is no doubt that the saving to suitors of the right of a common-law remedy leaves open the common-law jurisdiction of the state courts, and leaves some power of legislation at least, to the states. For the latter I need do no more than refer to state pilotage statutes, and to liens created by state laws in aid of maritime contracts. Nearer to the point, it is decided that a statutory remedy for causing death may be enforced by the state courts, although the death was due to a collision upon the high seas . . . As such a liability can be imposed where it was unknown not only to the maritime but to the common law, I can see no difference between one otherwise constitutionally created for death caused by accident and one for death due to fault . . .

No doubt there sometimes has been an air of benevolent gratuity in the admiralty's attitude about enforcing state laws. But of course there is no gratuity about it. Courts cannot give or withhold at pleasure. If the claim is enforced or recognized it is because the claim is a right, and if a claim depending upon a state statute is enforced it is because the state had constitutional power to pass the law. Taking it as established that a state has constitutional power to pass laws giving rights and imposing liabilities for acts done upon the high seas when there were no such rights or liabilities before, what is there to hinder its doing so in the case of a maritime tort? Not the existence of an inconsistent law emanating from a superior source, that is, from the United States. There is no

229

such law. The maritime law is not a corpus juris—it is a very limited body of customs and ordinances of the sea. The nearest to anything of the sort in question was the rule that a seaman was entitled to recover the expenses necessary for his cure when the master's negligence caused his hurt. The maritime law gave him no more. One may affirm with the sanction of that case that it is an innovation to allow suits in the admiralty by seamen to recover damages for personal injuries caused by the negligence of the master and to apply the common-law principles of tort.

Now, however, common-law principles have been applied to sustain a [suit] by a stevedore against the master for personal injuries suffered while loading a ship; and *The Osceola* recognizes that in some cases at least seamen may have similar relief. From what source do these new rights come? . . . I recognize without hesitation that judges do and must legislate, but they can do so only interstitially; they are confined from molar to molecular motions. A common-law judge could not say I think the doctrine of consideration a bit of historical nonsense and shall not enforce it in my court. No more could a judge exercising the limited jurisdiction of admiralty say I think well of the common-law rules of master and servant and propose to introduce them here en bloc. Certainly he could not in that way enlarge the exclusive jurisdiction of the district courts and cut down the power of the states. If admiralty adopts common-law rules without an act of Congress, it cannot extend the maritime law as understood by the Constitution. It must take the rights of the parties from a different authority, just as it does when it enforces a lien created by a state. The only authority available is the common law or statutes of a state. For from the often repeated statement that there is no common law of the United States, and from the principles recognized in *Atlantic Transport Co. v. Imbrovek* having been unknown to the maritime law, the natural inference is that in the silence of Congress this court has believed the very limited law of the sea to be supplemented here as in England by the common law, and that here that means, by the common law of the state . . .

The common law is not a brooding omnipresence in the sky but the articulate voice of some sovereign or quasi-sovereign that can be identified; although some decisions with which I have disagreed seem to me to have forgotten the fact. It always is the law of some state, and if the district courts adopt the common law of torts, as they have shown a tendency to do, they thereby assume that a law not of maritime origin and deriving its authority in that territory only from some particular state of this Union also governs maritime torts in that territory—and if the common law, the statute law has at least equal force, as the discussion in

The Osceola assumes. On the other hand the refusal of the district courts to give remedies coextensive with the common law would prove no more than that they regarded their jurisdiction as limited by the ancient lines—not that they doubted that the common law might and would be enforced in the courts of the states as it always has been . . .

Black & White Taxi Co. v. Brown & Yellow Taxi Co.
276 U.S. 518 (1928)
(Dissent)

This is a suit brought by the respondent, The Brown and Yellow Taxicab and Transfer Company, as plaintiff, to prevent the petitioner, The Black and White Taxicab and Transfer Company, from interfering with the carrying out of a contract between the plaintiff and the other defendant, The Louisville and Nashville Railroad Company. The plaintiff is a corporation of Tennessee. It had a predecessor of the same name which was a corporation of Kentucky. Knowing that the courts of Kentucky held contracts of the kind in question invalid and that the courts of the United States maintained them as valid, a family that owned the Kentucky corporation procured the incorporation of the plaintiff and caused the other to be dissolved after conveying all the corporate property to the plaintiff. The new Tennessee corporation then proceeded to make with the Louisville and Nashville Railroad Company the contract above mentioned, by which the railroad company gave to it exclusive privileges in the station grounds, and two months later the Tennessee corporation brought this suit. The circuit court of appeals, affirming a decree of the district court, granted an injunction and upheld this contract. It expressly recognized that the decisions of the Kentucky courts held that in Kentucky a railroad company could not grant such rights, but this being a 'question of general law' it went its own way regardless of the courts of this state.

The circuit court of appeals had so considerable a tradition behind it in deciding as it did that if I did not regard the case as exceptional I should not feel warranted in presenting my own convictions again after having stated them in *Kuhn v. Fairmont Coal Company.* But the question is important and in my opinion the prevailing doctrine has been accepted upon a subtle fallacy that never has been analyzed. If I am right the fallacy has resulted in an unconstitutional assumption of powers by the courts of the United States which no lapse of time or respectable array of opinion should make us hesitate to correct. Therefore I think it proper to state what I think the fallacy is. The often repeated proposition of this and the lower courts is that the parties are entitled to an independent judgment on matters of general law. By that phrase is meant matters that are not governed by any law of the United States or by any statute of the state—matters that in states other than Louisiana are governed in most respects by what is called the common law. It is through this phrase that what I think the fallacy comes in.

Books written about any branch of the common law treat it as a unit, cite cases from this Court, from the circuit courts of appeals, from the state courts, from England and the colonies of England indiscriminately, and criticize them as right or wrong according to the writer's notions of a single theory. It is very hard to resist the impression that there is one august corpus, to understand which clearly is the only task of any court concerned. If there were such a transcendental body of law outside of any particular state but obligatory within it unless and until changed by statute, the courts of the United States might be right in using their independent judgment as to what it was. But there is no such body of law. The fallacy and illusion that I think exist consist in supposing that there is this outside thing to be found. Law is a word used with different meanings, but law in the sense in which courts speak of it today does not exist without some definite authority behind it. The common law so far as it is enforced in a state, whether called common law or not, is not the common law generally but the law of that state existing by the authority of that state without regard to what it may have been in England or anywhere else. It may be adopted by statute in place of another system previously in force. But a general adoption of it does not prevent the state courts from refusing to follow the English decisions upon a matter where the local conditions are different. It may be changed by statute, as is done every day. It may be departed from deliberately by judicial decisions, as with regard to water rights, in states where the common law generally prevails. Louisiana is a living proof that it need not be adopted at all. (I do not know whether under the prevailing doctrine we should regard ourselves as authorities upon the general law of Louisiana superior to those trained in the system.) Whether and how far and in what sense a rule shall be adopted whether called common law or Kentucky law is for the state alone to decide.

If within the limits of the Constitution a state should declare one of the disputed rules of general law by statute there would be no doubt of the duty of all courts to bow, whatever their private opinions might be. I see no reason why it should have less effect when it speaks by its other voice. If a state constitution should declare that on all matters of general law the decisions of the highest court should establish the law until modified by statute or by a later decision of the same court, I do not perceive how it would be possible for a court of the United States to

refuse to follow what the state court decided in that domain. But whe[e]
the constitution of a state establishes a supreme court it by implication
does make that declaration as clearly as if it had said it in express words,
so far as it is not interfered with by the superior power of the United
States. The supreme court of a state does something more than make a
scientific inquiry into a fact outside of and independent of it. It says,
with an authority that no one denies, except when a citizen of another
state is able to invoke an exceptional jurisdiction, that thus the law is
and shall be. Whether it be said to make or to declare the law, it deals
with the law of the state with equal authority however its function may
be described.

Mr. Justice Story in *Swift v. Tyson*, evidently under the tacit domination of the fallacy to which I have referred, devotes some energy to
showing that §34 of the Judiciary Act of 1789 refers only to statutes
when it provides that except as excepted the laws of the several states
shall be regarded as rules of decision in trials at common law in courts
of the United States. An examination of the original document by a
most competent hand has shown that Mr. Justice Story probably was
wrong if anyone is interested to inquire what the framers of the instrument meant. But this question is deeper than that; it is a question of the
authority by which certain particular acts, here the grant of exclusive
privileges in a railroad station, are governed. In my opinion the authority and only authority is the state, and if that be so, the voice adopted by
the state as its own should utter the last word. I should leave *Swift v.
Tyson* undisturbed, as I indicated in *Kuhn v. Fairmont Coal Co.*, but I
would not allow it to spread the assumed dominion into new fields . . .

The Western Maid
257 U.S. 419 (1922)

These are petitions for prohibition to prevent district courts of the
United States from exercising jurisdiction of proceedings in rem* for
collisions that occurred while the vessels libeled were owned . . . by the
United States, and employed in the public service . . .

In deciding this question we must realize that however ancient may
be the traditions of maritime law, however diverse the sources from
which it has been drawn, it derives its whole and only power in this
country from its having been accepted and adopted by the United
States. There is no mystic overlaw to which even the United States must

*"In rem" jurisdiction is explained in Lecture I of *The Common Law*, reprinted below
(this chapter).—Ed.

bow. When a case is said to be governed by foreign law or by general maritime law that is only a short way of saying that for this purpose the sovereign power takes up a rule suggested from without and makes it part of its own rules. Also we must realize that the authority that makes the law is itself superior to it, and that if it consents to apply to itself the rules that it applies to others the consent is free and may be withheld. The sovereign does not create justice in an ethical sense, to be sure, and there may be cases in which it would not dare to deny that justice for fear of war or revolution. Sovereignty is a question of power, and no human power is unlimited. But from the necessary point of view of the sovereign and its organs whatever is enforced by it as law is enforced as the expression of its will.

The United States has not consented to be sued for torts, and therefore it cannot be said that in a legal sense the United States has been guilty of a tort. For a tort is a tort in a legal sense only because the law has made it so. If then we imagine the sovereign power announcing the system of its laws in a single voice it is hard to conceive it as declaring that while it does not recognize the possibility of its acts being a legal wrong and while its immunity from such an imputation of course extends to its property, at least when employed in carrying on the operations of the government, yet if that property passes into other hands, perhaps of an innocent purchaser, it may be seized upon a claim that had no existence before. It may be said that the persons who actually did the act complained of may or might be sued and that the ship for this purpose is regarded as a person. But that is a fiction not a fact and as a fiction is the creation of the law. It would be a strange thing if the law created a fiction to accomplish the result supposed. It is totally immaterial that in dealing with private wrongs the fiction, however originated, is in force. The personality of a public vessel is merged in that of the sovereign.

But it is said that the decisions have recognized that an obligation is created in the case before us. Legal obligations that exist but cannot be enforced are ghosts that are seen in the law but that are elusive to the grasp . . .

To Harold Laski

January 29, 1926

Dear Laski,

Two letters from you, delightful as usual, this week. The last this morning. I could not answer at the drop of the hat because I was so busy with the work here. But a recess comes on Monday, and all my opinions are written, up to date. Do you know I really am bothered by the old difference between us, if there is one, as to sovereignty, because as I understand the question it seems to me one that does not admit of argument. The thing to which I refer has nothing to do with the difficulty of finding out who the sovereign is, or the tacitly recognized *de facto* limits on the power of the most absolute sovereign that ever was. The issue is on this decision that you criticize, and even narrower than that. If you should say that the courts ought in these days to assume a consent of the U.S. to be sued, or to be liable in tort on the same principle as those governing private persons, I should have my reason for thinking you wrong, but should not care, as that would be an intelligible point of difference. But what I can't understand is the suggestion that the United States is bound by law even though it does not assent. What I mean by law in this connection is that which is or should be enforced by the courts and I can't understand how anyone should think that an instrumentality established by the United States to carry out its will, and that it can depose upon a failure to do so, should undertake to enforce something that *ex hypothesi* is against its will. It seems to me like shaking one's fist at the sky, when the sky furnishes the energy that enables one to raise the fist. There is a tendency to think of judges as if they were independent mouthpieces of the infinite, and not simply directors of a force that comes from the source that gives them their authority. I think our court has fallen into the error at times and it is that that I have aimed at when I have said that the common law is not a brooding omnipresence in the sky and that the U.S. is not subject to some mystic overlaw that it is bound to obey. When our U.S. circuit courts are backed up by us in saying that suitors have a right to their independent judgment as to the common law of a state, and so that the U.S. courts may disregard the decisions of the supreme court of the state, the fallacy is illustrated. The common law in a state is the common law of that state deriving all its authority from the state, as is shown by Louisiana where it does not prevail. But the late Harlan, Day, and a majority of others have treated the question as if they were invited to speculate about *the* common law *in abstracto*. I repeat that if you merely mean that we ought to imply a consent until it is denied in terms, I should think you were wrong and that I was better fitted to judge of that than outsiders, but that would be a specific question for a given situation, a difference about which could create no concern.

Wednesday I had to preside *vice* the C.J. absent at a funeral and again today as he had caught a cold and was advised to keep to the house. The newspapers laid hold of it for a paragraph, and even one chap got a photograph in the literal five minutes that I gave him. It came out in the evening paper—good but looking very old. It made me realize what a hungry lot the reporters are—every trifle that will make a paragraph is, I suppose, cash to them. The other day there was a railroad accident here and they were ferocious with the doctors and the nurses in a hospital who wouldn't let them interview the damaged engineer although they were told that it was a matter of life and death to keep him undisturbed . . .

Your suggestion of possible trouble about coming here worries me a little. They have made troubles that seemed queer, but I have assumed (in perfect ignorance) that the exclusions came from some hint on the part of a government. If I were you I would make sure beforehand that there will be no trouble. I was remarking to Brandeis the other day that speech was freer in England than here, now, whereas in 1866 or 7 it was freer here and he mentioned some writer who had made this same observation. I noted it as the striking of a bell when under Morley's editorship the Pall Mall spoke in a matter of course way of those who did not believe in Christianity . . .

To Frederick Pollock

March 5, 1881

My dear Pollock,

I have failed in all correspondence and have abandoned pleasure as well as a good deal of sleep for a year to accomplish a result which I now send you by mail in the form of a little book *The Common Law.* When a man is engaged all day at his office in practise it is a slow business to do work of this sort by night, but my heart has been deeply in it, and I am encouraged to hope by the way in which you have received articles which were precursors of parts of the volume that you will not think my time has been wasted. At any rate I have worked hard for results that seemed to me important. You are happy in being able to afford time to philosophy. I have to make my living by my profession and therefore have been compelled to approach philosophy indirectly through the door of a specialty, but all roads lead to Rome and I don't doubt that a man with the philosophic craving would find stuff to work upon if he was a hatter. I sometimes even think that there is a certain advantage in difficulties, and that one sails better with the wind on the quarter than when it is directly astern. I should like it very much if my book was noticed in England but I suppose there are few anywhere who interest themselves in such things. At least I find that Englishmen sometimes think that one has a better audience here for anything on the law which is not strictly practical, while I have been wont to look for companionship more to a few men on your side—although I should be unjust and ungrateful not to add some Americans in the same line.

THE COMMON LAW (1881)
Lecture I
Early Forms of Liability.

The object of this book is to present a general view of the Common Law. To accomplish the task, other tools are needed besides logic. It is something to show that the consistency of a system requires a particular result, but it is not all. The life of the law has not been logic: it has been experience. The felt necessities of the time, the prevalent moral and political theories, intuitions of public policy, avowed or unconscious, even the prejudices which judges share with their fellow-men, have had a good deal more to do than the syllogism in determining the rules by which men should be governed. The law embodies the story of a nation's development through many centuries, and it cannot be dealt with as if it contained only the axioms and corollaries of a book of mathematics. In order to know what it is, we must know what it has been, and what it tends to become. We must alternately consult history and existing theories of legislation. But the most difficult labor will be to understand the combination of the two into new products at every stage. The substance of the law at any given time pretty nearly corresponds, so far as it goes, with what is then understood to be convenient; but its form and machinery, and the degree to which it is able to work out desired results, depend very much upon its past.

In Massachusetts today, while, on the one hand, there are a great many rules which are quite sufficiently accounted for by their manifest good sense, on the other, there are some which can only be understood by reference to the infancy of procedure among the German tribes, or to the social condition of Rome under the Decemvirs.

I shall use the history of our law so far as it is necessary to explain a conception or to interpret a rule, but no further. In doing so there are two errors equally to be avoided both by writer and reader. One is that of supposing, because an idea seems very familiar and natural to us, that it has always been so. Many things which we take for granted have had to be laboriously fought out or thought out in past times. The other mistake is the opposite one of asking too much of history. We start with man full grown. It may be assumed that the earliest barbarian whose practices are to be considered had a good many of the same feelings and passions as ourselves.

The first subject to be discussed is the general theory of liability civil and criminal. The Common Law has changed a good deal since the beginning of our series of reports, and the search after a theory which may now be said to prevail is very much a study of tendencies. I believe that it will be instructive to go back to the early forms of liability, and to start from them.

It is commonly known that the early forms of legal procedure were grounded in vengeance. Modern writers have thought that the Roman law started from the blood feud, and all the authorities agree that the German law began in that way. The feud led to the composition, at first optional, then compulsory, by which the feud was bought off. The gradual encroachment of the composition may be traced in the Anglo-Saxon laws, and the feud was pretty well broken up, though not extinguished, by the time of William the Conqueror. The killings and house-burnings of an earlier day became the appeals of mayhem and arson. The appeals *de pace et plagis* and of mayhem became, or rather were in substance, the action of trespass which is still familiar to lawyers. But as the compensation recovered in the appeal was the alternative of vengeance, we might expect to find its scope limited to the scope of vengeance. Vengeance imports a feeling of blame, and an opinion, however distorted by passion, that a wrong has been done. It can hardly go very far beyond the case of a harm intentionally inflicted: even a dog distinguishes between being stumbled over and being kicked.

Whether for this cause or another, the early English appeals for personal violence seem to have been confined to intentional wrongs. Glanvill mentions mêlées, blows, and wounds—all forms of intentional violence. In the fuller description of such appeals given by Bracton it is made quite clear that they were based on intentional assaults. The appeal *de pace et plagis* laid an intentional assault, described the nature of the arms used, and the length and depth of the wound. The appellor also had to show that he immediately raised the hue and cry. So when Bracton speaks of the lesser offences, which were not sued by way of appeal, he instances only intentional wrongs, such as blows with the fist, flogging, wounding, insults, and so forth. The cause of action in the cases of trespass reported in the earlier Year Books and in the Abbreviatio Placitorum is always an intentional wrong. It was only at a later day, and after argument, that trespass was extended so as to embrace harms which were foreseen, but which were not the intended consequence of the defendant's act. Thence again it extended to unforeseen injuries.

It will be seen that this order of development is not quite consistent with an opinion which has been held, that it was a characteristic of early law not to penetrate beyond the external visible fact. It has been thought that an inquiry into the internal condition of the defendant, his culpability or innocence, implies a refinement of juridical conception equally foreign to Rome before the Lex Aquilia, and to England when trespass took its shape. I do not know any very satisfactory evidence that a man was generally held liable either in Rome or England for the accidental consequences even of his own act. But whatever may have been the early law, the foregoing account shows the starting-point of the system with which we have to deal. Our system of private liability for the consequences of a man's own acts, that is, for his trespasses, started from the notion of actual intent and actual personal culpability.

The original principles of liability for harm inflicted by another person or thing have been less carefully considered hitherto than those which governed trespass, and I shall therefore devote the rest of this Lecture to discussing them. I shall try to show that this liability also had its root in the passion of revenge, and to point out the changes by which it reached its present form. But I shall not confine myself strictly to what is needful for that purpose, because it is not only most interesting to trace the transformation throughout its whole extent, but the story will also afford an instructive example of the mode in which the law has grown, without a break, from barbarism to civilization. Furthermore, it will throw much light upon some important and peculiar doctrines which cannot be returned to later.

A very common phenomenon, and one very familiar to the student of history, is this. The customs, beliefs, or needs of a primitive time establish a rule or a formula. In the course of centuries the custom, belief, or necessity disappears, but the rule remains. The reason which gave rise to the rule has been forgotten, and ingenious minds set themselves to inquire how it is to be accounted for. Some ground of policy is thought of, which seems to explain it and to reconcile it with the present state of things; and then the rule adapts itself to the new reasons which have been found for it, and enters on a new career. The old form receives a new content, and in time even the form modifies itself to fit the meaning which it has received. The subject under consideration illustrates this course of events very clearly.

I will begin by taking a medley of examples embodying as many distinct rules, each with its plausible and seemingly sufficient ground of policy to explain it.

A man has an animal of known ferocious habits, which escapes and does his neighbor damage. He can prove that the animal escaped through no negligence of his, but still he is held liable. Why? It is, says the analytical jurist, because, although he was not negligent at the moment of escape, he was guilty of remote heedlessness, or negligence, or fault, in having such a creature at all. And one by whose fault damage is done ought to pay for it.

A baker's man, while driving his master's cart to deliver hot rolls of a morning, runs another man down. The master has to pay for it. And when he has asked why he should have to pay for the wrongful act of an independent and responsible being, he has been answered from the time of Ulpian to that of Austin, that it is because he was to blame for employing an improper person. If he answers, that he used the greatest possible care in choosing his driver, he is told that that is no excuse; and then perhaps the reason is shifted, and it is said that there ought to be a remedy against some one who can pay the damages, or that such wrongful acts as by ordinary human laws are likely to happen in the course of the service are imputable to the service.

Next, take a case where a limit has been set to liability which had previously been unlimited. In 1851, Congress passed a law, which is still in force, and by which the owners of ships in all the more common cases of maritime loss can surrender the vessel and her freight then pending to the losers; and it is provided that, thereupon, further proceedings against the owners shall cease. The legislators to whom we owe this act argued that, if a merchant embark a portion of his property upon a hazardous venture, it is reasonable that his stake should be confined to what he puts at risk—a principle similar to that on which corporations have been so largely created in America during the last fifty years.

It has been a rule of criminal pleading in England down into the present century, that an indictment for homicide must set forth the value of the instrument causing the death, in order that the king or his grantee might claim forfeiture of the deodand, "as an accursed thing," in the language of Blackstone.

I might go on multiplying examples; but these are enough to show the remoteness of the points to be brought together. As a first step towards a generalization, it will be necessary to consider what is to be found in ancient and independent systems of law.

There is a well-known passage in Exodus, which we shall have to remember later: "If an ox gore a man or a woman, that they die: then the ox shall be surely stoned, and his flesh shall not be eaten; but the owner of the ox shall be quit." When we turn from the Jews to the Greeks, we find the principle of the passage just quoted erected into a system. Plutarch, in his Solon, tells us that a dog that had bitten a man was to be delivered up bound to a log four cubits long. Plato made elaborate provisions in his Laws for many such cases. If a slave killed a man, he was to be given up to the relatives of the deceased. If he wounded a man, he was to be given up to the injured party to use him as he pleased. So if he did damage to which the injured party did not contribute as a joint cause. In either case, if the owner failed to surrender the slave, he was bound to make good the loss. If a beast killed a man, it was to be slain and cast beyond the borders. If an inanimate thing caused death, it was to be cast beyond the borders in like manner, and expiation was to be made. Nor was all this an ideal creation of merely imagined law, for it was said in one of the speeches of Æschines that "we banish beyond our borders stocks and stones and steel, voiceless and mindless things, if they chance to kill a man; and if a man commits suicide, bury the hand that struck the blow afar from its body." This is mentioned quite as an everyday matter, evidently without thinking it at all extraordinary, only to point an antithesis to the honors heaped upon Demosthenes. As late as the second century after Christ the traveller Pausanias observed with some surprise that they still sat in judgment on inanimate things in the Prytaneum. Plutarch attributes the institution to Draco.

In the Roman law we find the similar principles of the *noxæ deditio* gradually leading to further results. The Twelve Tables (451 B.C.) provided that, if an animal had done damage, either the animal was to be surrendered or the damage paid for. We learn from Gaius that the same rule was applied to the torts of children or slaves, and there is some trace of it with regard to inanimate things.

The Roman lawyers, not looking beyond their own system or their own time, drew on their wits for an explanation which would show that the law as they found it was reasonable. Gaius said that it was unjust that the fault of children or slaves should be a source of loss to their parents or owners beyond their own bodies, and Ulpian reasoned that *a fortiori* this was true of things devoid of life, and therefore incapable of fault.

This way of approaching the question seems to deal with the right of surrender as if it were a limitation of a liability incurred by a parent or owner, which would naturally and in the first instance be unlimited. But if that is what was meant, it puts the cart before the horse. The right of surrender was not introduced as a limitation of liability, but, in Rome and Greece alike, payment was introduced as the alternative of a failure to surrender.

The action was not based, as it would be nowadays, on the fault of the parent or owner. If it had been, it would always have been brought against the person who had control of the slave or animal at the time it did the harm complained of, and who, if any one, was to blame for not preventing the injury. So far from this being the course, the person to be sued was the owner at the time of suing. The action followed the guilty thing into whosesoever hands it came. And in curious contrast with the principle as inverted to meet still more modern views of public policy, if the animal was of a wild nature, that is, in the very case of the most ferocious animals, the owner ceased to be liable the moment it escaped, because at that moment he ceased to be owner. There seems to have been no other or more extensive liability by the old law, even where a slave was guilty with his master's knowledge, unless perhaps he was a mere tool in his master's hands . . .

All this shows very clearly that the liability of the owner was merely a way of getting at the slave or animal which was the immediate cause of offence. In other words, vengeance on the immediate offender was the object of the Greek and early Roman process, not indemnity from the master or owner. The liability of the owner was simply a liability of the offending thing. In the primitive customs of Greece it was enforced by a judicial process expressly directed against the object, animate or inanimate. The Roman Twelve Tables made the owner, instead of the thing itself, the defendant, but did not in any way change the ground of liability, or affect its limit. The change was simply a device to allow the owner to protect his interest.

But it may be asked how inanimate objects came to be pursued in this way, if the object of the procedure was to gratify the passion of revenge. Learned men have been ready to find a reason in the personification of inanimate nature common to savages and children, and there is much to confirm this view. Without such a personification, anger towards lifeless things would have been transitory, at most. It is noticeable that the commonest example in the most primitive customs and laws is that of a tree which falls upon a man, or from which he falls and is killed. We can conceive with comparative ease how a tree might have been put on the same footing with animals. It certainly was treated like them, and was delivered to the relatives, or chopped to pieces for the gratification of a real or simulated passion . . .

Another peculiarity to be noticed is that the liability seems to have been regarded as attached to the body doing the damage, in an almost physical sense. An untrained intelligence only imperfectly performs the analysis by which jurists carry responsibility back to the beginning of a chain of causation. The hatred for anything giving us pain, which wreaks itself on the manifest cause, and which leads even civilized man to kick a door when it pinches his finger, is embodied in the *noxae deditio* and other kindred doctrines of early Roman law . . .

. . . The Roman law dealt mainly with living creatures—with animals and slaves. If a man was run over, it did not surrender the wagon which crushed him, but the ox which drew the wagon. At this stage the notion is easy to understand. The desire for vengeance may be felt as strongly against a slave as against a freeman, and it is not without example nowadays that a like passion should be felt against an animal. The surrender of the slave or beast empowered the injured party to do his will upon them. Payment by the owner was merely a privilege in case he wanted to buy the vengeance off.

It will readily be imagined that such a system as has been described could not last when civilization had advanced to any considerable height. What had been the privilege of buying off vengeance by agreement, of paying the damage instead of surrendering the body of the offender, no doubt became a general custom. The Aquilian law, passed about a couple of centuries later than the date of the Twelve Tables, enlarged the sphere of compensation for bodily injuries. Interpretation enlarged the Aquilian law. Masters became personally liable for certain wrongs committed by their slaves with their knowledge, where previously they were only bound to surrender the slave. If a pack-mule threw off his burden upon a passer-by because he had been improperly overloaded, or a dog which might have been restrained escaped from his master and bit any one, the old noxal action, as it was called, gave way to an action under the new law to enforce a general personal liability.

Still later, shipowners and innkeepers were made liable as if they were wrongdoers for wrongs committed by those in their employ on board ship or in the tavern, although of course committed without their knowledge. The true reason for this exceptional responsibility was the exceptional confidence which was necessarily reposed in carriers and innkeepers. But some of the jurists, who regarded the surrender of children and slaves as a privilege intended to limit liability, explained this new liability on the ground that the innkeeper or shipowner was to a certain degree guilty of negligence in having employed the services of bad men. This was the first instance of a master being made unconditionally liable for the wrongs of his servant. The reason given for it was of general application, and the principle expanded to the scope of the reason.

The law as to shipowners and innkeepers introduced another and more startling innovation. It made them responsible when those whom they employed were free, as well as when they were slaves. For the first time one man was made answerable for the wrongs of another who was also answerable himself, and who had a standing before the law. This was a great change from the bare permission to ransom one's slave as a privilege. But here we have the history of the whole modern doctrine of master and servant, and principal and agent. All servants are now as free and as liable to a suit as their masters. Yet the principle introduced on special grounds in a special case, when servants were slaves, is now the general law of this country and England, and under it men daily have to pay large sums for other people's acts, in which they had no part and for which they are in no sense to blame. And to this day the reason offered by the Roman jurists for an exceptional rule is made to justify this universal and unlimited responsibility . . .

We will now follow the history of that branch of the primitive notion which was least likely to survive—the liability of inanimate things . . . In Edward the First's time some of the cases remind us of the barbarian laws at their rudest stage. If a man fell from a tree, the tree was deodand. If he drowned in a well, the well was to be filled up. It did not matter that the forfeited instrument belonged to an innocent person. "Where a man killeth another with the sword of John at Stile, the sword shall be forfeit as deodand, and yet no default is in the owner." That is from a book written in the reign of Henry VIII, about 1530. And it has been repeated from Queen Elizabeth's time to within one hundred years, that if my horse strikes a man, and afterwards I sell my horse, and after that the man dies, the horse shall be forfeited. Hence it is, that, in all indictments for homicide, until very lately it has been necessary to state the instrument causing the death and its value, as that the stroke was given by a certain penknife, value sixpence, so as to secure the forfeiture. It is said that a steam-engine has been forfeited in this way.

I now come to what I regard as the most remarkable transformation of this principle, and one which is a most important factor in our law as it is today. I must for the moment leave the common law and take up the doctrines of the Admiralty. In the early books which have just been referred to, and long afterwards, the fact of *motion* is adverted to as of much importance. A maxim of Henry Spigurnel, a judge in the time of Edward I, is reported, that "where a man is killed by a cart, or by the fall of a house, or in other like manner, and the thing in motion is the cause of the death, it shall be deodand". . .

The most striking example of this sort is a ship. And accordingly the old books say that, if a man falls from a ship and is drowned, the motion of the ship must be taken to cause the death, and the ship is forfeited— provided, however, that this happens in fresh water. For if the death took place on the high seas, that was outside the ordinary jurisdiction. This proviso has been supposed to mean that ships at sea were not forfeited; but there is a long series of petitions to the king in Parliament that such forfeitures may be done away with, which tell a different story.

The truth seems to be that the forfeiture took place, but in a different court . . .

A ship is the most living of inanimate things. Servants sometimes say "she" of a clock, but everyone gives a gender to vessels. And we need not be surprised, therefore, to find a mode of dealing which has shown such extraordinary vitality in the criminal law applied with even more striking thoroughness in the Admiralty. It is only by supposing the ship to have been treated as if endowed with personality that the arbitrary seeming peculiarities of the maritime law can be made intelligible, and on that supposition they at once become consistent and logical.

By way of seeing what those peculiarities are, take first a case of collision at sea. A collision takes place between two vessels, the Ticonderoga and the Melampus, through the fault of the Ticonderoga alone. That ship is under a lease at the time, the lessee has his own master in charge, and the owner of the vessel has no manner of control over it. The owner, therefore, is not to blame, and he cannot even be charged on the ground that the damage was done by his servants. He is free from personal liability on elementary principles. Yet it is perfectly settled that there is a lien on his vessel for the amount of the damage done, and this means that that vessel may be arrested and sold to pay the loss in any admiralty court whose process will reach her. If a livery-stable keeper lets a horse and wagon to a customer, who runs a man down by careless driving, no one would think of claiming a right to seize the horse and wagon. It would be seen that the only property which could be sold to pay for a wrong was the property of the wrongdoer.

But, again, suppose that the vessel, instead of being under lease, is in charge of a pilot whose employment is made compulsory by the laws of the port which she is just entering. The Supreme Court of the United States holds the ship liable in this instance also. The English courts would probably have decided otherwise, and the matter is settled in England by legislation. But there the court of appeal, the Privy Council, has been largely composed of common-law lawyers, and it has shown a marked tendency to assimilate common-law doctrine. At common law one who could not impose a personal liability on the owner could not bind a particular chattel to answer for a wrong of which it had been the instrument. But our Supreme Court has long recognized that a person may bind a ship, when he could not bind the owners personally, because he was not their agent.

It may be admitted that, if this doctrine were not supported by an appearance of good sense, it would not have survived. The ship is the only security available in dealing with foreigners, and rather than send one's own citizens to search for a remedy abroad in strange courts, it is easy to seize the vessel and satisfy the claim at home, leaving the foreign owners to get their indemnity as they may be able. I dare say some such thought has helped to keep the practice alive, but I believe the true historic foundation is elsewhere. The ship no doubt, like a sword, would have been forfeited for causing death, in whosesoever hands it might have been. So, if the master and mariners of a ship, furnished with letters of reprisal, committed piracy against a friend of the king, the owner lost his ship by the admiralty law, although the crime was committed without his knowledge or assent. It seems most likely that the principle by which the ship was forfeited to the king for causing death, or for piracy, was the same as that by which it was bound to private sufferers for other damage, in whose hands soever it might have been when it did the harm.

If we should say to an uneducated man today, "She did it and she ought to pay for it," it may be doubted whether he would see the fallacy, or be ready to explain that the ship was only property, and that to say, "The ship has to pay for it," was simply a dramatic way of saying that somebody's property was to be sold, and the proceeds applied to pay for a wrong committed by somebody else.

It would seem that a similar form of words has been enough to satisfy the minds of great lawyers. The following is a passage from a judgment by Chief Justice Marshall, which is quoted with approval by Judge Story in giving the opinion of the Supreme Court of the United States: "This is not a proceeding against the owner; it is a proceeding against the vessel for an offence committed by the vessel; which is not the less an offence, and does not the less subject her to forfeiture, because it was committed without the authority and against the will of the owner. It is true that inanimate matter can commit no offence. But this body is animated and put in action by the crew, who are guided by the master. The vessel acts and speaks by the master. She reports herself by the master. It is, therefore, not unreasonable that the vessel should be affected by this report." And again Judge Story quotes from another case: "The thing is here primarily considered as the offender, or rather the offence is primarily attached to the thing."

In other words, those great judges, although of course aware that a ship is no more alive than a mill-wheel, thought that not only the law did in fact deal with it as if it were alive, but that it was reasonable that the law should do so. The reader will observe that they do not say simply that it is reasonable on grounds of policy to sacrifice justice to the owner to security for somebody else, but that it is reasonable to deal with the vessel as an offending thing. Whatever the hidden ground of policy may be, their thought still clothes itself in personifying language . . .

Lecture II

The Criminal Law

. . . The desire for vengeance imports an opinion that its object is actually and personally to blame. It takes an internal standard, not an objective or external one, and condemns its victim by that. The question is whether such a standard is still accepted either in this primitive form, or in some more refined development, as is commonly supposed, and as seems not impossible, considering the relative slowness with which the criminal law has improved.

It certainly may be argued, with some force, that it has never ceased to be one object of punishment to satisfy the desire for vengeance. The argument will be made plain by considering those instances in which, for one reason or another, compensation for a wrong is out of the question.

Thus an act may be of such a kind as to make indemnity impossible by putting an end to the principal sufferer, as in the case of murder or manslaughter.

Again, these and other crimes, like forgery, although directed against an individual, tend to make others feel unsafe, and this general insecurity does not admit of being paid for.

Again, there are cases where there are no means of enforcing indemnity. In Macaulay's draft of the Indian Penal Code, breaches of contract for the carriage of passengers were made criminal. The palanquin-bearers of India were too poor to pay damages, and yet had to be trusted to carry unprotected women and children through wild and desolate tracts, where their desertion would have placed those under their charge in great danger.

In all these cases punishment remains as an alternative. A pain can be inflicted upon the wrongdoer, of a sort which does not restore the injured party to his former situation, or to another equally good, but which is inflicted for the very purpose of causing pain. And so far as this punishment takes the place of compensation, whether on account of the death of the person to whom the wrong was done, the indefinite number of persons affected, the impossibility of estimating the worth of the suffering in money, or the poverty of the criminal, it may be said that one of its objects is to gratify the desire for vengeance. The prisoner pays with his body.

The statement may be made stronger still, and it may be said, not only that the law does, but that it ought to, make the gratification of revenge an object. This is the opinion, at any rate, of two authorities so great, and so opposed in other views, as Bishop Butler and Jeremy

Bentham. Sir James Stephen says, "The criminal law stands to the passion of revenge in much the same relation as marriage to the sexual appetite."

The first requirement of a sound body of law is that it should correspond with the actual feelings and demands of the community, whether right or wrong. If people would gratify the passion of revenge outside of the law, if the law did not help them, the law has no choice but to satisfy the craving itself, and thus avoid the greater evil of private retribution. At the same time, this passion is not one which we encourage, either as private individuals or as lawmakers. Moreover, it does not cover the whole ground. There are crimes which do not excite it, and we should naturally expect that the most important purposes of punishment would be coextensive with the whole field of its application. It remains to be discovered whether such a general purpose exists, and if so what it is. Different theories still divide opinion upon the subject.

It has been thought that the purpose of punishment is to reform the criminal; that it is to deter the criminal and others from committing similar crimes; and that it is retribution. Few would now maintain that the first of these purposes was the only one. If it were, every prisoner should be released as soon as it appears clear that he will never repeat his offence, and if he is incurable he should not be punished at all. Of course it would be hard to reconcile the punishment of death with this doctrine.

The main struggle lies between the other two. On the one side is the notion that there is a mystic bond between wrong and punishment; on the other, that the infliction of pain is only a means to an end. Hegel, one of the great expounders of the former view, puts it, in his quasi mathematical form, that, wrong being the negation of right, punishment is the negation of that negation, or retribution. Thus the punishment must be equal, in the sense of proportionate to the crime, because its only function is to destroy it. Others, without this logical apparatus, are content to rely upon a felt necessity that suffering should follow wrongdoing.

It is objected that the preventive theory is immoral, because it overlooks the ill desert of wrongdoing, and furnishes no measure of the amount of punishment, except the lawgiver's subjective opinion in regard to the sufficiency of the amount of preventive suffering. In the language of Kant, it treats man as a thing, not as a person; as a means, not as an end in himself. It is said to conflict with the sense of justice, and to violate the fundamental principle of all free communities, that the members of such communities have equal rights to life, liberty, and personal security.

In spite of all this, probably most English-speaking lawyers would accept the preventive theory without hesitation. As to the violation of equal rights which is charged, it may be replied that the dogma of equality makes an equation between individuals only, not between an individual and the community. No society has ever admitted that it could not sacrifice individual welfare to its own existence. If conscripts are necessary for its army, it seizes them, and marches them, with bayonets in their rear, to death. It runs highways and railroads through old family places in spite of the owner's protest, paying in this instance the market value, to be sure, because no civilized government sacrifices the citizen more than it can help, but still sacrificing his will and his welfare to that of the rest.

If it were necessary to trench further upon the field of morals, it might be suggested that the dogma of equality applied even to individuals only within the limits of ordinary dealings in the common run of affairs. You cannot argue with your neighbor, except on the admission for the moment that he is as wise as you, although you may by no means believe it. In the same way, you cannot deal with him, where both are free to choose, except on the footing of equal treatment, and the same rules for both. The ever-growing value set upon peace and the social relations tends to give the law of social being the appearance of the law of all being. But it seems to me clear that the *ultima ratio,* not only *regum,* but of private persons, is force, and that at the bottom of all private relations, however tempered by sympathy and all the social feelings, is a justifiable self-preference. If a man is on a plank in the deep sea which will only float one, and a stranger lays hold of it, he will thrust him off if he can. When the state finds itself in a similar position, it does the same thing.

The considerations which answer the argument of equal rights also answer the objections to treating man as a thing, and the like. If a man lives in society, he is liable to find himself so treated. The degree of civilization which a people has reached, no doubt, is marked by their anxiety to do as they would be done by. It may be the destiny of man that the social instincts shall grow to control his actions absolutely, even in anti-social situations. But they have not yet done so, and as the rules of law are or should be based upon a morality which is generally accepted, no rule founded on a theory of absolute unselfishness can be laid down without a breach between law and working beliefs.

If it be true, as I shall presently try to show, that the general principles of criminal and civil liability are the same, it will follow from that alone that theory and fact agree in frequently punishing those who have been guilty of no moral wrong, and who could not be condemned by any standard that did not avowedly disregard the personal peculiarities of the individuals concerned. If punishment stood on the moral grounds which are proposed for it, the first thing to be considered would be those limitations in the capacity for choosing rightly which arise from abnormal instincts, want of education, lack of intelligence, and all the other defects which are most marked in the criminal classes. I do not say that they should not be, or at least I do not need to for my argument. I do not say that the criminal law does more good than harm. I only say that it is not enacted or administered on that theory.

There remains to be mentioned the affirmative argument in favor of the theory of retribution, to the effect that the fitness of punishment following wrongdoing is axiomatic, and is instinctively recognized by unperverted minds. I think that it will be seen, on self-inspection, that this feeling of fitness is absolute and unconditional only in the case of our neighbors. It does not seem to me that any one who has satisfied himself that an act of his was wrong, and that he will never do it again, would feel the least need or propriety, as between himself and an earthly punishing power alone, of his being made to suffer for what he had done, although, when third persons were introduced, he might, as a philosopher, admit the necessity of hurting him to frighten others. But when our neighbors do wrong, we sometimes feel the fitness of making them smart for it, whether they have repented or not. The feeling of fitness seems to me to be only vengeance in disguise, and I have already admitted that vengeance was an element, though not the chief element, of punishment.

But, again, the supposed intuition of fitness does not seem to me to be coextensive with the thing to be accounted for. The lesser punishments are just as fit for the lesser crimes as the greater for the greater. The demand that crime should be followed by its punishment should therefore be equal and absolute in both. Again, a *malum prohibitum* is just as much a crime as a *malum in se*. If there is any general ground for punishment, it must apply to one case as much as to the other. But it will hardly be said that, if the wrong in the case just supposed consisted of a breach of the revenue laws, and the government had been indemnified for the loss, we should feel any internal necessity that a man who had thoroughly repented of his wrong should be punished for it, except on the ground that his act was known to others. If it was known, the law would have to verify its threats in order that others might believe and tremble. But if the fact was a secret between the sovereign and the subject, the sovereign, if wholly free from passion, would undoubtedly see that punishment in such a case was wholly without justification.

On the other hand, there can be no case which the lawmaker makes certain conduct criminal without his thereby showing a wish and purpose to prevent that conduct. Prevention would accordingly seem to be the chief and only universal purpose of punishment. The law threatens certain pains if you do certain things, intending thereby to give you a new motive for not doing them. If you persist in doing them, it has to inflict the pains in order that its threats may continue to be believed.

If this is a true account of the law as it stands, the law does undoubtedly treat the individual as a means to an end, and uses him as a tool to increase the general welfare at his own expense. It has been suggested above that this course is perfectly proper; but even if it is wrong, our criminal law follows it, and the theory of our criminal law must be shaped accordingly.

Further evidence that our law exceeds the limits of retribution, and subordinates consideration of the individual to that of the public well-being, will be found in some doctrines which cannot be satisfactorily explained on any other ground.

The first of these is that even the deliberate taking of life will not be punished when it is the only way of saving one's own. This principle is not so clearly established as that next to be mentioned; but it has the support of very great authority. If that is the law, it must go on one of two grounds, either that self-preference is proper in the case supposed, or that, even if it is improper, the law cannot prevent it by punishment, because a threat of death at some future time can never be a sufficiently powerful motive to make a man choose death now in order to avoid the threat. If the former ground is adopted, it admits that a single person may sacrifice another to himself, and *a fortiori* that a people may. If the latter view is taken, by abandoning punishment when it can no longer be expected to prevent an act, the law abandons the retributive and adopts the preventive theory.

The next doctrine leads to still clearer conclusions. Ignorance of the law is no excuse for breaking it. This substantive principle is sometimes put in the form of a rule of evidence, that every one is presumed to know the law. It has accordingly been defended by Austin and others on the ground of difficulty of proof. If justice requires the fact to be ascertained, the difficulty of doing so is no ground for refusing to try. But every one must feel that ignorance of the law could never be admitted as an excuse, even if the fact could be proved by sight and hearing in every case. Furthermore, now that parties can testify, it may be doubted whether a man's knowledge of the law is any harder to investigate than many questions which are gone into. The difficulty, such as it is, would be met by throwing the burden of proving ignorance on the law-breaker.

The principle cannot be explained by saying that we are not only commanded to abstain from certain acts, but also to find out that we are commanded. For if there were such a second command, it is very clear that the guilt of failing to obey it would bear no proportion to that of disobeying the principal command if known, yet the failure to know would receive the same punishment as the failure to obey the principal law.

The true explanation of the rule is the same as that which accounts for the law's indifference to a man's particular temperament, faculties, and so forth. Public policy sacrifices the individual to the general good. It is desirable that the burden of all should be equal, but it is still more desirable to put an end to robbery and murder. It is no doubt true that there are many cases in which the criminal could not have known that he was breaking the law, but to admit the excuse at all would be to encourage ignorance where the lawmaker has determined to make men know and obey, and justice to the individual is rightly outweighed by the larger interests on the other side of the scales.

If the foregoing arguments are sound, it is already manifest that liability to punishment cannot be finally and absolutely determined by considering the actual personal unworthiness of the criminal alone. That consideration will govern only so far as the public welfare permits or demands. And if we take into account the general result which the criminal law is intended to bring about, we shall see that the actual state of mind accompanying a criminal act plays a different part from what is commonly supposed.

For the most part, the purpose of the criminal law is only to induce external conformity to rule. All law is directed to conditions of things manifest to the senses. And whether it brings those conditions to pass immediately by the use of force, as when it protects a house from a mob by soldiers, or appropriates private property to public use, or hangs a man in pursuance of a judicial sentence, or whether it brings them about mediately through men's fears, its object is equally an external result. In directing itself against robbery or murder, for instance, its purpose is to put a stop to the actual physical taking and keeping of other men's goods, or the actual poisoning, shooting, stabbing, and otherwise putting to death of other men. If those things are not done, the law forbidding them is equally satisfied, whatever the motive.

Considering this purely external purpose of the law together with the fact that it is ready to sacrifice the individual so far as necessary in order to accomplish that purpose, we can see more readily than before that the actual degree of personal guilt involved in any particular transgression cannot be the only element, if it is an element at all, in the liability incurred. So far from its being true, as is often assumed, that the condition of a man's heart or conscience ought to be more considered in determining criminal than civil liability, it might almost be said that it is the very opposite of truth. For civil liability, in its immediate working, is simply a redistribution of an existing loss between two individuals; and it will be argued in the next Lecture that sound policy lets losses lie where they fall, except where a special reason can be shown for interference. The most frequent of such reasons is that the party who is charged has been to blame.

It is not intended to deny that criminal liability, as well as civil, is founded on blameworthiness. Such a denial would shock the moral sense of any civilized community; or, to put it another way, a law which punished conduct which would not be blameworthy in the average member of the community would be too severe for that community to bear. It is only intended to point out that, when we are dealing with that part of the law which aims more directly than any other at establishing standards of conduct, we should expect there more than elsewhere to find that the tests of liability are external, and independent of the degree of evil in the particular person's motives or intentions. The conclusion follows directly from the nature of the standards to which conformity is required. These are not only external, as was shown above, but they are of general application. They do not merely require that every man should get as near as he can to the best conduct possible for him. They require him at his own peril to come up to a certain height. They take no account of incapacities, unless the weakness is so marked as to fall into well-known exceptions, such as infancy or madness. They assume that every man is as able as every other to behave as they command. If they fall on any one class harder than on another, it is on the weakest. For it is precisely to those who are most likely to err by temperament, ignorance, or folly that the threats of the law are the most dangerous . . .

Lecture III

Torts—Trespass and Negligence

. . . An act is always a voluntary muscular contraction, and nothing else. The chain of physical sequences which it sets in motion or directs to the plaintiff's harm is no part of it, and very generally a long train of such sequences intervenes. An example or two will make this extremely clear.

When a man commits an assault and battery with a pistol, his only act is to contract the muscles of his arm and forefinger in a certain way, but it is the delight of elementary writers to point out what a vast series of physical changes must take place before the harm is done. Suppose that, instead of firing a pistol, he takes up a hose which is discharging water on the sidewalk, and directs it at the plaintiff, he does not even set in motion the physical causes which must co-operate with his act to make a battery. Not only natural causes, but a living being, may intervene between the act and its effect. *Gibbons v. Pepper,* which decided that there was no battery when a man's horse was frightened by accident or a third person and ran away with him, and ran over the plaintiff, takes the distinction that, if the rider by spurring is the cause of the accident, then he is guilty. In *Scott v. Shepherd,* trespass was maintained against one who had thrown a squib into a crowd, where it was tossed from hand to hand in self-defence until it burst and injured the plaintiff. Here even human agencies were a part of the chain between the defendant's act and the result, although they were treated as more or less nearly automatic, in order to arrive at the decision.

Now I repeat that, if principle requires us to charge a man in trespass when his act has brought force to bear on another through a comparatively short train of intervening causes, in spite of his having used all possible care, it requires the same liability, however numerous and unexpected the events between the act and the result. If running a man down is a trespass when the accident can be referred to the rider's act of spurring, why is it not a tort in every case, seeing that it can always be referred more remotely to his act of mounting and taking the horse out?

Why is a man not responsible for the consequences of an act innocent in its direct and obvious effects, when those consequences would not have followed but for the intervention of a series of extraordinary, although natural events? The reason is that, if the intervening events are of such a kind that no foresight could have been expected to look out for them, the defendant is not to blame for having failed to do so. It seems to be admitted by the English judges that, even on the question whether the acts of leaving dry trimmings in hot weather by the side of a railroad, and then sending an engine over the track, are negligent—that is, are a ground of liability—the consequences which might reasonably be anticipated are material. Yet these are acts which, under the circumstances, can hardly be called innocent in their natural and obvious effects. The same doctrine has been applied to acts in violation of statute which could not reasonably have been expected to lead to the result complained of.

But there is no difference in principle between the case where a natural cause or physical factor intervenes after the act in some way not to be foreseen, and turns what seemed innocent to harm, and the case where such a cause or factor intervenes, unknown, at the time; as, for the matter of that, it did in the English cases cited. If a man is excused in the one case because he is not to blame, he must be in the other. The difference taken in *Gibbons v. Pepper* is not between results which are and those which are not the consequences of the defendant's acts: it is between consequences which he was bound as a reasonable man to contemplate, and those which he was not. Hard spurring is just so much more likely to lead to harm than merely riding a horse in the street that the court thought that the defendant would be bound to look out for the consequences of the one, while it would not hold him liable for those resulting merely from the other; because the possibility of being run away with when riding quietly, though familiar is comparatively slight. If, however, the horse had been unruly, and had been taken into a frequented place for the purpose of being broken, the owner might have been liable, because "it was his fault to bring a wild horse into a place where mischief might probably be done."

To return to the example of the accidental blow with a stick lifted in self-defence, there is no difference between hitting a person standing in one's rear and hitting one who was pushed by a horse within range of the stick just as it was lifted, provided that it was not possible, under the circumstances, in the one case to have known, in the other to have anticipated, the proximity. In either case there is wanting the only element which distinguishes voluntary acts from spasmodic muscular contractions as a ground of liability. In neither of them, that is to say, has there been an opportunity of choice with reference to the consequence complained of—a chance to guard against the result which has come to pass. A choice which entails a concealed consequence is as to that consequence no choice.

The general principle of our law is that loss from accident must lie where it falls, and this principle is not affected by the fact that a human being is the instrument of misfortune. But relatively to a given human being anything is accident which he could not fairly have been expected to contemplate as possible, and therefore to avoid. In the language of the late Chief Justice Nelson of New York: "No case or principle can be found, or if found can be maintained, subjecting an individual to liability for an act done without fault on his part . . . All the cases concede that an injury arising from inevitable accident, or, which in law or reason is the same thing, from an act that ordinary human care and foresight are unable to guard against, is but the misfortune of the sufferer, and lays no foundation for legal responsibility." If this were not so, any act would be sufficient, however remote, which set in motion or opened the door for a series of physical sequences ending in damage; such as riding the horse, in the case of the runaway, or even coming to a place where one is seized with a fit and strikes the plaintiff in an unconscious spasm. Nay, why need the defendant have acted at all, and why is it not enough that his existence has been at the expense of the plaintiff? The requirement of an act is the requirement that the defendant should have made a choice. But the only possible purpose of introducing this moral element is to make the power of avoiding the evil complained of a condition of liability. There is no such power where the evil cannot be foreseen. Here we reach the argument from policy . . . A man need not, it is true, do this or that act—the term *act* implies a choice—but he must act somehow. Furthermore, the public generally profits by individual activity. As action cannot be avoided, and tends to the public good, there is obviously no policy in throwing the hazard of what is at once desirable and inevitable upon the actor.

The state might conceivably make itself a mutual insurance company against accidents, and distribute the burden of its citizens' mishaps among all its members. There might be a pension for paralytics, and state aid for those who suffered in person or estate from tempest or wild beasts. As between individuals it might adopt the mutual insurance principle *pro tanto,* and divide damages when both were in fault, as in the *rusticum judicium* of the admiralty, or it might throw all loss upon the actor irrespective of fault. The state does none of these things, however, and the prevailing view is that its cumbrous and expensive machinery ought not to be set in motion unless some clear benefit is to be derived from disturbing the status quo. State interference is an evil, where it cannot be shown to be a good. Universal insurance, if desired, can be better and more cheaply accomplished by private enterprise. The undertaking to redistribute losses simply on the ground that they resulted from the defendant's act would not only be open to these objections, but, as it is hoped the preceding discussion has shown, to the still graver one of offending the sense of justice. Unless my act is of a nature to threaten others, unless under the circumstances a prudent man would have foreseen the possibility of harm, it is no more justifiable to make me indemnify my neighbor against the consequences, than to make me do the same thing if I had fallen upon him in a fit, or to compel me to insure him against lightning . . .

Supposing it now to be conceded that the general notion upon which liability to an action is founded is fault or blameworthiness in some sense, the question arises, whether it is so in the sense of personal moral shortcoming . . . Suppose that a defendant were allowed to testify that, before acting, he considered carefully what would be the conduct of a prudent man under the circumstances, and, having formed the best judgment he could, acted accordingly. If the story was believed, it would be conclusive against the defendant's negligence judged by a moral standard which would take his personal characteristics into account. But supposing any such evidence to have got before the jury, it is very clear that the court would say, Gentlemen, the question is not whether the defendant thought his conduct was that of a prudent man, but whether you think it was.

Some middle point must be found between the horns of this dilemma.

The standards of the law are standards of general application. The law takes no account of the infinite varieties of temperament, intellect, and education which make the internal character of a given act so different in different men. It does not attempt to see men as God sees them, for more than one sufficient reason. In the first place, the impossibility of nicely measuring a man's powers and limitations is far clearer than that of ascertaining his knowledge of law, which has been thought to account for what is called the presumption that every man knows the law. But a more satisfactory explanation is that, when men live in society, a certain average of conduct, a sacrifice of individual peculiarities going beyond a certain point, is necessary to the general welfare. If, for instance, a man is born hasty and awkward, is always having accidents and hurting himself or his neighbors, no doubt his congenital defects will be allowed for in the courts of Heaven, but his slips are no less troublesome to his neighbors than if they sprang from guilty neglect. His neighbors accordingly require him, at his proper peril, to come up to their standard, and the courts which they establish decline to take his personal equation into account.

The rule that the law does, in general, determine liability by blameworthiness is subject to the limitation that minute differences of character are not allowed for. The law considers, in other words, what would be blameworthy in the average man, the man of ordinary intelligence and prudence, and determines liability by that. If we fall below the level in those gifts, it is our misfortune; so much as that we must behave at our peril, for the reasons just given. But he who is intelligent and prudent does not act at his peril, in theory of law. On the contrary, it is only when he fails to exercise the foresight of which he is capable, or exercises it with evil intent, that he is answerable for the consequences.

There are exceptions to the principle that every man is presumed to possess ordinary capacity to avoid harm to his neighbors, which illustrate the rule, and also the moral basis of liability in general. When a man has a distinct defect of such a nature that all can recognize it as making certain precautions impossible, he will not be held answerable for not taking them. A blind man is not required to see at his peril; and although he is, no doubt, bound to consider his infirmity in regulating his actions, yet if he properly finds himself in a certain situation, the neglect of precautions requiring eyesight would not prevent his recovering for an injury to himself, and, it may be presumed, would not make him liable for injuring another. So it is held that, in cases where he is the plaintiff, an infant of very tender years is only bound to take the precautions of which an infant is capable; the same principle may be cautiously applied where he is defendant. Insanity is a more difficult matter to deal with, and no general rule can be laid down about it. There is no doubt that in many cases a man may be insane, and yet perfectly capable of taking the precautions, and of being influenced by the motives, which the circumstances demand. But if insanity of a pronounced type exists, manifestly incapacitating the sufferer from complying with the rule which he has broken, good sense would require it to be admitted as an excuse.

Taking the qualification last established in connection with the general proposition previously laid down, it will now be assumed that, on the one hand, the law presumes or requires a man to possess ordinary capacity to avoid harming his neighbors, unless a clear and manifest incapacity be shown; but that, on the other, it does not in general hold him liable for unintentional injury, unless possessing such capacity, he might and ought to have foreseen the danger, or, in other words, unless a man of ordinary intelligence and forethought would have been to blame for acting as he did. The next question is, whether this vague test is all that the law has to say upon the matter, and the same question in another form, by whom this test is to be applied.

Notwithstanding the fact that grounds of legal liability are moral to the extent above explained, it must be borne in mind that law only works within the sphere of the senses. If the external phenomena, the manifest acts and omissions, are such as it requires, it is wholly indifferent to the internal phenomena of conscience. A man may have as bad a heart as he chooses, if his conduct is within the rules. In other words, the standards of the law are external standards, and, however much it may take moral considerations into account, it does so only for the purpose of drawing a line between such bodily motions and rests as it permits, and such as it does not. What the law really forbids, and the only thing it forbids, is the act on the wrong side of the line, be that act blameworthy or otherwise.

Again, any legal standard must, in theory, be one which would apply to all men, not specially excepted, under the same circumstances. It is not intended that the public force should fall upon an individual accidentally, or at the whim of any body of men. The standard, that is, must be fixed. In practice, no doubt, one man may have to pay and another may escape, according to the different feelings of different juries. But this merely shows that the law does not perfectly accomplish its ends. The theory or intention of the law is not that the feeling of approbation or blame which a particular twelve may entertain should be the criterion. They are supposed to leave their idiosyncrasies on one side, and to represent the feeling of the community. The ideal average prudent man, whose equivalent the jury is taken to be in many cases, and whose culpability or innocence is the supposed test, is a constant, and his conduct under given circumstances is theoretically always the same.

Finally, any legal standard must, in theory, be capable of being known. When a man has to pay damages, he is supposed to have broken the law, and he is further supposed to have known what the law was.

If, now, the ordinary liabilities in tort arise from failure to comply with fixed and uniform standards of external conduct, which every man is presumed and required to know, it is obvious that it ought to be possible, sooner or later, to formulate these standards at least to some extent, and that to do so must at last be the business of the court. It is equally clear that the featureless generality, that the defendant was bound to use such care as a prudent man would do under the circumstances, ought to be continually giving place to the specific one, that he was bound to use this or that precaution under these or those circumstances. The standard which the defendant was bound to come up to was a standard of specific acts or omissions, with reference to the specific circumstances in which he found himself. If in the whole department of unintentional wrongs the courts arrived at no further utterance than the question of negligence, and left every case, without rudder or compass, to the jury, they would simply confess their inability to state a very large part of the law which they required the defendant to know, and would assert, by implication, that nothing could be learned by experience. But neither courts nor legislatures have ever stopped at that point.

From the time of Alfred to the present day, statutes and decisions have busied themselves with defining the precautions to be taken in certain familiar cases; that is, with substituting for the vague test of the care exercised by a prudent man, a precise one of specific acts or omissions. The fundamental thought is still the same, that the way prescribed is that in which prudent men are in the habit of acting, or else is one laid down for cases where prudent men might otherwise be in doubt.

It will be observed that the existence of the external tests of liability which will be mentioned, while it illustrates the tendency of the law of tort to become more and more concrete by judicial decision and by statute, does not interfere with the general doctrine maintained as to the grounds of liability. The argument of this Lecture, although opposed to the doctrine that a man acts or exerts force at his peril, is by no means opposed to the doctrine that he does certain particular acts at his peril. It is the coarseness, not the nature, of the standard which is objected to. If, when the question of the defendant's negligence is left to a jury, negligence does not mean the actual state of the defendant's mind, but a failure to act as a prudent man of average intelligence would have done, he is required to conform to an objective standard at his peril, even in that case. When a more exact and specific rule has been arrived at, he must obey that rule at his peril to the same extent. But, further, if the law is wholly a standard of external conduct, a man must always comply with that standard at his peril . . .

When a case arises in which the standard of conduct, pure and simple, is submitted to the jury, the explanation is plain. It is that the court, not entertaining any clear views of public policy applicable to the matter, derives the rule to be applied from daily experience, as it has been agreed that the great body of the law of tort has been derived. But the court further feels that it is not itself possessed of sufficient practical experience to lay down the rule intelligently. It conceives that twelve men taken from the practical part of the community can aid its judgment. Therefore it aids its conscience by taking the opinion of the jury.

But supposing a state of facts often repeated in practice, is it to be imagined that the court is to go on leaving the standard to the jury forever? Is it not manifest, on the contrary, that if the jury is, on the whole, as fair a tribunal as it is represented to be, the lesson which can be got from that source will be learned? Either the court will find that the fair teaching of experience is that the conduct complained of usually is or is not blameworthy, and therefore, unless explained, is or is not a ground of liability; or it will find the jury oscillating to and fro, and will see the necessity of making up its mind for itself. There is no reason why any other such question should not be settled, as well as that of liability for stairs with smooth strips of brass upon their edges. The exceptions would mainly be found where the standard was rapidly changing, as, for instance, in some questions of medical treatment . . .

It is perfectly consistent with the views maintained in this Lecture that the courts have been very slow to withdraw questions of negligence from the jury, without distinguishing nicely whether the doubt concerned the facts or the standard to be applied. Legal, like natural divisions, however clear in their general outline, will be found on exact scrutiny to end in a penumbra or debatable land. This is the region of the jury, and only cases falling on this doubtful border are likely to be carried far in court. Still, the tendency of the law must always be to narrow the field of uncertainty. That is what analogy, as well as the decisions on this very subject, would lead us to expect.

The growth of the law is very apt to take place in this way. Two widely different cases suggest a general distinction, which is a clear one when stated broadly. But as new cases cluster around the opposite poles, and begin to approach each other, the distinction becomes more difficult to trace; the determinations are made one way or the other on a very slight preponderance of feeling, rather than of articulate reason; and at last a mathematical line is arrived at by the contact of contrary decisions, which is so far arbitrary that it might equally well have been drawn a little farther to the one side or to the other, but which must have been drawn somewhere in the neighborhood of where it falls.

In this way exact distinctions have been worked out upon questions in which the elements to be considered are few. For instance, what is a reasonable time for presenting negotiable paper, or what is a difference in kind and what a difference only in quality, or the rule against perpetuities . . .

The same principle applies to negligence. If the whole evidence in the case was that a party, in full command of his senses and intellect, stood on a railway track, looking at an approaching engine until it ran him down, no judge would leave it to the jury to say whether the conduct was prudent. If the whole evidence was that he attempted to cross a level track, which was visible for half a mile each way, and on which no engine was in sight, no court would allow a jury to find negligence. Between these extremes are cases which would go to the jury. But it is obvious that the limit of safety in such cases, supposing no further elements present, could be determined almost to a foot by mathematical calculation.

The trouble with many cases of negligence is that they are of a kind not frequently recurring so as to enable any given judge to profit by long experience with juries to lay down rules, and that the elements are so complex that courts are glad to leave the whole matter in a lump for the jury's determination . . .

Lecture VIII

II. Elements of Contract

. . . It is now time to analyze the nature of a promise, which is the . . . most conspicuous element in a simple contract . . .

An assurance that it shall rain tomorrow, or that a third person shall paint a picture, may as well be a promise as one that the promisee shall receive from some source one hundred bales of cotton, or that the promisor will pay the promisee one hundred dollars. What is the difference in the cases? It is only in the degree of power possessed by the promisor over the event. He has none in the first case. He has equally little legal authority to make a man paint a picture, although he may have larger means of persuasion. He probably will be able to make sure that the promisee has the cotton. Being a rich man, he is certain to be able to pay the one hundred dollars, except in the event of some most improbable accident.

But the law does not inquire, as a general thing, how far the accomplishment of an assurance touching the future is within the power of the promisor. In the moral world it may be that the obligation of a promise is confined to what lies within reach of the will of the promisor (except so far as the limit is unknown on one side, and misrepresented on the other). But unless some consideration of public policy intervenes, I take it that a man may bind himself at law that any future event shall happen. He can therefore promise it in a legal sense. It may be said that when a man covenants that it shall rain tomorrow, or that A shall paint a picture, he only says, in a short form, I will pay if it does not rain, or if A does not paint a picture. But that is not necessarily so. A promise could easily be framed which would be broken by the happening of fair weather, or by A not painting. A promise, then, is simply an accepted assurance that a certain event or state of things shall come to pass.

But if this be true, it has more important bearings than simply to enlarge the definition of the word *promise*. It concerns the theory of contract. The consequences of a binding promise at common law are not affected by the degree of power which the promisor possesses over the promised event. If the promised event does not come to pass, the plaintiff's property is sold to satisfy the damages, within certain limits, which the promisee has suffered by the failure. The consequences are the same in kind whether the promise is that it shall rain, or that another man shall paint a picture, or that the promisor will deliver a bale of cotton.

If the legal consequence is the same in all cases, it seems proper that all contracts should be considered from the same legal point of view. In the case of a binding promise that it shall rain tomorrow, the immediate legal effect of what the promisor does is that he takes the risk of the event, within certain defined limits, as between himself and the promisee. He does no more when he promises to deliver a bale of cotton.

If it be proper to state the common-law meaning of promise and contract in this way, it has the advantage of freeing the subject from the superfluous theory that contract is a qualified subjection of one will to another, a kind of limited slavery. It might be so regarded if the law compelled men to perform their contracts, or if it allowed promisees to exercise such compulsion. If, when a man promised to labor for another, the law made him do it, his relation to the promisee might be called a servitude *ad hoc* with some truth. But that is what the law never does. It never interferes until a promise has been broken, and therefore cannot possibly be performed according to its tenor. It is true that in some instances equity does what is called compelling specific performance. But, in the first place, I am speaking of the common law, and, in the next, this only means that equity compels the performance of certain elements of the total promise which are still capable of performance. For instance, take a promise to convey land within a certain time, a court of equity is not in the habit of interfering until the time has gone by, so that the promise cannot be performed as made. But if the conveyance is more important than the time, and the promisee prefers to have it late rather than never, the law may compel the performance of that. Not literally compel even in that case, however, but put the promisor in prison unless he will convey. This remedy is an exceptional one. The only universal consequence of a legally binding promise is that the law makes the promisor pay damages if the promised event does not come to pass. In every case it leaves him free from interference until the time for fulfilment has gone by, and therefore free to break his contract if he chooses.

A more practical advantage in looking at a contract as the taking of a risk is to be found in the light which it throws upon the measure of damages. If a breach of contract were regarded in the same light as a tort, it would seem that if in the course of performance of the contract the promisor should be notified of any particular consequence which would result from its not being performed, he should be held liable for that consequence in the event of non-performance. Such a suggestion has been made. But it has not been accepted as the law. On the contrary, according to the opinion of a very able judge, which seems to be generally followed, notice, even at the time of making the contract, of special circumstances out of which special damages would arise in case of breach, is not sufficient unless the assumption of that risk is to be taken as having fairly entered into the contract. If a carrier should undertake to carry the machinery of a sawmill from Liverpool to Vancouver Island, and should fail to do so, he probably would not be held liable for the rate of hire of such machinery during the necessary delay, although he might know that it could not be replaced without sending to England, unless he was fairly understood to accept "the contract with the special condition attached to it."

It is true that, when people make contracts, they usually contemplate the performance rather than the breach. The express language used does not generally go further than to define what will happen if the contract is fulfilled. A statutory requirement of a memorandum in writing would be satisfied by a written statement of the promise as made, because to require more would be to run counter to the ordinary habits of mankind, as well as because the statement that the effect of a contract is the assumption of the risk of a future event does not mean that there is a second subsidiary promise to assume that risk, but that the assumption follows as a consequence directly enforced by the law, without the promisor's cooperation. So parol evidence would be admissible, no doubt, to enlarge or diminish the extent of the liability assumed for non-performance, where it would be inadmissible to affect the scope of the promise.

But these concessions do not affect the view here taken. As the relation of contractor and contractee is voluntary, the consequences attaching to the relation must be voluntary. What the event contemplated by the promise is, or in other words what will amount to a breach of contract, is a matter of interpretation and construction. What consequences of the breach are assumed is more remotely, in like manner, a matter of construction, having regard to the circumstances under which the contract is made. Knowledge of what is dependent upon performance is one of those circumstances. It is not necessarily conclusive, but it may have the effect of enlarging the risk assumed.

The very office of construction is to work out, from what is expressly said and done, what would have been said with regard to events not definitely before the minds of the parties, if those events had been considered. The price paid in mercantile contracts generally excludes the construction that exceptional risks were intended to be assumed. The foregoing analysis is believed to show that the result which has been reached by the courts on grounds of practical good sense falls in with the true theory of contract under the common law . . .

To Harold Laski

February 1, 1919

Dear Laski,

. . . As to Zane, if anyone takes the trouble to deal with him I think he should be handled lightly not wrathfully. A man who calls everybody a damn fool is like a man who damns the weather—he only shows that he is not adapted to his environment, not that the environment is wrong. As to the two points on which he falls foul of me, hitherto I have regarded those who doubted that the judges made law (interstitially) as simply incompetent or else carried away by a hobby. On the matter of sovereignty also I can't see a question about the proposition as I mean it. Of course I am not speaking of origins and don't care how far it may have been derived from *princeps legibus solutus* or how far that formula needs qualification—nor on the other hand is it material that every ultimate repository of ultimate political power *de facto* has limits beyond which it cannot go because the people would fight—that is fact not law. I simply say that the ultimate source of law when you find it is subject to such laws or resolutions only as it chooses to impose upon itself, from a legal point of view, and that therefore the State is not subject to legal claims except so far as it sees fit to submit itself to them—and I should think that that was obvious. Zane says the conclusion is right but it is simply a matter of convenience—who determines the convenience unless it is the mouthpiece of the State? He seems to me to fall back on dogmatic dissatisfaction, and hardly to show his own hand if he has one—but I speak from a hasty reading and have not his articles by me . . .

To recur to Zane there is one other point that I forgot. He is patronizing to the errors of my *Common Law.* I don't know whether it has serious ones or how many—but I think the material thing to be that I gathered the flax, made the thread, spun the cloth, and cut the garment—and started all the inquiries that since have gone over many matters therein. Every original book has the seeds of its own death in it, by provoking further investigation and clearer restatement, but it remains the original and I think it already is forgotten how far that is true of the *C.L.*

June 1, 1922

Dear Laski:

. . . You ask me what started my book. Of course I can't answer for unconscious elements. I don't think Maine had anything to do with it except to feed the philosophic passion. I think the movement came from within—from the passionate demand that what sounded so arbitrary in Blackstone, for instance, should give some reasonable meaning—that the law should be proved, if it could be, to be worthy of the interest of an intelligent man (that was the form the question took then). I went through much anguish of mind before I realized the answer to that question that I have often given since . . .

Globe Refining Co. v. Landa Cotton Oil Co.
190 U.S. 540 (1903)

This is an action of contract brought by the plaintiff in error [i.e., the appellant], a Kentucky corporation, against the defendant in error, a Texas corporation, for breach of a contract to sell and deliver crude oil. The defendant excepted to certain allegations of damage, and pleaded that the damages had been claimed and magnified fraudulently for the purpose of giving the United States circuit court jurisdiction, when in truth they were less than $2,000. The judge sustained the exceptions. He also tried the question of jurisdiction before hearing the merits, refused the plaintiff a jury, found that the plea was sustained, and dismissed the cause. The plaintiff excepted to all the rulings and action of the court, and brings the case here by writ of error . . .

The contract was made through a broker, it would seem by writing, and, at all events, was admitted to be correctly stated in the following letter:

Dallas, Texas, 7/30/97

Landa Oil Company
New Braunfels, Texas

Gentlemen:
Referring to the exchange of our telegrams today, we have sold for your account to the Globe Refining Company, Louisville, Kentucky, ten (10) tanks prime crude C/S oil at the price of 15-3/4 cents per gallon of 7-1/2 pounds, f.o.b. buyers' tank at your mill. Weights and quality guaranteed.

Terms: Sight draft without exchange b/ldg. attached. Sellers paying commission.

Shipment: Part last half August and balance first half September. Shipping instructions to be furnished by the Globe Refining Company.

Yours truly,
Thomas & Green, as Broker

Having this contract before us, we proceed to consider the allegations of special damage over and above the difference between the contract price of the oil and the price at the time of the breach, which was the measure adopted by the judge. These allegations must be read with care, for it is obvious that the pleader has gone as far as he dared to go, and to the verge of anything that could be justified under the contract, if not beyond.

It is alleged that it was agreed and understood that the plaintiff would send its tank cars to the defendant's mills, and that the defendant promptly would fill them with oil (so far, simply following the contract), and that the plaintiff sent tanks. "In order to do this, the plaintiff was under the necessity of obligating itself unconditionally to the railroad company (and of which the defendant had notice) to pay to it for the transportation of the cars from said Louisville to said New Braunfels in the sum of $900," which sum plaintiff had to pay, "and was incurred as an advancement on said oil contract." This is the first item. The last words quoted mean only that the sum paid would have been allowed by the railroad as part payment of the return charges had the tanks been filled and sent back over the same road.

Next it is alleged that the defendant, contemplating a breach of the contract, caused the plaintiff to send its cars a thousand miles, at a cost of $1,000; that defendant canceled its contract on the 2d of September, but did not notify the plaintiff until the 14th, when, if the plaintiff had known of the cancellation, it would have been supplying itself from other sources; that plaintiff (no doubt defendant is meant) did so willfully and maliciously, causing an unnecessary loss of $2,000.

Next it is alleged that, by reason of the breach of contract and want of notice, plaintiff lost the use of its tanks for thirty days—a loss estimated at $700 more. Next it is alleged that the plaintiff had arranged with its own customers to furnish the oil in question within a certain time, which contemplated sharp compliance with the contract by the defendant; "all of which facts, as above stated, were well known to the defendant, and defendant had contracted to that end with the plaintiff." This item is put at $740, with $1,000 more for loss of customers, credit, and reputation. Finally, at the end of the petition, it is alleged generally that it was known to defendant, and in contemplation of the contract, that plaintiff would have to send tanks at great expense from distant points, and that plaintiff "was required to pay additional freight in order to rearrange the destination of the various tanks and other points." Then it is alleged that by reason of the defendant's breach, the plaintiff had to pay $350 additional freight.

Whatever may be the scope of the allegations which we have quoted, it will be seen that none of the items was contemplated expressly by the words of the bargain. Those words are before us in writing, and go no further than to contemplate that when the deliveries were to take place the buyer's tanks should be at the defendant's mill. Under such circumstances the question is suggested how far the express terms of a writing, admitted to be complete, can be enlarged by averment and oral evidence; and, if they can be enlarged in that way, what averments are sufficient. When a man commits a tort, he incurs, by force of the law, a liability to damages, measured by certain rules. When a man makes a contract, he incurs, by force of the law, a liability to damages, unless a certain promised event comes to pass. But, unlike the case of torts, as the contract is by mutual consent, the parties themselves, expressly or by implication, fix the rule by which the damages are to be measured. The old law seems to have regarded it as technically in the election of the promisor to perform or to pay damages. It is true that, as people when contracting contemplate performance, not breach, they commonly say little or nothing as to what shall happen in the latter event, and the common rules have been worked out by common sense, which has established what the parties probably would have said if they had spoken about the matter. But a man never can be absolutely certain of performing any contract when the time of performance arrives, and, in many cases, he obviously is taking the risk of an event which is wholly, or to an appreciable extent, beyond his control. The extent of liability in such cases is likely to be within his contemplation, and, whether it is or not, should be worked out on terms which it fairly may be presumed he would have assented to if they had been presented to his mind. For instance, in the present case, the defendant's mill and all its oil might have been burned before the time came for delivery. Such a misfortune would not have been an excuse, although probably it would have prevented performance of the contract. If a contract is broken, the measure of damages generally is the same, whatever the cause of the breach. We have to consider, therefore, what the plaintiff would have been entitled to recover in that case, and that depends on what liability the defendant fairly may be supposed to have assumed consciously, or to have warranted the plaintiff reasonably to suppose that it assumed, when the contract was made . . .

The question arises, then. What is sufficient to show that the consequences were in contemplation of the parties, in the sense of the vendor taking the risk? . . . It may be said with safety that mere notice to a seller of some interest or probable action of the buyer is not enough necessarily and as matter of law to charge the seller with special damage on that account if he fails to deliver the goods. With that established, we recur to the allegations. With regard to the first, it is obvious that the plaintiff was free to bring its tanks from where it liked—a thousand miles away or an adjoining yard—so far as the contract was concerned. The allegation hardly amounts to saying that the defendant had notice that the plaintiff was likely to send its cars from a distance. It is not alleged that the defendant had notice that the plaintiff had to bind itself to pay $900, at the time when the contract was made, and it nowhere is alleged that the defendant assumed any liability in respect of this uncertain element of charge. The same observations may be made with regard to the claim for loss of use of the tanks and to the final allegations as to sending the tanks from distant points. It is true that this last was alleged to have been in contemplation of the contract, if we give the plaintiff the benefit of the doubt in construing a somewhat confused sentence. But, having the contract before us, we can see that this ambiguous expression cannot be taken to mean more than notice, and notice of a fact which would depend upon the accidents of the future.

It is to be said further, with regard to the foregoing items, that they were the expenses which the plaintiff was willing to incur for performance. If it had received the oil, these were deductions from any profit which the plaintiff would have made. But, if it gets the difference between the contract price and the market price, it gets what represents the value of the oil in its hands, and to allow these items in addition would be making the defendant pay twice for the same thing.

It must not be forgotten that we are dealing with pleadings, not evidence, and with pleadings which, as we have said, evidently put the plaintiff's case as high as it possibly can be put . . . It is a simple question of allegations which, by declining to amend, the plaintiff has admitted that it cannot reinforce. This consideration applies with special force to the attempt to hold the defendant liable for the breach of the plaintiff's contract with third persons. The allegation is that the fact that the plaintiff had contracts over was well known to the defendant, and that "defendant had contracted to that end with the plaintiff." Whether, if we were sitting as a jury, this would warrant an inference that the defendant assumed an additional liability, we need not consider. It is enough to say that it does not allege the conclusion of fact so definitely that it must be assumed to be true. With the contract before us it is in a high degree improbable that any such conclusion could have been made good . . .

LeRoy Fibre Company v. Chicago, Milwaukee & St. Paul Railway
232 U.S. 340 (1914)

Mr. Justice Holmes partially concurring.

The first two questions concern a standard of conduct and therefore that which in its nature and in theory is a question of law. In this, I gather, we all agree, although the proposition often is forgotten or denied. But while the standard is external to the judgment of the party concerned and must be known and conformed to by him at his peril, courts, by a practice that seems at first sight an abdication of their function where it is most needed but that I dare say is justified by good sense, in nice cases leave the standard to the jury as well as the facts. In the questions before us, however, the elements supposed are few and frequently recurring, so that but for what I have to say I should be very content to find that we were able to lay down the proper rule without a jury's aid. Furthermore, with regard to what that rule should be, I agree, for the purposes of argument, that as a general proposition people are entitled to assume that their neighbors will conform to the law; that a negligent tort is unlawful in as full a sense as a malicious one, and therefore that they are entitled to assume that their neighbors will not be negligent.

. . . If a man stacked his flax so near to a railroad that it obviously was likely to be set fire to by a well-managed train, I should say that he could not throw the loss upon the railroad by the oscillating result of an inquiry by the jury whether the road had used due care. I should say that although of course he had a right to put his flax where he liked upon his own land, the liability of the railroad for a fire was absolutely conditioned upon the stacks being at a reasonably safe distance from the train. I take it that probably many, certainly some, rules of law based on less than universal considerations are made absolute and universal in order to limit those over-refined speculations that we all deprecate, especially where such rules are based upon or affect the continuous physical relations of material things. The right that is given to inflict various inconveniences upon neighboring lands by building or digging is given, I presume, because of the public interest in making improvement free, yet it generally is made absolute by the common law. It is not thought worthwhile to let the right to build or maintain a barn depend upon the speculations of a jury as to motives. A defect in the highway, declared a defect in the interest of the least competent travelers that can travel unattended without taking legal risks, or in the interest of the average man, I suppose to be a defect as to all. And as in this case the distinction between the inevitable and the negligent escape of sparks is one of the most refined in the world, I think that I must be right so far, as to the law in the case supposed.

If I am right so far, a very important element in determining the right to recover is whether the plaintiff's flax was so near to the track as to be in danger from even a prudently managed engine. Here certainly, except in a clear case, we should call in the jury. I do not suppose that anyone would call it prudent to stack flax within five feet of the engines or imprudent to do it at a distance of half a mile, and it would not be absurd if the law ultimately should formulate an exact measure, as it has tended to in other instances; but at present I take it that if the question I suggest be material we should let the jury decide whether seventy feet was too near by the criterion that I have proposed . . .

I do not think we need trouble ourselves with the thought that my view depends upon differences of degree. Negligence is all degree—that of the defendant here degree of the nicest sort; and between the variations according to distance that I suppose to exist and the simple universality of the rules in the Twelve Tables or the Leges Barbarorum, there lies the culture of two thousand years.

United Zinc & Chemical Company v. Britt
258 U.S. 268 (1922)

This is a suit brought by the respondents against the petitioner to recover for the death of two children, sons of the respondents. The facts that for the purposes of decision we shall assume to have been proved are these. The petitioner owned a tract of about twenty acres in the outskirts of the town of Iola, Kansas. Formerly it had there a plant for the making of sulphuric acid and zinc spelter. In 1910 it tore the buildings down but left a basement and cellar, in which in July, 1916, water was accumulated, clear in appearance but in fact dangerously poisoned by sulphuric acid and zinc sulphate that had come in one way or another from the petitioner's works, as the petitioner knew. The respondents had been traveling and encamped at some distance from this place. A traveled way passed within 120 or 100 feet of it. On July 27, 1916, the children, who were eight and eleven years old, came upon the petitioner's land, went into the water, were poisoned and died. The petitioner saved the question whether it could be held liable. At the trial the judge instructed the jury that if the water looked clear but in fact was poisonous and thus the children were allured to it the petitioner was liable. The respondents got a verdict and judgment, which was affirmed by the circuit court of appeals.

. . . If the children had been adults they would have had no case. They would have been trespassers and the owner of the land would have owed no duty to remove even hidden danger; it would have been entitled to assume that they would obey the law and not trespass. The liability for spring guns and mantraps arises from the fact that the defendant has not rested on that assumption, but on the contrary has expected the trespasser and prepared an injury that is no more justified than if he had held the gun and fired it. Infants have no greater right to go upon other people's land than adults, and the mere fact that they are infants imposes no duty upon landowners to expect them and to prepare for their safety. On the other hand the duty of one who invites another upon his land not to lead him into a trap is well settled, and while it is very plain that temptation is not invitation, it may be held that knowingly to establish and expose, unfenced, to children of an age when they follow a bait as mechanically as a fish, something that is certain to attract them, has the legal effect of an invitation to them although not to an adult. But the principle if accepted must be very cautiously applied.

In *Railroad Co. v. Stout,* the well-known case of a boy injured on a turntable, it appeared that children had played there before, to the knowledge of employees of the railroad, and in view of that fact and the situation of the turntable near a road without visible separation, it seems to have been assumed without much discussion that the railroad owed a duty to the boy. Perhaps this was as strong a case as would be likely to occur of maintaining a known temptation, where temptation takes the place of invitation.

In the case at bar it is at least doubtful whether the water could be seen from any place where the children lawfully were and there is no evidence that it was what led them to enter the land. But that is necessary to start the supposed duty. There can be no general duty on the part of a landowner to keep his land safe for children, or even free from hidden dangers, if he has not directly or by implication invited or licensed them to come there . . . It does not appear that children were in the habit of going to the place; so that foundation also fails.

Union Pacific Ry. Co. v. McDonald is less in point. There a boy was burned by falling into burning coal slack close by the side of a path on which he was running homeward from other boys who had frightened him. It hardly appears that he was a trespasser and the path suggests an invitation; at all events boys habitually resorted to the place where he was. Also the defendant was under a statutory duty to fence the place sufficiently to keep out cattle. The decision is very far from establishing that the petitioner is liable for poisoned water not bordering a road, not shown to have been the inducement that led the children to trespass, if in any event the law would deem it sufficient to excuse their going there, and not shown to have been the indirect inducement because known to the children to be frequented by others. It is suggested that the roads across the place were invitations. A road is not an invitation to leave it elsewhere than at its end.

Judgment reversed.

Baltimore & Ohio Railroad v. Goodman
275 U.S. 66 (1927)

This is a suit brought by the widow and administratrix of Nathan Goodman against the petitioner for causing his death by running him down at a grade crossing. The defense is that Goodman's own negligence caused the death. At the trial the defendant asked the court to direct a verdict for it, but the request, and others looking to the same direction, were refused, and the plaintiff got a verdict and a judgment which was affirmed by the circuit court of appeals.

Goodman was driving an automobile truck in an easterly direction and was killed by a train running southwesterly across the road at a rate of not less than sixty miles an hour. The line was straight, but it is said by the respondent that Goodman "had no practical view" beyond a section house 243 feet north of the crossing until he was about twenty feet from the first rail, or, as the respondent argues, twelve feet from danger, and that then the engine was still obscured by the section house. He had been driving at the rate of ten or twelve miles an hour, but had cut down his rate to five or six miles at about forty feet from the crossing. It is thought that there was an emergency in which, so far as appears, Goodman did all that he could.

We do not go into further details as to Goodman's precise situation, beyond mentioning that it was daylight and that he was familiar with the crossing, for it appears to us plain that nothing is suggested by the evidence to relieve Goodman from responsibility for his own death. When a man goes upon a railroad track he knows that he goes to a place where he will be killed if a train comes upon him before he is clear of the track. He knows that he must stop for the train, not the train stop for him. In such circumstances it seems to us that if a driver cannot be sure otherwise whether a train is dangerously near he must stop and get out of his vehicle, although obviously he will not often be required to do more than to stop and look. It seems to us that if he relies upon not hearing the train or any signal and takes no further precaution he does so at his own risk. If at the last moment Goodman found himself in an emergency it was his own fault that he did not reduce his speed earlier or come to a stop. It is true that the question of due care very generally is left to the jury. But we are dealing with a standard of conduct, and when the standard is clear it should be laid down once for all by the courts.

Judgment reversed.

Brown v. United States
256 U.S. 335 (1921)

The petitioner was convicted of murder in the second degree committed upon one Hermis at a place in Texas within the exclusive jurisdiction of the United States, and the judgment was affirmed by the circuit court of appeals . . .

There had been trouble between Hermis and the defendant for a long time. There was evidence that Hermis had twice assaulted the defendant with a knife and had made threats communicated to the defendant that the next time, one of them would go off in a black box. On the day in question the defendant was at the place above mentioned superintending excavation work for a post office. In view of Hermis's threats he had taken a pistol with him and had laid it in his coat upon a dump. Hermis was driven up by a witness, in a cart to be loaded, and the defendant said that certain earth was not to be removed, whereupon Hermis came toward him, the defendant says, with a knife. The defendant retreated some twenty or twenty-five feet to where his coat was and got his pistol. Hermis was striking at him and the defendant fired four shots and killed him. The judge instructed the jury among other things that "it is necessary to remember, in considering the question of self-defense, that the party assaulted is always under the obligation to retreat so long as retreat is open to him, provided he can do so without subjecting himself to the danger of death or great bodily harm." The instruction was reinforced by the further intimation that unless "retreat would have appeared to a man of reasonable prudence, in the position of the defendant, as involving danger of death or serious bodily harm," the defendant was not entitled to stand his ground. An instruction to the effect that if the defendant had reasonable grounds of apprehension that he was in danger of losing his life or of suffering serious bodily harm from Hermis he was not bound to retreat was refused. So the question is brought out with sufficient clearness whether the formula laid down by the court and often repeated by the ancient law is adequate to the protection of the defendant's rights.

It is useless to go into the developments of the law from the time when a man who had killed another no matter how innocently had to get his pardon, whether of grace or of course. Concrete cases or illustrations stated in the early law in conditions very different from the present, like the reference to retreat in Coke, have had a tendency to ossify into specific rules without much regard for reason. Other examples may be found in the law as to trespass ab initio, and as to fresh complaint after rape. Rationally the failure to retreat is a circumstance to be considered with all the others in order to determine whether the defendant went farther than he was justified in doing; not a categorical proof of guilt. The law has grown, and even if historical mistakes have contributed to its growth it has tended in the direction of rules consistent with human nature. Many respectable writers agree that if a man reasonably believes that he is in immediate danger of death or grievous bodily harm from his assailant he may stand his ground and that if he kills him he has not exceeded the bounds of lawful self-defense. That has been the decision of this Court. Detached reflection cannot be demanded in the presence of an uplifted knife. Therefore in this Court, at least, it is not a condition of immunity that one in that situation should pause to consider whether a reasonable man might not think it possible to fly with safety or to disable his assailant rather than to kill him. The law of Texas very strongly adopts these views, as is shown by many cases . . .

Commonwealth v. Pierce
138 Mass. 165 (1884)

The defendant has been found guilty of manslaughter, on evidence that he publicly practised as a physician, and, being called to attend a sick woman, caused her, with her consent, to be kept in flannels saturated with kerosene for three days, more or less, by reason of which she died. There was evidence that he had made similar applications with favorable results in other cases, but that in one the effect had been to blister and burn the flesh as in the present case . . .

The court instructed the jury, that "it is not necessary to show an evil intent"; that, "if by gross and reckless negligence he caused the death, he is guilty of culpable homicide"; that "the question is whether the kerosene (if it was the cause of the death), either in its original application, renewal, or continuance, was applied as the result of foolhardy presumption or gross negligence on the part of the defendant"; and that the defendant was "to be tried by no other or higher standard of skill or learning than that which he necessarily assumed in treating her; that is, that he was able to do so without gross recklessness or foolhardy presumption in undertaking it." In other words, that the defendant's duty was not enhanced by any express or implied contract, but that he was bound at his peril to do no grossly reckless act when in the absence of any emergency or other exceptional circumstances he intermeddled with the person of another . . .

But recklessness in a moral sense means a certain state of consciousness with reference to the consequences of one's acts. No matter whether defined as indifference to what those consequences may be, or as a failure to consider their nature or probability as fully as the party might and ought to have done, it is understood to depend on the actual condition of the individual's mind with regard to consequences, as distinguished from mere knowledge of present or past facts or circumstances from which someone or everybody else might be led to anticipate or apprehend them if the supposed act were done. We have to determine whether recklessness in this sense was necessary to make the defendant guilty of felonious homicide, or whether his acts are to be judged by the external standard of what would be morally reckless, under the circumstances known to him, in a man of reasonable prudence.

More specifically, the questions raised by the foregoing requests and rulings are whether an actual good intent and the expectation of good results are an absolute justification of acts, however foolhardy they may be if judged by the external standard supposed, and whether the defendant's ignorance of the tendencies of kerosene administered as it was will excuse the administration of it.

So far as civil liability is concerned, at least, it is very clear that what we have called the external standard would be applied, and that, if a man's conduct is such as would be reckless in a man of ordinary prudence, it is reckless in him. Unless he can bring himself within some broadly defined exception to general rules, the law deliberately leaves his idiosyncrasies out of account, and peremptorily assumes that he has as much capacity to judge and to foresee consequences as a man of ordinary prudence would have in the same situation.

If this is the rule adopted in regard to the redistribution of losses, which sound policy allows to rest where they fall in the absence of a clear reason to the contrary, there would seem to be at least equal reason for adopting it in the criminal law, which has for its immediate object and task to establish a general standard, or at least general negative limits, of conduct for the community, in the interest of the safety of all . . .

If a physician is not less liable for reckless conduct than other people, it is clear, in the light of admitted principle and the later Massachusetts cases, that the recklessness of the criminal no less than that of the civil law must be tested by what we have called an external standard. In dealing with a man who has no special training, the question whether his act would be reckless in a man of ordinary prudence is evidently equivalent to an inquiry into the degree of danger which common experience shows to attend the act under the circumstances known to the actor. The only difference is, that the latter inquiry is still more obviously external to the estimate formed by the actor personally than the former. But it is familiar law that an act causing death may be murder, manslaughter, or misadventure, according to the degree of danger attending it. If the danger is very great, as in the case of an assault with a weapon found by the jury to be deadly, or an assault with hands and feet upon a woman known to be exhausted by illness, it is murder.

The very meaning of the fiction of implied malice in such cases at common law was, that a man might have to answer with his life for consequences which he neither intended nor foresaw. To say that he was presumed to have intended them is merely to adopt another fiction, and to disguise the truth. The truth was, that his failure or inability to predict them was immaterial, if, under the circumstances known to him, the court or jury, as the case might be, thought them obvious.

As implied malice signifies the highest degree of danger, and makes the act murder; so, if the danger is less, but still not so remote that it can be disregarded, the act will be called reckless, and will be manslaughter, as in the case of an ordinary assault with feet and hands, or a weapon not deadly, upon a well person. Or firing a pistol into the highway, when it does not amount to murder. Or slinging a cask over the highway in a customary, but insufficient mode. Or careless driving.

If the principle which has thus been established both for murder and manslaughter is adhered to, the defendant's intention to produce the opposite result from that which came to pass leaves him in the same position with regard to the present charge that he would have been in if he had had no intention at all in the matter. We think that the principle must be adhered to, where, as here, the assumption to act as a physician was uncalled for by any sudden emergency, and no exceptional circumstances are shown; and that we cannot recognize a privilege to do acts manifestly endangering human life, on the ground of good intentions alone.

We have implied, however, in what we have said, and it is undoubtedly true, as a general proposition, that a man's liability for his acts is determined by their tendency under the circumstances known to him, and not by their tendency under all the circumstances actually affecting the result, whether known or unknown . . . But knowledge of the dangerous character of a thing is only the equivalent of foresight of the way in which it will act. We admit that, if the thing is generally supposed to be universally harmless, and only a specialist would foresee that in a given case it would do damage, a person who did not foresee it, and who had no warning, would not be held liable for the harm. If men were held answerable for everything they did which was dangerous in fact, they would be held for all their acts from which harm in fact ensued. The use of the thing must be dangerous according to common experience, at least to the extent that there is a manifest and appreciable chance of harm from what is done, in view either of the actor's knowledge or of his conscious ignorance. And therefore, again, if the danger is due to the specific tendencies of the individual thing, and is not characteristic of the class to which it belongs, which seems to have been the view of the common law with regard to bulls, for instance, a person to be made liable must have notice of some past experience, or, as is commonly said, "of the quality of his beast." But if the dangers are characteristic of the class according to common experience, then he who uses an article of the class upon another cannot escape on the ground that he had less than the common experience. Common experience is necessary to the man of ordinary prudence, and a man who assumes to act as the defendant did must have it at his peril. When the jury are asked whether a stick of a certain size was a deadly weapon, they are not asked further whether the defendant knew that it was so. It is enough that he used and saw it such as it was. So as to an assault and battery by the use of excessive force. So here. The defendant knew that he was using kerosene. The jury have found that it was applied as the result of foolhardy presumption or gross negligence, and that is enough. Indeed, if the defendant had known the fatal tendency of the prescription, he would have been perilously near the line of murder. It will not be necessary to invoke the authority of those exceptional decisions in which it has been held, with regard to knowledge of the circumstances, as distinguished from foresight of the consequences of an act, that, when certain of the circumstances were known, the party was bound at his peril to inquire as to the others, although not of a nature to be necessarily inferred from what were known.

The remaining questions may be disposed of more shortly. When the defendant applied kerosene to the person of the deceased in a way which the jury have found to have been reckless, or, in other words, seriously and unreasonably endangering life according to common experience, he did an act which his patient could not justify by her consent, and which therefore was an assault notwithstanding that consent . . .

As we have intimated above, an allegation that the defendant knew of the deadly tendency of the kerosene was not only unnecessary, but improper. An allegation that the kerosene was of a dangerous tendency is superfluous, although similar allegations are often inserted in indictments, it being enough to allege the assault, and that death did in fact result from it. It would be superfluous in the case of an assault with a staff, or where the death resulted from assault combined with exposure . . . The instructions to the jury on the standard of skill by which the defendant was to be tried, stated above, were as favorable to him as he could ask . . .

Hamilton v. West End Street Railway Company
163 Mass. 199, 39 N.E. 1010 (1895)

The plaintiff seeks to charge the defendant for personal injuries suffered by her, on the ground that its car ought to have avoided a runaway herdic* which ran into it and did the damage. The grounds, however stated, are pure matter of guesswork. It is conjecture whether the driver knew that the herdic was coming. It would be prejudice to say that he ought to have known, if he did not. There is no evidence on either point which amounts to anything except the relative situations. The time during which the herdic was in sight before the accident must have been very short. During the last part of that time, if not the whole of it, the car was making a sharp turn into Cambridge Street on the opposite side from Joy Street, down which the herdic came, and the driver was stopping for passengers on his side, so that his attention naturally was drawn away from Joy Street. But suppose the driver had known the danger; it was just as prudent for him to be where he was as to be anywhere else where he could have been. It is said that if he had gone a little faster the herdic would have cleared the rear platform, which it struck, or that if he had stopped in Chambers Street there would have been no collision. This is very well after the event; but beforehand the driver could not tell where the horse would go. A horse car cannot be handled like a rapier. Within the narrow limits of the possible, so far as the evidence shows, a prudent man had no reason to think one spot safer than another.

Butler v. New York, New Haven & Hartford Railroad Company
177 Mass. 191, 58 N.E. 592 (1900)

This is an action to recover for the death of a boy killed by the defendant's cars. The case is here upon an exception to a refusal to take the case from the jury. There was evidence tending to show that the boy was killed on a grade crossing by one of the rear cars of a freight train which had broken apart before reaching the crossing, and that the forward part of the train had gone by, leaving an interval of from thirty-two feet to two hundred yards. It is not argued that there was not evidence of negligence on the part of the defendant subject to the almost inseparable question of the boy's due care. But the boy was only four years and seven months old, and it is contended that there was a lack of due care on his part and on the part of his mother. His mother was a poor woman and was alone in the house. Five minutes before the accident she left the boy eating on her front doorstep with her two other children aged nine and

*A small horse-drawn carriage.—Ed.

seven, told them to sit down and stay there, and went in to her washing. The house was about two hundred feet from the track and the earth was banked up on the side of the track so that cars could not be seen until one was very near. The track, however, was straight. The children, or the boy and his sister, went towards the track, and according to her the boy went on the track and took off his hat and said good-by to the part of the train that had passed. She called to him to come back, saying the cars were coming, and he replied, "Why, the car has gone by . . . It is passed now, and so there is no more."

The boy's answer shows that he understood the danger from a train in motion to one upon the track. But we assume in favor of the defendant that he was not exercising such care as an adult would be bound to exercise under similar circumstances. The cars that killed him could have been seen before they reached the crossing if he had looked. On the other hand, the danger from detached cars following a train from which they have broken is so unusual, and the passing of the front part of the train had such a tendency to suggest that the track was safe, as from his answer the boy believed, that we cannot say as matter of law that he was not exercising the care of a prudent boy of his years. The only question, therefore, is with regard to the care shown by his mother. That must be considered, because an injury to a child cannot be recovered for, although the child has used all the care to be expected of it, if it has not shown the prudence required of an adult, and if it ought not to have been left where it was without the oversight of an elder.

The lines between liability and immunity are fixed, at least in part, by legislative considerations of policy. While it may not be a sufficient reason for making greater requirements of a defendant that the plaintiff was disabled by poverty from taking certain precautions, the circumstances and limited powers of a large part of the community may be taken into account in determining what persons who use or cross the highways must look out for, and what they shall be held entitled to expect from those whom they meet and may injure. The poor cannot always keep their children in the house or always see that they are attended when out of doors. In this case the evidence warranted a finding that the mother reasonably might expect her children to obey her, and that leaving them where she did for the short time that she left them there, occupied as they were, was not negligence, in view of the facts that one of them was nine, and that the boy had the degree of intelligence which his answer proved. The case falls into that border region between two extremes which we leave to the jury.

Burt v. Advertiser Newspaper Company
154 Mass. 238, 28 N.E. 1 (1891)

In this case [a libel suit] there must be a new trial. We shall state the grounds on which we come to this conclusion, and shall discuss such of the rulings as dealt with questions which are likely to come up again. Some matters not likely to recur we shall pass over. The first question which we shall consider is raised by the presiding judge's refusal to rule that the articles were privileged. The requests referred to each article as a whole. Each article contained direct and indirect allegations of fact touching the plaintiff, and highly detrimental to him, charging him with being a party to alleged frauds in the New York custom-house. Some or all of these allegations we must take to be false. Therefore the ruling asked was properly refused.

We agree with the defendant that the subject was of public interest, and that in connection with the administration of the custom-house the defendant would have a right to make fair comments on the conduct of private persons affecting that administration in the way alleged. But there is an important distinction to be noticed between the so-called privilege of fair criticism upon matters of public interest, and the privilege existing in the case, for instance, of answers to inquiries about the character of a servant. In the latter case, a bona fide statement not in excess of the occasion is privileged, although it turns out to be false. In the former, what is privileged, if that is the proper term, is criticism, not statement, and however it might be if a person merely quoted or referred to a statement as made by others, and gave it no new sanction, if he takes upon himself in his own person to allege facts otherwise libelous, he will not be privileged if those facts are not true. The reason for the distinction lies in the different nature and degree of the exigency and of the damage in the two cases. In these, as in many other instances, the law has to draw a line between conflicting interests, both intrinsically meritorious. When private inquiries are made about a private person, a servant, for example, it is often impossible to answer them properly without stating facts, and those who settled the law thought it more important to preserve a reasonable freedom in giving necessary information than to insure people against occasional unintended injustice, confined as it generally is to one or two persons. But what the interest of private citizens in public matters requires is freedom of discussion rather than of statement. Moreover, the statements about such matters which come before the courts are generally public statements, where the harm done by a falsehood is much greater than

in the other case. If one private citizen wrote to another that a high official had taken a bribe, no one would think good faith a sufficient answer
to an action. He stands no better, certainly, when he publishes his writing to the world through a newspaper, and the newspaper itself stands
no better than the writer . . .

Hanson v. Globe Newspaper Company

159 Mass. 293, 34 N.E. 462 (1893)

(Dissent)

I am unable to agree with the decision of the majority of the court, and
as the question is of some importance in its bearing on legal principles,
and as I am not alone in my views, I think it proper to state the considerations which have occurred to me . . .

The facts are that libelous matter was published in an article by the
defendant about "H. P. Hanson, a real estate and insurance broker of
South Boston," that the plaintiff bore that name and description, and,
so far as appears, that no one else did, but that the defendant did not
know of his existence, and intended to state some facts about one
Andrew P. H. Hanson, also a real estate and insurance broker of South
Boston, concerning whom the article was substantially true.

The article described the subject of it as a prisoner in the criminal
dock, and states that he was fined, and this makes it possible to speak of
the article as one describing the conduct of a prisoner. But this mode of
characterization seems to me misleading. In form it describes the plight
and conduct of "H. P. Hanson, a real estate and insurance broker of
South Boston." The statement is, "H. P. Hanson, a real estate and insurance broker of South Boston, emerged from the seething mass of humanity that filled the dock," etc. In order to give it any different
subject, or to give the subject any further qualifications or description,
you have to resort to the predicate, to the very libelous matter itself. It is
not necessary to say that this never can be done, but it must be done
with great caution. The very substance of the libel complained of is the
statement that the plaintiff was a prisoner in the criminal dock, and was
fined. The object of the article, which is a newspaper criminal court report, is to make that statement. The rest of it amounts to nothing, and is
merely an attempt to make the statement amusing. If an article should
allege falsely that A murdered B with a knife, it would not be a satisfactory answer to an action by A that it was a description of the conduct of
the murderer of B, and was true concerning him. The public, or all except the few who may have been in court on the day in question, or who

consult the criminal records, have no way of telling who was the prisoner except by what is stated in the article, and the article states that it was "H. P. Hanson, a real estate and insurance broker of South Boston."

If I am right so far, the words last quoted, and those words alone, describe the subject of the allegation, in substance as well as in form. Those words also describe the plaintiff, and no one else. The only ground, then, on which the matters alleged of and concerning that subject can be found not to be alleged of and concerning the plaintiff, is that the defendant did not intend them to apply to him; and the question is narrowed to whether such a want of intention is enough to warrant the finding, or to constitute a defense, when the inevitable consequence of the defendant's acts is that the public, or that part of it which knows the plaintiff, will suppose that the defendant did use its language about him.

On general principles of tort, the private intent of the defendant would not exonerate it. It knew that it was publishing statements purporting to be serious, which would be hurtful to a man if applied to him. It knew that it was using as the subject of those statements words which purported to designate a particular man, and would be understood by its readers to designate one. In fact, the words purported to designate, and would be understood by its readers to designate, the plaintiff. If the defendant had supposed that there was no such person, and had intended simply to write an amusing fiction, that would not be a defense, at least unless its belief was justifiable. Without special reason, it would have no right to assume that there was no one within the sphere of its influence to whom the description answered. The case would be very like firing a gun into a street, and, when a man falls, setting up that no one was known to be there. So, when the description which points out the plaintiff is supposed by the defendant to point out another man whom in fact it does not describe, the defendant is equally liable as when the description is supposed to point out nobody. On the general principles of tort, the publication is so manifestly detrimental that the defendant publishes it at the peril of being able to justify it in the sense in which the public will understand it . . .

I feel some difficulty in putting my finger on the precise point of difference between the minority and majority of the court. I understand, however, that a somewhat unwilling assent is yielded to the general views which I have endeavored to justify, and I should gather that the exact issue was to be found in the statement that the article was one describing the conduct of a prisoner brought before the municipal court of Boston, coupled with the later statement that the language, taken in connection with the publicly known circumstances under which it was written, showed at once that the article referred to A. P. H. Hanson, and that the name of H. P. Hanson was used by mistake. I have shown why it seems to me that these statements are misleading. I only will add on this point, that I do not know what the publicly known circumstances are. I think it is a mistake of fact to suppose that the public generally know who was before the municipal criminal court on a given day. I think it is a mistake of law to say that, because a small part of the public have that knowledge, the plaintiff cannot recover for the harm done him in the eyes of the greater part of the public, probably including all his acquaintances, who are ignorant about the matter; and I also think it no sufficient answer to say that they might consult the criminal records, and find out that probably there was some error. If the case should proceed further on the facts, it might appear that, in view of the plaintiff's character and circumstances, all who knew him would assume that there was a mistake, that the harm to him was merely nominal, and that he had been too hasty in resorting to an action to vindicate himself. But that question is not before us . . .

Arizona Employers' Liability Cases
250 U.S. 400 (1919)
(Concurrence)

The plaintiff was employed in the defendant's mine, was hurt in the eye in consequence of opening a compressed air valve and brought the present suit. The injury was found to have been due to risks inherent to the business and so was within the Employers' Liability Law of Arizona. By that law as construed the employer is liable to damages for injuries due to such risks in specified hazardous employments when guilty of no negligence. There was a verdict for the plaintiff, judgment was affirmed by the supreme court of the state, and the case comes here on the single question whether, consistently with the Fourteenth Amendment, such liability can be imposed. It is taken to exclude "speculative, exemplary and punitive damages," but to include all loss to the employee caused by the accident, not merely in the way of earning capacity, but of disfigurement and bodily or mental pain.

There is some argument made for the general proposition that immunity from liability when not in fault is a right inherent in free government. But if it is thought to be public policy to put certain voluntary conduct at the peril of those pursuing it, whether in the interest of safety or upon economic or other grounds, I know of nothing to hinder. A man employs a servant at the peril of what that servant may do in the course of his employment and there is nothing in the Constitution to limit the principle to that instance. There are cases in which even the criminal law requires a man to know facts at his peril. Indeed, the criterion which is thought to be free from constitutional objection, the criterion of fault, is the application of an external standard, the conduct of a prudent man in the known circumstances, that is, in doubtful cases, the opinion of the jury, which the defendant has to satisfy at his peril and which he may miss after giving the matter his best thought.

I do not perceive how the validity of the law is affected by the fact that the employee is a party to the venture. There is no more certain way of securing attention to the safety of the men, an unquestionably constitutional object of legislation, than by holding the employer liable for accidents. Like the crimes to which I have referred they probably will happen a good deal less often when the employer knows that he must answer for them if they do. I pass, therefore, to the other objection urged and most strongly pressed. It is that the damages are governed by the rules governing an action of tort—that is, as we have said, that they may include disfigurement and bodily or mental pain. Natural observations are made on the tendency of juries when such elements are allowed. But if it is proper to allow them of course no objection can be founded on the supposed foibles of the tribunal that the Constitution of the United States and the states have established. Why then, is it not proper to allow them? It is said that the pain cannot be shifted to another. Neither can the loss of a leg. But one can be paid for as well as the other. It is said that these elements do not constitute an economic loss, in the sense of diminished power to produce. They may. But whether they do or not they are as much part of the workman's loss as the loss of a limb. The legislature may have reasoned thus. If a business is unsuccessful it means that the public does not care enough for it to make it pay. If it is successful the public pays its expenses and something more. It is reasonable that the public should pay the whole cost of producing what it wants and a part of that cost is the pain and mutilation incident to production. By throwing that loss upon the employer in the first instance we throw it upon the public in the long run and that is just. If a legislature should reason in this way and act accordingly it seems to me that it is within constitutional bounds. It is said that the liability is unlimited, but this is not true. It is limited to a conscientious valuation of the loss suffered. Apart from the control exercised by the judge it is to be hoped that juries would realize that unreasonable verdicts would tend to make the business impossible and thus to injure those whom they might wish to help. But whatever they may do we must accept the tribunal, as I have said, and are bound to assume that they will act rightly and confine themselves to the proper scope of the law . . .

9 · INTERPRETATION

Towne v. Eisner
245 U.S. 418 (1918)

. . . It is not necessarily true that income means the same thing in the Constitution and the act. A word is not a crystal, transparent and unchanged; it is the skin of a living thought and may vary greatly in color and content according to the circumstances and the time in which it is used . . .

Johnson v. United States
163 Fed. 30 (1st Cir. 1908)

HOLMES, Circuit Justice. The plaintiff in error, hereafter called the defendant, was indicted for concealing from the trustee of his estate in bankruptcy property belonging to the estate . . . The government, after putting in the creditors' petition filed against the defendant, the order appointing a receiver, notice to the bankrupt, the adjudication, the appointment of the trustee, the order of reference and the list of debts, offered the schedules of assets and liabilities filed by the bankrupt in the district court. The defendant objected, the objection was overruled, the schedules were admitted, and the defendant excepted. It is said that the grounds of the objection should have been stated, but we are of opinion that the only possible ground was sufficiently obvious to entitle the defendant in fairness to have it considered by us upon its merits.

The ground, of course, was Rev. St. §860:

No pleading of a party, nor any discovery or evidence obtained from a party or witness by means of a judicial proceeding in this or any foreign country, shall be given in evidence, or in any manner used against him or his property or estate, in any court of the United States, in any criminal proceeding, or for the enforcement of any penalty or forfeiture: Provided, that this section shall not exempt any party or witness from prosecution and punishment for perjury committed in discovering or testifying as aforesaid.

The government argues that the schedules are not pleadings, discovery or evidence, and that therefore the section does not apply; but we are not satisfied that the fagot can be taken to pieces and broken stick by stick in this manner so easily. We quite agree that vague arguments as to the spirit of a constitution or statute have little worth. We recognize that courts have been disinclined to extend statutes modifying the common law beyond the direct operation of the words used, and that at times this disinclination has been carried very far. But it seems to us that there may be statutes that need a different treatment. A statute may indicate or require as its justification a change in the policy of the law, although it expresses that change only in the specific cases most likely to occur to the mind. The legislature has the power to decide what the policy of the law shall be, and if it has intimated its will, however indirectly, that will should be recognized and obeyed. The major premise of the conclusion expressed in a statute, the change of policy that induces the enactment, may not be set out in terms, but it is not an adequate discharge of duty for courts to say: We see what you are driving at, but you have not said it, and therefore we shall go on as before.

This section of the Revised Statutes goes beyond and outside of the Fifth Amendment. It applies, even to a sworn bill or answer in chancery, what is said to be the rule of common law, that pleadings are not evidence against the party concerned. It makes this a general provision, and its object seems to us clear. We think that object was to prevent the required steps of the written procedure in court preliminary to trial from being used against the party for whom they were filed. We should be surprised if an allegation in a writ should be held to be outside the protection of the statute, if there should be a case in which that protection was needed. On the same principle we think that schedules in bankruptcy are protected. We can see no reason that would apply to an answer in equity that does not apply to them. They are required by the law. They are a regular step in the written procedure preliminary to the proof of facts. If necessary, it might be argued that they are pleadings within the meaning of the act. Bankruptcy is a proceeding in rem. The schedules indicate those who are to be made parties to the proceeding, the extent of their supposed claims, and the subject-matter of the distribution. They have such characteristics of pleadings as are possible at that stage of a proceeding of this kind against all the world . . .

International Stevedoring Company v. Haverty
272 U.S. 50 (1926)

This is an action brought in a state court seeking a common law remedy for personal injuries sustained by the plaintiff, the respondent here, upon a vessel at dock in the harbor of Seattle. The plaintiff was a long-shoreman engaged in stowing freight in the hold. Through the negligence of the hatch tender, no warning was given that a load of freight was about to be lowered, and when the load came down the plaintiff was badly hurt. The plaintiff and the hatch tender both were employed by the defendant stevedore, the petitioner here, and the defendant asked for a ruling that they were fellow servants and that therefore the plaintiff could not recover. The court ruled that if the failure of the hatch tender to give a signal was the proximate cause of the injury the verdict must be for the plaintiff. A verdict was found for him and a judgment on the verdict was affirmed by the supreme court of the state . . .

The petitioner argues that the case is governed by the admiralty law; that the admiralty law has taken up the common law doctrine as to fellow servants, and that by the common law the plaintiff would have no case. Whether this last proposition is true we do not decide. The petitioner cites a number of decisions . . . It also refers to an intimation of this Court that, whether the established doctrine be good or bad, it is not open to courts to do away with it upon their personal notions of what is expedient. It is open to Congress, however, to change the rule, and in our opinion it has done so. By the Act of June 5, 1920, c. 250, §20, "any seaman who shall suffer personal injury in the course of his employment may, at his election, maintain an action for damages at law, with the right of trial by jury, and in such action all statutes of the United States modifying or extending the common law right or remedy in cases of personal injury to railway employees shall apply." It is not disputed that the statutes do away with the fellow-servant rule in the case of personal injuries to railway employees. The question, therefore, is how far the Act of 1920 should be taken to extend.

It is true that for most purposes, as the word is commonly used, stevedores are not "seamen." But words are flexible. The work upon which the plaintiff was engaged was a maritime service formerly rendered by the ship's crew. We cannot believe that Congress willingly would have allowed the protection to men engaged upon the same maritime duties to vary with the accident of their being employed by a stevedore rather than by the ship. The policy of the statute is directed to the safety of the men and to treating compensation for injuries to them as properly part of the cost of the business. If they should be protected in the one case they should be in the other. In view of the broad field in which Congress has disapproved and changed the rule introduced into the common law within less than a century, we are of opinion that a wider scope should be given to the words of the act, and that in this statute "seamen" is to be taken to include stevedores employed in maritime work on navigable waters, as the plaintiff was, whatever it might mean in laws of a different kind.

Judgment affirmed.

Boston Sand & Gravel Co. v. United States
278 U.S. 41 (1928)

This is a libel in admiralty brought by the petitioner to recover for damages done to its steam lighter *Cornelia* by a collision with the United States destroyer *Bell*. It is brought against the United States by authority of a special Act of May 15, 1922, c. 192, 42 Stat. 1590. There has been a trial in which both vessels ultimately were found to have been in fault and it was ordered that the damages should be divided. Thereafter the damages were ascertained and the petitioner sought to be allowed interest upon its share. (There was no cross libel.) The circuit court of appeals, going on the words of the statute, parallel legislation, and the general understanding with regard to the United States, held that no interest could be allowed . . .

The material words of the Act are that the district court "shall have jurisdiction to hear and determine the whole controversy and to enter a judgment or decree for the amount of the legal damages sustained by reason of said collision, if any shall be found to be due either for or against the United States, upon the same principle and measure of liability with costs as in like cases in admiralty between private parties with the same rights of appeal." On a hasty reading one might be led to believe that Congress had put the United States on the footing of a private person in all respects. But we are of opinion that a scrutiny leads to a different result. It is at least possible that the words fixing the extent of the government's liability were carefully chosen, and we are of opinion that they were. We start with the rule that the United States is not liable to interest except where it assumes the liability by contract or by the express words of a statute, or must pay it as part of the just compensation required by the Constitution. Next we notice that when this special act was passed there was a recent general statute on the books allowing suits in admiralty to be brought against the United States, in which it was set forth specifically that interest was to be allowed upon money judgments and the rate was four per cent, not the six per cent that the petitioner expects to get. The later general statute passed as a substitute for special bills like the one before us allows suits in admiralty for damages done by public vessels but excludes interest in terms.

We are satisfied by the argument for the government that the policy thus expressed in the Act of 1925 had been the policy of the United States for years before 1922, and that the many private acts like the present generally have been understood, before and since the act now in question, not to carry interest by the often repeated words now before us. This was stated by the Attorney General in a letter to the Chairman of the Senate Committee on Claims when the Act of 1925 was under consideration and the bill was amended so as to remove all doubt. The Act of March 2, 1901, believed to be the first of the private acts in the present form, was passed after an amendment striking out an allowance of interest, thus showing that the words now relied upon then were understood not to allow it. The same thing has happened repeatedly with later acts, and when by exception interest has been allowed it has been allowed by express words. Before 1901, since 1871, such cases had been referred to the Court of Claims, which was forbidden by statute to allow interest. It is said that when the meaning of language is plain we are not to resort to evidence in order to raise doubts. That is rather an axiom of experience than a rule of law, and does not preclude consideration of persuasive evidence if it exists. If Congress has been accustomed to use a certain phrase with a more limited meaning than might be attributed to it by common practice, it would be arbitrary to refuse to consider that fact when we come to interpret a statute. But, as we have said, the usage of Congress simply shows that it has spoken with careful precision, that its words mark the exact spot at which it stops, and that it distinguishes between the damages caused by the collision and the later loss caused by delay in paying for the first—between damages and "the allowance of interest on damages," as it is put by Mr. Justice Bradley in *The Scotland*.

What the Act authorizes the court to ascertain and allow is the "amount of the legal damages sustained by reason of said collision." Of these, interest is no part. It might be in case of the detention of money. But this is not a claim for the detention of money, nor can any money be said to have been detained. When a jury finds a man guilty of a tort or a crime, it may determine not only the facts but also a standard of conduct that he is presumed to have known and was bound at his peril to follow. But legal fiction never reached the height of holding a defendant bound to know the estimate that a jury would put upon the damage that he had caused. As the cause of action is the damage, not the detention of the money to be paid for it, it could be argued in a respectable court, as late as 1886, that at common law, even as a matter of discretion, interest could not be allowed. And although it commonly is allowed in admiralty, still the element of discretion is not wholly absent there. As stated by Mr. Justice Bradley in *The Scotland*, "The allowance of interest on damages is not an absolute right." When the government is concerned, there is no obligation until the statute is passed and the foregoing considerations gain new force.

It has been urged that the United States would claim interest and that, as the statute speaks of "damages due either for or against the

United States," the claims on the two sides stand alike. But that is not true. The United States did not need the statute, and it has been held that, even in the adjustment of mutual claims between an individual and the government, while the latter is entitled to interest on its credits, it is not liable for interest on the charges against it.

The mention of costs and the omission of interest again helps the conclusion to which we come.

Decree affirmed.

Gompers v. United States
233 U.S. 604 (1914)

[A federal statute provided that offenses, unless capital, must be prosecuted within three years of their commission. The defendants were prosecuted (and convicted) for criminal contempts committed more than three years before the prosecution was instituted. The question was whether the three-year statute of limitations applied to criminal contempts—in other words whether they were offenses within the meaning of the statute.]

. . . It is urged in the first place that contempts cannot be crimes, because, although punishable by imprisonment and therefore, if crimes, infamous, they are not within the protection of the Constitution and the amendments giving a right to trial by jury, etc., to persons charged with such crimes. But the provisions of the Constitution are not mathematical formulas having their essence in their form; they are organic, living institutions transplanted from English soil. Their significance is vital not formal; it is to be gathered not simply by taking the words and a dictionary, but by considering their origin and the line of their growth. It does not follow that contempts of the class under consideration are not crimes, or rather, in the language of the statute, offenses, because trial by jury as it has been gradually worked out and fought out has been thought not to extend to them as a matter of constitutional right. These contempts are infractions of the law, visited with punishment as such. If such acts are not criminal, we are in error as to the most fundamental characteristic of crimes as that word has been understood in English speech. So truly are they crimes that it seems to be proved that in the early law they were punished only by the usual criminal procedure and that at least in England it seems that they still may be and preferably are tried in that way.

We come then to the construction of the statute. It has been assumed that the concluding words "unless the indictment is found or the information is instituted within three years" limit the offenses given the benefit of the act to those usually prosecuted in that way, and the counsel for the petitioners were at some pains to argue that the charges of the committee amounted to an information—a matter that opens vistas of antiquarian speculation. But this question is not one to be answered by refinements and curious inquiries. In our opinion the proper interpretation of the statute begins with the substantive not with the adjective part. The substantive portion of the section is that no person shall be tried for any offense not capital except within a certain time. Those words are of universal scope. What follows is a natural way of expressing that the proceedings must be begun within three years; indictment and information being the usual modes by which they are begun and very likely no other having occurred to those who drew the law. But it seems to us plain that the dominant words of the act are "no person shall be prosecuted, tried, or punished for any offence not capital" unless.

No reason has been suggested to us for not giving to the statute its natural scope. The English courts seem to think it wise, even when there is much seeming reason for the exercise of a summary power, to leave the punishment of this class of contempts to the regular and formal criminal process. Maintenance of their authority does not often make it really necessary for courts to exert their own power to punish, as is shown by the English practice in more violent days than these, and there is no more reason for prolonging the period of liability when they see fit to do so than in the case where the same offense is proceeded against in the common way. Indeed the punishment of these offenses peculiarly needs to be speedy if it is to occur. The argument loses little of its force if it should be determined hereafter, a matter on which we express no opinion, that in the present state of the law an indictment would not lie for a contempt of a court of the United States.

Even if the statute does not cover the case by its express words, as we think it does, still, in dealing with the punishment of crime a rule should be laid down, if not by Congress by this Court. The power to punish for contempt must have some limit in time, and in defining that limit we should have regard to what has been the policy of the law from the foundation of the government. By analogy if not by enactment the limit is three years . . .

Missouri v. Holland
252 U.S. 416 (1920)

This is a bill in equity brought by the State of Missouri to prevent a game warden of the United States from attempting to enforce the

Migratory Bird Treaty Act of July 3, 1918. The ground of the bill is that the statute is an unconstitutional interference with the rights reserved to the states by the Tenth Amendment, and that the acts of the defendant done and threatened under that authority invade the sovereign right of the state and contravene its will manifested in statutes.

. . . By Article VI [of the Constitution] treaties made under the authority of the United States, along with the Constitution and laws of the United States, made in pursuance thereof, are declared the supreme law of the land . . . [But] it is said that a treaty cannot be valid if it infringes the Constitution, that there are limits, therefore, to the treaty-making power, and that one such limit is that what an act of Congress could not do unaided, in derogation of the powers reserved to the states, a treaty cannot do . . .

. . . Acts of Congress are the supreme law of the land only when made in pursuance of the Constitution, while treaties are declared to be so when made under the authority of the United States. It is open to question whether the authority of the United States means more than the formal acts prescribed to make the convention. We do not mean to imply that there are no qualifications to the treaty-making power; but they must be ascertained in a different way. It is obvious that there may be matters of the sharpest exigency for the national well being that an act of Congress could not deal with but that a treaty followed by such an act could, and it is not lightly to be assumed that, in matters requiring national action, "a power which must belong to and somewhere reside in every civilized government" is not to be found . . . We are not yet discussing the particular case before us but only are considering the validity of the test proposed. With regard to that we may add that when we are dealing with words that also are a constituent act, like the Constitution of the United States, we must realize that they have called into life a being the development of which could not have been foreseen completely by the most gifted of its begetters. It was enough for them to realize or to hope that they had created an organism; it has taken a century and has cost their successors much sweat and blood to prove that they created a nation. The case before us must be considered in the light of our whole experience and not merely in that of what was said a hundred years ago. The treaty in question does not contravene any prohibitory words to be found in the Constitution. The only question is whether it is forbidden by some invisible radiation from the general terms of the Tenth Amendment. We must consider what this country has become in deciding what that amendment has reserved.

The state as we have intimated founds its claims of exclusive authority upon an assertion of title to migratory birds, an assertion that is embodied in statute. No doubt it is true that as between a state and its inhabitants the state may regulate the killing and sale of such birds, but it does not follow that its authority is exclusive of paramount powers. To put the claim of the state upon title is to lean upon a slender reed. Wild birds are not in the possession of anyone; and possession is the beginning of ownership. The whole foundation of the state's rights is the presence within their jurisdiction of birds that yesterday had not arrived, tomorrow may be in another state and in a week a thousand miles away. If we are to be accurate we cannot put the case of the state upon higher ground than that the treaty deals with creatures that for the moment are within the state borders, that it must be carried out by officers of the United States within the same territory, and that but for the treaty the state would be free to regulate this subject itself.

As most of the laws of the United States are carried out within the states and as many of them deal with matters which in the silence of such laws the state might regulate, such general grounds are not enough to support Missouri's claim. Valid treaties of course "are as binding within the territorial limits of the states as they are effective throughout the dominion of the United States." No doubt the great body of private relations usually falls within the control of the state, but a treaty may override its power . . .

Here a national interest of very nearly the first magnitude is involved. It can be protected only by national action in concert with that of another power. The subject-matter is only transitorily within the state and has no permanent habitat therein. But for the treaty and the statute there soon might be no birds for any powers to deal with. We see nothing in the Constitution that compels the government to sit by while a food supply is cut off and the protectors of our forests and our crops are destroyed. It is not sufficient to rely upon the states. The reliance is vain, and were it otherwise, the question is whether the United States is forbidden to act. We are of opinion that the treaty and statute must be upheld.

Springer v. Philippine Islands
277 U.S. 183 (1928)

(Dissent)

The great ordinances of the Constitution do not establish and divide fields of black and white. Even the more specific of them are found to terminate in a penumbra shading gradually from one extreme to the other. Property must not be taken without compensation, but with the help of a phrase (the police power) some property may be taken or destroyed for public use without paying for it, if you do not take too much.

When we come to the fundamental distinctions it is still more obvious that they must be received with a certain latitude or our government could not go on.

To make a rule of conduct applicable to an individual who but for such action would be free from it is to legislate—yet it is what the judges do whenever they determine which of two competing principles of policy shall prevail. At an early date it was held that Congress could delegate to the courts the power to regulate process, which certainly is lawmaking so far as it goes. With regard to the Executive, Congress has delegated to it or to some branch of it the power to impose penalties, to make conclusive determination of dutiable values, to establish standards for imports, to make regulations as to forest reserves, and other powers not needing to be stated in further detail. Congress has authorized the President to suspend the operation of a statute, even one suspending commercial intercourse with another country, and very recently it has been decided that the President might be given power to change the tariff. It is said that the powers of Congress cannot be delegated, yet Congress has established the Interstate Commerce Commission, which does legislative, judicial and executive acts, only softened by a *quasi;* makes regulations, issues reparation orders, and performs executive functions in connection with Safety Appliance Acts, Boiler Inspection Acts, etc. Congress also has made effective excursions in the other direction. It has withdrawn jurisdiction of a case after it has been argued. It has granted an amnesty, notwithstanding the grant to the President of the power to pardon. A territorial legislature has granted a divorce. Congress has declared lawful an obstruction to navigation that this Court has declared unlawful. Parallel to the case before us, Congress long ago established the Smithsonian Institution, to question which would be to lay hands on the Ark of the Covenant; not to speak of later similar exercises of power hitherto unquestioned, so far as I know.

It does not seem to need argument to show that however we may disguise it by veiling words we do not and cannot carry out the distinction between legislative and executive action with mathematical precision and divide the branches into watertight compartments, were it ever so desirable to do so, which I am far from believing that it is, or that the Constitution requires . . .

The Theory of Legal Interpretation
12 *Harvard Law Review* 417 (1899)

. . . It is true that in theory any document purporting to be serious and to have some legal effect has one meaning and no other, because the known object is to achieve some definite result. It is not true that in practice (and I know no reason why theory should disagree with the facts) a given word or even a given collocation of words has one meaning and no other. A word generally has several meanings, even in the dictionary. You have to consider the sentence in which it stands to decide which of those meanings it bears in the particular case, and very likely will see that it there has a shade of significance more refined than any given in the wordbook. But in this first step, at least, you are not troubling yourself about the idiosyncrasies of the writer, you are considering simply the general usages of speech. So when you let whatever galvanic current may come from the rest of the instrument run through the particular sentence, you still are doing the same thing.

How is it when you admit evidence of circumstances and read the document in the light of them? Is this trying to discover the particular intent of the individual, to get into his mind and to bend what he said to what he wanted? No one would contend that such a process should be carried very far, but, as it seems to me, we do not take a step in that direction. It is not a question of tact in drawing a line. We are after a different thing. What happens is this. Even the whole document is found to have a certain play in the joints when its words are translated into things by parol evidence, as they have to be. It does not disclose one meaning conclusively according to the laws of language. Thereupon we ask, not what this man meant, but what those words would mean in the mouth of a normal speaker of English, using them in the circumstances in which they were used, and it is to the end of answering this last question that we let in evidence as to what the circumstances were. But the normal speaker of English is merely a special variety, a literary form, so to speak, of our old friend the prudent man. He is external to the particular writer, and a reference to him as the criterion is simply another instance of the externality of law.

But then it is said, and this is thought to be the crux, in the case of a gift of Blackacre to John Smith, when the donor owned two Blackacres and the directory reveals two John Smiths, you may give direct evidence of the donor's intention, and it is only an anomaly that you cannot give the same evidence in every case. I think, on the contrary, that the exceptional rule is a proof of the instinctive insight of the judges who established it. I refer again to the theory of our language. By the theory of our language, while other words may mean different things, a proper name means one person or thing and no other. If language perfectly performed its function, as Bentham wanted to make it, it would point out the person or thing named in every case. But under our random system it sometimes happens that your name is *idem sonans* with mine, and it may be the same even in spelling. But it never means you or me indifferently. In theory of speech your name means you and my name means me, and the two names are different. They are different words . . . In such a case we let in evidence of intention not to help out what theory recognizes as an uncertainty of speech, and to read what the writer meant into what he has tried but failed to say, but, recognizing that he has spoken with theoretic certainty, we inquire what he meant in order to find out what he has said. It is on this ground that there is no contract when the proper name used by one party means one ship, and that used by the other means another. The mere difference of intent as such is immaterial. In the use of common names and words a plea of different meaning from that adopted by the court would be bad, but here the parties have said different things and never have expressed a contract. If the donor, instead of saying "Blackacre," had said "my gold watch" and had owned more than one, inasmuch as the words, though singular, purport to describe any such watch belonging to the speaker, I suppose that no evidence of intention would be admitted. But I dare say that evidence of circumstances sufficient to show that the normal speaker of English would have meant a particular watch by the same words would be let in.

I have stated what I suppose to be our general theory of construction. It remains to say a few words to justify it. Of course, the purpose of written instruments is to express some intention or state of mind of those who write them, and it is desirable to make that purpose effectual, so far as may be, if instruments are to be used. The question is how far the law ought to go in aid of the writers. In the case of contracts, to begin with them, it is obvious that they express the wishes not of one person but of two, and those two adversaries. If it turns out that one meant one thing and the other another, speaking generally, the only choice possible for the legislator is either to hold both parties to the judge's interpretation of the words in the sense which I have explained, or to allow the contract to be avoided because there has been no meeting of minds. The latter course not only would greatly enhance the difficulty of enforcing contracts against losing parties, but would run against a plain principle of justice. For each party to a contract has notice that the other will understand his words according to the usage of the normal speaker of English under the circumstances, and therefore cannot complain if his words are taken in that sense.

Different rules conceivably might be laid down for the construction of different kinds of writing. In the case of a statute, to turn from contracts to the opposite extreme, it would be possible to say that as we are dealing with the commands of the sovereign the only thing to do is to find out what the sovereign wants. If supreme power resided in the person of a despot who would cut off your hand or your head if you went wrong, probably one would take every available means to find out what was wanted. Yet in fact we do not deal differently with a statute from our way of dealing with a contract. We do not inquire what the legislature meant; we ask only what the statute means. In this country, at least, for constitutional reasons, if for no other, if the same legislature that passed it should declare at a later date a statute to have a meaning which in the opinion of the court the words did not bear, I suppose that the declaratory act would have no effect upon intervening transactions unless in a place and case where retrospective legislation was allowed. As retrospective legislation it would not work by way of construction except in form.

So in the case of a will. It is true that the testator is a despot, within limits, over his property, but he is required by statute to express his commands in writing, and that means that his words must be sufficient for the purpose when taken in the sense in which they would be used by the normal speaker of English under his circumstances.

I may add that I think we should carry the external principle of construction even further than I have indicated. I do not suppose that you could prove, for purposes of construction as distinguished from avoidance, an oral declaration or even an agreement that words in a dispositive instrument making sense as they stand should have a different meaning from the common one; for instance, that the parties to a contract orally agreed that when they wrote five hundred feet it should mean one hundred inches, or that Bunker Hill Monument should signify Old South Church. On the other hand, when you have the security of a local or class custom or habit of speech, it may be presumed that the writer conforms to the usage of his place or class when that is what a normal person in his situation would do. But these cases are remote from the point of theory upon which I started to speak.

It may be, after all, that the matter is one in which the important thing, the law, is settled, and different people will account for it by such theory as pleases them best, as in the ancient controversy whether the finder of a thing which had been thrown away by the owner got a title in privity by gift, or a new title by abandonment. That he got a title no one denied. But although practical men generally prefer to leave their major premises inarticulate, yet even for practical purposes theory generally turns out the most important thing in the end. I am far from saying that it might not make a difference in the old question to which I have referred.

Opinion of the Justices to the House of Representatives
178 Mass. 605, 60 N.E. 129 (1901)

The ground for doubt as to the power of the general court [i.e., the Massachusetts Legislature] under the constitution of the commonwealth is to be found in the requirement that representatives "shall be chosen by written votes". . .

We assume that the voting machines which the honorable house has in mind vary in their mode of recording votes, that all of them dispense with the use of a separate piece of paper for each vote, that some of them register a large number of successive votes by successive punches upon one strip of paper in separate lines for separate candidates, with the names, if necessary, against the lines, and that some of them abandon the use of paper altogether in recording, each vote being marked by the partial revolution of a cog-wheel or other similar device, and the total number being shown by some easily adapted index. If necessary, however, in this class of machines the names of the candidates may appear in writing attached to the point where the voter registers his vote, in such manner as to indicate that his turning a particular key or pressing a particular knob expresses a vote for the name written above . . .

[I]t is not so important to consider what picture the framers of the constitution had in their minds as what benefits they sought to secure, or evils to prevent—what they were thinking against in their affirmative requirement of writing, and what they would have prohibited if they had put the clause in a negative form . . . No doubt the picture in the minds of those who used the words was that of a piece of paper with the names of the candidates voted for written upon it in manuscript, but the thing which they meant to stop was oral or hand voting, and the benefits which they meant to secure were the greater certainty and permanence of a material record of each voter's act and the relative privacy incident to doing that act in silence. They did not require the signature of the voter, or any means of identifying his vote as his after it had been cast. It was settled by *Henshaw v. Foster* that they did not require manuscript. In our opinion they did not require a separate piece of paper for each voter. That is to say, by requiring writing they did not prevent the legislature from authorizing several voters to use a single ballot if the voters all signed it, or in some way sufficiently indicated that a single paper expressed the act and choice of each. It seems to us that the object and even the words of the constitution in requiring "written votes" are satisfied when the voter makes a change in a material object—for instance, by causing a wheel to revolve a fixed distance—if the material object changed is so connected with or related to a written or printed name purporting to be the name of a candidate for office that, by the understanding of all, the making of the change expresses a vote for the candidate whose name is thus connected with the device . . .

Storti v. Commonwealth
175 Mass. 549, 60 N.E. 210 (1901)

These proceedings are respectively a writ of error and a petition for a writ of habeas corpus. Both are intended to raise the same issue, that the punishment, death by electricity, to which the said Storti has been sentenced, is "cruel or unusual" within article 26 of the Massachusetts Declaration of Rights . . .

Taking all the preliminaries most favorably for the prisoner, we are clearly of opinion that the constitution is not contravened by the act, and we render our opinion at once that we may avoid delaying the course of the law and raising false hopes in his mind. The answer to the whole argument which has been presented is that there is but a single punishment, death. It is not contended that if this is true the statute is invalid, but it is said that it is not true, and that you cannot separate the means from the end in considering what the punishment is, any more when the means is a current of electricity than when it is a slow fire. We should have thought that the distinction was plain. In the latter case the means is adopted not solely for the purpose of accomplishing the end of death but for the purpose of causing other pain to the person concerned. The so-called means is also an end of the same kind as the death itself, or in other words is intended to be a part of the punishment. But when, as here, the means adopted are chosen with just the contrary intent, and are devised for the purpose of reaching the end proposed as swiftly and painlessly as possible, we are of opinion that they are not forbidden by the constitution although they should be discoveries of recent science and never should have been heard of before. Not only is the prohibition addressed to what in a proper sense may be called the punishment but, further, the word "unusual" must be construed with the word "cruel" and cannot be taken so broadly as to prohibit every humane improvement not previously known in Massachusetts.

The suggestion that the punishment of death, in order not to be unusual, must be accomplished by molar rather than by molecular motion seems to us a fancy unwarranted by the constitution.

No doubt a means might be adopted which, although adopted only as a means, practically would be part of the punishment and would have to be considered as such. But such a case is not presented by a means chosen precisely because it is instantaneous. There was a hint at an argument based on mental suffering, but the suffering is due not to its being more horrible to be struck by lightning than to be hanged with the chance of slowly strangling, but to the general fear of death. The suffering due to that fear the law does not seek to spare. It means that it shall be felt . . .

10 · LIBERTY

McAuliffe v. Mayor and Board of Aldermen of New Bedford
155 Mass. 216, 29 N.E. 517 (1892)

This is a petition for mandamus to restore the petitioner to the office of policeman in New Bedford. He was removed by the mayor upon a written complaint, after a hearing, the mayor finding that he was guilty of violating Rule 31 of the police regulations of that city. The part of the rule which the petitioner seems certainly to have violated is as follows: "No member of the department shall be allowed to solicit money or any aid, on any pretence, for any political purpose whatever" . . . It is argued by the petitioner that the mayor's finding did not warrant the removal, that the part of the rule violated was invalid as invading the petitioner's right to express his political opinions, and that a breach of it was not a cause sufficient under the statutes.

One answer to this argument, assuming that the statute does not make the mayor the final judge of what cause is sufficient, and that we have a right to consider it, is that there is nothing in the constitution or the statute to prevent the city from attaching obedience to this rule as a condition to the office of policeman, and making it part of the good conduct required. The petitioner may have a constitutional right to talk politics, but he has no constitutional right to be a policeman. There are few employments for hire in which the servant does not agree to suspend his constitutional rights of free speech, as well as of idleness, by the implied terms of his contract. The servant cannot complain, as he takes the employment on the terms which are offered him. On the same principle, the city may impose any reasonable condition upon holding offices within its control. This condition seems to us reasonable, if that be a question open to revision here . . .

Otis v. Parker
187 U.S. 606 (1903)

This is an action . . . for margins paid to the defendants as stock brokers on contracts to buy and sell mining stocks . . . The basis of the action is the following provision of the California constitution: "All contracts for the sales of shares of the capital stock of any corporation or association, on margin, or to be delivered at a future day, shall be void, and any money paid on such contracts may be recovered by the party paying it by suit in any court of competent jurisdiction". . .

The objection urged against the provision in its literal sense is that this prohibition of all sales on margin bears no reasonable relation to the evil sought to be cured, and therefore falls within the first section of the Fourteenth Amendment. It is said that it unduly limits the liberty of adult persons in making contracts which concern only themselves, and cuts down the value of a class of property that often must be disposed of under contracts of the prohibited kind if it is to be disposed of to advantage, thus depriving persons of liberty and property without due process of law, and that it unjustifiably discriminates against property of that class, while other familiar objects of speculation, such as cotton or grain, are not touched, thus depriving persons of the equal protection of the laws.

It is true, no doubt, that neither a state legislature nor a state constitution can interfere arbitrarily with private business or transactions, and that the mere fact that an enactment purports to be for the protection of public safety, health or morals, is not conclusive upon the courts. But general propositions do not carry us far. While the courts must exercise a judgment of their own, it by no means is true that every law is void which may seem to the judges who pass upon it excessive, unsuited to its ostensible end, or based upon conceptions of morality with which they disagree. Considerable latitude must be allowed for differences of view as well as for possible peculiar conditions which this court can know but imperfectly, if at all. Otherwise a constitution, instead of embodying only relatively fundamental rules of right, as generally understood by all English-speaking communities, would become the partisan of a particular set of ethical or economical opinions, which by no means are held *semper ubique et ab omnibus*.

Even if the provision before us should seem to us not to have been justified by the circumstances locally existing in California at the time when it was passed, it is shown by its adoption to have expressed a deep-seated conviction on the part of the people concerned as to what that policy required. Such a deep-seated conviction is entitled to great respect. If the state thinks that an admitted evil cannot be prevented except by prohibiting a calling or transaction not in itself necessarily objectionable, the courts cannot interfere, unless, in looking at the substance of the matter, they can see that it "is a clear, unmistakable infringement of rights secured by the fundamental law." No court would declare a usury law unconstitutional, even if every member of it believed that Jeremy Bentham had said the last word on that subject, and had shown for all time that such laws did more harm than good. The Sunday laws, no doubt, would be sustained by a bench of judges, even if every one of them thought it superstitious to make any day holy. Or, to take cases where opinion has moved in the opposite direction, wagers may be declared illegal without the aid of statute, or lotteries forbidden by express enactment, although at an earlier day they were thought pardonable at least. The case would not be decided differently if lotteries had been lawful when the Fourteenth Amendment became law, as indeed they were in some civilized states.

We cannot say that there might not be conditions of public delirium in which at least a temporary prohibition of sales on margins would be a salutary thing. Still less can we say that there might not be conditions in which it reasonably might be thought a salutary thing, even if we disagreed with the opinion. Of course, if a man can buy on margin he can launch into a much more extended venture than where he must pay the whole price at once. If he pays the whole price he gets the purchased article, whatever its worth may turn out to be. But if he buys stocks on margin he may put all his property into the venture, and being unable to keep his margins good if the stock market goes down, a slight fall leaves him penniless, with nothing to represent his outlay, except that he has had the chances of a bet. There is no doubt that purchases on margin may be and frequently are used as a means of gambling for a great gain or a loss of all one has. It is said that in California, when the constitution was adopted, the whole people were buying mining stocks in this way with the result of infinite disaster. If at that time the provision of the constitution, instead of being put there, had been embodied in a temporary act, probably no one would have questioned it, and it would be hard to take a distinction solely on the ground of its more permanent form. Inserting the provision in the constitution showed, as we have said, the conviction of the people at large that prohibition was a proper means of stopping the evil . . .

Lochner v. New York

198 U.S. 45 (1905)

(Dissent)

I regret sincerely that I am unable to agree with the judgment in this case [invalidating a statute limiting the hours of work in bakeries], and that I think it my duty to express my dissent.

This case is decided upon an economic theory which a large part of the country does not entertain. If it were a question whether I agreed with that theory, I should desire to study it further and long before making up my mind. But I do not conceive that to be my duty, because I strongly believe that my agreement or disagreement has nothing to do with the right of a majority to embody their opinions in law. It is settled by various decisions of this Court that state constitutions and state laws may regulate life in many ways which we as legislators might think as injudicious or if you like as tyrannical as this, and which equally with this interfere with the liberty to contract. Sunday laws and usury laws are ancient examples. A more modern one is the prohibition of lotteries. The liberty of the citizen to do as he likes so long as he does not interfere with the liberty of others to do the same, which has been a shibboleth for some well-known writers, is interfered with by school laws, by the Post Office, by every state or municipal institution which takes his money for purposes thought desirable, whether he likes it or not. The Fourteenth Amendment does not enact Mr. Herbert Spencer's Social Statics. The other day we sustained the Massachusetts vaccination law. United States and state statutes and decisions cutting down the liberty to contract by way of combination are familiar to this Court. Two years ago we upheld the prohibition of sales of stock on margins or for future delivery in the constitution of California. The decision sustaining an eight-hour law for miners is still recent. Some of these laws embody convictions or prejudices which judges are likely to share. Some may not. But a constitution is not intended to embody a particular economic theory, whether of paternalism and the organic relation of the citizen to the state or of laissez faire. It is made for people of fundamentally differing views, and the accident of our finding certain opinions natural and familiar or novel and even shocking ought not to conclude our judgment upon the question whether statutes embodying them conflict with the Constitution of the United States.

General propositions do not decide concrete cases. The decision will depend on a judgment or intuition more subtle than any articulate major premise. But I think that the proposition just stated, if it is accepted, will carry us far toward the end. Every opinion tends to become a law. I think that the word liberty in the Fourteenth Amendment is perverted when it is held to prevent the natural outcome of a dominant opinion, unless it can be said that a rational and fair man necessarily would admit that the statute proposed would infringe fundamental principles as they have been understood by the traditions of our people and our law. It does not need research to show that no such sweeping condemnation can be passed upon the statute before us. A reasonable man might think it a proper measure on the score of health. Men whom I certainly could not pronounce unreasonable would uphold it as a first instalment of a general regulation of the hours of work. Whether in the latter aspect it would be open to the charge of inequality I think it unnecessary to discuss.

Adkins v. Children's Hospital
261 U.S. 525 (1923)
(Dissent)

The question in this case is the broad one, whether Congress can establish minimum rates of wages for women in the District of Columbia with due provision for special circumstances, or whether we must say that Congress has no power to meddle with the matter at all. To me, notwithstanding the deference due to the prevailing judgment of the Court, the power of Congress seems absolutely free from doubt. The end—to remove conditions leading to ill health, immorality and the deterioration of the race—no one would deny to be within the scope of constitutional legislation. The means are means that have the approval of Congress, of many states, and of those governments from which we have learned our greatest lessons. When so many intelligent persons, who have studied the matter more than any of us can, have thought that the means are effective and are worth the price, it seems to me impossible to deny that the belief reasonably may be held by reasonable men. If the law encountered no other objection than that the means bore no relation to the end or that they cost too much I do not suppose that anyone would venture to say that it was bad. I agree, of course, that a law answering the foregoing requirements might be invalidated by specific provisions of the Constitution. For instance it might take private property without just compensation. But in the present instance the only objection that can be urged is found within the vague contours of the Fifth Amendment, prohibiting the depriving any person of liberty or property without due process of law. To that I turn.

The earlier decisions upon the same words in the Fourteenth Amendment began within our memory and went no farther than an unpretentious assertion of the liberty to follow the ordinary callings. Later that innocuous generality was expanded into the dogma, Liberty of Contract. Contract is not specially mentioned in the text that we have to construe. It is merely an example of doing what you want to do, embodied in the word liberty. But pretty much all law consists in forbidding men to do some things that they want to do, and contract is no more exempt from law than other acts. Without enumerating all the restrictive laws that have been upheld I will mention a few that seem to me to have interfered with liberty of contract quite as seriously and directly as the one before us. Usury laws prohibit contracts by which a man receives more than so much interest for the money that he lends. Statutes of frauds restrict many contracts to certain forms. Some Sunday laws prohibit practically all contracts during one-seventh of our whole life. Insurance rates may be regulated . . . Finally women's hours of labor may be fixed, *Muller v. Oregon;* and the principle was extended to men with the allowance of a limited overtime to be paid for "at the rate of time and one-half of the regular wage."

I confess that I do not understand the principle on which the power to fix a minimum for the wages of women can be denied by those who admit the power to fix a maximum for their hours of work. I fully assent to the proposition that here as elsewhere the distinctions of the law are distinctions of degree, but I perceive no difference in the kind or degree of interference with liberty, the only matter with which we have any concern, between the one case and the other. The bargain is equally affected whichever half you regulate. *Muller v. Oregon,* I take it, is as good law today as it was in 1908. It will need more than the Nineteenth Amendment to convince me that there are no differences between men and women, or that legislation cannot take those differences into account. I should not hesitate to take them into account if I thought it necessary to sustain this act. But after *Bunting v. Oregon,* I had supposed that it was not necessary, and that *Lochner v. New York* would be allowed a deserved repose.

This statute does not compel anybody to pay anything. It simply forbids employment at rates below those fixed as the minimum requirement of health and right living. It is safe to assume that women will not be employed at even the lowest wages allowed unless they earn them, or unless the employer's business can sustain the burden. In short the law in its character and operation is like hundreds of so-called police laws that have been upheld. I see no greater objection to using a board to apply the standard fixed by the act than there is to the other commissions with which we have become familiar, or than there is to the requirement of a license in other cases. The fact that the statute warrants classification, which like all classifications may bear hard upon some individuals, or in exceptional cases, notwithstanding the power given to the board to issue a special license, is no greater infirmity than is incident to all law. But the ground on which the law is held to fail is fundamental and therefore it is unnecessary to consider matters of detail.

The criterion of constitutionality is not whether we believe the law to be for the public good. We certainly cannot be prepared to deny that a reasonable man reasonably might have that belief in view of the legislation of Great Britain, Victoria and a number of the states of this Union. The belief is fortified by a very remarkable collection of documents submitted on behalf of the appellants, material here, I conceive, only as showing that the belief reasonably may be held. In Australia the power to fix a minimum for wages in the case of industrial disputes extending beyond the limits of any one state was given to a court, and its President wrote a most interesting account of its operation. If a legislature should adopt what he thinks the doctrine of modern economists of all schools, that "freedom of contract is a misnomer as applied to a contract between an employer and an ordinary individual employee," I could not pronounce an opinion with which I agree impossible to be entertained by reasonable men. If the same legislature should accept his further opinion that industrial peace was best attained by the device of a court having the above powers, I should not feel myself able to contradict it, or to deny that the end justified restrictive legislation quite as adequately as beliefs concerning Sunday or exploded theories about usury. I should have my doubts, as I have them about this statute—but they would be whether the bill that has to be paid for every gain, although hidden as interstitial detriments, was not greater than the gain was worth: a matter that is not for me to decide.

I am of opinion that the statute is valid and that the decree should be reversed.

Hammer v. Dagenhart
247 U.S. 251 (1918)
(Dissent)

The single question in this case is whether Congress has power to prohibit the shipment in interstate or foreign commerce of any product of a cotton mill situated in the United States, in which within thirty days before the removal of the product children under fourteen have been employed, or children between fourteen and sixteen have been employed more than eight hours in a day, or more than six days in any week, or between seven in the evening and six in the morning. The objection urged against the power is that the states have exclusive control over their methods of production and that Congress cannot meddle with them, and taking the proposition in the sense of direct intermeddling I agree to it and suppose that no one denies it. But if an act is within the powers specifically conferred upon Congress, it seems to me that it is not made any less constitutional because of the indirect effects that it may have, however obvious it may be that it will have those effects, and that we are not at liberty upon such grounds to hold it void . . .

The notion that prohibition is any less prohibition when applied to things now thought evil I do not understand. But if there is any matter upon which civilized countries have agreed—far more unanimously than they have with regard to intoxicants and some other matters over which this country is now emotionally aroused—it is the evil of premature and excessive child labor. I should have thought that if we were to introduce our own moral conceptions where in my opinion they do not belong, this was preeminently a case for upholding the exercise of all its powers by the United States.

But I had thought that the propriety of the exercise of a power admitted to exist in some cases was for the consideration of Congress alone and that this Court always had disavowed the right to intrude its judgment upon questions of policy or morals. It is not for this Court to pronounce when prohibition is necessary to regulation if it ever may be necessary—to say that it is permissible as against strong drink but not as against the product of ruined lives.

The act does not meddle with anything belonging to the states. They may regulate their internal affairs and their domestic commerce as they like. But when they seek to send their products across the state line they are no longer within their rights. If there were no Constitution and no Congress their power to cross the line would depend upon their neighbors. Under the Constitution such commerce belongs not to the states but to Congress to regulate. It may carry out its views of public policy whatever indirect effect they may have upon the activities of the states. Instead of being encountered by a prohibitive tariff at her boundaries the state encounters the public policy of the United States which it is for Congress to express. The public policy of the United States is shaped with a view to the benefit of the nation as a whole . . . The national welfare as understood by Congress may require a different attitude within its sphere from that of some self-seeking state. It seems to me entirely constitutional for Congress to enforce its understanding by all the means at its command.

Truax v. Corrigan

257 U.S. 312 (1921)

(Dissent)

The dangers of a delusive exactness in the application of the Fourteenth Amendment have been adverted to before now. Delusive exactness is a source of fallacy throughout the law. By calling a business "property" you make it seem like land, and lead up to the conclusion that a statute cannot substantially cut down the advantages of ownership existing before the statute was passed. An established business no doubt may have pecuniary value and commonly is protected by law against various unjustified injuries. But you cannot give it definiteness of contour by calling it a thing. It is a course of conduct and like other conduct is subject to substantial modification according to time and circumstances both in itself and in regard to what shall justify doing it a harm. I cannot understand the notion that it would be constitutional to authorize boycotts and the like in aid of the employees' or the employers' interest by statute when the same result has been reached constitutionally without statute by courts with whom I agree. In this case it does not even appear that the business was not created under the laws as they now are.

I think further that the selection of the class of employers and employees for special treatment, dealing with both sides alike, is beyond criticism on principles often asserted by this Court. And especially I think that without legalizing the conduct complained of the extraordinary relief by injunction may be denied to the class. Legislation may begin where an evil begins. If, as many intelligent people believe, there is more danger that the injunction will be abused in labor cases than elsewhere I can feel no doubt of the power of the legislature to deny it in such cases . . .

I must add one general consideration. There is nothing that I more deprecate than the use of the Fourteenth Amendment beyond the absolute compulsion of its words to prevent the making of social experiments that an important part of the community desires, in the insulated chambers afforded by the several states, even though the experiments may seem futile or even noxious to me and to those whose judgment I most respect . . .

Tyson & Bro. v. Banton
273 U.S. 418 (1927)
(Dissent)

We fear to grant power and are unwilling to recognize it when it exists. The states very generally have stripped jury trials of one of their most important characteristics by forbidding the judges to advise the jury upon the facts, and when legislatures are held to be authorized to do anything considerably affecting public welfare it is covered by apologetic phrases like the police power, or the statement that the business concerned has been dedicated to a public use. The former expression is convenient, to be sure, to conciliate the mind to something that needs explanation: the fact that the constitutional requirement of compensation when property is taken cannot be pressed to its grammatical extreme; that property rights may be taken for public purposes without pay if you do not take too much; that some play must be allowed to the joints if the machine is to work. But police power often is used in a wide sense to cover and, as I said, to apologize for the general power of the legislature to make a part of the community uncomfortable by a change.

I do not believe in such apologies. I think the proper course is to recognize that a state legislature can do whatever it sees fit to do unless it is restrained by some express prohibition in the Constitution of the United States or of the state, and that courts should be careful not to extend such prohibitions beyond their obvious meaning by reading into them conceptions of public policy that the particular court may happen to entertain. Coming down to the case before us I think that the notion that a business is clothed with a public interest and has been devoted to the public use is little more than a fiction intended to beautify what is disagreeable to the sufferers. The truth seems to me to be that, subject to compensation when compensation is due, the legislature may forbid or restrict any business when it has a sufficient force of public opinion behind it. Lotteries were thought useful adjuncts of the state a century or so ago; now they are believed to be immoral and they have been stopped. Wine has been thought good for man from the time of the Apostles until recent years. But when public opinion changed it did not need the Eighteenth Amendment, notwithstanding the Fourteenth, to enable a state to say that the business should end. What has happened to lotteries and wine might happen to theaters in some moral storm of the future, not because theaters were devoted to a public use, but because people had come to think that way.

But if we are to yield to fashionable conventions, it seems to me that theaters are as much devoted to public use as anything well can be. We have not that respect for art that is one of the glories of France. But to many people the superfluous is the necessary, and it seems to me that government does not go beyond its sphere in attempting to make life livable for them. I am far from saying that I think this particular law* a wise and rational provision. That is not my affair. But if the people of the State of New York speaking by their authorized voice say that they

*The law invalidated by the Court was a regulation of ticket scalping.—Ed.

want it, I see nothing in the Constitution of the United States to prevent their having their will.

Baldwin v. Missouri
281 U.S. 586 (1930)
(Dissent)

Although this decision hardly can be called a surprise after *Farmers Loan & Trust Co. v. Minnesota* and *Safe Deposit & Trust Co. v. Virginia,* and although I stated my views in those cases, still, as the term is not over, I think it legitimate to add one or two reflections to what I have said before. I have not yet adequately expressed the more than anxiety that I feel at the ever-increasing scope given to the Fourteenth Amendment in cutting down what I believe to be the constitutional rights of the states. As the decisions now stand, I see hardly any limit but the sky to the invalidating of those rights if they happen to strike a majority of this Court as for any reason undesirable. I cannot believe that the amendment was intended to give us carte blanche to embody our economic or moral beliefs in its prohibitions. Yet I can think of no narrower reason that seems to me to justify the present and the earlier decisions to which I have referred. Of course the words "due process of law," if taken in their literal meaning, have no application to this case; and while it is too late to deny that they have been given a much more extended and artificial signification, still we ought to remember the great caution shown by the Constitution in limiting the power of the states, and should be slow to construe the clause in the Fourteenth Amendment as committing to the Court, with no guide but the Court's own discretion, the validity of whatever laws the states may pass. In this case the bonds, notes and bank accounts were within the power and received the protection of the State of Missouri; the notes, so far as appears, were within the considerations that I offered in the earlier decisions mentioned, so that logically Missouri was justified in demanding a quid pro quo; the practice of taxation in such circumstances I think has been ancient and widespread and the tax was warranted by decisions of this Court. (I suppose that these cases and many others now join *Blackstone v. Miller* on the Index Expurgatorius—but we need an authoritative list.) It seems to me to be exceeding our powers to declare such a tax a denial of due process of law.

And what are the grounds? Simply, so far as I can see, that it is disagreeable to a bondowner to be taxed in two places. Very probably it might be good policy to restrict taxation to a single place, and perhaps the technical conception of domicile may be the best determinant. But it seems to me that if that result is to be reached it should be reached through understanding among the states, by uniform legislation or otherwise, not by evoking a constitutional prohibition from the void of "due process of law," when logic tradition and authority have united to declare the right of the state to lay the now prohibited tax.

Schenck v. United States
249 U.S. 47 (1919)

This is an indictment in three counts. The first charges a conspiracy to violate the Espionage Act of June 15, 1917, by causing and attempting to cause insubordination, etc., in the military and naval forces of the United States, and to obstruct the recruiting and enlistment service of the United States, when the United States was at war with the German Empire; to wit, that the defendant willfully conspired to have printed and circulated to men who had been called and accepted for military service under the Act of May 18, 1917, a document set forth and alleged to be calculated to cause such insubordination and obstruction. The count alleges overt acts in pursuance of the conspiracy, ending in the distribution of the document set forth. The second count alleges a conspiracy to commit an offense against the United States; to wit, to use the mails for the transmission of matter declared to be nonmailable by title 12, §2, of the Act of June 15, 1917, to wit, the above-mentioned document, with an averment of the same overt acts. The third count charges an unlawful use of the mails for the transmission of the same matter and otherwise as above. The defendants were found guilty on all the counts. They set up the First Amendment to the Constitution, forbidding Congress to make any law abridging the freedom of speech or of the press, and, bringing the case here on that ground, have argued some other points also of which we must dispose.

The document in question, upon its first printed side, recited the first section of the Thirteenth Amendment, said that the idea embodied in it was violated by the Conscription Act, and that a conscript is little better than a convict. In impassioned language it intimated that conscription was despotism in its worst form and a monstrous wrong against humanity, in the interest of Wall Street's chosen few. It said: "Do not submit to intimidation;" but in form at least confined itself to peaceful measures, such as a petition for the repeal of the act. The other and later printed side of the sheet was headed, "Assert Your Rights." It stated reasons for alleging that anyone violated the Constitution when he refused to recognize "your right to assert your opposition to the draft," and went on: "If you do not assert and support your rights, you are helping to deny or disparage rights which it is the solemn duty of all citizens and residents of the United States to retain." It described the arguments on the other side as coming from cunning politicians and a mercenary capitalist press, and even silent consent to the Conscription Law as helping to support an infamous conspiracy. It denied the power to send our citizens away to foreign shores to shoot up the people of other lands, and added that words could not express the condemnation such cold-blooded ruthlessness deserves, etc., etc., winding up, "You must do your share to maintain, support, and uphold the rights of the people of this country." Of course the document would not have been sent unless it had been intended to have some effect, and we do not see what effect it could be expected to have upon persons subject to the draft except to influence them to obstruct the carrying of it out. The defendants do not deny that the jury might find against them on this point.

But it is said, suppose that that was the tendency of this circular, it is protected by the First Amendment to the Constitution. Two of the strongest expressions are said to be quoted respectively from well-known public men. It well may be that the prohibition of laws abridging the freedom of speech is not confined to previous restraints, although to prevent them may have been the main purpose. We admit that in many places and in ordinary times the defendants, in saying all that was said in the circular, would have been within their constitutional rights. But the character of every act depends upon the circumstances in which it is done. The most stringent protection of free speech would not protect a man in falsely shouting fire in a theater, and causing a panic. It does not even protect a man from an injunction against uttering words that may have all the effect of force. The question in every case is whether the words used are used in such circumstances and are of such a nature as to create a clear and present danger that they will bring about the substantive evils that Congress has a right to prevent. It is a question of proximity and degree. When a nation is at war many things that might be said in time of peace are such a hindrance to its effort that their utterance will not be endured so long as men fight, and that no court could regard them as protected by any constitutional right. It seems to be admitted that if an actual obstruction of the recruiting service were proved, liability for words that produced that effect might be enforced. The Statute of 1917, in §4, punishes conspiracies to obstruct as well as actual obstruction. If the act (speaking, or circulating a paper), its tendency and the intent with which it is done, are the same, we perceive no ground for saying that success alone warrants making the act a crime . . .

To Harold Laski

March 16, 1919

Dear Laski,

. . . I sent you yesterday some opinions in the [Eugene] Debs and other similar cases [including *Schenk*]. I greatly regretted having to write them—and (between ourselves) that the government pressed them to a hearing. Of course I know that donkeys and knaves would represent us as concurring in the condemnation of Debs because he was a dangerous agitator. Of course, too, so far as that is concerned, he might split his guts without my interfering with him or sanctioning interference. But on the only questions before us I could not doubt about the law. The federal judges seem to me (again between ourselves) to have got hysterical about the war. I should think the President when he gets through with his present amusements might do some pardoning. I have been interrupted and so perhaps have been less coherent than I should have been.

Abrams v. United States

250 U.S. 616 (1919)

(Dissent)

This indictment is founded wholly upon the publication of two leaflets which I shall describe in a moment. The first count charges a conspiracy pending the war with Germany to publish abusive language about the form of government of the United States, laying the preparation and publishing of the first leaflet as overt acts. The second count charges a conspiracy pending the war to publish language intended to bring the form of government into contempt, laying the preparation and publishing of the two leaflets as overt acts. The third count alleges a conspiracy to encourage resistance to the United States in the same war and to attempt to effectuate the purpose by publishing the same leaflets. The fourth count lays a conspiracy to incite curtailment of production of things necessary to the prosecution of the war and to attempt to accomplish it by publishing the second leaflet to which I have referred.

The first of these leaflets says that the President's cowardly silence about the intervention in Russia reveals the hypocrisy of the plutocratic gang in Washington. It intimates that "German militarism combined with allied capitalism to crush the Russian revolution"; goes on that the tyrants of the world fight each other until they see a common enemy— working class enlightenment—when they combine to crush it; and that now militarism and capitalism combined, though not openly, to crush the Russian revolution. It says that there is only one enemy of the workers of the world and that is capitalism; that it is a crime for workers of America, etc., to fight the workers' republic of Russia, and ends "Awake! Awake, you workers of the world! Revolutionists." A note adds "It is absurd to call us pro-German. We hate and despise German militarism more than do you hypocritical tyrants. We have more reasons for denouncing German militarism than has the coward of the White House."

The other leaflet, headed "Workers—Wake Up," with abusive language says that America together with the Allies will march for Russia to help the Czecko-Slovaks in their struggle against the Bolsheviki, and that this time the hypocrites shall not fool the Russian emigrants and friends of Russia in America. It tells the Russian emigrants that they now must spit in the face of the false military propaganda by which their sympathy and help to the prosecution of the war have been called forth and says that with the money they have lent or are going to lend "they will make bullets not only for the Germans but also for the worker soviets of Russia," and further, "Workers in the ammunition factories, you are producing bullets, bayonets, cannon to murder not only the Germans, but also your dearest, best, who are in Russia fighting for freedom." It then appeals to the same Russian emigrants at some length not to consent to the "inquisitionary expedition in Russia," and says that the destruction of the Russian Revolution is "the politics of the march on Russia." The leaflet winds up by saying "Workers, our reply to this barbaric intervention has to be a general strike!" and after a few words on the spirit of revolution, exhortations not to be afraid, and some usual tall talk ends "Woe unto those who will be in the way of progress. Let solidarity live! The Rebels."

No argument seems to me necessary to show that these pronunciamentos in no way attack the form of government of the United States, or that they do not support either of the first two counts. What little I have to say about the third count may be postponed until I have considered the fourth. With regard to that it seems too plain to be denied that the suggestion to workers in the ammunition factories that they are producing bullets to murder their dearest, and the further advocacy of a general strike, both in the second leaflet, do urge curtailment of production of things necessary to the prosecution of the war within the meaning of the Act of May 16, 1918. But to make the conduct criminal that statute requires that it should be "with intent by such curtailment to cripple or hinder the United States in the prosecution of the war." It seems to me that no such intent is proved.

I am aware of course that the word intent as vaguely used in ordinary legal discussion means no more than knowledge at the time of the act that the consequences said to be intended will ensue. Even less than that will satisfy the general principle of civil and criminal liability. A man may have to pay damages, may be sent to prison, at common law might be hanged, if at the time of his act he knew facts from which common experience showed that the consequences would follow, whether he individually could foresee them or not. But, when words are used exactly, a deed is not done with intent to produce a consequence unless the consequence is the aim of the deed. It may be obvious, and obvious to the actor, that the consequence will follow, and he may be liable for it even if he regrets it, but he does not do the act with intent to produce it unless the aim to produce it is the proximate motive of the specific act, although there may be some deeper motive behind.

It seems to me that this statute must be taken to use its words in a strict and accurate sense. They would be absurd in any other. A patriot might think that we were wasting money on aeroplanes, or making more cannon of a certain kind than we needed, and might advocate curtailment with success, yet even if it turned out that the curtailment hindered and was thought by other minds to have been obviously likely to hinder the United States in the prosecution of the war, no one would hold such conduct a crime. I admit that my illustration does not answer all that might be said but it is enough to show what I think and to let me pass to a more important aspect of the case. I refer to the First Amendment to the Constitution that Congress shall make no law abridging the freedom of speech.

. . . I do not doubt for a moment that by the same reasoning that would justify punishing persuasion to murder, the United States constitutionally may punish speech that produces or is intended to produce a clear and imminent danger that it will bring about forthwith certain substantive evils that the United States constitutionally may seek to prevent. The power undoubtedly is greater in time of war than in time of peace because war opens dangers that do not exist at other times.

But as against dangers peculiar to war, as against others, the principle of the right to free speech is always the same. It is only the present danger of immediate evil or an intent to bring it about that warrants Congress in setting a limit to the expression of opinion where private rights are not concerned. Congress certainly cannot forbid all effort to change the mind of the country. Now nobody can suppose that the surreptitious publishing of a silly leaflet by an unknown man, without more, would present any immediate danger that its opinions would hinder the success of the government arms or have any appreciable tendency to do so. Publishing those opinions for the very purpose of obstructing, however, might indicate a greater danger and at any rate would have the quality of an attempt. So I assume that the second leaflet if published for the purposes alleged in the fourth count might be punishable. But it seems pretty clear to me that nothing less than that would bring these papers within the scope of this law. An actual intent in the sense that I have explained is necessary to constitute an attempt, where a further act of the same individual is required to complete the substantive crime. It is necessary where the success of the attempt depends upon others because if that intent is not present the actor's aim may be accomplished without bringing about the evils sought to be checked. An intent to prevent interference with the revolution in Russia might have been satisfied without any hindrance to carrying on the war in which we were engaged.

I do not see how anyone can find the intent required by the statute in any of the defendants' words. The second leaflet is the only one that affords even a foundation for the charge, and there, without invoking the hatred of German militarism expressed in the former one, it is evident from the beginning to the end that the only object of the paper is to help Russia and stop American intervention there against the popular government—not to impede the United States in the war that it was carrying on. To say that two phrases taken literally might import a suggestion of conduct that would have interference with the war as an indirect and probably undesired effect seems to me by no means enough to show an attempt to produce that effect.

I return for a moment to the third count. That charges an intent to provoke resistance to the United States in its war with Germany. Taking the clause in the statute that deals with that in connection with the other elaborate provisions of the act, I think that resistance to the United States means some forcible act of opposition to some proceeding of the United States in pursuance of the war. I think the intent must be the specific intent that I have described and for the reasons that I have given I think that no such intent was proved or existed in fact. I also think that there is no hint at resistance to the United States as I construe the phrase.

In this case sentences of twenty years' imprisonment have been imposed for the publishing of two leaflets that I believe the defendants had as much right to publish as the government has to publish the Constitution of the United States now vainly invoked by them. Even if I am technically wrong and enough can be squeezed from these poor and puny anonymities to turn the color of legal litmus paper—I will add, even if what I think the necessary intent were shown—the most nominal punishment seems to me all that possibly could be inflicted, unless the defendants are to be made to suffer not for what the indictment alleges but for the creed that they avow—a creed that I believe to be the creed of ignorance and immaturity when honestly held, as I see no reason to doubt that it was held here, but which, although made the subject of examination at the trial, no one has a right even to consider in dealing with the charges before the Court.

Persecution for the expression of opinions seems to me perfectly logical. If you have no doubt of your premises or your power and want a certain result with all your heart you naturally express your wishes in law and sweep away all opposition. To allow opposition by speech seems to indicate that you think the speech impotent, as when a man says that he has squared the circle, or that you do not care wholeheartedly for the result, or that you doubt either your power or your premises. But when men have realized that time has upset many fighting faiths, they may come to believe even more than they believe the very foundations of their own conduct that the ultimate good desired is better reached by free trade in ideas—that the best test of truth is the power of the thought to get itself accepted in the competition of the market, and that truth is the only ground upon which their wishes safely can be carried out. That at any rate is the theory of our Constitution. It is an experiment, as all life is an experiment. Every year if not every day we have to wager our salvation upon some prophecy based upon imperfect knowledge. While that experiment is part of our system I think that we should be eternally vigilant against attempts to check the expression of opinions that we loathe and believe to be fraught with death, unless they so imminently threaten immediate interference with the lawful and pressing purposes of the law that an immediate check is required to save the country. I wholly disagree with the argument of the government that the First Amendment left the common law as to seditious libel in force. History seems to me against the notion. I had conceived that the United States through many years had shown its repentance for the Sedition Act of 1798, by repaying fines that it imposed. Only the emergency that makes it immediately dangerous to leave the correction of evil counsels to time warrants making any exception to the sweeping command, "Congress shall make no law . . . abridging the freedom of speech." Of course I am speaking only of expressions of opinion and exhortations, which were all that were uttered here, but I regret that I cannot put into more impressive words my belief that in their conviction upon this indictment the defendants were deprived of their rights under the Constitution of the United States.

To Harold Laski

October 26, 1919

Dear Laski,
 . . . I fear we have less freedom of speech here than they have in England. Little as I believe in it as a theory I hope I would die for it and I go as far as anyone whom I regard as competent to form an opinion, in favor of it. Of course when I say I don't believe in it as a theory I don't mean that I do believe in the opposite as a theory. But on their premises it seems to me logical in the Catholic Church to kill heretics and the Puritans to whip Quakers—and I see nothing more wrong in it from our ultimate standards than I do in killing Germans when we are at war. When you are thoroughly convinced that you are right, wholeheartedly desire an end, and have no doubt of your power to accomplish it, I see nothing but municipal regulations to interfere with your using your power to accomplish it. The sacredness of human life is a formula that is good only inside a system of law—and so of the rest—all which apart from its *banalité* I fear seems cold talk if you have been made to feel popular displeasure. I should not be cold about that—nor do I in any way shrink from saying what I think—but I can't spare the energy necessary to deal with extralegal themes . . .

Gitlow v. New York
268 U.S. 652 (1925)
(Dissent)

Mr. Justice Brandeis and I are of opinion that this judgment should be reversed. The general principle of free speech, it seems to me, must be taken to be included in the Fourteenth Amendment, in view of the scope that has been given to the word "liberty" as there used, although perhaps it may be accepted with a somewhat larger latitude of interpretation than is allowed to Congress by the sweeping language that governs or ought to govern the laws of the United States . . . If what I think the correct test is applied, it is manifest that there was no present danger of an attempt to overthrow the government by force on the part of the admittedly small minority who shared the defendant's views. It is said that this manifesto was more than a theory, that it was an incitement. Every idea is an incitement. It offers itself for belief and if believed it is acted on unless some other belief outweighs it or some failure of energy stifles the movement at its birth. The only difference between the expression of an opinion and an incitement in the narrower sense is the speaker's enthusiasm for the result. Eloquence may set fire to reason. But whatever may be thought of the redundant discourse before us it had no chance of starting a present conflagration. If in the long run the beliefs expressed in proletarian dictatorship are destined to be accepted by the dominant forces of the community, the only meaning of free speech is that they should be given their chance and have their way.

If the publication of this document had been laid as an attempt to induce an uprising against government at once and not at some indefinite time in the future it would have presented a different question. The object would have been one with which the law might deal, subject to the doubt whether there was any danger that the publication could produce any result, or in other words whether it was not futile and too remote from possible consequences. But the indictment alleges the publication and nothing more.

To Lewis Einstein

Beverly Farms, July 11, 1925

Dear Einstein,

Your letter, just arrived, gives me the usual pleasure. What you quote from Dizzy [Disraeli] comes in apropos as I was just writing a day or two ago to a friend who repeated a criticism of my opinions that they might be literature but were not the proper form of judicial exposition. My notion was that longwinded expositions of the obvious were as out of place in opinions as elsewhere. This however is not intended as a hit at the judgment of the majority in the Gitlow case. I had my whack on free speech some years ago in the case of one Abrams, and therefore did no more than lean to that and add that an idea is always an incitement. To show the ardor of the writer is not a sufficient reason for judging him. I regarded my view as simply upholding the right of a donkey to drool. But the usual notion is that you are free to say what you like if you don't shock *me*. Of course the value of the constitutional right is only when you do shock people . . .

United States v. Schwimmer

279 U.S. 644 (1929)

(Dissent)

The applicant seems to be a woman of superior character and intelligence, obviously more than ordinarily desirable as a citizen of the United States. It is agreed that she is qualified for citizenship except so far as the views set forth in a statement of facts "may show that the applicant is not attached to the principles of the Constitution of the United States and well disposed to the good order and happiness of the same, and except insofar as the same may show that she cannot take the oath of allegiance without a mental reservation." The views referred to are an extreme opinion in favor of pacifism and a statement that she would not bear arms to defend the Constitution. So far as the adequacy of her oath is concerned I hardly can see how that is affected by the statement, inasmuch as she is a woman over fifty years of age, and would not be allowed to bear arms if she wanted to. And as to the opinion, the whole examination of the applicant shows that she holds none of the now-dreaded creeds but thoroughly believes in organized government and prefers that of the United States to any other in the world. Surely it cannot show lack of attachment to the principles of the Constitution that she thinks that it can be improved. I suppose that most intelligent people think that it might be. Her particular improvement looking to the abolition of war seems to me not materially different in its bearing on this case from a wish to establish cabinet government as in England, or a single house, or one term of seven years for the President. To touch a more burning question, only a judge mad with partisanship would exclude because the applicant thought that the Eighteenth Amendment should be repealed.

Of course the fear is that if a war came the applicant would exert activities such as were dealt with in *Schenck v. United States.* But that seems to me unfounded. Her position and motives are wholly different from those of Schenck. She is an optimist and states in strong and, I do not doubt, sincere words her belief that war will disappear and the impending destiny of mankind is to unite in peaceful leagues. I do not share that optimism nor do I think that a philosophic view of the world would regard war as absurd. But most people who have known it regard it with horror, as a last resort, and even if not yet ready for cosmopolitan efforts, would welcome any practicable combinations that would increase the power on the side of peace. The notion that the applicant's optimistic anticipations would make her a worse citizen is sufficiently answered by her examination, which seems to me a better argument for her admission than any that I can offer. Some of her answers might excite popular prejudice, but if there is any principle of the Constitution that more imperatively calls for attachment than any other it is the principle of free thought—not free thought for those who agree with us but freedom for the thought that we hate. I think that we should adhere to that principle with regard to admission into, as well as to life within this country. And recurring to the opinion that bars this applicant's way, I would suggest that the Quakers have done their share to make the country what it is, that many citizens agree with the applicant's belief and that I had not supposed hitherto that we regretted our inability to expel them because they believe more than some of us do in the teachings of the Sermon on the Mount.

Hyde v. United States
225 U.S. 347 (1909)
(Dissent)

This is an indictment for a conspiracy to defraud the United States. The petitioners were tried and convicted in the District of Columbia, the conviction was affirmed by the court of appeals, and thereupon a writ of certiorari was granted by this Court. The scheme was to obtain by fraudulent devices from the states of California and Oregon school lands lying within forest reserves, to exchange for public lands of the United States open to selection, and then to sell the lands so obtained. Hyde and Schneider were in California and never were actually in the District in aid of the conspiracy, but overt acts are alleged to have been done there to effect the objects in view. Most of these acts are innocent, taken by themselves, consisting mainly of the entry of appearance by Hyde's lawyer in the matter of different selections, the filing of papers concerning them, and letters urging speed. Hyde is alleged to have caused some documents affecting the same to be transmitted from California to the Commissioner at Washington, and in the last six counts payments to employees in the Land Office are alleged to have been made with corrupt purpose and in aid of the plan by a person who was included in the indictment as a conspirator, but whom the jury did not convict.

The court instructed the jury that if the defendants agreed to accomplish their purpose by having any of the alleged overt acts done in the District of Columbia, and any of those acts were done there, the conspiracy was in the District, whether the defendants were there or not. The defendants excepted to this instruction, as well as to many others.

. . . It is not enough to say that as the overt act was one that was contemplated by the conspirators, it is treated as the act of them all, and that this is equivalent to saying that they were constructively present . . . To speak of constructive presence is to use the language of fiction, and so to hinder precise analysis. When a man is said to be constructively present where the consequences of an act done elsewhere are felt, it is meant that for some special purpose he will be treated as he would have been treated if he had been present, although he was not. For instance, if a man, acting in one state, sets forces in motion that kill a man in another, or produces or induces some consequence in that other that it regards as very hurtful and wishes to prevent, the latter state is very likely to say that, if it can catch him, it will punish him, although he was not subject to its laws when he did the act. But as states usually confine their threats to those within the jurisdiction at the time of the act, the symmetry of general theory is preserved by saying that the offender was constructively present in the case supposed. We must not forget facts, however. He was not present in fact, and in theory of law he was present only so far as to be charged with the act.

Obviously the use of this fiction or form of words must not be pushed to such a point in the administration of the national law as to transgress the requirement of the Constitution that the trial of crimes shall be held in the state and district where the crimes shall have been committed. With the country extending from ocean to ocean, this requirement is even more important now than it was a hundred years ago, and must be enforced in letter and spirit if we are not to make impossible hardships amounting to grievous wrongs. In the case of conspiracy the danger is conspicuously brought out. Every overt act done in aid of it, of course, is attributed to the conspirators; and if that means that the conspiracy is present as such wherever any overt act is done, it might be at the choice of the government to prosecute in any one of twenty states in none of which the conspirators had been. And as wherever two or more have united for the commission of a crime there is a conspiracy, the opening to oppression thus made is very wide indeed. It is even wider if success should be held not to merge the conspiracy in the crime intended and achieved. I think it unnecessary to dwell on oppressions that I believe had been practised, or on the constitutional history impressively adduced by Mr. Worthington to show that this is one of the wrongs that our forefathers meant to prevent.

No distinction can be taken based on the gravity of the overt act, or the fact that it was contemplated, or that it is important for the accomplishment of the substantive evil that the conspiracy aims to bring about and the law seeks to prevent. That would be carrying over the law of attempts to where it does not belong. Although both are adjective crimes, a conspiracy is not an attempt, even under Rev. Stat. §5440, which requires an overt act. When I first read that section I thought that it was an indefinite enlargement of the law of attempts. But reflection and the decisions both convinced me that I was wrong. The statute simply did away with a doubt as to the requirements of the common law. An attempt, in the strictest sense, is an act expected to bring about a substantive wrong by the forces of nature. With it is classed the kindred offense where the act and the natural conditions present or supposed to be present are not enough to do the harm without a further act, but where it is so near to the result that, if coupled with an intent to produce that result, the danger is very great. But combination, intention, and overt act may all be present without amounting to a criminal attempt— as if all that were done should be an agreement to murder a man fifty miles away, and the purchase of a pistol for the purpose. There must be dangerous proximity to success. But when that exists the overt act is the essence of the offense. On the other hand, the essence of the conspiracy is being combined for an unlawful purpose; and if an overt act is required, it does not matter how remote the act may be from accomplishing the purpose, if done to effect it; that is, I suppose, in furtherance of it in any degree. In this case the statute treats the conspiracy as the crime and the indictment follows the statute.

The cases in this court have agreed that the statute has not made the overt act a part of the crime, which still remains the conspiracy alone . . . The overt act is simply evidence that the conspiracy has passed beyond the words and is on foot when the act is done. As a result of actuality it is made a condition to punishment; but it is no more a part of the crime than it was at common law, where it was customary to allege such an act; or than is the fact that the statute of limitations has not run . . .

The defendants were in California and never left the state, so far as this case is concerned. The fraud, assuming as I do, for the purposes of decision, that there was one, was to get land from the United States there and elsewhere on the Pacific coast. If successful it would be punished there. The crime with which the defendants are charged is having been engaged in or members of a conspiracy, nothing else; no act, other than what is implied as necessary to signify their understanding to each other. It is punished only to create a further obstacle to the ultimate crime in California. The defendants never were members of a conspiracy within a thousand miles of the District in fact. Yet if a lawyer entered his appearance there in a case before the Land Department, and the defendants directed it and expected to profit by it in carrying out their plans, it is said that we should feign that they were here in order to warrant their being taken across the continent and tried in this place. The Constitution is not to be satisfied with a fiction. When a man causes an unlawful act, as in the case of a prohibited use of the mails, it needs no fiction to say that the crime is committed at the place of the act, wherever the man may be. But when the offense consists solely in a relation to other men with a certain intent, it is pure fiction to say that the relation is maintained and present in the case supposed. If the government, instead of prosecuting for the substantive offense, charges only conspiracy to commit it, trial ought to be where the conspiracy exists in fact . . .

The intimations that are to be found, opposed to the view that I take, appear to have been induced by the confusion that I have tried to dispel, and to assume that an overt act creates jurisdiction over a conspiracy on the same ground that causing a death may give jurisdiction in murder; or, perhaps, to proceed on the dangerous analogy of treasonable conspiracies to levy war or compass the death of the sovereign. The *dictum* in that case gains no new force from the repetition by text writers. It is one of the misfortunes of the law that ideas become encysted in phrases and thereafter for a long time cease to provoke further analysis . . . At least, in the absence of clear statutory words, I am of opinion that logic and the policy and general intent of the Constitution agree in refusing to extend the fiction of constructive presence to a case like this . . .

Silverthorne Lumber Co. v. United States
251 U.S. 385 (1920)

This is a writ of error brought to reverse a judgment of the district court fining the Silverthorne Lumber Company two hundred and fifty dollars for contempt of court and ordering Frederick W. Silverthorne to be imprisoned until he should purge himself of a similar contempt. The contempt in question was a refusal to obey subpoenas and an order of court to produce books and documents of the company before the grand jury to be used in regard to alleged violation of the statutes of the United States by the said Silverthorne and his father. One ground of the refusal was that the order of the court infringed the rights of the parties under the Fourth Amendment of the Constitution of the United States.

The facts are simple. An indictment upon a single specific charge having been brought against the two Silverthornes mentioned, they both were arrested at their homes early in the morning of February 25, 1919, and were detained in custody a number of hours. While they were thus detained representatives of the Department of Justice and the United States marshal without a shadow of authority went to the office of their company and made a clean sweep of all the books, papers and documents found there. All the employees were taken or directed to go to the office of the District Attorney of the United States to which also the books, etc., were taken at once. An application was made as soon as might be to the district court for a return of what thus had been taken unlawfully. It was opposed by the District Attorney so far as he had found evidence against the plaintiffs in error, and it was stated that the evidence so obtained was before the grand jury. Color had been given by the District Attorney to the approach of those concerned in the act by an invalid subpoena for certain documents relating to the charge in the indictment then on file. Thus the case is not that of knowledge acquired through the wrongful act of a stranger, but it must be assumed that the government planned or at all event ratified the whole performance. Photographs and copies of material papers were made and a new indictment was framed based upon the knowledge thus obtained. The district court ordered a return of the originals but impounded the photographs and copies. Subpoenas to produce the originals then were served and on the refusal of the plaintiffs in error to produce them the court made an order that the subpoenas should be complied with, although it had found that all the papers had been seized in violation of the parties' constitutional rights. The refusal to obey this order is the contempt alleged. The government now, while in form repudiating and condemning the illegal seizure, seeks to maintain its right to avail itself of the knowledge obtained by that means which otherwise it would not have had.

The proposition could not be presented more nakedly. It is that although of course its seizure was an outrage which the government now regrets, it may study the papers before it returns them, copy them, and then may use the knowledge that it has gained to call upon the owners in a more regular form to produce them; that the protection of the Constitution covers the physical possession but not any advantages that the government can gain over the object of its pursuit by doing the forbidden act. *Weeks v. United States,* to be sure, had established that laying the papers directly before the grand jury was unwarranted, but it is taken to mean only that two steps are required instead of one. In our opinion such is not the law. It reduces the Fourth Amendment to a form of words. The essence of a provision forbidding the acquisition of evidence in a certain way is that not merely evidence so acquired shall not be used before the court but that it shall not be used at all.* Of course this does not mean that the facts thus obtained become sacred and inaccessible. If knowledge of them is gained from an independent source they may be proved like any others, but the knowledge gained by the government's own wrong cannot be used by it in the way proposed . . .

To Harold Laski

Beverly Farms, August 24, 1927

My dear Laski,

Your last letter shows you stirred up like the rest of the world on the Sacco Vanzetti case. I cannot but ask myself why this so much greater interest in red than black. A thousand-fold worse cases of negroes come up from time to time, but the world does not worry over them. It is not a mere simple abstract love of justice that has moved people so much. I never have read the evidence except on the limited points that came before me. As I remember the time of the trial I always have appreciated the difficulty in getting a dispassionate verdict when everyone was as excited as everyone was in those days. I also appreciate what I believe was the generous knight-errantry of Felix in writing his book. But I see no adequate available reasons for the world outside the U.S. taking up the matter and I think your public and literary men had better have kept their mouths shut. There were two applications for habeas corpus to me, the first presented by Arthur Hill, the last on different grounds the night before the execution, by other counsel, both of which I denied, as I thought them beyond my power, on the case made. There was also an application for a stay until the full Court could consider granting of a certiorari, which also I denied, as I thought no shadow of a ground was shown on which the writ should be granted. There was no way that I knew of in which the merits of the case could be brought before us. Of course I got lots of letters—some abusive, some precatory (and emotion from women) all more or less assuming that I had the power of Austin's sovereign over the matter. (Forgive my mentioning so contemptible a personage.) The most sensible talk I have seen was a letter by Norman Hapgood, who recognized the humbug of talking as if justice alone was thought of. Not having read the record I do not consider myself entitled to an opinion on the case—my prejudices are against the convictions, but they are still stronger against the run of the shriekers. The lovers of justice have emphasized their love by blowing

---

*See also Holmes's dissent in the *Olmstead* case (above, in chapter 7).—Ed.

up a building or two and there are guards in all sorts of places, including one for this house for a few days, which left to myself I should not have thought of . . .

Frank v. Mangum
237 U.S. 309 (1915)

Mr. Justice Hughes and I are of opinion that the judgment should be reversed. The only question before us is whether the petition shows on its face that the writ of habeas corpus should be denied, or whether the district court should have proceeded to try the facts. The allegations that appear to us material are these. The trial began on July 28, 1913, at Atlanta, and was carried on in a court packed with spectators and surrounded by a crowd outside, all strongly hostile to the petitioner. On Saturday, August 23, this hostility was sufficient to lead the judge to confer in the presence of the jury with the Chief of Police of Atlanta and the Colonel of the Fifth Georgia Regiment stationed in that city, both of whom were known to the jury. On the same day, the evidence seemingly having been closed, the public press, apprehending danger, united in a request to the court that the proceedings should not continue on that evening. Thereupon the court adjourned until Monday morning. On that morning when the Solicitor General entered the court he was greeted with applause, stamping of feet and clapping of hands, and the judge before beginning his charge had a private conversation with the petitioner's counsel in which he expressed the opinion that there would be "probable danger of violence" if there should be an acquittal or a disagreement, and that it would be safer for not only the petitioner but his counsel to be absent from court when the verdict was brought in. At the judge's request they agreed that the petitioner and they should be absent, and they kept their word. When the verdict was rendered, and before more than one of the jurymen had been polled there was such a roar of applause that the polling could not go on until order was restored. The noise outside was such that it was difficult for the judge to hear the answers of the jurors although he was only ten feet from them. With these specifications of fact, the petitioner alleges that the trial was dominated by a hostile mob and was nothing but an empty form.

We lay on one side the question whether the petitioner could or did waive his right to be present at the polling of the jury. That question was apparent in the form of the trial and was raised by the application for a writ of error; and although after the application to the full Court we thought that the writ ought to be granted, we never have been impressed by the argument that the presence of the prisoner was required by the Constitution of the United States. But habeas corpus cuts through all forms and goes to the very tissue of the structure. It comes in from the outside, not in subordination to the proceedings, and although every form may have been preserved opens the inquiry whether they have been more than an empty shell.

The argument for the appellee in substance is that the trial was in a court of competent jurisdiction, that it retains jurisdiction although, in fact, it may be dominated by a mob, and that the rulings of the state court as to the fact of such domination cannot be reviewed. But the argument seems to us inconclusive. Whatever disagreement there may be as to the scope of the phrase "due process of law," there can be no doubt that it embraces the fundamental conception of a fair trial, with opportunity to be heard. Mob law does not become due process of law by securing the assent of a terrorized jury. We are not speaking of a mere disorder, or mere irregularities in procedure, but of a case where the processes of justice are actually subverted. In such a case, the federal court has jurisdiction to issue the writ. The fact that the state court still has its general jurisdiction and is otherwise a competent court does not make it impossible to find that a jury has been subjected to intimidation in a particular case. The loss of jurisdiction is not general but particular, and proceeds from the control of a hostile influence.

When such a case is presented, it cannot be said, in our view, that the state court decision makes the matter *res judicata*.* The state acts when by its agency it finds the prisoner guilty and condemns him. We have held in a civil case that it is no defence to the assertion of the federal right in the federal court that the state has corrective procedure of its own—that still less does such procedure draw to itself the final determination of the federal question. We see no reason for a less liberal rule in a matter of life and death. When the decision of the question of fact is so interwoven with the decision of the question of constitutional right that the one necessarily involves the other, the federal court must examine the facts. Otherwise, the right will be a barren one. It is significant that the argument for the state does not go so far as to say that in no case would it be permissible on application for habeas corpus to override the findings of fact by the state courts. It would indeed be a most serious thing if this Court were so to hold, for we could not but regard it as a removal of what is perhaps the most important guaranty of the federal Constitution. If, however, the argument stops short of

*Adjudicated and not open to relitigation.—Ed.

this, the whole structure built upon the state procedure and decisions falls to the ground.

To put an extreme case and show what we mean, if the trial and the later hearing before the supreme court had taken place in the presence of an armed force known to be ready to shoot if the result was not the one desired, we do not suppose that this Court would allow itself to be silenced by the suggestion that the record showed no flaw. To go one step further, suppose that the trial had taken place under such intimidation and that the supreme court of the state on writ of error had discovered no error in the record, we still imagine that this Court would find a sufficient one outside of the record, and that it would not be disturbed in its conclusion by anything that the supreme court of the state might have said. We therefore lay the suggestion that the supreme court of the state has disposed of the present question by its judgment on one side along with the question of the appellant's right to be present. If the petition discloses facts that amount to a loss of jurisdiction in the trial court, jurisdiction could not be restored by any decision above. And notwithstanding the principle of comity and convenience (for in our opinion it is nothing more) that calls for a resort to the local appellate tribunal before coming to the courts of the United States for a writ of habeas corpus, when, as here, that resort has been had in vain, the power to secure fundamental rights that had existed at every stage becomes a duty and must be put forth.

The single question in our minds is whether a petition alleging that the trial took place in the midst of a mob savagely and manifestly intent on a single result, is shown on its face unwarranted, by the specifications, which may be presumed to set forth the strongest indications of the fact at the petitioner's command. This is not a matter for polite presumptions; we must look facts in the face. Any judge who has sat with juries knows that in spite of forms they are extremely likely to be impregnated by the environing atmosphere. And when we find the judgment of the expert on the spot, of the judge whose business it was to preserve not only form but substance, to have been that if one juryman yielded to the reasonable doubt that he himself later expressed in court as the result of most anxious deliberation, neither prisoner nor counsel would be safe from the rage of the crowd, we think the presumption overwhelming that the jury responded to the passions of the mob. Of course we are speaking only of the case made by the petition, and whether it ought to be heard. Upon allegations of this gravity in our opinion it ought to be heard, whatever the decision of the state court may have been, and it did not need to set forth contradictory evidence, or matter of rebuttal, or to explain why the motions for a new trial and to set aside the verdict were overruled by the state court. There is no reason to fear an impairment of the authority of the state to punish the guilty. We do not think it impracticable in any part of this country to have trials free from outside control. But to maintain this immunity it may be necessary that the supremacy of the law and of the federal Constitution should be vindicated in a case like this. It may be that on a hearing a different complexion would be given to the judge's alleged request and expression of fear. But supposing the alleged facts to be true, we are of opinion that if they were before the supreme court it sanctioned a situation upon which the courts of the United States should act, and if for any reason they were not before the supreme court, it is our duty to act upon them now and to declare lynch law as little valid when practiced by a regularly drawn jury as when administered by one elected by a mob intent on death.

Moore v. Dempsey
261 U.S. 86 (1923)

. . . The appellants are five negroes who were convicted of murder in the first degree and sentenced to death by the court of the State of Arkansas. The ground of the petition for the writ is that the proceedings in the state court, although a trial in form, were only a form, and that the appellants were hurried to conviction under the pressure of a mob without any regard for their rights and without according to them due process of law.

The case stated by the petition is as follows, and it will be understood that while we put it in narrative form, we are not affirming the facts to be as stated but only what we must take them to be, as they are admitted by the demurrer: On the night of September 30, 1919, a number of colored people assembled in their church were attacked and fired upon by a body of white men, and in the disturbance that followed a white man was killed. The report of the killing caused great excitement and was followed by the hunting down and shooting of many negroes and also by the killing on October 1 of one Clinton Lee, a white man, for whose murder the petitioners were indicted. They seem to have been arrested with many others on the same day. The petitioners say that Lee must have been killed by other whites, but that we leave on one side as what we have to deal with is not the petitioners' innocence or guilt but solely the question whether their constitutional rights have been preserved. They say that their meeting was to employ counsel for protection against extortions practiced upon them by the landowners and

that the landowners tried to prevent their effort, but that again we pass
by as not directly bearing upon the trial. It should be mentioned however that O. S. Bratton, a son of the counsel who is said to have been
contemplated and who took part in the argument here, arriving for
consultation on October 1, is said to have barely escaped being
mobbed; that he was arrested and confined during the month on a
charge of murder and on October 31 was indicted for barratry,* but
later in the day was told that he would be discharged but that he must
leave secretly by a closed automobile to take the train at West Helena,
four miles away, to avoid being mobbed. It is alleged that the judge of
the court in which the petitioners were tried facilitated the departure
and went with Bratton to see him safely off.

A Committee of Seven was appointed by the Governor in regard to
what the committee called the "insurrection" in the county. The newspapers daily published inflammatory articles. On the 7th a statement
by one of the committee was made public to the effect that the present
trouble was a "deliberately planned insurrection of the negroes against
the whites, directed by an organization known as the 'Progressive
Farmers and Household Union of America' established for the purpose of banding negroes together for the killing of white people." According to the statement the organization was started by a swindler to
get money from the blacks.

Shortly after the arrest of the petitioners a mob marched to the jail
for the purpose of lynching them but were prevented by the presence
of United States troops and the promise of some of the Committee of
Seven and other leading officials that if the mob would refrain, as the
petition puts it, they would execute those found guilty in the form of
law. The Committee's own statement was that the reason that the people refrained from mob violence was "that this Committee gave our
citizens their solemn promise that the law would be carried out." According to affidavits of two white men and the colored witnesses on
whose testimony the petitioners were convicted, produced by the petitioners since the last decision of the supreme court hereafter mentioned, the Committee made good their promise by calling colored
witnesses and having them whipped and tortured until they would say
what was wanted, among them being the two relied on to prove the petitioners' guilt. However this may be, a grand jury of white men was organized on October 27 with one of the Committee of Seven and, it is
alleged, with many of a posse organized to fight the blacks, upon it, and
on the morning of the 29th the indictment was returned. On November

*Improperly stirring up litigation.—Ed.

3 the petitioners were brought into court, informed that a certain lawyer was appointed their counsel and were placed on trial before a white jury—blacks being systematically excluded from both grand and petit juries. The court and neighborhood were thronged with an adverse crowd that threatened the most dangerous consequences to anyone interfering with the desired result. The counsel did not venture to demand delay or a change of venue, to challenge a juryman or to ask for separate trials. He had had no preliminary consultation with the accused, called no witnesses for the defence although they could have been produced, and did not put the defendants on the stand. The trial lasted about three-quarters of an hour and in less than five minutes the jury brought in a verdict of guilty of murder in the first degree. According to the allegations and affidavits there never was a chance for the petitioners to be acquitted; no juryman could have voted for an acquittal and continued to live in Phillips County and if any prisoner by any chance had been acquitted by a jury he could not have escaped the mob.

The averments as to the prejudice by which the trial was environed have some corroboration in appeals to the Governor, about a year later, earnestly urging him not to interfere with the execution of the petitioners. One came from five members of the Committee of Seven, and stated in addition to what has been quoted heretofore that "all our citizens are of the opinion that the law should take its course." Another, from a part of the American Legion, protests against a contemplated commutation of the sentence of four of the petitioners and repeats that a "solemn promise was given by the leading citizens of the community that if the guilty parties were not lynched, and let the law take its course, that justice would be done and the majesty of the law upheld." A meeting of the Helena Rotary Club attended by members representing, as it said, seventy-five of the leading industrial and commercial enterprises of Helena, passed a resolution approving and supporting the action of the American Legion post. The Lions Club of Helena at a meeting attended by members said to represent sixty of the leading industrial and commercial enterprises of the city passed a resolution to the same effect. In May of the same year, a trial of six other negroes was coming on and it was represented to the Governor by the white citizens and officials of Phillips County that in all probability those negroes would be lynched. It is alleged that in order to appease the mob spirit and in a measure secure the safety of the six the Governor fixed the date for the execution of the petitioners at June 10, 1921, but that the execution was stayed by the proceedings in court and, we presume, the proceedings before the Chancellor, to which we shall advert.

In *Frank v. Mangum*, it was recognized of course that if in fact a trial is dominated by a mob so that there is an actual interference with the course of justice, there is a departure from due process of law; and that "if the State, supplying no corrective process, carries into execution a judgment of death or imprisonment based upon a verdict thus produced by mob domination, the State deprives the accused of his life or liberty without due process of law." We assume in accordance with that case that the corrective process supplied by the state may be so adequate that interference by habeas corpus ought not to be allowed. It certainly is true that mere mistakes of law in the course of a trial are not to be corrected in that way. But if the case is that the whole proceeding is a mask—that counsel, jury and judge were swept to the fatal end by an irresistible wave of public passion, and that the state courts failed to correct the wrong, neither perfection in the machinery for correction nor the possibility that the trial court and counsel saw no other way of avoiding an immediate outbreak of the mob can prevent this Court from securing to the petitioners their constitutional rights.

In this case a motion for a new trial on the ground alleged in this petition was overruled and upon exceptions and appeal to the supreme court the judgment was affirmed. The supreme court said that the complaint of discrimination against petitioners by the exclusion of colored men from the jury came too late and by way of answer to the objection that no fair trial could be had in the circumstances stated that it could not say "that this must necessarily have been the case"; that eminent counsel was appointed to defend the petitioners, that the trial was had according to law, the jury correctly charged, and the testimony legally sufficient. On June 8, 1921, two days before the date fixed for their execution, a petition for habeas corpus was presented to the Chancellor and he issued the writ and an injunction against the execution of the petitioners; but the supreme court of the state held that the Chancellor had no jurisdiction under the state law whatever might be the law of the United States. The present petition perhaps was suggested by the language of the court: "What the result would be of an application to a Federal Court we need not inquire." It was presented to the district court on September 21. We shall not say more concerning the corrective process afforded to the petitioners than that it does not seem to us sufficient to allow a judge of the United States to escape the duty of examining the facts for himself when if true as alleged they make the trial absolutely void . . .

INDEX